St. Louis de Montfort's True Devotion

Consecration to
Mary

Fr. Helmuts Libietis

Angelus
Press

PO Box 217 | Saint Marys, KS 66536

Library of Congress Cataloging-in-Publication Data

Consecration to Mary : St. Louis de Montfort's True devotion :
[complete five-week preparation : prayers, daily meditations, spiritual
guidance, ceremony / compiled] by Helmuts Libietis.
    p. cm.
    ISBN 0-935952-44-6
    1. Mary, Blessed Virgin, Saint--Prayer-books and devotions-English. I.
Libietis, Helmuts. II. Grignion de Montfort, Louis-Marie, Saint, 1673-1716.
Traité de la vraie dévotion à la Sainte Vierge.
BX2160.3.C66 1999
232.91--DC21

99–14060
CIP

ANGELUS PRESS
PO Box 217
Saint Marys, Kansas 66536
Phone (816) 753-3150
FAX (816) 753-3557
Order Line 1-800-966-7337
www.angeluspress.org

ISBN 978-0-935952-44-5
FIRST PRINTING—January 1998
NINTH PRINTING—April 2023

Printed in the United States of America

Contents

PREFACE

It is hoped that this book will be of assistance to those wishing to make St. Louis de Montfort's *True Devotion Consecration to the Blessed Virgin*. Until now, it was impossible for anyone making the *True Devotion Consecration,* to find all the readings—recommended by St. Louis—in a single, easy-to-follow and manageable work. Instead, they had to do all kinds of gymnastics, by jumping around from their Bible to the *Imitation of Christ,* flipping backwards and forwards through the *True Devotion to Mary, etc.,* not to mention having to carry all these books around with them! There are, of course, summarized compilations available on the market, but they are mostly inadequate for the serious and thorough preparation envisaged and recommended by St. Louis de Montfort.

This book has been compiled in order to fill that void. It is, for the moment, the most complete single-volumed book available, explaining: *(a)* how to prepare for, *(b)* how to make and *(c)* how to daily live the *True Devotion Consecration* after having made it. It contains almost all the readings and every single prayer originally recommended by the Saint. We have also added appropriate extracts from other works of St. Louis de Montfort, such as *The Love of Eternal Wisdom, The Secret of the Rosary, The Secret of Mary,* and *Letter to the Friends of the Cross*—which St. Louis almost certainly would have recommended in his day, but could not, since his own writings were not widely available at that time. We feel the inclusion of these extracts to be very important for who is better qualified to explain the spirit of his *True Devotion Consecration* than St. Louis himself?

We have specially arranged and divided all these readings into an easy-to-follow series of daily meditations. All *you* have to do is meditate! For those who find meditation difficult, there are tips on *how* to meditate. We think you will appreciate having St. Louis' recommended spiritual reading already arranged, edited and divided into a series of daily meditations covering the entire preparatory period. This leaves you free to focus on the meditations and preparation. You need not necessarily make *all* the meditations, since, of course, both the length of preparation and list of spiritual reading are only *suggested* by St. Louis de Montfort. *However, do at least try to read them all.* Nor are our selected readings meant to be exclusive. You may also incorporate other suitable spiritual reading with that found in this book.

You will also find a very thorough examination of conscience to help you with Confession—of a depth rarely found elsewhere these days. We have also included Appendices dealing with the Rosary and the Brown Scapular—of which Our Lady is reported to have said to St. Dominic: "*One day, through the Rosary and the Scapular, I will save the world.*" In short, this book will truly supply you with all the basics needed to prepare for, make and live a *True Devotion to Mary.*

St. Louis de Montfort suggests a 33-day preparation for the Consecration to Mary—adding, however, that this may be lengthened or shortened at will. We have extended the recommended 33-days by two days, making it a more manageable period of five weeks.

The first week is spent in recognizing and rejecting the *Spirit of the World*; the second in *Knowing Oneself*; the third in *Knowing Mary*; and the fourth week in *Knowing Jesus.* The fifth and final week is devoted to *Final Preparations for the Consecration.*

During the first week, we are encouraged to look around and see what exactly constitutes the Spirit of the World so as to develop both an awareness and a revulsion for a spirit that is so radically opposed to the Spirit of Christ.

The second week encourages us to examine our lives in order to see and correct the ravages brought about by effects of Original Sin and the Spirit of the World. The negative aspect of the first two weeks is complemented by the positive and pleasing aspect of the remaining weeks, whereby....

In the third week we come to a better knowledge and love of the Blessed Virgin Mary. We look at what constitutes a *True Devotion* towards her and examine some of the practical aspects of such a devotion.

The fourth week will lead us to a greater knowledge and love of Our Lord Jesus Christ, especially with regard to the Cross and the Eucharist, both of which are joined together in the Holy Mass—which is both a Sacrifice and a Sacrament.

It is interesting to see how this *True Devotion* fits in with the well-known vision of St. John Bosco, wherein he sees the Church, represented by a ship, avoiding the perils of both storms and pirates, by anchoring Herself with chains to two pillars. Upon one pillar was the Blessed Virgin Mary, while upon the other was the Holy Eucharist. We, too, can avoid the dangers and shipwreck of this world, by anchoring and chaining ourselves to Jesus and Mary through this *True Devotion Consecration.*

Finally, the fifth week will prepare us for the day of Consecration itself, with a series of meditations upon the words of our Act of Consecration, while also pointing out our obligations after having made the Consecration.

We are, without doubt, currently living in the *Age of Mary* and heaven most certainly requires of mankind a *True Devotion* to the Mother of God. At Fatima, 80 years ago, Our Lady said that God wishes to establish in the world devotion to her Immaculate Heart—adding that, in the end, her Immaculate Heart would triumph over the evil in the world today.

That triumph can also take place in our own personal lives. An immense increase in our devotion to Mary can transform our lives. In the preface of his translation of St. Louis' *True Devotion to Mary*, Fr. Faber writes:

> All those who are likely to read this book love God and lament that they do not love Him more. All desire something for His glory—the spread of some good work, the success of some devotion, the coming of some good time. One man has been striving for years to overcome a particular fault, but has not succeeded. Another mourns that so few of his relations and friends have been converted to the Faith. One grieves that he has not enough devotion; another grieves that he has a cross to carry, which seems to be

an impossible cross to him. Another has domestic troubles and family unhappiness, which seem incompatible with his salvation. Yet for all these things, prayer appears to bring so little remedy.

But what is the remedy that is wanted? What is the remedy indicated by God Himself? If we may rely on the disclosures of the saints, then it is *an immense increase in devotion to Our Blessed Lady; but remember, nothing short of an immense one.* Mary is not half enough preached. Devotion to her is low and thin and poor....Hence it is that Jesus is not loved. Jesus is obscured, because Mary is kept in the background. Thousands of souls perish, because Mary is withheld from them. It is the miserable, unworthy shadow which we call our devotion to the Blessed Virgin, that is the cause of all these wants and blights, these evils and omissions and declines.

Yet, if we are to believe the revelations of the saints, God is pressing for a greater, a wider, a stronger, quite another devotion to His Blessed Mother. I cannot think of a higher work or a broader vocation for anyone than the simple spreading of this peculiar devotion of St. Louis de Montfort. Let a man but try it for himself, and his surprise at the graces it brings with it and the transformations it causes in his soul, will soon convince him of its incredible efficacy as a means of salvation for men and for the coming of the kingdom of Christ!" (Fr. Faber's Preface to the *True Devotion to Mary*).

Finally, I dedicate this book in gratitude to and in honor of the Most Sorrowful and Immaculate Heart of Mary. I hope it helps transform your soul by generating, as Fr. Faber says, *"an immense increase in devotion to Our Blessed Lady"* and may that resulting increase in devotion hasten the promised Triumph of the Immaculate Heart of Mary. To Jesus through Mary!

Fr. Helmuts Libietis
December 8, 1997
Feast of the Immaculate Conception

TIPS ON PRAYER AND MEDITATION

The modern world cannot do without God. This is the root of its ills. The great truth is that we have an absolute need of God...He normally bestows His grace only in response to prayer. Since our need exists at all times...."We ought always to pray and not to faint" (Lk. 18:1)....The true nature of Christian prayer is perfectly expressed in the following definition given by St. John Damascene and St. Thomas Aquinas: prayer is "a raising of the mind and heart towards God" to offer Him our homage and to ask Him for all those things of which we stand in need (Dom Marmion, *Christ—The Ideal of the Priest*, chap. 15).

The saints say many wonderful things about prayer:

"By prayer, man gives to God the greatest glory possible" (St. Peter Julian Emyard). "As the body cannot live without nourishment, so our soul cannot be spiritually kept alive without prayer" (St. Augustine). "It is simply impossible to live a virtuous life without prayer" (St. John Chrysostom). "He knows how to live well who knows how to pray well" (St. Augustine). "He who does not give up prayer, cannot possibly continue to offend God habitually. Either he will give up prayer, or he will stop sinning" (St. Alphonsus Liguori). "When prayer is poured forth, sins are covered" (St. Peter Julian Emyard). "He who prays most, receives most" (St. Alphonsus Liguori). "The power of prayer is really tremendous" (St. Therese of Lisieux).

Preparation for Prayer

We should neither tempt God, nor offend Him, by rushing into prayer unprepared. Firstly, we should have an intention for our prayer. The word ALTAR presents us with the main motives for prayer.

The letter "A" is for *adoration*, which is the primary of duty of man toward God. Just look at the power of God's creation! A simple study of the sciences manifests His greatness! What miracles He has wrought throughout history! Let us adore Him! The "L" is for *love*. God *is* love. He created us in love, to share His love with us. God so loved the world that he sent His only begotten Son to die for us. Love is reciprocal. That love must be returned. Greater love no man has than he who lays down his life for his friends. Jesus laid down His life for us, we should do the same out of love for Him. The "T" is for *thanksgiving*. Our Lord would often give thanks to His heavenly Father, thus giving us the example of gratitude. Thank Him for general and particular graces. Thank Him for His mercy and His providence. The second "A" is for *asking*. Our Lord commanded us: "Ask and you shall receive....All things whatsoever you shall ask in prayer, believing, you shall receive." Let us pray for the Church, for our country, our community, our family and ourselves. Let us pray for the living and the dead, for our friends and enemies. Finally, the "R" is for *reparation*. If we say we have no sins, then we are liars. We are all sinners who need to do penance and prayer is a form of penance.

The Presence of God

St. Francis de Sales gives us some useful ways of placing ourselves in the presence of God before praying:

> Begin all your prayers, whether mental or vocal, in the presence of God. Keep to this rule without any exception and you will quickly see how helpful it will be....To help you place yourself in God's presence, I propose four practical means that you can use [pick only one each time you pray]:

> The first consists of a lively, attentive realization of God's absolute presence, that is God in all things and all places. There is no place or thing in this world where He is not truly present. Just as wherever birds fly they always encounter air, so also wherever we go, or wherever we are, we find God present. Everyone knows this truth, but everyone does not try to bring it home to himself....Although Faith assures us of His presence, yet because we do not see Him with our eyes, we often forget about Him and behave as if God were far distant from us.

> The second way to place yourself in God's presence is to remember that not only is He present in the same place you are, but that He is present, in a most particular way, in your heart and in

the very center of your spirit. He enlivens and animates it by His divine presence, for He is there as the heart of your heart and the spirit of your spirit.

A third way is to consider how our Savior, in His humanity, gazes down from heaven on all mankind and particularly on Christians, who are His children, and most especially on those who are at prayer, whose actions and conduct He observes. This is by no means a figment of the imagination, but the very truth.

A fourth method consists in the use of a simple imagination as we represent to ourselves the Savior in His sacred humanity as if He were near us, just as we sometimes imagine a friend to be present and say: "I can imagine so and so doing this or that." If the Blessed Sacrament is present, then Christ's presence is real and not purely imaginary. Hence, you can employ one of these four means of placing yourself in the presence of God before prayer. Do not use them all at once, but only one at a time, and that briefly and simply" (*Introduction to the Devout Life*, Part 2, chap. 1).

Dignity, Attention and Devotion in Prayer

People often pray without realizing what it is they are doing, or Whom it is that they are addressing! God so rightly complains in Scripture saying: "This people honoureth me with their lips, but their heart is far from Me" (Mt. 15:7).

> It happens to some souls that when they have recited many formulas, they realize that they have said nothing to God from the bottom of their hearts. Our mind may be far distant from the words that fall from our lips....In our prayer we must give up to God our whole heart and our whole mind....Just as the sanctuary light burns itself up without reserving anything, so our soul in its conversation with God, must be entirely dedicated to the Almighty. We must free ourselves from preoccupations and from vain thoughts, which tie the soul down to earth and prevent it from being entirely given over to the Lord (Dom Marmion, *Christ— The Ideal of the Priest*, chap. 15).

Our prayers should be said:

With Dignity: Our external posture often reflects the interior disposition of our soul. Dignity does not always mean kneeling. Sometimes we can pray as we are walking or even working, but we should always reserve time for prayer in a formal, dignified and humble position. Since the exterior can influence the

interior, a humble posture is often useful and necessary—such as
kneeling or even lying flat on your face (though only in private)
as the priest does at the start of the Good Friday ceremonies.

With Attention: Don't rush into prayer without thinking what
you are about to do or Whom you are about to address. Place
yourself in the presence of God. Formulate an intention for your
prayer. We don't leave our homes without having a reason for
doing so, neither should we start praying without an intention.
The word ALTAR will help supply an intention. Do not fear distractions. They often make prayer more powerful and meritorious when we are faithful in driving them away and thus showing
our desire to remain in the presence of God.

With Devotion: It helps if we *really want* what we are praying
for; or if we *really appreciate* God and what He has done for us; or
if we are *really sorry* for our past sins.

Mental Prayer Is Better Than Vocal Prayer

St. Francis de Sales, writing on prayer, says:

> Do not hurry along and say many things, but try to speak
> from your heart. A single *Our Father* said with feeling has greater
> value than many said quickly and hurriedly....However, if you have
> the gift of mental prayer, you should always give it first place.
> Afterwards, if you cannot say your vocal prayers because of your
> many duties or some other reason, don't be disturbed on that ac-
> count. During vocal prayer, if you find your heart drawn and in-
> vited to interior or mental prayer, don't refuse to take it up. Let
> your mind turn very gently in that direction and don't be con-
> cerned at not finishing the vocal prayers you intended to say. The
> mental prayer you substitute for them is more pleasing to God
> and more profitable for your soul. I make an exception for the
> Divine Office, if you are obliged to say it, for in that case you must
> fulfill your obligation (*Introduction to the Devout Life*, Part 2,
> chap. 1).

Prayer Means Effort

Many find prayer difficult. That is only natural, since we are
trying to communicate with the supernatural world:

> Prayer always requires a certain effort, even from those who
> find in it their delight, because a certain strain is involved in the
> concentration necessary to speak to God; it is always more or less

difficult to maintain the soul in an atmosphere which is above its usual level. That is why prayer can serve as a sacramental penance. We must not be surprised at this difficulty in applying ourselves to prayer: for to raise ourselves towards God, even in the smallest degree, is to exceed our natural powers (Dom Marmion, *Christ— The Ideal of the Priest*, chap. 15).

Is There Room for God?

Too many people limit prayer to an isolated part of the day— first thing in the morning or last thing at night. Yet God should be part of our whole day, not just a mere ten minutes:

> Prayer in our life, must not be limited to a number of iso- lated, passing incidents. We must cultivate *a spirit of prayer*. What must we understand by this? A spirit of prayer is an habitual dis- position of soul whereby, in our troubles and discouragements, as well as in our joys and successes, our hearts turn towards Our Lady and Our Lord, as to our best friends and most intimate con- fidants of our feelings. And it is not only in the morning and in the evening that the soul should be raised heavenwards, but al- ways: "My eyes are ever towards the Lord" (Ps. 24:15) (Dom Marmion, *Christ—The Ideal of the Priest*, chap. 15).

The Power of Prayer of Petition

> Do we believe in the power of prayer? We know the common teaching of theologians: that true prayer—by which we ask some- thing for ourselves with humility, confidence and perseverance, the graces necessary for salvation—is infallibly efficacious (St. Thomas Aquinas, *Summa Theologica*, IIa IIae, Q.83, A.15, ad 2). We know this doctrine, and yet it seems to us at times that we have truly prayed without being heard. We believe in, or rather we see, the power of a machine, of an army, of money and of knowledge; but we do not believe strongly enough in the efficacy of prayer. At times we seem to think that prayer is a force by which we would try bending the will of God by persuasion. Yet God's will has been made up from all eternity—nothing can change it (Rev. Fr. Garrigou-Lagrange, *The Three Ages of the Interior Life*, chap.23).

Prayer is actually a bending of our will towards the will of God. He wishes the salvation of all, but all will not be saved— and one of the contributory causes is a lack of prayer; a lack of prayer by those who will be damned and a lack of prayer on the part of others for the conversion of those unfortunate souls.

For material harvests, God prepared the seed, the rain that must help it germinate, the sun that will ripen the fruits of the earth. Likewise, for spiritual harvest, He has prepared spiritual seeds, the divine graces necessary for sanctification and salvation. Prayer is one of the causes meant to produce that sanctification and salvation (Rev. Fr. Garrigou-Lagrange, *The Three Ages of the Interior Life*, chap.23).

St. Gregory the Great says: "Men ought by prayer to dispose themselves to receive what Almighty God from eternity has decided to give them" (*Dialogues*, Bk.1, chap. 8). Thus Christ, wishing to convert the Samaritan woman, led her to pray by saying to her: "If thou didst know the gift of God!" In the same way, He granted Mary Magdalen a strong and gentle actual grace which inclined her to repentance and to prayer. He acted in the same way to Zacheus and the Good Thief. It is, therefore, as necessary to pray in order to obtain the help of God, as it is necessary to sow seed in order to have wheat. To those who say that what was to happen would happen, whether they prayed or not, is as foolish as to maintain that whether or not we sowed seed, wheat would still appear once summer came! Therefore, prayer is necessary to obtain the help of God, as seed is necessary for the harvest (Rev. Fr. Garrigou-Lagrange, *The Three Ages of the Interior Life*, chap. 23)

The problems we face arise from the fact that God is prepared to give far more than we are prepared to ask for—we are so lazy and negligent, lacking in confidence and perseverance, that we receive only a fraction of what God is prepared to give. The efficacy of prayer, correctly made, is infallibly assured by Christ:

Ask, and it shall be given to you; seek, and you shall find; knock and it shall be opened to you....And which of you, if he ask his father bread, will he give him a stone? Or a fish, will he give him a serpent?...If you then, being evil, know how to give good gifts to your children, how much more will your Father from heaven give the good Spirit to them that ask Him? (Lk.11:9-13).

The problem does not lie with the Giver, but with us.

Getting Our Prayers Answered

Many of us become discouraged with prayer because our prayers are rarely, if ever heard. Yet there are ways in which we can almost infallibly get our prayers answered. The spiritual writers list the following cardinal points as "infallible" means of having our prayers favorably heard and answered:

1. Pray for what is <u>good and not sinful or harmful</u> to our salvation—We should always remember that what we *want* is not always what we *need*. At times adversity is a better route to heaven than prosperity. St. Augustine says: "We ought to be persuaded that what God refuses to our prayer, He grants to our salvation."

2. Our prayer must be <u>humble</u>—Remember the prayer of the Pharisee and the Publican. Remember, too, Our Lady's prayer, the *Magnificat*, wherein she says that God has "regarded the humility of His handmaid...He hath put down the mighty from their seat and hath exalted the humble." The Old Testament says: "...nor from the beginning have the proud been acceptable to Thee: but the prayer of the humble and the meek hath always pleased Thee" (Jud. 9:16). "May the Lord destroy all deceitful lips, and the tongue that speaketh proud things" (Ps. 11:4). "Thou hast rebuked the proud" (Ps.118:21). "Every proud man is an abomination to the Lord" (Prov. 16:5).

3. Our prayer must be <u>fervent</u>—Too often our prayers are said listlessly, routinely, mechanically; our heart is not in them. Of such Our Lord said: "This people honoureth me with their lips, but their heart is far from me" (Mt. 15:7). Our prayers should be like grains of incense, placed on the hot coals of our hearts.

4. We should <u>amend our life</u> — If we persist in leading a life of sin, then we greatly handicap the chances of having our prayers heard. "He who turns his ears from hearing the law, his prayer is an abomination" (Prov. 28:9).

5. We should <u>forgive those who have injured us</u> — This was the example of Christ dying on the cross: "Father, forgive them..." "If therefore thou offer thy gift at the altar, and there thou rememberest that thy brother hath any thing against thee—Leave there thy offering before the altar, and go first to be reconciled to thy brother: and then coming thou shalt offer thy gift" (Mt. 5:23-24). "Blessed are the merciful, for they shall obtain mercy" (Mt. 5:7). "Forgive thy neighbor if he hath hurt thee, and then shall thy sins be forgiven to thee when thou prayest" (Eccles. 28:2).

6. Our prayer should be <u>united to good works or sacrifices</u> — "Prayer is good with fasting and alms" (Tob. 12:8).

7. We should __pray with confidence__ — Our Lord praised the faith and confidence of persons on many occasions, saying: "Go, thy faith has made thee whole…" (Mt. 9:22; Mk. 5:34; 10:52; Lk. 17:19; 18:42). He also told us that "all things whatsoever you shall ask in prayer, believing, you shall receive" (Mt. 21:22). Do we have that confidence in prayer? Lord, I believe, increase my belief!

8. We should __pray with perseverance__ — "He defers the granting to increase our desire and appreciation" says St. Augustine. Our Lord Himself said: "Yet if he shall continue knocking, I say to you, although he will not rise and give him because he is his friend; yet, because of his importunity, he will rise and give him as many as he needeth. And I say to you: Ask, and it shall be given you: seek, and you shall find: knock, and it shall be opened to you" (Lk. 11:8-9).

If we would only pray in the above manner, we would be amazed at the response our prayers would bring from heaven! Keep in mind the words of the Little Flower: "The power of prayer is really tremendous."

MEDITATION

In speaking of heaven, Jesus said: "In My Father's house there are many mansions" (Jn. 14:2). The same may be said of the life of prayer: there are many stages in it. To help you in your ascent to God, here are three different points of departure from which the soul can ascend. All three lead to the Father's house. We can ascend to the Lord either by *(a)* contemplation of the created world, or *(b)* by meditation on the revealed truths contained in Scripture and on the life of Jesus, or finally *(c)* by attaching ourselves to Christ with a lively faith in His power to introduce us into the bosom of the Father. We are quite free to make use of any one of these manners of approach to God, according to our own personal disposition and to the circumstances we find ourselves in (Dom Marmion, *Christ—The Ideal of the Priest*, chap. 15).

1. Meditation Based on Nature

Does not St. Paul invite us to admire these created things when he says: "The invisible things of Him…are clearly seen, being understood by the things that are made"? (Rom. 1:20). You may ask: "Can one pray by considering the beauties of nature?"— And why not? God is the supreme artist. Creation bears the mark of its Author. Some souls find their satisfaction in contemplating the great spectacles of the work of God: the immensity of the ocean, the peaks of the mountains, the majesty of the landscape, the beauty of a sunset and other such things move them to pray. Why? Because behind the curtain of nature, they divine the hidden presence of God. The whole universe cries out to them: "He made us, and not we ourselves" (Ps. 99:3). The prophet Baruch wrote: "The stars have given light in their watches and rejoiced. They were called and said: 'Here we are!' and with cheerfulness they have shined forth to Him that made them" (Bar. 3:34-35). You also can look on the starry sky and by this spectacle raise your soul to the love of Him Who has created the space of the worlds (Dom Marmion, *Christ—The Ideal of the Priest*, chap. 15).

2. Meditation Based on the Gospel and the Writings of the Saints

It is possible to read Holy Scripture and find nothing in it to arouse one to prayer, but it is also possible to read it humbly as a child of God, in such a way that the prayer of our soul, enlightened by the divine words, becomes truly fervent....In fact, when we take the trouble to meditate on the words and actions of Jesus, we give God the opportunity to communicate Himself to us. If with humility, hope and love, we read the divine words of Scripture, which are spirit and life, they contain for us a special grace that daily inclines us more to imitate the virtues of Christ: His meekness, patience and heroic love on the cross. The mere recollection of Jesus is sanctifying. You can meditate on the Gospel scenes as if you were by the side of Jesus, as if you were listening to His words with your own ears, or seeing Him with your eyes. You can kneel down before the crib with the shepherds; with His disciples you can accompany Him on His journeys. Consider Christ in the Garden of Olives, in His Passion and, above all, on the cross (Dom Marmion, *Christ—The Ideal of the Priest*, chap. 15).

Next to the Scriptures, the reading of the spiritual works of the saints greatly enlightens and warms the soul, because these works, though not composed under infallible inspiration, were written with the lights and the unction of the Holy Ghost (Rev. Fr. Garrigou-Lagrange, *The Three Ages of the Interior Life*, chap.16).

3. The Contemplation of Faith

You will have some idea of this prayer if you recall to mind the old farmer, whom the Curé of Ars used to see every evening in the church, with his eyes fixed on the tabernacle, saying nothing. Eventually, he asked him what he was doing just sitting there and the farmer replied: "I say nothing to God. I look at Him and He looks at me." That is the prayer of simple consideration: one looks, loves and is silent. Every faithful soul should attain to this form of prayer after a certain time. In its initial stages it is still dependent on acquired prayer, that is to say, prayer in which our own efforts enable us, with the help of grace, to find our repose in God.

What is it that prevents souls...from attaining this prayer? Trifles—it is sad to have to admit it, but we spend hours on matters which are of no importance, we think a lot about ourselves, we become attached to all sorts of trifles, and time passes. Never forget that our prayer is the reflection or expression of the true state of the soul. Ordinarily, even for very holy souls, prayer begins on the outer threshold. There, our work, helped by grace, disposes us to make Christ our all. When God invites man to enter further into the contemplation of pure faith, He lets him experience his absolute incapacity to raise himself by his own resources....We would only spoil his work if we tried to achieve this resemblance to the Son of God by ourselves. It is only according as we die to ourselves that the Lord acts on us (Dom Marmion, *Christ—The Ideal of the Priest*, chap. 15).

Method and Meditation?

As regards the manner of meditating:

Many souls employ a method for their meditation; if they find it satisfactory, they would do wrong to abandon it. The Church has freely proclaimed the usefulness of many of these methods. Yet, it would be a mistake to identify the method with prayer itself, as though the prayer could not exist outside such a framework. Methods are only means to an end (Dom Marmion, *Christ— The Ideal of the Priest*, chap.15).

Methods can be very useful, especially at the beginning of the spiritual life, for, adapted to the temperament of each one, they sustain and guide the efforts of souls. They are beneficial only on condition that one knows how to abandon the multiple and ordered acts that they prescribe when one has arrived at the end— namely, intimacy with God.

Sometimes, unfortunately, these methods are badly understood. One considers the work of the faculties that they require, much more than the friendly intercourse to which they lead. One confounds the mode of prayer with the prayer itself. To make a prayer, they think, is to construct an imaginary framework, to feel, to hear, to see, to have strong impressions, or again to formulate considerations, or to have before their eyes some truth to contemplate. They devote all their efforts to work out the method that has been imposed or chosen; they deprive themselves of the liberty of soul that is necessary for the life of love.

The accessory has become the essential to the point that they forget that prayer is an exchange, and that they are no longer even thinking of God, to Whom they ought to speak. The soul is enclosed in a particular method of prayer, or rather is making vain efforts to keep itself there; and, not succeeding, it gives up discouraged, with the conviction that it is not made for a life of mental prayer. If one finds in a soul signs of the action of God, namely, humility and progress in virtue, one must not disturb it in its modes of prayer; it has a right to its liberty (Rev. Fr. Marie-Eugène, O.C.D., *I Want To See God*, chap. 4).

Meditating with the Spiritual Masters

In early times, learning meditation meant, primarily, acquiring the habit of pausing in the course of one's reading of Holy Scripture or of a pious work. During these pauses, the soul thought, reflected and convinced itself of the truths proposed, realized its duties, made acts of conformity to the divine will, and gave expression to its hopes and its petitions. When these sentiments of faith, confidence and love were exhausted, one resumed quite simply the reading of the sacred text.

This was the approach to meditation as the fathers of the desert, those great masters of holiness, understood it. With St. Benedict, the monks of the West simply carried on this tradition. St. Teresa of Avila also recommends this method. It is a very simple method, but it has the advantage of being within the capacity of everyone, and it lessens distractions. Considering that so many souls have been introduced to contemplation in the past by this way, why should it not lead us to this same grace?

Everyone must consider for themselves how they can meditate. Be careful that your meditation is adapted to your spiritual needs, to the weaknesses you have to surmount, the duties which you have to accomplish, and make sure that it develops an ever-growing loyalty to God in your soul. In the beginning, a certain amount of groping is inevitable; that is why you must not hesitate to seek the aid of a book. In the antiphon for the feast of St. Cecilia we read: "She bore the Gospel of Christ in her heart, and never ceased from prayer and divine conversation." *She bore the Gospel of Christ, not in her pocket, but in her heart.* It is in the humble and affectionate meditation of the Gospels, the Epistles and other books of Holy Scripture that you will find, little by little, the spirit of prayer. After having made an act of contrition and having put yourself in the presence of God, expose yourself fully to the sanctifying influence of Jesus [and Mary] and to the action of the Holy Ghost, then read a little, making pauses during the reading, and in this way your soul will learn unconsciously to speak with its Lord (Dom Marmion, *Christ—The Ideal of the Priest*, chap. 15).

Stages of Prayer and Meditation

St. Teresa of Avila, in the book of her *Life*, gave a well known classification of the degrees of prayer:

> It seems to me that the garden can be watered in four ways: by manually drawing the water from a well, which costs us great labor; or by a water-wheel and buckets, when the water is drawn by a windlass—it is less laborious than the other and gives more water; or by a stream or a brook, which waters the ground much better, for it saturates it more thoroughly and there is less need to water it often, so that the gardener's labor is much less; or by heavy rain, when the Lord waters it with no labor of ours, a way which is incomparably better than any of those which have been described. Beginners in prayer, we may say, are those who draw up the water out of the well: this, as I have said, is a very laborious process, for it will fatigue them to keep their senses recollected, which is a great labor, because they have been accustomed to a life of distraction....Then they have to try to meditate upon the life of Christ and this fatigues their minds....This is what is meant by beginning to draw up water from the well" (*Life*, xi; Peers I, pp.65-66).

Do not expect every day to be a profitable day of meditation. Sometimes the well can be dry. Sometimes the tensions of daily life make the rope break. Let us not be afraid of the labor, for God seeing our good intentions and perseverance will presently come with a deluge of heavenly graces and raise us to a higher level of prayer.

WEEK ONE

INTRODUCTION TO WEEK ONE:
THE SPIRIT OF THE WORLD

We are all the children of our age. It is said that you cannot leave clothes in a smoky room, without them taking on the smell of smoke. Similarly, by living in an age whose spirit is radically opposed to that of Christ, it is only to be expected that most of us will become tainted by that spirit in one way or another, to a greater or lesser degree.

In this first period of preparation, we are encouraged to look around and see what exactly constitutes the Spirit of the World, so as to develop both an awareness and a revulsion for a Spirit so radically opposed to the Spirit of Christ. This Spirit is usually manifested through a desire of independence from God; and is visible by the concupiscence of the flesh, the concupiscence of the eyes and the pride of life. It disobeys the laws of God and all lawful authority; it abuses created things. Its works can be seen to flow from the Seven Capital Sins—Pride, Covetousness, Gluttony, Anger, Lust, Envy and Sloth. Its works darken our mind; seduce, weaken and corrupt our will.

Through this Spirit of the World, the devil makes sin look splendid, charming and alluring in persons, places and things. To overcome this Spirit, we must be able to recognize it in those selfsame persons, places and things; and we must pray and mortify ourselves to purify ourselves of its effects.

At the start of the week, we will firstly give a summary of the Spirit of Christ, which is so beautifully expounded in Christ's Sermon on the Mount from chapters 5, 6 and 7 of St. Matthew's

Gospel. We will then allow St. Louis de Montfort to paint a picture of the Spirit of the World, taking extracts from his book *The Love of Eternal Wisdom*. This theme will be continued by a series of meditations upon the *Seven Deadly Sins* and the week will end with some of the meditations suggested by St. Louis—taken from that great spiritual classic *The Imitation of Christ*. The recommended prayers, to be said each day during this first week, are the *Veni Creator* and the *Ave Maris Stella*.

RECOMMENDED PRAYERS FOR WEEK ONE

(Try to say the *Veni Creator* before and the *Ave Maris Stella* after each meditation; or say them both at least once a day. Both prayers are also fruitful sources of meditation.)

Veni Creator

Come, O Creator Spirit blest!
And in our souls take up Thy rest;
Come with Thy grace and heavenly aid,
And fill the hearts which Thou hast made.

Great Paraclete! To Thee we cry,
O highest gift of God most high!
O font of life! O fire of love!
And sweet anointing from above.

Thou in Thy sevenfold gifts art known,
The finger of God's hand we own;
The promise of the Father, Thou!
Who dost the tongue with power endow.

Kindle our senses from above,
And make our hearts overflow with love;
With patience firm and virtue high,
The weakness of our flesh supply.

Far from us drive the foe we dread,
And grant us Thy true peace instead;
So shall we not, with Thee for guide,
Turn from the path of life aside.

O may Thy grace on us bestow
The Father and the Son to know,
And Thee, through endless times confessed,
Of both, the eternal Spirit blest.

All glory while the ages run,
Be to the Father and the Son,
Who rose from death; the same to Thee,
O Holy Ghost, eternally. Amen.

Ave Maris Stella

Hail, bright star of ocean,
God's own Mother blest,
Ever sinless Virgin,
Gate of heavenly rest.

Taking that sweet Ave,
Which from Gabriel came,
Peace confirm within us,
Changing Eva's name.

Break the captives' fetters,
Light on blindness pour,
All our ills expelling,
Every bliss implore.

Show thyself a Mother;
May the Word Divine,
Born for us thy Infant,
Hear our prayers through thine.

Virgin all excelling,
Mildest of the mild,
Freed from guilt, preserve us,
Pure and undefiled.

Keep our life all spotless,
Make our way secure,
Till we find in Jesus,
Joy forevermore.

Through the highest heaven
To the Almighty Three,
Father, Son and Spirit,
One same glory be. Amen.

DAILY MEDITATIONS TO HELP US REJECT THE SPIRIT OF THE WORLD AND ACQUIRE THE SPIRIT OF CHRIST

The Sermon on the Mount is a wonderful summary of Christian Doctrine and is, thus, an excellent indication and reflection of the Spirit of Christ. Yet, within its three chapters (Matthew 5, 6 and 7), we also see the ugly head of the Spirit of the World appear—either explicitly, in the condemnations made by Our Lord, or implicitly, as the vices opposed to the virtues that Our Lord extols. He directly attacks pride, covetousness, gluttony, anger, lust, revenge and hypocrisy. He recommends humility, meekness, compassion, justice, mercy, purity.

He calls us the "salt of the earth" and "the light of the world," so as to encourage us to enlighten the world and prevent its corruption. He proposes the revolutionary idea of not only bearing with one's enemies, but He also says that we must turn the other cheek and even pray for them! He then teaches us how to pray and how to abandon ourselves to Divine Providence. These three chapters are certainly little treasures. Let us read them often and reflect upon them.

WEEK 1: DAY 1–FIRST MEDITATION

St. Matthew, Chapter 5: The Sermon on the Mount

The Beatitudes

1 And seeing the multitudes, he went up into a mountain, and when he was set down, his disciples came unto him.

2 And opening his mouth, he taught them, saying:

3 Blessed are the poor in spirit: for theirs is the kingdom of heaven.

4 Blessed are the meek: for they shall possess the land.

5 Blessed are they that mourn: for they shall be comforted.

6 Blessed are they that hunger and thirst after justice: for they shall have their fill.

7 Blessed are the merciful: for they shall obtain mercy.

8 Blessed are the clean of heart: for they shall see God.

9 Blessed are the peacemakers: for they shall be called the children of God

10 Blessed are they that suffer persecution for justice' sake: for theirs is the kingdom of heaven.

11 Blessed are ye when they shall revile you, and persecute you, and speak all that is evil against you, untruly, for my sake:

12 Be glad and rejoice, for your reward is very great in heaven. For so they persecuted the prophets that were before you.

We Are the Salt of the Earth and the Light of the World

13 You are the salt of the earth. But if the salt loses its savor, wherewith shall it be salted? It is good for nothing anymore but to be cast out, and to be trodden on by men.

14 You are the light of the world. A city seated on a mountain cannot be hid.

15 Neither do men light a candle and put it under a bushel, but upon a candlestick, that it may shine to all that are in the house.

16 So let your light shine before men, that they may see your good works, and glorify your Father, Who is in heaven.

17 Do not think that I am come to destroy the law, or the prophets. I am not come to destroy, but to fulfill.

18 For amen I say unto you, till heaven and earth pass, one jot, or one tittle shall not pass of the law, till all be fulfilled.

19 He therefore that shall break one of these least commandments, and shall so teach men, shall be called the least in the kingdom of heaven. But he that shall do and teach, he shall be called great in the kingdom of heaven.

20 For I tell you, that unless your justice abound more than that of the Scribes and Pharisees, you shall not enter into the kingdom of heaven.

Our Dealings with Our Fellow Men

21 You have heard that it was said to them of old: Thou shalt not kill, and whosoever shall kill shall be in danger of the judgment.

22 But I say to you, that whosoever is angry with his brother, shall be in danger of the judgment. And whosoever shall say to his brother, "Raca," shall be in danger of the council. And whosoever shall say, "Thou fool," shall be in danger of hell fire.

23 If therefore thou offer thy gift at the altar, and there thou remember that thy brother hath any thing against thee;

24 Leave there thy offering before the altar, and go first to be reconciled to thy brother: and then coming thou shalt offer thy gift.

25 Be at agreement with thy adversary betimes, whilst thou art in the way with him: lest perhaps the adversary deliver thee to the judge, and the judge deliver thee to the officer, and thou be cast into prison.

26 Amen I say to thee, thou shalt not go out from thence, till thou repay the last farthing.

WEEK 1: DAY 1–SECOND MEDITATION

St. Matthew, Chapter 5

The Dangers of Impurity and Adultery

27 You have heard that it was said of them of old: Thou shalt not commit adultery.

28 But I say to you, that whosoever shall look on a woman to

lust after her, hath already committed adultery with her in his heart.

29 And if thy right eye scandalize thee, pluck it out and cast it from thee. For it is expedient for thee that one of thy members should perish, rather than that thy whole body be cast into hell.

30 And if thy right hand scandalize thee, cut it off, and cast it from thee: for it is expedient for thee that one of thy members should perish, rather than that thy whole body go into hell.

31 And it hath been said, Whosoever shall put away his wife, let him give her a bill of divorce.

32 But I say to you, that whosoever shall put away his wife, excepting for the cause of fornication, maketh her to commit adultery and he that shall marry her that is put away, committeth adultery.

Care in Our Speech

33 Again you have heard that it was said to them of old, Thou shalt not forswear thyself: but thou shalt perform thy oaths to the Lord.

34 But I say to you not to swear at all, neither by heaven, for it is the throne of God:

36 Nor by the earth, for it is his footstool: nor by Jerusalem, for it is the city of the great king:

36 Neither shalt thou swear by thy head, because thou canst not make one hair white or black.

37 But let your speech be yea, yea: no, no: and that which is over and above these, is of evil.

Dealings with Our Enemies

38 You have heard that it hath been said, An eye for an eye, and a tooth for a tooth.

39 But I say to you not to resist evil: but if one strike thee on thy right cheek, turn to him also the other:

40 And if a man will contend with thee in judgment, and take away thy coat, let go thy cloak also unto him.

41 And whosoever will force thee one mile, go with him another two.

42 Give to him that asketh of thee and from him that would borrow of thee turn not away.

43 You have heard that it hath been said, Thou shalt love thy neighbor, and hate thy enemy.

44 But I say to you, Love your enemies: do good to them that hate you and pray for them that persecute and calumniate you:

45 That you may be the children of your Father who is in heaven, who maketh his sun to rise upon the good and bad, and raineth upon the just and the unjust.

46 For if you love them that love you, what reward shall you have? Do not even the publicans this?

47 And if you salute your brethren only, what do you more? Do not also the heathens do this?

48 Be you therefore perfect, as also your heavenly Father is perfect.

WEEK 1: DAY 1–THIRD MEDITATION

Taken from the Gospel according to St. Matthew, Chapter 6

Avoiding Hypocritical Ostentation

1 Take heed that you do not your justice before men, to be seen by them: otherwise you shall not have a reward of your Father who is in heaven.

2 Therefore when thou dost an almsdeed, sound not a trumpet before thee, as the hypocrites do in the synagogues and in the streets, that they may be honored by men. Amen I say to you, they have received their reward.

3 But when thou dost alms, let not thy left hand know what thy right hand doth.

4 That thy alms may be in secret, and thy Father who seeth in secret will repay thee.

5 And when ye pray, you shall not be as the hypocrites, that love to stand and pray in the synagogues and corners of the streets, that they may be seen by men: Amen I say to you, they have received their reward.

6 But thou when thou shalt pray, enter into thy chamber, and having shut the door, pray to thy Father in secret: and thy Father who seeth in secret will repay thee.

7 And when you are praying, speak not much, as the heathens. For they think that in their much speaking they may be heard.

8 Be not you therefore like to them, for your Father knoweth what is needful for you, before you ask him.

9 Thus therefore shall you pray: Our Father who art in heaven, hallowed be thy name.

10 Thy kingdom come. Thy will be done on earth as it is in heaven.

11 Give us this day our daily bread.

12 And forgive us our debts, as we also forgive our debtors.

13 And lead us not into temptation. But deliver us from evil. Amen.

14 For if you will forgive men their offences, your heavenly Father will forgive you also your offences.

15 But if you will not forgive men, neither will your Father forgive you your offences.

16 And when you fast, be not as the hypocrites, sad. For they disfigure their faces, that they may appear unto men to fast. Amen I say to you, they have received their reward.

17 But thou, when thou fastest anoint thy head, and wash thy face;

18 That thou appear not to men to fast, but to thy Father who is in secret: and thy Father who seeth in secret, will repay thee.

Valuing the Things of Heaven More Than the Things of This Earth

19 Lay not up to yourselves treasures on earth: where the rust, and moth consume, and where thieves break through and steal.

20 But lay up to yourselves treasures in heaven: where neither the rust nor moth doth consume, and where thieves do not break through, nor steal.

21 For where thy treasure is, there is thy heart also.

22 The light of thy body is thy eye. If thy eye be single, thy whole body shall be lightsome.

23 But if thy eye be evil thy whole body shall be darksome. If then the light that is in thee, be darkness: the darkness itself how great shall it be!

24 No man can serve two masters. For either he will hate the one, and love the other: or he will sustain the one, and despise the other. You cannot serve God and mammon.

Trusting in Divine Providence

25 Therefore I say to you, be not solicitous for your life, what you shall eat, nor for your body, what you shall put on. Is not the life more than the meat: and the body more than the raiment?

26 Behold the birds of the air, for they neither sow, nor do they reap, nor gather into barns: and your heavenly Father feedeth them. Are not you of much more value than they?

27 And which of you by taking thought, can add to his stature one cubit?

28 And for raiment why are you solicitous? Consider the lilies of the field, how they grow: they labor not, neither do they spin.

29 But I say to you, that not even Solomon in all his glory was arrayed as one of these.

30 And if the grass of the field, which is today, and tomorrow is cast into the oven, God doth so clothe: how much more you, O ye of little faith?

31 Be not solicitous therefore, saying, What shall we eat: or what shall we drink, or wherewith shall we be clothed?

32 For after all these things do the heathens seek. For your Father knoweth that you have need of all these things.

33 Seek ye therefore first the kingdom of God, and his justice, and all these things shall be added unto you.

34 Be not therefore solicitous for tomorrow; for the morrow will be solicitous for itself. Sufficient for the day is the evil thereof.

WEEK 1: DAY 1–FOURTH MEDITATION

Taken from the Gospel according to St. Matthew, Chapter 7

Judging Others

1 Judge not, that you may not be judged.

2 For with what judgment you judge, you shall be judged: and with what measure you mete, it shall be measured to you again.

3 And why seest thou the mote that is in thy brother's eye; and seest not the beam that is in thy own eye?

4 Or how sayest thou to thy brother: Let me cast the mote out of thy eye; and behold a beam is in thy own eye?

5 Thou hypocrite, cast out first the beam out of thy own eye, and then shalt thou see to cast out the mote out of thy brother's eye.

Ask, Seek and Knock....

6 Give not that which is holy to dogs; neither cast ye your pearls before swine, lest perhaps they trample them under their feet, and, turning upon you, they tear you.

7 Ask, and it shall be given you: seek, and you shall find: knock, and it shall be opened to you.

8 For every one that asketh, receiveth: and he that seeketh, findeth: and to him that knocketh, it shall be opened.

9 Or what man is there among you, of whom if his son shall ask bread, will he reach him a stone?

10 Or if he shall ask him a fish, will he reach him a serpent?

11 If you then being evil, know how to give good gifts to your children: how much more will your Father who is in heaven, give good things to them that ask him?

12 All things therefore whatsoever you would that men should do to you, do you also to them. For this is the law and the prophets.

The Roads that Lead to Heaven and Hell

13 Enter ye in at the narrow gate: for wide is the gate, and broad is the way that leadeth to destruction, and many there are who go in thereat.

14 How narrow is the gate, and strait is the way that leadeth to life: and few there are that find it!

15 Beware of false prophets, who come to you in the clothing of sheep, but inwardly they are ravening wolves.

16 By their fruits you shall know them. Do men gather grapes of thorns, or figs or thistles?

17 Even so every good tree bringeth forth good fruit, and the evil tree bringeth forth evil fruit.

18 A good tree cannot bring forth evil fruit, neither can an evil tree bring forth good fruit.

19 Every tree that bringeth not forth good fruit, shall be cut down, and shall be cast into the fire.

20 Wherefore by their fruits you shall know them.

Not Everyone that Says Lord, Lord, Shall Go to Heaven

21 Not every one that saith to me, Lord, Lord, shall enter into the kingdom of heaven: but he that doth the will of my Father who is in heaven, he shall enter into the kingdom of heaven.

22 Many will say to me in that day: Lord, Lord, have not we prophesied in thy name, and cast out devils in thy name, and done many miracles in thy name?

23 And then will I profess unto them: I never knew you depart from me, you that work iniquity.

24 Every one therefore that heareth my words, and doth them, shall be likened to a wise man that built his house upon a rock,

25 And the rain fell, and the floods came, and the winds blew, and they beat upon that house, and it fell not, for it was founded on a rock.

26 And every one that heareth these my words, and doth them not, shall be like a foolish man that built his house upon the sand,

27 And the rain fell, and the floods came, and the winds blew, and they beat upon that house, and it fell, and great was the fall thereof.

28 And it came to pass when Jesus had fully ended these words, the people were in admiration at his doctrine.

29 For he was teaching them as one having power, and not as the Scribes and Pharisees.

THE SPIRIT OF THE WORLD ACCORDING TO ST. LOUIS DE MONTFORT'S BOOK *THE LOVE OF ETERNAL WISDOM*

Christ lives in all Christians who are in the state of grace. In the great majority, however, the Christian life is only, as it were, in its embryonic stage. St. Louis de Montfort's aim is to develop that embryo until Christ has come to the fullness of His age in us. That is, until we have become perfect Christians. According to St. Louis de Montfort, this perfect Christian life is acquired by an ardent desire for sanctity, continual prayer, universal mortification and a tender and true devotion to the Blessed Virgin Mary. Among these four means, St. Louis stresses devotion to Mary as the surest, the easiest and the quickest way to the perfect development of the Christ-like life in us. In the extracts that follow, wherever St. Louis speaks of the *Wisdom* we can substitute the words "Spirit of Christ," or where he refers to "the Eternal Wisdom," or "the Divine Wisdom," we can read the words "Jesus Christ."

WEEK 1: DAY 2–FIRST MEDITATION

Taken from St. Louis de Montfort's book *The Love of Eternal Wisdom,* §1ff.

The Excellence of Wisdom

Wisdom is better than strength; and a wise man is better than a strong man. Hear therefore, ye kings, and understand: learn, ye that are judges of the ends of the earth. Give ear, you that rule the people, and that please yourselves in multitudes of nations....

Wisdom is glory and never fadeth away; and is easily seen by them that love her; and is found by them that seek her. She guides them that covet her, so that she first showeth herself unto them. He that awaketh early to seek her shall not labor: for he shall find her sitting at his door. To think therefore upon her is perfect understanding; and he that watcheth for her shall quickly be secure. For she goeth about seeking such as are worthy of her; and she showeth herself to them cheerfully in the ways and meeteth them with all providence.

The Danger of Power, Wealth and Pleasure

Great is the misfortune of the mighty and the rich if they do not love Eternal Wisdom. The words He speaks to them are terrifying. They cannot be rendered in our language. "Horribly and speedily will He appear to you...the mighty shall be mightily tormented...a greater punishment is ready for the more mighty" (Wis. 6:6-9).

To these words let us add a few which He spoke to them after His Incarnation. "Woe to you that are rich....It is easier for a camel to pass through the eye of a needle than for a rich man to enter into the kingdom of God....Go now, ye rich man, weep and howl in your miseries, which shall come upon you" (Mt. 19; Mk. 10; Lk. 18).

These last words were so often repeated by Divine Wisdom when He lived on earth that three Evangelists have quoted them without variation, which ought to make the rich weep and wail and lament. But, alas, they have their earthly comforts, they are as it were, bewitched by their pleasures and riches; they do not see the evils which hang over their heads.

The World and Worldlings Do not Love Christ Because They Do not Know Him

Is it possible for man to love that which he does not know? Can he love ardently that which he knows but imperfectly? Why, then, is the adorable Jesus—Eternal and Incarnate Wisdom—loved so little? Because He is not known, or known but little.

Very few of us, like St. Paul, make a sincere study of the supereminent science of Jesus, which is, nevertheless, the most noble, the most consoling, the most useful and the most necessary of all sciences in heaven and on earth. To know Jesus Christ, the Eternal Wisdom, is to know everything...to know everything and not to know Him, is, in reality, to know nothing.

What does it avail an archer to know how to hit the outer parts of the target, if he does not know how to hit the center?

What will it avail us to know all other sciences necessary for salvation, if we do not know the only essential one, the center to which all others must converge, Jesus Christ?

Although St. Paul was a man of varied knowledge and well versed in human sciences, he said: "I judge not myself to know anything among you but Jesus Christ and Him crucified" (I Cor. 2:2).

I now see and appreciate that this knowledge is so excellent, so delightful, so profitable and so admirable, that I take no account of all that pleased me before. All else is void of meaning, absurd and a waste of time. "This I say, that no man may deceive you by loftiness of words. Beware lest any man cheat you by philosophy and vain deceit" (Col. 2:4; 2:8).

WEEK 1: DAY 2–SECOND MEDITATION

Taken from St. Louis de Montfort's book
The Love of Eternal Wisdom, §13ff.

True and False Wisdom

There are several kinds of Wisdom. First there is true and false wisdom. True wisdom is fondness of truth, without guile or dissimulation. False wisdom is fondness of falsehood, disguised under the appearance of truth. This false wisdom is the wisdom of the world, which, according to the Holy Spirit, is threefold "Earthly, sensual and devilish wisdom" (Jas. 3:15). True wisdom is natural and supernatural. Natural wisdom is knowledge, in an eminent degree, of natural things in their principles; supernatural wisdom is knowledge of supernatural and divine things in their origin.

But we must be beware of being mistaken in our choice, for there are several kinds of wisdom. There is the Wisdom of God— the only true Wisdom, that deserves to be loved as a great treasure. There is also the wisdom of the corrupt world, which must be condemned and detested as evil and pernicious. Moreover, there is the wisdom of the philosophers, which we must despise when it is not true philosophy and because it is often dangerous to salvation.

So far, following the advice of St. Paul, we have spoken of the Wisdom of God to chosen souls, but lest they should be deceived by the false luster of worldly wisdom, let us expose its deceit and malice. The wisdom of the world is that of which it is written: "I will destroy the wisdom of the wise" (I Cor. 1:19) according to the world. "The wisdom of the flesh is an enemy to God....This is not the wisdom descending from above but earthly, sensual, devilish" (Rom. 8:7, Jas. 3:15).

Examples of the Spirit of the World

This worldly wisdom consists in the exact compliance with the maxims and the fashions of the world; in a continuous trend toward greatness and esteem. It is a secret and unceasing pursuit of pleasures and personal interests, not in a gross and open manner, so as to cause scandal, but in a secret, deceitful and scheming fashion. Otherwise, it would not be what the world calls wisdom, but rank licentiousness.

Those who proceed according to the wisdom of the world, are those who know how to manage well their affairs and to arrange things to their temporal advantage, without appearing to do so;

—who know the art of deceiving and how to cleverly cheat without it being noticed; who say or do one thing and have another thing in mind;

—who are thoroughly acquainted with the way and the flattery of the world;

—who know how to please everybody, in order to reach their goal, not troubling much about the honor and interests of God;

—who make a secret, but deadly, fusion of truth with untruth; of the Gospel with the world; of virtue with vice; of Jesus Christ with Satan;

—who wish to pass for honest people, but not as religious men; who despise and corrupt; or readily condemn every religious practice which does not conform to their own.

In short, the worldly-wise are those who, being guided only by their human senses and reason, seek only to *appear* as Christian and honest folk, without troubling much to please God, or to do penance for the sins which they have committed against His divine Majesty. The worldling bases his conduct upon his *honor*, upon *what people say*, upon *convention*, upon *good cheer*, upon *personal interest*, upon *refined manners*, upon *witty jokes*. These are the seven innocent incentives, so he thinks, upon which he can rely, so that he may lead an easy life. He has virtues of his own, for which he is canonized by the world. These are *manliness*, *finesse*, *diplomacy*, *tact*, *gallantry*, *politeness and sprightliness*. He considers as serious sins such traits as lack of feeling, silliness, dullness and sanctimoniousness.

WEEK 1: DAY 2–THIRD MEDITATION

Taken from St. Louis de Montfort's book
The Love of Eternal Wisdom, §78ff.

The Ten Commandments of the Worldly Man

1. Thou shalt be well acquainted with the world.
2. Thou shalt appear to be an honest man.
3. Thou shalt be successful in business.
4. Thou shalt keep what is thine.
5. Thou shalt get on in the world.
6. Thou shalt make friends.
7. Thou shalt be a society man.
8. Thou shalt make merry.
9. Thou shalt not be a killjoy.
10. Thou shalt avoid singularity, dullness and an air of piety.

Never was the world so corrupt as it is now, because it was never so astute, so wise in its own conceit and so cunning. It is so skillful in deceiving the soul seeking perfection, that it makes use of truth to foster untruth, of virtue to authorize vice and it even distorts the meaning of Christ's own truths, to give authority to its own maxims. "The number of those who are fools, according to God, is infinite" (Eccles.1:15).

Time for the World...No Time for God

The earthly wisdom, spoken of by St. James, is an excessive striving for worldly goods. The worldly-wise make a secret profession of this type of wisdom when they allow themselves to become attached to their earthly possessions; when they strive to become rich; when they go to law and bring useless actions against others, in order to acquire or to keep temporal goods; when their every thought, word and deed is mainly directed toward obtaining or retaining something temporal. As to working out their eternal salvation and making use of the means to do so—such as reception of the Sacraments and prayer—they accomplish these duties only carelessly, in a very offhand manner, once in a while and for the sake of appearances.

Sensual Pleasure

Sensual wisdom is a lustful desire for pleasure. The worldly-wise make a profession of it, when they seek only the satisfaction of the senses; when they are inordinately fond of entertainment; when they shun whatever mortifies and inconveniences the body, such as fasting and other austerities; when they continually think of eating, drinking, playing, laughing, amusing themselves and having an agreeable time; when they eagerly seek after soft beds, merry games, sumptuous feasts and fashionable society.

Then, after having unscrupulously indulged in all these pleasures—perhaps without displeasing the world or injuring their health—they look for "the least scrupulous" confessor (such is the name they give to those easy going confessors who shirk their duty) that they may receive from him, at little cost, the peaceful sanction of their soft and effeminate life, and a plenary indulgence for all their sins. I say, at little cost, for these, sensually wise, want, as penance, the recitation of only a few prayers, or the giving of an alms, because they dislike what afflicts the body.

Devilish Search for Greatness, Honor, Praise and Applause

Devilish wisdom consists in an unlawful striving for human esteem and honors. This is the wisdom which the worldly-wise profess when they aim, although not openly, at greatness, honors, dignities and high positions; when they wish to be seen, esteemed, praised and applauded by men; when in their studies, their works, their endeavors their words and actions, they seek only the good opinion and praise of men, so that they may be looked upon as pious people, as men of learning, as great leaders, as clever lawyers, as people of boundless and distinguished merit, or deserving of high consideration; while they cannot bear an insult, or a rebuke; or they cover up their faults and make a show of their fine qualities.

With Our Lord Jesus Christ, the Incarnate Wisdom, we must detest and condemn these three kinds of false wisdom if we wish to acquire the true one, which does not seek its own interest, which is not found on this earth, nor in the heart of those who lead a comfortable life, but which abhors all that which is great and high in the estimation of men.

WEEK 1: DAY 2–FOURTH MEDITATION

Taken from St. Louis de Montfort's book
The Love of Eternal Wisdom, §133ff.

How to Acquire the Spirit and Wisdom of Christ

To come to the perfect possession of Divine Wisdom we must accept and follow His teaching. We must begin renouncing ourselves and keeping the great commandment of loving God and our neighbor. We must renounce the flesh, the world and its temporal goods. Above all we must renounce our self-will. To do this, we must humbly pray, we must do penance and suffer persecution. For all this we need the help of Divine Wisdom, Who invites us to go to Him.

With His help we need not fear, provided we be clean of heart. To succeed we must persevere and not look back; we must

walk in the light and act according to the teachings of Divine
Wisdom; we must be vigilant and avoid the maxims of the false
prophets; we must not fear what may be done to our body and
reputation, but only be solicitous about the kingdom of God,
which we can only enter by the narrow gate. Therefore, we must
keep in mind the Eight Beatitudes and we must be thankful to
God for having taught us these heavenly truths.

Acquired by Self-Denial

The Spirit of Christ is admirably summed up by examining
the words that Christ Himself speaks to us through the Gospels:

> If any man will come after Me, let him deny himself, and take
> up his cross daily and follow Me (Mt. 16:24)....If any man love
> Me, he will keep My word, and My Father will love him and we
> will come to him (Jn. 14:23)....If thou offer thy gift at the altar,
> and there thou remember that thy brother hath anything against
> thee; leave there thy offering before the altar and go first to be
> reconciled to thy brother (Mt. 5:23).

> If any man come to Me and hate not his father and mother
> and wife and children and brethren and sisters, yea, and his own
> life also, he cannot be My disciple (Lk. 14:26)....Every one that
> hath left house, or brethren, or sisters, or father or mother or wife
> or children or lands for My name's sake, shall receive a hundred-
> fold, and shall possess life everlasting (Mt. 19:29)....If thou wilt
> be perfect, go sell what thou hast, and give to the poor, and thou
> shalt have treasure in heaven (Mt. 19:21).

> Not every one that shall say to Me, Lord, Lord, shall enter
> into the kingdom of heaven, but he that doth the will of My Fa-
> ther, Who is in heaven, he shall enter into the kingdom of heaven
> (Mt. 7:21)....Every one therefore that heareth My words, and doth
> them, shall be likened to a wise man that built his house upon a
> rock (Mt. 7:24)....Amen, I say to you, unless you be converted,
> and become as little children, you shall not enter into the king-
> dom of heaven (Mt. 18:3)....Learn from Me because I am meek
> and humble of heart, and you shall find rest to your souls (Mt.
> 11:29).

WEEK 1: DAY 3–FIRST MEDITATION

Taken from St. Louis de Montfort's book
The Love of Eternal Wisdom, §136ff.

Acquired by Prayer

Let us again listen to words of Our Lord, that He spoke to us while on this earth, in order to better understand and acquire His Spirit:

> When ye pray, you shall not be as the hypocrites that love to stand and pray in the synagogues, that they may be seen by men. When you are praying, speak not much as the heathens, for your Father knoweth what is needful for you, before you ask Him....When you shall stand to pray, forgive, if you have aught against any man, that your Father who is in heaven, may forgive you your sins....All things whatsoever you ask when ye pray, believe that you shall receive, and they shall come to you.

Acquired by Penance

> When you fast be not as the hypocrites, sad. For they disfigure their faces, that they may appear unto men to fast. Amen I say to you they have received their reward.

> There shall be joy in heaven upon one sinner that doth penance, more than upon the ninety-nine just who need not penance. I come not to call the just, but sinners to penance.

> Blessed are they that suffer persecution for justice sake; for theirs is the kingdom of heaven. Blessed are ye when they shall hate you, and when they shall separate you, and shall reproach you and cast you out for the Son of man's sake. Be glad in that day and rejoice for behold your reward is great in heaven. If the world hate you, know ye that it hath hated Me before you. If you had been of the world, the world would love its own; but because I have chosen you out of the world, therefore the world hateth you.

Acquired by God's Help

> Come to Me all you that labor and are burdened, and I will refresh you. I am the living bread which came down from heaven....If any man eat of this bread, he shall live for ever, and the bread that I will give is My flesh. My flesh is meat indeed and

My blood is drink indeed. He that eateth My flesh and drinketh My blood, abideth in Me and I in him

You shall be hated by all men for My name's sake....But a hair of your head shall not perish....No man can serve two masters. For either he will hate the one and love the other, or he will sustain the one and despise the other.

Acquired by Clean of Heart

From the heart come forth evil thoughts that defile a man; but to eat with unwashed hands doth not defile a man. A good man out of a good treasure bringeth forth good things and an evil man out of an evil treasure bringeth forth evil things.

No man putting his hand to the plough and looking back, is fit for the kingdom of God....Yea, the very hairs of your head are all numbered. Fear not therefore, you are of more value than many sparrows....God sent not His Son into the world to judge the world, but that the world may be saved by Him.

WEEK 1: DAY 3–SECOND MEDITATION

Taken from St. Louis de Montfort's book
The Love of Eternal Wisdom, §145ff.

Acquired by Following His Teachings

It is by listening to others that we uncover the spirit that moves them. Let us listen, once more, to Our Lord speaking to us:

Every one that doth evil hateth the light and cometh not to the light, that his works may not be reproved....God is a spirit and they that adore Him, must adore Him in spirit and in truth....It is the spirit that quickeneth, the flesh profiteth nothing....The words that I have spoken to you, are spirit and life.

Whosoever committeth sin is the servant of sin; now the servant abideth not in the house for ever....He that is faithful in that which is least, is faithful also in that which is greater; and he that is unjust in that which is little, is unjust also in that which is greater....It is easier for heaven and earth to pass away than one tittle of the law to fall.

So let your light shine before men, that they may see your good works and glorify your Father who is in heaven.

Unless your justice abound more than that of the Scribes and Pharisees, you shall not enter into the kingdom of heaven....If thy right eye scandalize thee, pluck it out and cast it from thee, for it is expedient for thee that one of thy members should perish, rather than that thy whole body be cast into hell....The kingdom of heaven suffereth violence and the violent bear it away.

Lay not up to yourselves treasures on earth, where the rust and moth consume and where thieves break through and steal. But lay up to yourselves treasures in heaven, where neither the rust nor moth consume and where thieves do not break through nor steal....Judge not that you may not be judged; for with what judgment you judge, you shall be judged.

False Prophets

Beware of false prophets who come to you in the clothing of sheep, but inwardly they are ravening wolves. By their fruits you shall know them....See that you despise not one of these little ones, for I say to you that their angels in heaven always see the face of My Father who is in heaven....Watch ye therefore because you know not the day nor the hour (when the Lord will come).

Be not afraid of them that kill the body and after that have no more they can do; but fear Him who after He hath killed, hath power to cast into hell....Be not solicitous for your life what you shall eat, nor for your body what you shall put on. Your Father knoweth that you have need of these things....There is not anything secret that shall not be made manifest, nor hidden that shall not be known.

WEEK 1: DAY 3–THIRD MEDITATION

Taken from St. Louis de Montfort's book
The Love of Eternal Wisdom, §149ff.

The Narrow Gate of Poverty and Humility

Our Lord continues to transform our spirit into His, by the following words taken from the Gospels:

Whosoever will be the greater among you, let him be your minister; and he that will be the first among you, shall be your servant....How hardly shall they that have riches enter into the kingdom of God. It is easier for a camel to pass through the eye of a needle, than for a rich man to enter into the kingdom of God....I say to you, love your enemies; do good to them that hate you, and pray for them that persecute and calumniate you.

Woe to you that are rich; for you have your consolation....Enter ye in at the narrow gate, for wide is the gate and broad is the way that leadeth to destruction, and many there are who go in thereat. How narrow is the gate and strait is the way that leadeth to life, and few there are that find it....The last shall be first and the first last, for many are called but few are chosen.

It is a more blessed thing to give rather than to receive....If one strike thee on the right cheek, turn to him also the other; and if a man will contend with thee in judgment and take away thy coat, let go thy cloak also to him....We ought always to pray and not to faint....Watch ye and pray that ye enter not into temptation....Give alms and, behold, all things are clean unto you.

Every one that exalteth himself shall be humbled, and he that humbleth himself shall be exalted....If thy hand or thy foot scandalize thee, cut it off and cast it from thee. It is better for thee to go into life maimed, or lame, than having two hands or two feet, to be cast into everlasting fire. And if thy eye scandalize thee, pluck it out and cast it from thee. It is better for thee having one eye to enter into life, than having two eyes to be cast into hell fire.

Eight Beatitudes

Blessed are the poor in spirit: for theirs is the kingdom of heaven.

Blessed are the meek: for they shall possess the land.

Blessed are they that mourn: for they shall be comforted.

Blessed are they that hunger and thirst after justice: for they shall have their fill.

Blessed are the merciful: for they shall obtain mercy.

Blessed are the clean of heart: for they shall see God.

Blessed are the peacemakers: for they shall be called the children of God.

Blessed are they that suffer persecution for justice' sake: for theirs is the kingdom of heaven.

I confess to Thee, O Father, Lord of heaven and earth, because Thou hast hidden these things from the wise and prudent,
and hast revealed them to little ones. Yea, Father; for so hath it
seemed good in Thy sight.

Such is the summary of the great and important truths which
the Eternal Wisdom came to teach us on earth—after having first
practiced them Himself—in order to cure us from the blindness
and the aberrations into which our sins had led us.

WEEK 1: DAY 3–FOURTH MEDITATION

Taken from St. Louis de Montfort's
The Love of Eternal Wisdom, §194 ff.

Gratification of the Senses Drives Away
the Spirit of Christ

"Wisdom," the Holy Spirit declares, "is not found in the land
of them that live in delights," who gratify all the desires of their
passions and bodily senses, for "they who are in the flesh cannot
please God" and because "the wisdom of the flesh is an enemy to
God." "My Spirit shall not remain in man, because he is flesh"
(Job 28:13; Rom. 8:8,7; Gen. 6:3).

All those who belong to Christ, the Incarnate Wisdom, have
crucified their flesh, with its vices and concupiscences. They ever
bear about in their bodies the mortification of Jesus. They continually do violence to themselves, carry their cross every day, die
daily and bury themselves in Christ. These words of the Holy
Spirit show more clearly than the light of day that to possess Incarnate Wisdom, Jesus Christ, we must practice mortification,
renounce the world and self.

Do not think that this Wisdom, purer than the rays of the
sun, will enter a soul and a body sullied by the pleasures of the
senses. Do not believe that He will grant His rest and ineffable
peace to those who love the company and the vanities of the world.
He tells us, "to him that overcometh the world and himself....I
will give the hidden Manna" (Apoc. 2:17). This lovable Prince,
though He knows and sees all things in a trice by His infinite

light, yet seeks for persons worthy of Him. He seeks because there are so few, that He can scarcely find any sufficiently detached from the world, sufficiently interior and mortified to be worthy of His Person, of His riches and of union with Him.

This Wisdom, to communicate Himself, is not satisfied with a half-hearted mortification, or a mortification of a few days, but He requires universal, continuous, courageous and prudent mortification.

To Obtain Possession of Wisdom, It is Necessary...

1. Either to give up entirely the possessions of the world, as did the Apostles, the Disciples, the first Christians and Religious—and this is the best, quickest, and surest means to possess Wisdom—or, at the very least, to be detached in heart from all worldly goods. This detachment permits us to possess worldly goods as though not possessing them, without being eager to acquire, or being anxious to retain any; not complaining or worrying when possessions are lost. This is very difficult to accomplish.

2. Not to follow the showy fashions of worldlings in dress, in furniture, in dwellings, in banquets, or any other worldly modes and ways of living. "Be not conformed to this world" (Rom. 12:2). This practice is more necessary than is generally thought.

3. Not to believe or to follow the false maxims of the world; not to think, to speak, or to act as do the people of the world. Worldly doctrine is as opposed to that of the Incarnate Wisdom, as darkness is opposed to light and death to life. Consider well the opinions and the words of the worldlings. They think and speak evil of all the great truths of religion. True, they do not tell brazen lies. They cover their lying with a cloak of truth. They are not conscious of telling untruths, yet they lie. Nor do they usually teach sinful doctrines openly, but they speak of them as of virtue and propriety, or else as doctrines of indifference and of little consequence. This cunning, which the devil has taught the world in order to cover up the heinousness of sin and lying, is the wickedness spoken of by St. John, when he writes: "The whole world is seated in wickedness" (I Jn. 5:19). This is true now, more than ever.

4. We must flee, as much as possible, from the company of men, not only from that of worldlings, which is hurtful and dangerous, but even from that of devout persons, when association with them is useless and a waste of time. He who wishes to become wise and perfect, must put into practice these three golden counsels, which Eternal Wisdom spoke to St. Arsenius: "Flee, hide, be silent....Flee as much as possible from the company of men, as the greatest saints have done." (*Imitation of Christ*, bk.I, ch.20, no.1). Let your life be hidden with Christ in God; be silent in the company of men that you may converse with Divine Wisdom. "He who knows how to keep silent is a wise man" (Sir. 20:5).

WEEK 1: DAY 4–FIRST MEDITATION

Taken from St. Louis de Montfort's
The Love of Eternal Wisdom §201 ff.

Mortify the body

To obtain possession of this Wisdom, we must mortify the body, not only by enduring patiently our bodily ailments and the sufferings which the natural elements bring upon us, but, also, by freely imposing upon ourselves some penances and mortifications. We may fast, watch before the Blessed Sacrament, talk with God during the silent hours of the night and practice other austerities, as exemplified in the lives of holy penitents.

It requires courage to do this, because the body naturally idolizes itself, and the world considers as useless all corporal penances and rejects them. The world does everything possible to deter people from practicing the austerities of the saints. Of each one of the saints it is said, in due proportion: "The wise, or the saintly man, has brought his body into subjection by continual watchings, fastings, disciplines, cold, insufficient clothing and every kind of austerity. He made a compact with it not to give it any rest in this world" (Rom. Brev., Oct. 19, St. Peter of Alcantara). The Holy Spirit declares of all the saints: "They hated the spotted garment which is carnal" (Jude 1:23).

Mortify the soul

In order that exterior and voluntary mortification be good, it is necessary that it be accompanied by mortification of the judgment and the will, and by holy obedience. Without this obedience, all exterior mortification is spoiled by self-love and it often becomes more pleasing to the devil than to God. Hence, no considerable mortification should be undertaken without taking counsel. "I, Wisdom, dwell in counsel" (Prov. 8:12).

"He that trusteth in his own heart is a fool....The prudent man doth all things with counsel" (Prov. 28:26). And the great counsel of the Holy Spirit is this: "My son, do thou nothing without counsel, and thou shalt not repent when thou hast done....Seek counsel always of a wise man" (Tob. 4:19).

By this holy obedience, we do away with self-love, which spoils everything. By holy obedience, the least of our actions become meritorious. It shields us from the illusions of the devil. It makes us conquer our enemies and brings us safely, as peacefully as if we were sleeping, into the harbor of salvation. All that I have just said, is comprised in this one great counsel: "Leave all things and you will find all things, in finding Jesus Christ, the Incarnate Wisdom" (*Imitation of Christ*, Bk.III, chap. 32, no.1).

THE SEVEN CAPITAL SINS
MANIFEST THE SPIRIT OF THE WORLD

WEEK 1: DAY 4–SECOND MEDITATION

Pride

The satanic sin of pride! The terrible sin of our first parents! Those cries of pride that rang out from Satan and our first parents: "I will not serve! I want to be like God!" It is a vice that can bear neither superior, nor equal, nor rival. Those same cries can be heard around the world today, not only in the distant world, but in our own personal world—at work, at school, at home and even in our own hearts and minds!

Pride is the root of all sin. Whenever we sin, our pride has paved the way. We too, have cried out: "I will not serve! I will not do this! I will not do that! You can't tell me what to do!" Pride is indeed an evil thing, but only when it goes to extremes. For there is a virtuous pride and an evil pride.

There is nothing wrong in being proud of the good that we do, and of the good that is in us—but this must always be in acknowledging the source or first principle of that good—which is God, not ourselves! It is when we deviate from this basic truth, that sinful pride rears its ugly head. It is when we think that we, ourselves, are the cause of all our goodness, our talents, our success and our achievements—it is then that we sin.

Neither is there anything wrong in letting others see the good that is in us, if the motive for this is God's glory: "So let your light shine before men that they may see your good works, and glorify your Father Who in heaven" (Mt. 5:16). But if we are tempted to show off the good that is in us, for motives of self-glorification, then again pride rears its sinful, ugly head. For we fall into a species of idolatry by worshipping ourselves. Sometimes we recognize, in theory, that God exists and that we depend upon Him—but, very often, this truth is not apparent in the way we live our lives.

In theory, we need God, but, in practice, He is pushed aside, as we glory in whatever goods and talents that He may have given us: our intellect, wit, dexterity, health, beauty, strength, *etc*. Look at the excessive amount of time people spend bathing and basking in these secondary qualities, while almost totally forgetting what really matters—God and their salvation.

Similarly, we tend to exaggerate our personal qualities, while ignoring our defects. We have the eye of an eagle, when it comes to our qualities, but are blind as bats, when it comes to our sins. Yet with regard to our neighbors, the reverse principle is true! We have an eagle eye for their faults, but are blind to their virtues!

This pride is the source of many faults: through pride we are unyielding, even when in the wrong; we become caustic and sarcastic in speech; we get involved in harsh and heated discussions, which bring about dissension and discord; which then lead to bitter words, unjust words and actions against our rivals, in order to belittle them. Hence, the bitter criticism of superiors and a refusal to obey their orders. Hence, too, the demi-god obstinacy and lack of humility in superiors, by never admitting a fault, or changing a course of action, when they realize that they are in the wrong. This is far from imitating and learning from Jesus, the Superior of all superiors, Who was "meek and humble of heart." This pride of life leads and keeps us within an atmosphere of anxiety and unhappiness, wherein we find no peace, nor any real lasting contentment, because we want to excel in all things and lord it over all others.

The remedy for pride is humility. We are nothing! We came from dust! We will return, as the Ash Wednesday liturgy says, into dust! Without God we can do nothing good! As St. Paul says: what have we to glory about, except our sins? What is it that we achieved when left totally to ourselves? Nothing but sin!

What can I do without the help of others? How much success would I have had, were it not for the help and talents of others? How much success would I have had, without the agreement and help of God's Providence? Nothing happens without God putting his signature to it! Absolutely nothing! Was I the source of my own existence? Did I survive without the care of parents? Did I teach myself? Did I create all the talents that I have? Will I avoid all illness and suffering? Will I escape death? Will I escape the final judgement? Will I create and build a heaven for myself in hell? No! Remember, man, that thou art dust, and to dust thou shalt return!

WEEK 1: DAY 4–THIRD MEDITATION

Covetousness

Covetousness, avarice, greed—they all come down to the same thing: an inordinate desire and love of earthly goods. There has never been such an enormous store of earthly goods as there is today, in this over-materialistic twentieth century. The whole economy revolves around an ever increasing creation and consumption of earthly goods. Much of family life revolves around the same thing. Even sacred feasts such as Christmas, have seen the spiritual aspect take a distant second place to the material aspect!

Many of us fall into this sin of covetousness. If we cannot satisfy our greed, by actually possessing the thing we desire, then we at least encourage that greed, by avidly gorging everything with our eyes.

It is undeniable that we *do* require certain material goods to help us live in a way that will help, rather than hinder, our salvation. Yet this appetite, when uncontrolled, soon runs rampant. We start to pursue money, wealth and goods with great eagerness, using all kinds of means, regardless of the rights or needs of others, in order to get them. We risk our health and livelihood, or that of our employees, by overwork or taking too many financial risks. We become stingy and mean in spending our money, because we wish to accumulate more and more. We give little or nothing to charitable concerns or the poor, for the same reason.

It finally gets to the point where we idolize money or material goods, hoarding them beyond sane measure. This kind of attitude is sinful, because it makes a god of what is simply a means to salvation. It also refuses to rely upon Divine Providence. What did Our Lord say upon the matter?...

> Therefore I say to you, be not solicitous for your life, what you shall eat, nor for your body, what you shall put on. Is not the life more than the meat: and the body more than the raiment? Behold the birds of the air, for they neither sow, nor do they reap, nor gather into barns: and your heavenly Father feedeth them. Are not you of much more value than they? And which of you by taking thought, can add to his stature one cubit? And for raiment why are you solicitous? (Mt. 6:25-28).

> Consider the lilies of the field, how they grow: they labor not, neither do they spin. But I say to you, that not even Solomon in all his glory was arrayed as one of these. And if the grass of the field, which is today, and tomorrow is cast into the oven, God doth so clothe: how much more you, O ye of little faith? Be not solicitous therefore, saying, What shall we eat: or what shall we drink, or wherewith shall we be clothed? For after all these things do the heathens seek. For your Father knoweth that you have need

of all these things. Seek ye therefore first the kingdom of God, and his justice, and all these things shall be added unto you (Mt. 6:28-33).

WEEK 1: DAY 4–FOURTH MEDITATION

Gluttony

Gluttony is akin to covetousness, in that it is greed for specific things—namely, food and drink. Gluttony is a disordered love of the pleasures of the table. It is an abuse of those legitimate pleasures that God has attached to eating and drinking, which are the necessary means of self-preservation. We violate this legitimate pleasure in any of the following ways:

(*a*) By eating when there is no need; eating between meals and for no other reason than that of indulging our greed.

(*b*) Seeking delicacies or daintily prepared food, for the sole reason of obtaining greater pleasure from it.

(*c*) Going beyond either appetite or need, gorging ourselves with food or drink to the point where it endangers our health or prevents us from doing our duties.

(*d*) Eating in a greedy, over-eager or animalistic manner.

What gluttony does: it makes us slaves of our bodies, it brutalizes us, it dulls and then weakens our intellectual and moral life, and gradually prepares the way for lust and impurity—because, through gluttony, we give in to the craving of the body in the realm of food, which is but one step away from giving in to the craving of the body in the sexual domain.

Intemperance at table also leads to intemperance in speech. How many things have been said at table, that would have better been left unsaid? How many secrets and confidences have been betrayed over a meal or a bottle of wine? How many reputations tarnished, or even ruined? Perhaps, by doing so, we have even tarnished, or even ruined our own reputation!

The guiding principle, in our struggle against gluttony, must be one of mortification and penance. Remember Our Lord saying that certain kinds of devils are only cast out by prayer and *fasting*. We eat and drink to live, and not vice-versa! Too much food and drink weighs down the mind and will, then a certain laziness and sluggishness creeps in and this takes over both the physical and spiritual domains.

Mortify yourself in the realm of quantity—it is a good principle to always leave the table still feeling *slightly* hungry. Put less on your plate at the start of the meal. Take the smaller piece, rather than the larger. Do not be in a hurry to start eating. Eat and drink more slowly. Drink water instead of some favorite beverage. Avoid putting ice in your drink, if you prefer a cool drink. Perhaps over-salt, or over-spice your food a little, so as to take away some of the pleasurable taste; or, take less seasoning if you have a liking for spicy food. Give your favorite dessert to another. Do not eat between meals. Do not buy the most extravagant or costly foods. Do not throw food away, but re-use it. Given a choice between two equally nourishing dishes, sometimes take the less tasty dish. These are just some of the many ways in which we can mortify ourselves with regard to food and drink.

WEEK 1: DAY 5–FIRST MEDITATION

Anger

Anger is not always a sin. There is a lawful sentiment of anger, a just indignation, which is an ardent, but rational, desire to punish a guilty party with some form of just retribution. As an example of this, we see Our Lord, with a whip, angrily cast out the money-changers from the Temple. Whereas, on the other hand, we see the high-priest Heli, severely rebuked for *not showing enough anger* in correcting his sons.

Thus for anger to be legitimate, it must be: *(a)* Just—by punishing only those that deserve punishment; *(b)* Tempered—by moderation in the degree of the punishment that is given; by giving a punishment that fits the crime and not exceeding that; *(c)* Charitable—not vented out of a spirit of hatred, revenge or animosity, but out of a sincere desire of helping the wrongdoer.

Anger is sinful when it is unjust, immoderate or uncharitable. Sometimes, we have a violent and inordinate desire to punish someone, regardless of the conditions we have mentioned above. Our anger is accompanied by hatred, which does not merely seek to correct, but seeks to exact some form of revenge. There are several degrees of intensity within anger, which are worth remembering:

(a) Interior Anger of the Mind:

Firstly, we become increasingly impatient with others, whereby the least annoying thing, or the smallest degree of failure, causes dissatisfaction.

This is followed by agitation, producing an unnecessary irritation, which we manifest outwardly in some way—facial expressions, agitation, *etc.*

Then, by brooding upon the facts, this anger or irritation can become so deep rooted, that it engenders sentiments of varying degrees that pass from resentment, to bitterness, hatred and eventually a desire for revenge.

(b) Exterior Anger

The interior anger manifests itself outwardly, beginning with exterior signs of impatience. The earlier anger manifests itself, the weaker it shows the person to be. This exterior anger can, if uncontrolled, easily develop into violence, which in turn can lead to an insane rage, wherein we no longer know what we are saying or doing.

(c) Sinfulness of anger

When anger is impulsive and spontaneous, it is usually a venial sin. If it is so intense that self-control is lost and grave insult is shown to neighbor, then it would be mortal, but this is often not the case. Anger that goes as far as hatred and rancor, when it is deliberate and wilful, is, of itself, a mortal sin.

WEEK 1: DAY 5–SECOND MEDITATION

Lust

Our Lady of Fatima said that, in this age, more souls are condemned to hell through sins of lust than any other sin. In itself, there is nothing wrong with the sexual appetite. Just as God has attached pleasurable sensations to the act of eating and drinking in order to help self-preservation, so, too, has He attached pleasurable feelings to the act of procreation in order to guarantee the propagation of the human race.

Yet, this pleasure is only allowed within the scope of marriage—whose prime purpose is the procreation of children. Outside of marriage, all such pleasure is forbidden. Not only are extra-marital sexual actions forbidden, but so too is the interior desire for those very things. Did not Our Lord say: "But I say to you, that whosoever shall look on a woman, to lust after her, hath already committed adultery with her in his heart" (Mt. 5:28).

From the point of view of perfection, next to pride, there is no greater obstacle to spiritual growth than the vice of impurity. It can very easily make slaves of us and, through lust, we lose any desire for the spiritual. We pray little, or not at all. We become very selfish. True love dies and is replaced by a carnal love. The lustful desires become an obsession. The right balance of our faculties is destroyed. Lust takes command over reason. The will also becomes a slave of this shameful passion. The mind becomes dull and weak. Taste for any serious study or work is lost. The imagination dwells on earthly things. The person increasingly needs base things to satisfy itself. Finally, salvation itself is greatly risked.

To withstand and fight such a dangerous passion, we need a true appreciation of our bodies as being temples of the Holy Ghost. We should behave, in our body, as we do in church. We should also avoid the occasions of sin. This, first and foremost, means keeping a guard over our eyes—which are the windows and doors of our soul. It only takes a few seconds to absorb an image, but it can take weeks, months or years to cleanse our mind or imagination of that selfsame image!

We must also avoid certain friends—charming, witty, intelligent, alluring though they may be—but who may, like the proverbial Pied Piper, lead us a merry dance to hell! Finally, there are certain places or things that also need to be avoided. One of the most dangerous ones that comes to mind is the TV, with its frequent temptations to impurity. The same can be said for certain types of music, whose lyrics glorify or encourage the impure. Similarly, many magazines and books sow the seed of lust in the mind, and must be avoided at all costs.

To the above we must also add *sincere* prayer and mortification. Do not pamper your body, whether it be in the domain of food and drink, or in the realm of fashion, or in the trappings of the home. Undue comfort makes us soft and weakens our will. Also, mortify your imagination by refusing to dwell upon past pleasures. All these things, if seriously undertaken, will greatly fortify us against this vicious and dangerous vice.

WEEK 1: DAY 5–THIRD MEDITATION

Envy

This vice proceeds from pride—which can bear neither rival nor superior. As a result, we are saddened by another person's qualities, possessions or achievements, as though they constituted an affront to our own "superiority" or standing. Often it leads us to the desire of seeing that person lose that quality or possession, and a wish that they experience failure. Because of our pride, we are convinced of our own imagined superiority and, consequently, we feel offended, or threatened, when we encounter someone better gifted, or more successful than ourselves. We know that we are prey to and, perhaps, even guilty of this vice, when it pains us to hear others acknowledged, praised, congratulated, honored, *etc.* We can be sure that we are guilty of this vice, if we then indulge in a needless and unjust criticism of the person thus honored!

The effects of envy can be very serious. It can stir up a hatred towards the person whom we envy and can, as a result, lead us to speaking ill of them, sowing discord, blackening their character, sowing suspicion and, eventually, wishing some evil to befall them—if not actually carrying out that very evil ourselves! It can destroy family life, community life, civic life and even religious life! We need only recall the story of Joseph and his many brothers, who became so envious of him, that they sought to kill him—eventually settling for the option of selling him into slavery. Similarly, we see the envy that the religious leaders had for Jesus—their own countryman. The little seed of envy can grow into a evil tree bringing forth much bad fruit. It is better weeded out before it can exert a stranglehold grip upon our souls.

Some of the ways in which we can weed it out are by remembering that the more God gives to someone, then the more He expects in return. God is the perfect economist and entrepreneur—He wastes nothing and He expects a full return on His investments! Think of the parable of the talents! Therefore, the person whom you envy so much, will be all the more strictly judged upon his use or misuse of what he has been given. Being given more, he must do all the more with it! With the little that *you* have, you also have less to worry about. Thank God for the little you have and pray for the persons who have much. For to whom more is given, more is also expected.

Another way to avoid envy, is to try and imitate the person whom you are tempted to envy. This prompts us, with the help of God's grace, to a holy envy, whereby we seek to imitate and even surpass our neighbor in virtuous things—all for the glory of God and not out of pride. Thus, no sin is committed and, on the contrary, a greater good can result. To do so, is to enter into the spirit of the Church, who proposes so many saints for our emulation.

WEEK 1: DAY 5–FOURTH MEDITATION

Sloth

Sloth is connected to sensuality, because, due to an inordinate attachment to pleasure, it makes us fear and avoid effort and hardship—both of which seem to be opposed to our notion of pleasure. There is, in all of us, a tendency to follow the line of least resistance, or to adhere to the law of the minimum. We want the maximum results for the minimum effort. Much of our economy is based upon that pernicious law—produce at the lowest possible cost and sell it for the highest possible price that you can get away with!

There are various degrees of laziness. Firstly, we take up our duties reluctantly and perform them indifferently, without zeal and attention, with the result that the work is invariably done poorly. The next stage is one of, not outright refusal, but of procrastination—seeking to put off the accepted task. The spirit is willing, but the flesh is weak and, consequently, a prolonged procrastination leads to the task being put-off indefinitely. Finally we have the truly lazy man, who does not want to work, who refuses to work and who deliberately seeks ways of avoiding having to work. He lies and seeks excuses so as to avoid doing his duty.

This laziness is seen in the work place, whereby we are busy only when a supervisor or boss is present. Yet once he leaves, we drop down a gear or two in our effort. In doing so, do we really give a fair day's work for a fair day's pay?

This laziness can also be seen in the home life, where parents have neither studied how to raise children, nor have they been successful in raising children that are a credit to themselves, the Church and society. We then later see their laziness reproduced in their children, who will imitate them perfectly!

That same laziness is even seen in their duties towards God and His Church. Some are slow to pray, lazy about coming to Mass, neglectful of their spiritual duties. They forget the wise proverb: *The Devil makes work for idle hands!* If they fail to find work for themselves, the devil will most certainly find some for them, but the wages will not be heavenly!

God has put us here to *work out* our salvation. He even said to Adam:

> Cursed is the earth in thy work; with labor and toil shalt thou eat thereof all the days of thy life. Thorns and thistles shall it bring forth to thee; and thou shalt eat the herbs of the earth. In the sweat of thy face shalt thou eat bread till thou return to the earth out of which thou wast taken (Gen. 3:17-19).

We shall reap what we sow. Therefore, it is important that we cultivate, in our children, from their earliest days, an appreciation and a love of work, but they will only have that if they see the virtue of diligence and industry working in their parents.

THE SPIRIT OF THE CHRIST

WEEK 1: DAY 6–FIRST MEDITATION

Based on *The Imitation of Christ*, Book 1, Chapter 1

On the Imitation of Christ and Contempt for the Vanities of the World

1. "He who follows Me, does not walk in darkness," says the Lord (Jn. 8:12). These are the words of Christ, by which we are advised to imitate His life and ways, if we truly desire to be enlightened and freed from all blindness of heart. Let it, therefore, be our chief preoccupation to dwell upon the life of Jesus Christ.

2. The teaching of Christ surpasses all the teaching of holy men, and he who has Christ's spirit will find there "the hidden manna" (Apoc. 2:17). But it happens that many, though frequently hearing the Gospel, are little affected by it, because they have not the spirit of Christ. But he who wishes, with relish, to fully understand the words of Christ, must strive to bring his whole life in conformity to that of Christ.

3. What does it profit you to argue profoundly about the Trinity, if you lack humility and so become displeasing to the Trinity? Truly, deep words do not make a man holy and just. It is a virtuous life that makes a man dear to God. I would rather feel contrition than define the word. If you know the whole Bible by heart and the sayings of all the philosophers, what would all this profit you without the grace of God? "Vanity of vanities, all is vanity," (Eccles. 1:2) except to love God and serve Him alone. This is the highest wisdom—despising the world so as to reach for the Kingdom of heaven.

4. It is vanity, therefore, to seek riches that shall perish and to put one's hope in them. It is vanity also to be ambitious for honors and to raise oneself to high station. It is vanity to follow the lusts of the flesh and to desire that for which you will later be grievously punished. It is vanity to hope for a long life and to take little care of leading a good life. It is vanity to attend only to the present life and not look forward to the things to come. It is vanity to love that which speedily passes away and not to hasten there where endless joy abides.

5. Often remember that proverb: "The eye is not satisfied with seeing, nor the ear filled with hearing" (Eccles.1:8). Be zealous, therefore, to withdraw your heart from the love of visible things and to turn it towards invisible things, for those who follow their carnal nature, defile their conscience and lose the grace of God.

WEEK 1: DAY 6–SECOND MEDITATION

Based on *The Imitation of Christ*, Book 1, Chapter 18

On the Examples of the Holy Fathers

1. Consider the living examples of the holy fathers—in whom shone real perfection and religion—and you will see how little, or virtually nothing, is that which we do. Alas, what is our life if it be compared to theirs? Saints and friends of Christ, they served the Lord in hunger and thirst, in cold and nakedness, in toil and weariness, in watchings and fastings, in prayers and holy meditations, in persecutions and many reproaches (Heb. 11:37).

2. O, how many and grievous tribulations did the Apostles, Martyrs, Confessors, Virgins and others suffer, in their desire to follow the steps of Christ! They hated their lives in this world, so as to possess them for eternity. O, what a strict and renounced a life did the holy fathers in the desert live! What long and grievous temptations they endured! So often were they attacked by the enemy! What frequent and fervent prayers did they offer up to God! What a rigorous abstinence did they undergo! What great zeal and fervor they had for their spiritual progress. What strong wars they waged against the tyranny of their vices! With what pure and upright effort did they reach for God! By day they labored and at night they gave themselves to long prayers, though, while they labored, they ceased not at all from mental prayer.

3. They spent all their time profitably, every hour seemed short to spend with God; and in the great sweetness of divine contemplation, they even forgot their need of bodily refreshment. They renounced all riches, dignities, honors, friends and relations; they desired to have nothing from the world; they scarcely took the bare necessities of life; they were grieved to serve the body, even in necessity. Therefore, they were poor in earthly things, but most rich in grace and virtues. Outwardly they were in need, but inwardly they were refreshed with God's graces and consolation.

4. To the world they were strangers, but to God they were neighbors and familiar friends. To themselves they seemed as nothing, and despised by this world; but in the eyes of God they were precious and beloved. They stood in true humility, they lived in simple obedience, they walked in love and patience; and so, day by day, they advanced in spirit and obtained great favor with God. They are an example to all men...and should inspire us to make good progress, more than the number of the lukewarm calls us to careless living.

5. O, how great was the fervor of all religious at the start of their holy institution! O, what devoutness of prayer! What rivalry of virtue! How great a discipline flourished! What reverence and obedience flourished under the rule of their superiors! The traces remaining bear witness that they were truly holy and mature men, who, waging war so stoutly, trod the world underfoot. Yet, today, a man is thought great if he merely avoids sin and if he can patiently endure what he has undertaken.

6. O, the lukewarmness and negligence of our state, wherein we so quickly fall away from our former fervor and have become weary of life through sloth and lukewarmness! May progress in the virtues be not entirely asleep in you, who have so often witnessed the example of such devoted men.

WEEK 1: DAY 6–THIRD MEDITATION

Based on *The Imitation of Christ*, Book 1, Chapter 22

On Considering Man's Wretchedness

1. You are unhappy wherever you are and in whatever direction you turn, unless you turn to God. Why are you troubled that things do not turn out for you just as you wish and desire? Who is there who has everything according to his wish? Neither I, nor you, nor anyone on earth. There is no one on earth free from trouble or anguish, be he king or Pope. Who is he who has a better lot in life? Most certainly he who has the strength to suffer something for God.

2. Many foolish weaklings say: "Look, what a good life that man has, how rich, how great, how powerful and famous he is!" But give your attention to the good things of heaven, and you will see that all those temporal things are worth nothing, but are utterly uncertain and very burdensome, because they are never owned without anxiety and fear. Our happiness is not in having temporal things in abundance—moderation in those things is enough for us. It is truly misery to live upon earth. The more a soul desires to be spiritual, the more bitter the present life becomes to it, because it better understands and clearly sees the shortcomings of man's corruption. For to eat, to drink, to stay awake, to sleep, to rest, to labor and to submit to the other necessities of nature, is truly a source of misery and affliction to a devout soul, who would gladly be released from these things and freed from all sin.

3. For in this world, those who lead interior lives are greatly burdened by the demands of the body. And so the Prophet devoutly asks for strength to be free from them, saying: "The troubles of my heart are multiplied; deliver me from my necessities" (Ps. 24:17). But woe to them who do not recognize their wretchedness and even more woe to them who love this wretched and perishable life. For there are some who cling to this life so much that, even though they have to toil or beg for the bare necessities of life, they would, if it were only possible, prefer to live on earth forever, showing no interest for the kingdom of God.

4. O, senseless and faithless people, who lie buried so deep in earthly things, as to relish nothing other than the things of the flesh! Miserable wretches! In the end they will find, to their cost, how cheap and worthless was that which they loved. But the saints of God and all devoted friends of Christ, gave no thought to the things which pleased the flesh, nor to those things which flourished in this life, but their whole hope and intention aspired towards the good things of eternity. Their whole desire was borne upwards to the things eternal and invisible, lest the love of things visible should pull them down to things below.

5. Do not become discouraged with your lack of spiritual progress; you still have time and opportunity. Why do you wish to put off your progress till tomorrow? Arise, begin this very moment and say: "Now is the time for action, now is the time to fight, now is the proper time to amend my life." When you are troubled and afflicted, then is the time for merit. You must go through fire and water before finding refreshment. Unless you force yourself, you will never conquer vice. As long as we are in this frail body, we cannot be without sin, nor live without weariness and sorrow. We would gladly have rest from all misery, but because, through sin, we have lost our innocence, we have also lost our true blessedness. And so we must be patient and await the mercy of God, until all iniquity pass away and this mortality be swallowed up by eternal life.

6. O, how great is human frailty, which is ever prone to vice! Today you confess your sins and, tomorrow, you again commit the sins you have confessed. At this very moment, you are resolved to be on your guard, yet, after an hour, you act as if you had never made any resolutions. Deservedly, then, can we humble ourselves and never hold any high opinion of ourselves, because

we are so frail and unstable. What will yet become of us in the end, when we grow lukewarm so soon? Woe to us if we wish to turn aside, in order to rest, as if we had already arrived at peace and safety, but without there being any trace of true holiness in our words and actions (I Thess. 5:3).

WEEK 1: DAY 6–FOURTH MEDITATION

Based on the *Imitation of Christ*, Book 1, Chapter 25

On the Fervent Amendment of Our Whole Life

1. Be watchful and diligent in the service of God, and often reflect: "Why have I come here? And why have I abandoned the world? Was it not that I might live for God and become a spiritual person?" Therefore be ardent for your spiritual progress, for you will soon receive the reward for your labors and, then, neither fear nor sorrow shall come within your borders any more. You will labor a little now and you will find great rest and everlasting joy. And if you remain ardent and faithful in what you do, God, without doubt, will be faithful in rewarding you. You must hold on to the hope that you will win the crown, but you must not become over-confident, lest you become lazy and proud.

2. On one occasion, when a certain anxious man, overwhelmed with sadness and often wavering between fear and hope, threw himself down in a church before an altar, saying as he turned these matters in his mind: "O, if I only knew that it was still worthwhile persevering!" He immediately heard God's reply in his heart: "And if you knew that it was worthwhile, what would you do? Do now what you would do then and you will be perfectly safe." Immediately comforted and strengthened, he committed himself to God's will and his anxious wavering ceased. Henceforth, he had no desire to curiously search to know what would happen to him in the future, but strove to learn what God's "well-pleasing and perfect" will might be, here and now, for the beginning and accomplishing of every good work.

3. "Trust in the Lord and do good," says the Prophet, "and dwell in the land and thou shalt be fed with its riches" (Ps. 36:3).

There is one thing that keeps many back from spiritual progress and sincere amendment of life: that is a dread of the difficulty or the toil of the struggle involved. And they indeed advance in virtue, more than all others, who more manfully strive to overcome those things which are more troublesome and opposed to them. For, the more we overcome ourselves and mortify our spirit, the more we make progress and merit more abundant grace.

4. But all people have not equal difficulties to overcome and mortify. Yet, a zealous imitator of Christ will make greater progress, even though he may have more passions to fight against, than someone who has fewer passions to overcome, but is less zealous in the pursuit of virtue. Two things, especially, help to bring about a great amendment of life: namely, to forcibly withdraw oneself from that to which our nature is viciously inclined and to earnestly labor in acquiring those virtues which we lack the most.

Strive, too, to guard against and overcome those things which displease you most in others. Try to make progress at all times and in all places, so that, if you hear or see good examples, you may be inspired to imitate them. But if you have thought anything blameworthy in others, take care lest you do the same; or, if at times you have done so, be zealous in quickly correcting yourself.

How pleasant and how sweet it is to see brethren, fervent and devout, well-mannered and disciplined! How sad and grievous to see them indisciplined and not practising those things to which they were called! How hurtful it is to neglect the purpose of their calling and to turn the heart to that which is not their business!

5. Be mindful of your purpose in life and set before you the image of the Crucified. You can be truly ashamed when you look upon the life of Jesus Christ, because you have not shown zeal in imitating Him, even though you have been His disciple for many a year. The soul that exercises itself intensely and devotedly, in the most holy life and passion of the Lord, will find there an abundance of things useful and necessary for itself. Nor is there need to seek anything better outside Jesus. O, if Jesus crucified should come into our hearts, how quickly and adequately should we learn!

6. The fervent soul bears and takes well all things that may be

commanded. The negligent and lukewarm soul has tribulation upon tribulation and suffers anguish on every side, because it lacks inner consolation and is forbidden to seek exterior consolations. The soul that lives an indisciplined life, is exposed to grievous ruin. Whoever seeks after easier and less restrained things, will always be in trouble, because one thing or the other will always be displeasing.

7. How do so many other souls manage, who live a disciplined life? They seldom go out, live apart, eat in the poorest fashion, dress roughly, labor much, speak little, keep long vigil, rise early, prolong prayer, read much and keep themselves in all discipline. Consider the Carthusians, the Cistercians, and the monks and nuns of other religious orders: how they rise each night to sing praises to the Lord. What a terrible thing it would be for you to grow slothful in such holy work, when such a host of religious people are beginning to sing praise to God.

8. O, if only there were no other obligation laid upon us, other than to praise the Lord our God with the whole heart and voice! O, if you should never need to eat, or drink or sleep, but could always praise God and be free for spiritual pursuits alone! Then you would be much more happy than now, when you serve the flesh and every sort of need. Would to God those needs did not exist, but only the spiritual refreshments of the soul, which, alas, we savor rarely enough.

9. When a soul reaches this point, whereby it seeks its consolation from no created thing, then first does God begin perfectly to content that soul; then, too, will the soul be content with every outcome of events. For neither will it rejoice over riches, nor be sorrowful in poverty, but will commit itself wholly and trustingly to God, Who is all in all; to Whom, assuredly, nothing is lost or perishes, but all things live for Him and at His nod instantly obey.

10. Remember always the end and that time lost does not return. Without care and diligence you will never acquire virtues. If you begin to grow lukewarm, you will start to deteriorate. But if you give yourself to zeal, you will find great peace and will feel labor lighter, for the grace of God and the love of virtue. An

ardent and diligent man is ready for everything. It is a greater toil to resist vices and passions, than to sweat at bodily labors. He who does not shun small faults, gradually slips into greater. You will always rejoice in the evening, if you spend the day fruitfully. Watch over yourself, stir yourself up, admonish yourself and whatever may be the case with others, do not neglect yourself. You will progress in proportion to violence that you will exert on yourself.

WEEK 1: DAY 7–FIRST MEDITATION

Based on *The Imitation of Christ*, Book 3, Chapter 18

Temporal Miseries are to be Borne with Patience, After the Example of Jesus Christ

1. Son, I came down from heaven for your salvation. I took up your sufferings, not because I had to, but because love drew Me, that you might learn patience, and not unworthily bear the sufferings of life. For, from the hour of My birth to My death upon the cross, I never ceased to bear sorrow and had great lack of temporal things. I often heard many reproaches against Me. I gently bore contradictions and harsh words; for benefits I received ingratitude, blasphemies for miracles, and for teaching I was censured.

2. Lord, because Thou wert patient during Thy life, chiefly in thus fulfilling Thy Father's command, it is fitting that I, a poor and wretched sinner, should bear myself patiently according to Thy will and carry, while it is Thy will, for my salvation, the burden of mortal life. For though the present life seems burdensome, it is, however, so full of merit and, by Thy grace and by Thine example and the footsteps of Thy saints, more bearable and brighter to the weak; but it is also much fuller of consolation than it had been of old under the ancient Law, when heaven's gate stayed shut and the way to heaven seemed more hard to find; when so few cared to seek the kingdom of the heavens. But not even those, who then were just and worthy of salvation, could enter the heavenly kingdom before Thy passion and the ransom of Thy holy death.

3. O, what great thanks am I bound to render Thee, because Thou deigned to show me and all the faithful, the straight and good way to Thine eternal kingdom! For Thy way is our way; and through Thy holy patience we walk to Thee, Who art our crown. If Thou hadst not gone before and taught us, who would care to follow? Alas, how far back would they remain, had they not in view Thy shining example! Behold, we are still lukewarm, although we have heard of Thy many miracles and teachings; what then would happen, had we not so great a light by which to follow Thee?

WEEK 1: DAY 7–SECOND MEDITATION

Based on *The Imitation of Christ*, Book 1, Chapter 13

On Resisting Temptations

1. So long as we live in the world we cannot be without tribulation and temptation. That is why it is written in Job: "The life of man upon earth is warfare" (Job 7:1). And therefore everyone must be concerned about their temptations and watchful in prayer, lest the devil find opportunity for deception; for he never sleeps but "goes about seeking whom he may devour." No one is so mature and holy, that he does not sometimes have temptations, nor can we be completely free from them.

2. Nevertheless, temptations are often very useful to us, hard and heavy though they may be, because in them we are made humble, cleansed and instructed. All the saints passed through many tribulations and temptations and made progress. And those who were unable to bear temptations were rejected and fell away. There is no Religious Order so sacred, no place so secluded, that there are no temptations and adversities there.

3. There is no one completely free from temptations as long as they live, because the source of temptation is within us. For we were born in sinful desire; one temptation or tribulation passes and another is on its way; and we shall always have something to suffer, for we have lost the gift of our original happiness. Many seek to escape temptations, only to more grievously fall into them.

We cannot win by flight alone, but only by patience and true humility are we made stronger than all our foes.

4. A soul, merely turning temptation aside outwardly and not tearing it out at the root, will make little progress. No, indeed, temptations will return all the more quickly and you will feel all the worse. With the help of God, little by little, with patience and endurance of spirit, you will win a better victory than by the harshness and force of your own determination. Seek counsel more often in temptation and do not deal harshly with someone who is tempted, but pour in comfort as you might wish done to yourself.

5. The beginning of all evil temptations is instability of mind and little trust in God. Just as a ship, without a helm, is tossed this way and that way by the waves, so too is a negligent man, who has abandoned his resolution, tempted in various ways. Fire tests iron and temptation tests the just man. Often we do not know what we can do, but temptation reveals what we are made of. Nevertheless, we must watch, especially at the beginning of temptation, for then the foe is more easily overcome, when he is in no way allowed to enter the door of the soul, but, as soon as he has knocked, is met and withstood outside on the doorstep. Whence someone has said: "Resist thou the beginnings; too late comes the remedy. When ills, through long delays, have grievous grown to be."

6. At first, the mere thought occurs to the mind, then comes the strong push of the imagination, afterwards pleasure, evil action and assent. And so, little by little, the malicious foe gains total entrance when he is not resisted at the beginning. And the longer a man is inactive in resisting, the weaker each day he grows in himself and the enemy grows stronger against him.

7. Some people suffer their most grievous temptations at the beginning of their Christian life; others at the end. Some are much troubled throughout their whole life. Some are tempted lightly enough, according to the wisdom and justice of God's Providence, which weighs the standing and the worth of men, ordering all things beforehand for the salvation of his chosen ones. Some are preserved from great temptations and are often overcome in little daily ones; so that, being humbled, they may never presume on themselves in great things, when they see themselves so weak in such small things.

8. We must not, therefore, despair when we are tempted, but we should pray to God with all the more fervor, that He might help us in all tribulations; Who, according to St. Paul, will "make such issue with the temptation, that we may be able to bear it" (I Cor. 10:13). Let us therefore humble our souls under the hand of God in all temptations and tribulations—for the humble in spirit He will save and exalt.

WEEK 1: DAY 7–THIRD MEDITATION

Based on *The Imitation of Christ*, Book 3, Chapter 22

On Remembering God's Manifold Blessings

1. Lord, open my heart to Thy law and teach me to walk in Thy precepts (II Mac. 1:4). Grant me to understand Thy will and, with great reverence and careful consideration, to be mindful of Thy benefits, both those granted widely and those to me alone; so that I may worthily give thanks to Thee. Truly I know and confess that I am unable to pay due praise for even the least of Thy mercies. I do not deserve any of the benefits bestowed upon me. And when I think of Thy majesty, my spirit faints faced with its greatness.

2. All things, which I have in soul and in body and whatever I possess, exterior or interior, natural or supernatural, are Thy benefits and show Thee, from Whom I receive all good things, to be bountiful, merciful and good. Though one has received more and another less, all benefits, nevertheless, are Thine and, without Thee, not the least can be possessed. He who has received greater, cannot boast of deserving them, nor lift himself above others, nor hold the lesser in contempt, because he is the greater and the better who attributes less to himself and, by returning thanks, is the more humble and devout. And he who counts himself to be the least of all and judges himself more unworthy, is fitter to receive greater.

3. He who has received less must not be saddened, nor take it amiss, nor envy the richer, but rather look to Thee and most greatly praise Thy goodness, because so richly, so freely and generously, "without respect of persons," Thou bestowest Thy gifts. All things are from Thee and that is why, in all things, Thou art to be praised. Thou knowest what each one should be given and it is not for us to question why this one should have less and that one more, for that is for Thee to discern, to Whom it is clear what each one deserves.

4. That is why, Lord God, I even consider it a great blessing not to have much of that which, outwardly in the opinion of men, may be thought praise and glory; so that each one, his poverty and worthlessness considered, should not only conceive no grief, nor sadness, nor dejection from it, but rather consolation and great gladness, because Thou hast chosen for Thyself, as friends and intimates, the poor and humble and those despised in this world.

Thine Apostles are themselves witnesses, whom Thou hast made princes over all the earth. Yet they lived in this world without complaint, so humble and gentle, without any malice or guile, that they even "rejoiced to suffer reproaches for Thy name" and embraced with joy those things the world hates.

5. Nothing, therefore, ought to give such great joy to him that loves Thee and knows Thy benefits, as the accomplishment of Thy will in himself and the acceptance of Thy providence. He should find, therein, such content and comfort, that he should desire to be the least, as others desire to be the greatest; and as peaceful and contented in the very last place as in the first; and as willing to be despised and rejected, even to the point of losing one's name and reputation, as others are willing to be more honored and thought greater in the world. For Thy will and the love of Thine honor must go before everything and should console and please him more than all the benefits already given, or to those that may be given him in the future.

WEEK 1: DAY 7–FOURTH MEDITATION

Based on *The Imitation of Christ*, Book 3, Chapter 25

The Secret of Peace of Heart and Progress

1. Son, I have said: "Peace I leave with you, My peace I give unto you; not as the world giveth, do I give unto you" (Jn. 14:27). All long for peace, but not all care for that which belongs to true peace. My peace is with the humble and the lowly of heart. Your peace will be in much patience. If you have heard Me and followed my voice, you will be able to enjoy much peace.

2. What, therefore, shall I do, Lord?

3. In all things watch over yourself, what you do and what you say. Direct all your attention to this, that you may please Me alone and, outside of Me, desire or seek nothing. Also, make no rash judgment about what others say or do. Do not become involved in matters not committed to you and you will find that you will be disturbed but little or rarely. To never feel any disturbance, to never suffer any affliction of heart or of body, does not belong to the present time, but is the state of eternal rest. Do not, therefore, conclude that you have found true peace if you feel no grief; nor that all is good if you suffer from no enemy; nor to have found perfection if all things go according to your desires. Do not think that you are something great, or that you are specially loved if you find yourself in a state of great fervor or sweetness of spirit, for it is not in such things that the true lover of virtue is known, nor does the progress and perfection of man consist in such things.

4. In what, then, Lord, does it consist in?

5. In offering yourself wholeheartedly to God's will; in not seeking the things which are your own, small or great, in time or in eternity. So that you remain calm, rendering thanks both in prosperity and adversity, weighing all things with an even balance. If you shall be so strong and long-suffering in hope, so that if inner consolation is removed, you still prepare your heart for fuller endurance and do not justify yourself—thinking you ought not to suffer trials so great as these, but rather justify Me in all that I ordain and praise my holiness—then you are walking in the true straight way of peace and in the undoubted hope and knowledge that you will again see my face in joy (Job 33:26). If you have come to utter contempt of self, know that then you will enjoy an abundance of peace, as much as is possible in this state of banishment.

WEEK 1: DAY 7–FIFTH MEDITATION

Based on the *Imitation of Christ*, Book 3, Chapter 10

It is Sweet to Serve God

1. Now once more shall I speak, Lord, and not be silent; I shall say in the ears of my God and my King: "How great is the abundance of Thy sweetness, O Lord, which Thou hast hidden for them that fear Thee" (Ps. 30:20). But how much more is there for those who love Thee? And what of those who serve Thee with their whole heart? Truly unutterable is the sweetness of the contemplation of Thee, which Thou bestowest upon those who love Thee. In this Thou hast revealed to me the sweetness of Thy love, that when I was not, Thou didst make me; and when I wandered far from Thee, Thou didst bring me back that I might serve Thee and Thou hast commanded me to love Thee.

2. O fount of never-ending love, what shall I say about Thee? How shall I be able to forget Thee, Who deigned to remember me, even after I fell away and was lost? Beyond all hope Thou didst show mercy to Thy servant and, beyond all merit, revealed grace and friendship. What shall I return to Thee for this Thy grace? For it is not a grace given to everyone, to abandon all things, to renounce the world and to live for Thee. Is it a great thing that I should serve Thee, Whom everything created is bound to serve? I should not think it a great thing for me to serve Thee, I should rather be in wonderment that Thou didst deign to receive, as a servant, one so poor and unworthy and to include him with Thy beloved ones.

3. All things which I have and with which I serve Thee, are Thine. Yet, on the contrary, Thou servest me more than I serve

Thee. For, heaven and earth, which Thou didst make to serve man, are at Thy hand and each day they do whatever Thou command. And this is a small thing: for Thou hast even created and set up angels to serve man! But it goes beyond all this that *Thou hast Thyself* deigned to serve man and have promised to give Thyself to him.

4. What shall I give Thee for Thy thousand benefits? Would that I could serve Thee all the days of my life! Would that I were able, for even one day, to show worthy service! Truly, Thou are worthy of all service, all honor and praise eternal. Truly, Thou art my Lord and God, and I Thy poor servant, who, with all my strength, am bound to serve Thee and never must I grow weary in praising Thee. Such is my desire, such my longing and whatever is lacking in me do Thou deign to supply.

5. It is a great honor and a great glory to serve Thee and to despise all things for Thy sake. For they shall have great grace, who, of their own will, shall subject themselves to Thy most holy service. They will find the sweetest consolations of the Holy Spirit, who, for love of Thee, have cast every carnal joy aside. They shall attain great liberty of mind, who, for Thy name's sake, enter on the narrow way, and have put aside all worldly cares.

6. O, pleasing and delightful service of God, by which a man is truly made free and holy! O, holy state of religious servitude, which makes a man equal to the angels, pleasing to God, a terror to demons and praiseworthy to all the faithful. O, servitude to be embraced and ever prayed for, by which the highest good is won and joy gained, which shall abide for evermore. Amen.

WEEK TWO

INTRODUCTION TO WEEK TWO:
KNOWING ONESELF

True Devotion to Mary Is a Secret of Grace

The practice which I am about to disclose is one of these secrets of grace, unknown to the greater number of Christians, known even to few of the devout, and practiced and relished by a lesser number still (*True Devotion*, §82).

Those who wish to enter into this particular devotion, which is not at present erected into a confraternity (though that were to be wished), after having, as I said in the first part of this preparation for the reign of Jesus Christ, employed twelve days at least in ridding themselves of the spirit of the world, which is contrary to the spirit of Jesus Christ, should employ three weeks in filling themselves with Jesus Christ by the holy Virgin. They can follow this order: (*True Devotion*, §227).

Pray to Know Thyself

They should then offer up all their prayers and pious actions to ask for a knowledge of themselves and contrition for their sins; and they should do this in a spirit of humility. For that end they can, if they choose, meditate on what I have said before of our inward corruption. They can look upon themselves during...this week as snails, crawling things, toads, swine, serpents and unclean animals; or they can reflect on these three considerations of St. Bernard: the vileness of our origin, the dishonors of our present state, and our ending as the food of worms (*True Devotion*, §228).

They should pray Our Lord and the Holy Ghost to enlighten them; and for that end they might use the ejaculations, *"Lord, that*

I may see!" (Lk. 18:41); or *"May I know myself!"* or *"Come, Holy Ghost,"* together with the Litany of the Holy Ghost and the prayer which follows....They should have recourse to the Blessed Virgin and ask her to grant them this immense grace, which must be the foundation of all the others; for this end, they should say the *Ave Maris Stella* and the Litany of the Blessed Virgin (*True Devotion,* §228).

We now enter the second week of preparation—a period dedicated to knowledge of self; something indispensable for our progress in the spiritual life. Too often we have only a superficial knowledge of ourselves—imagining ourselves to be what we are not. The purpose of this week is to see ourselves as we really are—to see ourselves as God sees us. How shall we achieve this knowledge of ourselves? By....

PRAYER—asking God for the grace to see ourselves as we really are. True knowledge of self, will only be achieved by the grace of God and this grace will only come if we ask it of God, through humble and sincere prayer.

EXAMINING OUR LIFE—to see how we have spent or misspent our lives. To help you examine your life thoroughly, we have included an extensive examination of conscience for Day Two of this week. This covers all the Ten Commandments and various sins based on different states in life. It is also an ideal way to prepare for Confession. We recommend that you make a general confession of your whole life, or at least from the time of your last general confession. However, this is only recommended, *not obligatory,* and it suffices to make a regular confession in preparation for the Consecration. Realizing that it can sometimes be difficult to find both the priest and the time for a general confession, we suggest that you make your confession at any time during the five-week preparatory period—or in cases of impossibility, at any time before or after the Consecration.

REFLECTION—on why we were created? By Whom? Where we came from? Where are we going? Everyone ends up in one of two places—heaven or hell. Reflect upon the fact that we cannot serve God *and* the world. Which one do we *really* put first? Are we *really* committed to serving God? Is it only on Sundays and in private? Or only in those things that we find to our liking?

ACTS OF MORTIFICATION—in order to atone for our past sins and to draw down God's favor and graces upon ourselves. Remember, there is more joy in heaven over one sinner doing penance, than ninety-nine just men who need no penance! Our Lord also warns us that unless we do penance, we will also perish.

ACTS OF CONTEMPT TOWARDS OURSELVES—showing contempt for our sins and our past life; showing contempt for our inclination to do evil and neglect good; contempt for the way we have misspent our lives in offending God; contempt for those things that could lead us back to such a sinful life:

> Christians in a state of grace, who begin to give themselves to the service of God, have an initial knowledge of themselves; little by little they discern the defects they have, the remains of sins that have already been forgiven, and the new failings that are more or less deliberate and voluntary. If these beginners are generous, they seek, not to excuse themselves, but to correct themselves. God shows them their wretchedness and spiritual poverty, making them understand that they must consider it in the light of divine mercy, which exhorts them to advance spiritually. They must daily examine their consciences and learn to overcome themselves, so that they may not follow the impulses of their passions.

> However, as yet, they only know themselves in a superficial way. They have not discovered what a treasure baptism placed in their souls and are ignorant of all the self-love and the often unconscious egoism still continuing in them—revealing itself from time to time under the sting of a sharp reproach or vexation. Often, they have a clearer perception of this self-love in others than in themselves; they ought to remember Christ's words in such cases: "Why seest thou the mote that is in thy brother's eye; and seest not the beam that is in thy own eye?" (Mt. 7:3). The beginner bears in himself a diamond embedded in a mass of gross material and he does not yet know the value of the diamond or all the defects of the other material. God loves him far more than he believes, but with a strong love that has its exigencies and which demands abnegation of the soul to reach true liberty of spirit (Rev. Fr. Garrigou-Lagrange, O.P., *The Three Ages of the Interior Life*, ch.18).

A true knowledge of ourselves will never be pleasant and all this self-examination can become quite depressing. Yet, even though we have to cast a *glance* at our past, our *focus* should be on the future, not on the past. We only look at our sinful past so as to flee from it to a virtuous future. Let us confidently place ourselves at the feet of our merciful and compassionate Mother, the Refuge of Sinners. From her we will obtain the light to leave our present darkness. Next to her, we will see our true state without despairing. If she could accept into her company, a repentant Mary Magdalen (once possessed by seven devils), then she will accept us also.

The recommended prayers for this week are the Litanies of the Holy Ghost and the Blessed Virgin, together with the *Ave Maris Stella*. We have also added the Litany of Humility. You will find all these prayers on the following pages. If you have time, then say all of them each day. If not, then say what you are able, or at least say one of those prayers daily, taking a different prayer each day. Remember, you do not have to meditate on all the readings in this book, but *do at least try to read them all*—while meditating on as many as you are able. To Jesus through Mary!

RECOMMENDED PRAYERS FOR WEEK TWO

Litany of the Holy Ghost
Litany of the Blessed Virgin Mary
Ave Maris Stella
Litany of Humility
(Each prayer need not be said daily.)

Litany of the Holy Ghost

Lord, have mercy on us,
Christ, have mercy on us
Lord, have mercy on us
Father, all powerful,
Have mercy on us.
Jesus, Eternal Son of the Father,
Redeemer of the world, *Save us.*
Spirit of the Father and the Son, boundless life of both,
Sanctify us.
Holy Trinity, *Hear us.*
Holy Ghost, Who proceedest
from the Father and the Son, *Enter our hearts.*
Holy Ghost, Who art equal to the Father and the Son,
Enter our hearts.
Promise of God the Father, *Have mercy on us.*
Ray of heavenly light,
Author of all good,
Source of heavenly water,
Consuming fire,
Ardent charity,
Spiritual unction,
Spirit of love and truth,
Spirit of wisdom and understanding,
Spirit of counsel and fortitude,
Spirit of knowledge and piety,
Spirit of the fear of the Lord,
Spirit of grace and prayer,
Spirit of peace and meekness,
Spirit of modesty and innocence,
Holy Ghost, the Comforter,
Holy Ghost, the Sanctifier,
Holy Ghost, Who governest the Church,
Gift of God, the Most High,
Spirit Who fillest the universe,
Spirit of the adoption of the children of God,
Holy Ghost, *inspire us with horror of sin.*

Holy Ghost, *come and renew the face of the earth.*
Holy Ghost, *shed Thy light in our souls.*
Holy Ghost, *engrave Thy law in our hearts.*
Holy Ghost, *inflame us with the flame of Thy love.*
Holy Ghost, *open to us the treasures of Thy graces.*
Holy Ghost, *teach us to pray well.*
Holy Ghost, *enlighten us with Thy heavenly inspirations.*
Holy Ghost, *lead us in the way of salvation.*
Holy Ghost, *grant us the only necessary knowledge.*
Holy Ghost, *inspire in us the practice of good.*
Holy Ghost, *grant us the merits of all virtues.*
Holy Ghost, *make us persevere in justice.*
Holy Ghost, *be Thou our everlasting reward.*

Lamb of God, Who takest away the sins of the world,
    Send us Thy Holy Ghost.
Lamb of God, Who takest away the sins of the world,
    Pour down into our souls the gifts of the Holy Ghost.
Lamb of God, Who takest away the sins of the world,
    Grant us the Spirit of wisdom and piety.

V. Come, Holy Ghost! Fill the hearts of Thy faithful.
R. And enkindle in them the fire of Thy Love.

Let us pray

Grant, O merciful Father, that Thy Divine Spirit enlighten, inflame and purify us, that He may penetrate us with His heavenly dew and make us fruitful in good works; through our Lord Jesus Christ, Thy Son, Who with Thee, in the unity of the same Spirit, liveth and reigneth forever and ever. *R. Amen.*

Litany of the Blessed Virgin Mary

Lord, have mercy on us.
Christ, have mercy on us.
Lord, have mercy on us.
Christ, hear us.
Christ, graciously hear us.
God the Father of heaven, *Have mercy on us.*
God the Son, Redeemer of the world,
God the Holy Ghost,
Holy Trinity, one God,
Holy Mary, *Pray for us.*
Holy Mother of God,
Holy Virgin of virgins,
Mother of Christ,
Mother of divine grace,
Mother most pure,
Mother most chaste,
Mother inviolate,
Mother undefiled,
Mother most amiable,
Mother most admirable,
Mother of good counsel,
Mother of our Creator,
Mother of our Savior,
Virgin most prudent,
Virgin most venerable,
Virgin most renowned,
Virgin most powerful,
Virgin most merciful,
Virgin most faithful,
Mirror of justice,
Seat of wisdom,
Cause of our joy,
Spiritual vessel,
Vessel of honor,
Singular vessel of devotion,
Mystical rose,

Tower of David,
Tower of ivory,
House of gold,
Ark of the covenant,
Gate of heaven,
Morning Star,
Health of the sick,
Refuge of sinners,
Comforter of the afflicted,
Help of Christians,
Queen of angels,
Queen of patriarchs,
Queen of prophets,
Queen of Apostles,
Queen of martyrs,
Queen of confessors,
Queen of virgins,
Queen of all saints,
Queen conceived without original sin,
Queen assumed into heaven,
Queen of the most holy Rosary,
Queen of peace,

Lamb of God, Who takes away the sins of the world,
    Spare us, O Lord.
Lamb of God, Who takes away the sins of the world,
    Graciously hear us, O Lord.
Lamb of God, Who takes away the sins of the world,
    Have mercy on us.

V. Pray for us, O holy Mother of God.
R. That we may be made worthy of the promises of Christ.

Let us pray

Grant unto us, Thy servants, we beseech Thee, O Lord God, at all times to enjoy health of soul and body; and by the glorious intercession of Blessed Mary, ever virgin, when freed from the sorrows of this present life, to enter into that joy which hath no end. Through Christ our Lord. *R. Amen.*

Ave Maris Stella

Hail, bright star of ocean,
God's own Mother blest,
Ever sinless Virgin,
Gate of heavenly rest.

Taking that sweet Ave
Which from Gabriel came,
Peace confirm within us,
Changing Eva's name.

Break the captives' fetters,
Light on blindness pour,
All our ills expelling,
Every bliss implore.

Show thyself a Mother;
May the Word Divine,
Born for us thy Infant,
Hear our prayers through thine.

Virgin all excelling,
Mildest of the mild,
Freed from guilt, preserve us,
Pure and undefiled.

Keep our life all spotless,
Make our way secure,
Till we find in Jesus
Joy forevermore.

Through the highest heaven
To the Almighty Three,
Father, Son and Spirit,
One same glory be. Amen.

Litany of Humility

O Jesus, meek and humble of heart, *Hear me.*
From the desire of being esteemed, *Deliver me, O Jesus.*
From the desire of being loved,
From the desire of being extolled,
From the desire of being honored,
From the desire of being praised,
From the desire of being preferred to others,
From the desire of being consulted,
From the desire of being approved,
From the fear of being humiliated,
From the fear of being despised,
From the fear of suffering rebukes,
From the fear of being calumniated,
From the fear of being forgotten,
From the fear of being ridiculed,
From the fear of being wronged,
From the fear of being suspected,
That others may be loved more than I,
> *Jesus, grant me the grace to desire it.*

That others may be esteemed more than I,
> *Jesus, grant me the grace to desire it.*

That, in the opinion of the world,
others may increase and I may decrease,
> *Jesus, grant me the grace to desire it.*

That others may be chosen and I set aside,
> *Jesus, grant me the grace to desire it.*

That others may be praised and I go unnoticed,
> *Jesus, grant me the grace to desire it.*

That others may be preferred to me in everything,
> *Jesus, grant me the grace to desire it.*

That others may become holier than I,
Provided that I may become as holy as I should,
> *Jesus, grant me the grace to desire it. Amen.*

DAILY MEDITATIONS TO HELP US GROW IN THE KNOWLEDGE OF OURSELVES

WEEK 2: DAY 1–FIRST MEDITATION

Knowledge of Self is the Foundation of Sanctity

The first thing we must impress upon ourselves is that *we are creatures*. There is a great deal more in this thought than may at first appear. We were created by a holy God and for a holy purpose. In his book, the Secret of Mary, St. Louis de Montfort says, quite bluntly:

> Chosen soul, living image of God and redeemed by the Precious Blood of Jesus Christ, God wants you to become holy like Him in this life, and glorious like Him in the next....It is certain that growth in the holiness of God is your vocation. All your thoughts, words, actions, everything you suffer or undertake, must lead you towards that end. Otherwise you are resisting God, in not doing the work for which He created you and for which He is even now keeping you in being (*Secret of Mary*, §3).

This is nothing other than what Our Lord meant, when He said: "Be you therefore perfect, as also your heavenly Father is perfect" (Mt. 5:48).

We therefore belong entirely to Him; and it is our duty to fulfill His desire that we become perfect—for, after all, it is *only* saints that go to heaven. That sanctity is achieved here below, or in the fires of Purgatory. Ask yourself candidly: "Have I always looked upon myself in that light?" When you have performed any seemingly great act of self-sacrifice, *etc.*, have you regarded it as a small thing and nothing more than your duty? If this is how you approach the things you do for God, well and good. It is the right light in which to view what you do, because it is a truthful light.

Many people—and they are well-intentioned people—endeavor to hide what they do; they trouble themselves a great deal for fear of giving way to vanity; they think they are bound not to know what they have done. To these good people I would say: pray for the grace to know yourself, and then you will not fear vanity; God, Who is truth itself, does not wish you to be un-truthful. He wishes you to know yourself, as far as it is possible.

This self-knowledge will go on increasing until the day of your death. *Nevertheless, if you earnestly strive to spend this week in the endeavor to know yourself, you will have made a great step in laying the foundation-stone of all sanctity, which is self-knowledge, the lowly sentiment of yourself as a creature, or in other words, the virtue of humility.* Perhaps, until now, you have not been aware how much you needed this virtue.

Let the fruit of this meditation be a very earnest desire to know yourself, with *some* of the knowledge with which God knows you. I say, with *some* of the knowledge, because you never will know your own nothingness as God does. Our Lord once said to one of His saints—"If you saw yourself as I saw you, then you would die out of fright!" We imagine ourselves to be far better than we really are. Ask God to let you see yourself in a more truthful light—without the "die out of fright" part! Direct to this end all your works, penances, and prayers—always in union with Mary—to obtain from God this great grace.

WEEK 2: DAY 1–SECOND MEDITATION

Slaves of Christ...Unprofitable Servants

We were made by God, therefore we belong to Him with all that we do, all our thoughts, words and works. You are obliged to devote yourself to His service and seek His will in all things. You belong by right to God. You are—I will not say a servant, for a servant has rights—but I will say clearly that you are a slave of God. If there was any other word, any more forcible word, by which I could express more strongly the absolute dominion God has over you, I would use it.

Consider well the truth of this and you will acknowledge that God has greater rights over you than a master, in former times, had over his slaves. Yet, you may object that Our Lord Himself says: "I will not now call you servants (more correctly translated, slaves), but I will call you friends." That is true, indeed, but we are not to forget that our true position is evident from His words: "When you have done all these things that are commanded, say that you are unprofitable servants."

If Our Lord, in His great love and goodness, raises us up and calls us His friends, He does not mean, on that account, that we should forget our true position and say: "We are slaves to no one!" Yet how often this *is* said, even by those whose knowledge of theology should not hinder the truth! *Mancipia Christi* —*slaves of Christ*—are the words used in the Council of Trent concerning Christians. Let this truth, though perhaps unpalatable to you at first, sink into your mind. Put yourself in the presence of God in your true position as His creature and His slave. Remember your past rebelliousness, through sin, and regret that disobedience. He will love you with a special love, because you place yourself before Him, without any pretence, in your true position.

What Has God Done for Us?
What Have We Done for Him?

Indeed, it is true that we are children of God and, if children, heirs also. But we must remember we are children only by adoption. If a master had released and raised one of his slaves to the rank of his child and heir, would he be pleased if that slave totally forgot his former position and never thought of it, even so far as to never thank the good master, to whom he was indebted for his freedom and present position as heir? No, most certainly the master would not be pleased: the slave would be considered to have become proud by his self-elevation and would probably be held in disgrace. He would also be considered and would, in fact, be ungrateful. I think it is St. Thomas who says that true gratitude consists in esteeming a benefit as it deserves, and endeavoring to make our benefactor an adequate return (St. Thomas Aquinas, *Summa Theologica*, IIa IIae, Q.106, A.3).

Therefore, a person who will not acknowledge what he owes another, who endeavors to banish it from his mind, cannot be a grateful person any more than he is a trustful person. This, then, would be another reason for making us discover our own nothingness, because it makes us more grateful to God. If we thor-

oughly search into what we are—creatures of God made to glorify Him and bound by the fact of our creation to do so, as the
sun or any other work of God is bound to fulfill the end of its
creation—it will make us think very little of what we do for God.

Furthermore, when we consider what He has done for us—
raising us up from the rank of slaves to that of His adopted children—then it will make us all the more humble in the thought
that we never can make Him anything like an adequate return.
Imprint this thought on your mind, or, rather, ask Mary to give
you a portion of her wonderful humility, that precious gift for
which the King of kings regarded this chosen one with a look of
love, beyond that given to any other creature; raised her above the
highest of the angels and made her their Queen.

We Are Still Unprofitable Servants

We have considered that, being creatures and subjects, we are
bound to give service; and, in giving that service, we do no more
than our duty. This is what Our Lord would have us understand
when He tells us that, when we have done all that is commanded
of us, "we are still unprofitable servants." These are the words of
Truth Incarnate, pronouncing a truth that cannot be exagger-
ated; and to those who possess a truthful knowledge of themselves, there is no difficulty in understanding it. We must give to
God what is due to Him—but we give Him no profit, that is to
say, nothing over and above what is due, therefore we are "unprofitable servants."

This is a simple plain truth, but not considered enough; and
for that reason do people spend their time, "laboring, fasting,
watching, praying, working—and take nothing," or very little.
They think too much of what they are doing: they believe they
have made great sacrifices and deserve much more from God as a
consequence. They spoil many of their works, which are not pleasing to God, by contaminating them with pride.

WEEK 2: DAY 1–THIRD MEDITATION

We Have Betrayed God

Having considered that if we do all that is commanded of us, we shall still be unprofitable servants, what, then, must we be if we are *still not doing all that is commanded of us?* What should we be called, when, far from fulfilling all that God commands us to do, we, on the contrary, break many of His commandments! We, who have dared to stand in God's presence and cry out with Satan, *"I will not serve."* What are we? Sinners, we call ourselves—but that word does not express the utter degradation of our state. As Catholics, our sins, in a certain sense, take on a greater culpability.

What images can we use to make ourselves see more clearly the evil we have done by our sins? Soul, what have you done in breaking the law of God? He is the Creator of your soul. He loved it and, by His continued love, keeps it in existence. Yet you have committed spiritual adultery of sorts, by leaving God for a mere creation of God's—preferring it to God Himself! Instead of returning His love, you spat in His face, you threw Him out of your soul, you drove a lance into His heart and obstinately continued in your evil ways. United to Him in Baptism, you quickly forsook Him for something else. Made a Soldier of Christ in Confirmation, you struck a treacherous blow against Him, instead of the enemy with whom you live at peace. Drawn to a more intimate union with Him in the Eucharist, like Judas, you stole out into the dark night to betray His love.

Flee the Ugliness of Sin

Some are tempted to flee from the presence of the diseased, the crippled, the handicapped, *etc.*, because they see a certain lack of physical perfection that they cannot cope with. Yet such diseases and handicaps are nothing compared to the soul crippled by sin. Others have the same desire to flee when faced with the worst and vilest of criminals. The lack of moral perfection repels them. Imagine what a wife or a husband becomes in the sight of their once loved spouse and children, once they have committed adultery—a filthy wretch who has betrayed trusting love and scandalized innocent children. How much more despicable is the terrible act of spiritual adultery that we commit, when we turn away from God in order to commit sin. There is no greater evil than sin and there is nothing so ugly as a soul in the state of mortal sin.

Shamefully place yourself at the feet of the Blessed Mother, the Refuge of sinners. Turn to her like Mary Magdalen turned to Christ. A mother can put up with the most gruesome sights and situations, when the good of her child is at stake. Mary will receive you, like a prodigal child, the moment you realize what you have done by your sins. She will console you with the thought of the new spiritual birth, for which you are now preparing. She will tell you that, as the Mother of Mercy, she has a special role to play in the conversion of sinners and in bringing about their reconciliation with God.

The greater the sinner, the greater the achievement there will be when he eventually becomes a saint—and there have been some great sinners who have become great saints: St. Mary Magdalen, the Good Thief on the cross, St. Augustine, St. John of God, St. Matthew Talbot and many, many more. What God did for them, He will also do for us—if only we let Him. You need Mary like you need mercy. For she is the Mother of Mercy.

WEEK 2: DAY 1–FOURTH MEDITATION

Catholic Sinners are Worse than Pagan Sinners

In the last meditation, we saw that a soul in a state of mortal sin is, in the eyes of God and His holy angels, a very ugly being. Yet , how much worse is the mortal sin of a Catholic? We sometimes call ourselves great sinners, but have we realized what an abomination a *Catholic* sinner is.

Many sinners in the world may have never been baptized; never taught the Faith; never received the extra graces and inspirations of God as we have; never had the many helps and structures that the Church gives us and surrounds us with. Yet we are temples of the Holy Ghost, temples of an all-pure and all-holy

God! We were consecrated to the service of God at our baptism and we have desecrated that temple by sin! We have committed a sacrilege of sorts! I doubt if there are very many Catholics who have sufficiently considered this truth. Very few Catholics have considered their sins to be more serious than those of non-Catholics—people who have never been taught the Faith, nor received the sacraments and their graces. We often read of fearful crimes that strike terror in our hearts. Yet, never for an instant do we stop to weigh our sins alongside those crimes. Yet, perhaps, in the sight of God, some of our sins are worse than the many terrible crimes we read about.

St. Thomas Aquinas states that:

> A sin is deemed so much the more grievous as the sinner is held to be a more excellent person....Firstly, because a more excellent person, *e.g.*, one who excels in knowledge and virtue, can more easily resist sin; hence Our Lord said (Lk. 12:47) that the *"servant who knew the will of his lord...and did it not...shall be beaten with many stripes."* Secondly, on account of ingratitude, because every good in which a man excels, is a gift of God, to Whom man is ungrateful when he sins: and in this respect any excellence, even in temporal goods, aggravates a sin, according to Wis. 6:7: *"The mighty shall be mightily tormented."* Thirdly, on account of the sinful act being specially inconsistent with the excellence of the person sinning: for instance, if a prince were to violate justice, whereas he is set up as the guardian of justice, or if a priest were to be a fornicator, whereas he has taken the vow of chastity. Fourthly, on account of the example or scandal; because, as Gregory says (*Pastor.* i, 2): "Sin becomes much more scandalous, when the sinner is honored for his position" (St. Thomas Aquinas, *Summa Theologica,* Ia IIae, Q.73, A.10).

Let us also remember that God sees, not only what is, but what also *could be*. Therefore, if some criminal had been given all the graces and helps that I have received, then he might be a much holier person than I presently am. God may also see that if I found myself in the same circumstances as the criminals that I detest, then I might actually be far worse than they are! As the saying goes: "There, but for the grace of God, go I."

Think of this truth and while you consider it, forget not to return thanks to the remarkable providence of God, that so guarded you from the evils and temptations which would have been too strong for you. While you are considering what you are in the sight of God, be sure to thank Him for Our Lady, who turned out to be the only created person never to offend Him by the ingratitude of sin. Thank Him for bringing you, by His grace, to this special moment in your life, whereby this spotless and powerful masterpiece of God's, will take you under her protection and guidance.

Leave the Past and Yourself Behind

Finally, since we are seeking knowledge of ourselves, it would be well to consider the greatness of our dignity before the fall of our first parents into Original Sin. We all have an unfortunate habit of exaggerating things and it is quite probable that the preceding meditations have induced us to take too grim and low a view of human nature. We may even be somewhat depressed by the exercise so far! That is not the object of this week's meditations.

Despite Original Sin and our own actual sins, we were, nevertheless, made a *"little lower than the angels"* —we are, so to speak, their younger brethren. In Adam, we were all created potentially immaculate. Had Adam and Eve not sinned, their children could have been born in the state of sanctifying grace. They would all have had the same chance as their parents of not-dying, providing they avoided sin! Yet it was sin that brought death and tragedy into the world. Through the sin of one man, death entered the world.

We were created potentially immaculate in Adam, yet through Adam we sinned. Through that one sin, there came the source of all the crimes and outrages that are daily committed in this world. Yet, even though we were created a little below the angels, we have, in some respects, stooped down to the level of devils, because, by our behavior, we have imitated the fallen angels. Our fallen state, in some respects, resembles the rebellious nature of devils. We were endowed with the treasure of sanctifying grace, yet, like the Prodigal Son, we have lost our treasure and turned to husks of swine.

Think of the union between God and yourself, first entered into at Baptism, when you became a temple of the Holy Ghost. Think of the intimate union achieved at your first Holy Communion. Yet, how have we treated God since that day? Let us now, at least for the future, resolve to do better than we have in the past. The purpose of looking so deeply into our past, is to make us so horrified of what we have done, so that we really seek to leave its sinfulness and horror behind us, as we turn towards a new and better life of serving Him within the ranks of His Heavenly Mother's army.

Below, you will find an extensive examination of conscience. This will be very useful in examining our lives, to see how much we have offended God and, thereby, puncture the inflated and false notions we have of our own worth. The whole of this second day should be spent in a detailed examination of conscience. Ask the Holy Ghost for the grace to see yourself as He sees you, while also asking the Refuge of Sinners to prevent you from becoming discouraged, or even despairing, at the true evaluation of your past sins.

WEEK 2: DAY 2–AN ALL-DAY EXAMINATION OF CONSCIENCE

There are no meditations today, just an examination of conscience. Divide the following examination into manageable sections for the entire day. If you are to make a general confession, you may wish to photocopy the examination of conscience and mark the sins that apply to you—destroying the sheets afterwards.

How long ago did you make your last general confession? [A general confession is recommended, but is not obligatory—consult your confessor if in doubt as to what to do].
Did you receive absolution?
Did you perform your penance?
Did you willfully conceal a mortal sin, or confessed without true sorrow, or without a firm purpose of amendment, or without intending to perform your penance?
Did you, after this bad confession, receive Holy Communion in the state of mortal sin?
How many such sacrilegious Confessions and Communions have you made?
Have you, whilst in a state of mortal sin, received any other Sacraments?

FIRST COMMANDMENT:

I Am the Lord Thy God, Thou Shalt Not Have Strange Gods Before Me

Have you denied the Catholic Faith, openly rejected, or spoken against any doctrines of the Catholic Church?
Have you disbelieved or willfully indulged in doubts against any article of Faith, or suggested, or encouraged such doubts in others?
Have you betrayed the Catholic Faith by saying that all religions are good, that a man may choose to be saved in any religion whatsoever?

Have you read the Protestant Bible, heretical tracts or books, or sold, or lent them?

Have you attended, or joined in false worship? Have you played or sung in places of false worship? Have you listened to heretical or pagan preachers or lectures? How many times?

Have you exposed your Faith to danger by evil associations? Have you joined any secret society forbidden by the Church? Do you still belong to it? Have you through your own fault, remained ignorant of the doctrines and duties of your religion?

Have you remained a long time—a whole month, or longer— without saying any prayers, or performing any acts of devotion towards God?

Have you committed a sin in a holy place, the church, the graveyard? Have you been guilty of great irreverence in Church, by immodest conversation, by an unbecoming way of dressing, or by other gross misconduct?

Have you consulted fortune-tellers, or seriously made use of superstitious practices, love-potions, charms, horse-shoes, horoscopes, *etc.*. Read, kept, given, lent or sold dream-books, fortune-telling books and the like?

Have you sinned and remained in sin, thinking that because God is good, He is bound to forgive you?

Have you given way to despair?

Have you made an idol out of sports, or any other activity or creature?

Have you been ashamed of your Faith?

SECOND COMMANDMENT:

Thou Shalt Not Take the Name
of the Lord Thy God in Vain

Have you been guilty of blasphemy by angry, injurious or insulting words against God or any of His perfections, or against the Catholic Church, the Most Blessed Virgin Mary or any saints? Did you ever hate God?

Have you pronounced, in a blasphemous or irreverent manner, or in anger, the Holy Name of God, the Name of Our Lord Jesus Christ, or abused the words of Holy Scripture by any indecent or grossly irreverent application?

Have you sworn falsely? Have you done so to the prejudice of your neighbor? Have you joined an oath-bound secret society? How many oaths did you take in the society? Did you take an oath to be revenged or to commit some other crime? Have you induced others to swear falsely or unnecessarily, or to break a lawful oath?

Have you cursed yourself or your neighbor? Did you mean it? Was this sin habitual?

Have you made any rash vows? Have you broken or neglected a lawful vow, or changed it without permission?

THIRD COMMANDMENT:

Remember Thou Keep Holy the Lord's Day

The Precepts of the Church

1. To assist at Mass on Sundays and Holy Days of Obligation.
2. To fast and abstain on the days appointed.
3. To confess your sins at least once a year.
4. To go to Communion during Easter time.
5. To contribute to the support of the Church.
6. To observe the laws of the Church concerning marriage.

Have you on Sundays and Holy Days of Obligation willfully missed Mass, or arrived late, or left before Mass was over? Have you talked, laughed and gazed about during Mass?

Have you been habitually absent from the sermons and instructions?

Have you performed unnecessary servile work on Sundays and Holy Days of Obligation, or caused others to do so?

Have you desecrated these days, by frequenting ungodly company, by sinful amusements, gambling, immodest dancing, or drinking to excess?

Have you, without necessity, eaten meat or caused others to eat meat on days of abstinence? Have you broken the laws of fasting?

Have you neglected to contribute, according to your means, to the support of the Church and Her priests?

Have you been married before a civil magistrate, or even before an heretical preacher?

Have you ever, without the Church's dispensation, married a relative or a non-Catholic person?

Have you contracted marriage in any way forbidden by the Church?

FOURTH COMMANDMENT:

Honor Thy Father and Thy Mother

Have you despised, or even hated your parents, wished their death, or hoped that some other misfortune should befall them?

Have you insulted, mocked, ridiculed or cursed them?

Have you threatened them, or even lifted your hand to strike them?

Have you disobeyed them in serious matters when they forbade you to keep bad company, read bad books and papers and so on? Have you sorely grieved your parents by your ingratitude, or misconduct?

Have you, while still a minor, promised or even contracted marriage without your parents' knowledge and consent?

Have you neglected or refused to help them in their wants? Have you been ashamed of them on account of their poverty, class or appearance?

Have you faithfully accomplished their last will? Have you neglected to pray for them?

Have you been disrespectful and disobedient to your spiritual superiors, the Pope, the bishops and priests of the Church? Have you behaved towards them in a haughty and insulting manner? Did you refuse to pray for them, or for their conversion?

Do you pray for your country, for your government? Have you placed your country above God?

Have you taken part with the disaffected and seditious (revolutionary activities)? Have you ever joined a Communist or a Liberal association?

Have you resisted the lawful authorities of the country, taken part in any mob violence, or disturbed public peace?

FIFTH COMMANDMENT:

Thou Shalt Not Kill

Have you by act, participation, instigation, counsel, consent or silence, been guilty of anyone's death or bodily injury?

Have you intended or attempted to take another's life?

Have you been guilty of the sin of abortion? Have you counseled or helped another person obtain an abortion?

Have you intended or attempted to take your own life?

Have you injured your health by excess in eating or drinking?

Have you been drunk or been the cause of drunkenness in others?

Have you used drugs? Have you introduced others to drugs?

Have you by act, advice or consent done anything to hinder or to destroy life?

Have you wished the death of your neighbor, or that some other misfortune befall him? Have you injured, or attempted to injure, or ill-treat others?

Have you been at enmity with your neighbor? Have you refused to speak to him or salute him? Are you reconciled with him?

Have you ever been wildly angry, beyond reason? Have you excited others to anger or revenge?

Have you through avarice, passion or revenge, engaged in vexatious or unjust lawsuits?

Have you harmed anyone's soul by giving scandal, destroying this soul through bad example? Have you, by wicked words, deeds or bad example, ruined innocent persons, taught them bad habits or things they should not know?

Have you exposed yourself or others to temptation?

Have you watched bad movies? Have you listened to bad music? Have you kept and read bad magazines? Have you allowed your children to do these things?

Have you dressed in an improper or indecent manner (mini skirts, tight pants, plunging necklines, see-through blouses and skirts, bikinis, *etc...*)?

Have you thrown temptation in the way of the weak? Have you tried to dissuade or discourage those who were willing to repent and reform?

Have you dated when you should not have done so, when you were not mature enough to get married? Did you offend God during your courtship?

Have you neglected to give alms according to your means, or to relieve those in distress?

SIXTH AND NINTH COMMANDMENTS:

Thou Shalt Not Commit Adultery
Thou Shalt Not Covet Thy Neighbor's Wife

You must mention those circumstances that change the nature of your sin: the sex, the relationship and the condition, whether married, single or bound by a vow; and whether you were married or single at the time of committing the sin?

Have you dwelt with willful pleasure on impure thoughts or imaginations, or consented to them in your heart?

Have you willfully desired to see or do anything impure?

Have you made use of impure language, allusions, or words of double meaning? How many were listening to you?

Have you listened with willful pleasure to immodest language? Have you sung immodest songs or listened to them?

Have you boasted of your immorality?

Have you read immoral books or papers, or lent or sold them to others? Have you written, sent or received improper letters or messages? Have you gazed with willful pleasure on improper objects, images or cards, or shown them to others?

Have you voluntarily exposed yourself to the occasions of sin by sinful curiosity, by keeping dangerous company, by frequenting dangerous places, dangerous or sinful amusements; by immodest dances and indecent plays; by undue familiarity with persons of the opposite sex?

Do you keep sinful company now? Have you in the past, or do you now, live with someone who is not your spouse in the eyes of God?

Have you by your freedom of manners, your immodest dress, *etc.*, been the cause of temptation to others?

Have you ruined an innocent person by introducing them to immorality?

Have you been guilty of improper liberties with others? How far have you carried your sinful conduct?

Have you been guilty of seduction or rape? Did you accomplish your designs by a false promise of marriage? Have you refused to repair the injury done?

Have you been addicted to solitary sexual sins (masturbation)? Did it become habitual?

Have you committed unnatural sexual sins?

Have you taken part in, or facilitated, the sins of others?

Have you been guilty of the sin of fornication, or adultery?

Have you used artificial birth control? Have you used natural birth control without sufficient reason? Have you tried to cheat God and His Law?

SEVENTH AND TENTH COMMANDMENTS:

Thou Shalt Not Steal
Thou Shalt Not Covet Thy Neighbor's Goods

As regards sins of theft, you should tell the priest, as exactly as possible, the value of what you took, or the amount of damage caused by your injustice, so that the priest may judge whether your sins are mortal or not, and what restitution you have to make.

Have you stolen money or anything of value? What was its value? Is it still in your possession? How much did you take each time?

Have you stolen anything consecrated to God, or from a holy place? This is a sacrilege, as well as theft.

Have you charged exorbitant prices, or made out false bills, or falsified the quality of your goods?

Have you cheated in games? Have you been in the habit of gambling, if so to what extent?

Have you engaged in deceitful speculations or enterprises to the injury of the simple and unwary?

Have you defrauded your creditors? Have you been guilty of forgery or swindling? Have you charged exorbitant interest?

Have you robbed the poor?

Have you passed counterfeit or mutilated money? Have you been guilty of bribery, or taking bribes?

Have you kept things you found without inquiring for the owner? Have you retained any of the money entrusted to you?

Have you failed to return things borrowed? Have you neglected to pay your debts? Have you contracted debts without any reasonable hope of paying?

Have you bought, received, or concealed things you knew to be stolen?

Have you caused ruin or damage to the property of another? Did you allow your livestock to injure the neighbor's crop, *etc...*?

Have you squandered the money of your husband, wife, parents, *etc*...in buying costly dresses, jewelry, in drinking, in drugs, *etc*...? Have you been careless of goods entrusted to your charge?

Have you received pay for work or service you have never done, or have done it so poorly that it had to be done over again?

Have you sought to gain your cause by bribery, threats, or other unjust means?

Have you damaged or destroyed (*e.g.*, by fire) your property and kept the insurance money?

Have you, in your dealings, taken advantage of the simple, the poor, the young and inexperienced? Have you made hard bargains with the poor, or those in distress?

Have you been guilty of fraud or embezzlement in any public office or private trust?

Have you caused any injury or loss by your negligence, or culpable ignorance, in the discharge of your profession or employment?

Have you, in any way, taken part in another's theft, fraud or injustice? Have you concealed the injustice of others, when it was your duty to report it?

Have you attempted, or intended, or willfully desired to rob, steal, defraud or commit any kind of injustice?

Have you, by calumny, or other unjust means, caused anyone to lose his position or reputation?

Have you voted for anyone you knew to be unfit for office?

Examine whether you have repaired all the injustice you have done. Your sins will not be pardoned so long as you refuse or knowingly and willfully neglect to make restitution. If what you have unjustly acquired is no longer in your possession, return the value of it.

If you cannot restore the whole, restore at least a part without delay. If you cannot restore it at once, you must have the firm and sincere resolution to do so as soon as possible and also strive earnestly to acquire the means of doing so. The obligation of restitution is binding until it is fully discharged. Restitution must be made to the owner. If the owner cannot be found, you must give the money to the poor, the Church, or some charity.

EIGHTH COMMANDMENT:

Thou Shalt Not Bear False Witness
Against Thy Neighbor

Have you taken a false oath or advised others to do so?

Have you signed false papers or documents, or forged any writings? What injury have you done thereby?

Have you been guilty of malicious lying? Have you put into circulation, or repeated any scandalous report, you knew or believed to be false?

Have you been guilty of detraction in serious matters, by making known your neighbor's secret sins or defects?

Have you done anything to blacken his character or injure his interests?

Have you caused ill-feeling between others by tale-bearing? Have you revealed an important or a professional secret?

Have you, without authority, read another's letters?

Have you endeavored to repair the harm you have done, by contradicting your false reports? Have you honestly tried to restore the good name that you have injured?

Have you spoken against a member of the clergy, because he is consecrated to God? This is also a sacrilege .

Have you been guilty of unjust suspicions and rash judgments?

THE SEVEN CAPITAL SINS

Pride, Avarice, Lust, Envy, Gluttony, Anger, Sloth.

THE SIX SINS AGAINST
THE HOLY GHOST

(1) To despair of your own salvation; *(2)* to presume to be saved without merits; *(3)* to fight the truth knowingly; *(4)* to be

envious of the graces of another; *(5)* to be obstinate in sin; *(6)* to die unrepentant.

THE PARTICULAR DUTIES OF YOUR STATE

Parents and Guardians

Have you failed to always take proper care of the life and health of your children? Have you exposed them to great danger before their birth? Have you failed to provide for their wants? Have you given them proper food, clothing, *etc...*? Have you ever deserted them?

Have you failed to teach them a trade or profession, so that they could gain an honest livelihood?

Have you manifested an unjust preference for one, to the prejudice of the others? Have you been neglectful, unkind and even cruel to your children, stepchildren or wards?

Have you forced your children into a state of life for which they had no vocation? Have you hindered them from following their vocation to the religious or ecclesiastical state?

Have you, without reasonable cause, opposed their inclination with regard to marriage?

Have you failed to procure for them a good and Catholic education according to your means?

Have you neglected to teach them their prayers? Have you neglected to inspire them, in their tender years, with the love of God and a horror of sin?

Have you delayed their baptism too long? Have you neglected to have them prepared and brought, at the proper age, to Confession, Holy Communion and Confirmation?

Have you neglected their religious instruction, or sent them to heretical or Godless schools? Have you failed to take them to Mass on Sundays and Holy Days?

Have you caused them not to observe abstinence on the days prescribed?

Have you placed them in a situation where they could not practice their religion, or where their faith or their virtue was in danger?

Have you exposed their innocence to danger by letting the different sexes sleep together, or by keeping them at night in your own bedroom?

Have you kept watch on their conduct carefully? Have you seen where they spend their time, with what companions they associate, and if they are addicted to any secret vice? Have you allowed them to wander where they would? Have you entrusted them to the care of servants that were irreligious or of loose morals?

Have you allowed them to read unbecoming stories, trashy novels and other dangerous books? Have you allowed them to take part in sinful or dangerous amusements, or to watch bad television?

Have you let them date when they were not mature enough to do so, or when they were not old enough to get married?

Have you allowed them unnecessary freedom with persons of the other sex; visits alone, or at improper hours, or to stay out late at night? Have you allowed immodest dances in your house? Have you allowed them to dance immodestly?

Have you failed to correct and punish them when they deserved it? Have you allowed them to curse, or use improper language without punishing them?

Have you, through indifference or misguided affection, left them without restraint? Have you on the contrary cursed them in anger; treated them brutally, or exasperated or scandalized them by violent or foul language, abusive names, *etc*...?

Have you scandalized them by bad example, by neglecting your religion?

The Married

Did you enter into the state of matrimony for bad and non-Catholic motives?

Have you, by your conduct, been the cause of jealousy and grief to your spouse?

Have you profaned the sanctity of matrimony by misuse, or by trying to hinder its lawful end—namely, the procreation of children?

Have you sinned against each other by angry words, opprobrious names, or even by quarrels and blows?

Have you without just cause and lawful permission, abandoned your spouse in life, lived separately or remained long absent?

Husband

Have you been faithless to your marriage vows?

Have you treated your wife in a gross, cruel or tyrannical manner, beaten her, or abused her in your anger? Have you made her unhappy by your coldness, stinginess, neglect and unfeeling conduct, or by spending your leisure time too often away from home? Have you failed to treat her with attention and forbearance, when she was in a delicate condition?

Have you compelled her to act against her conscience to sin against the laws of nature in the marital act?

Have you neglected to support your wife and children? Have you squandered your earnings, or the property of your wife?

Have you caused discord by your selfishness and jealousy, and by your unfriendly conduct towards her relatives?

Have you made your home disagreeable by your ill temper, abusive language and fault-finding, or by pretended or imaginary ailments?

Wife

Have you broken your marriage vows? Have you given rise to jealousy by your levity, or by trying to win the admiration and affection of others?

Have you, unknown to your husband, made useless and extravagant expenses for yourself or relatives?

Have you caused discord by your selfishness and jealousy and by your unfriendly conduct towards his relatives?

Have you been respectful and obedient to him in all things reasonable and lawful?

Have you made your home disagreeable by your ill temper, scolding and fault-finding, or by pretended or imaginary ailments?

Have you without just cause refused him his marriage rights? Have you induced him to offend God and act contrary to the laws of nature in the sexual domain?

Have you done your part towards the support of the family, or have you, on the contrary, been idle and neglectful of your household duties?

Students

Have you failed to study seriously and with diligence? Have you failed to spend enough time on your studies? Have you missed an exam because of laziness?

Have you abused the liberty you have at college or university, because you are far away from your family?

Have you spent too much money on useless things and entertainment?

Have you spent too much time on your intellectual training, forgetting about your spiritual life?

Have you failed to avoid the evil influences of any bad teachers, books or companions? Have you failed to act as a Catholic with your acquaintances? Have you been ashamed of your faith?

Young Ladies and Young Men

Have you been helpful, assisting in your home, or, on the contrary, been a hindrance?

Have you been too concerned with the way you look, and do you spend too much time with these frivolities?

Have you dressed decently, with dignity, simplicity, and modesty? Are you superficial and worldly?

Have you kept any occasions of sin in your life, or are you an occasion of sin for someone else?

Have you cultivated your intelligence with good reading, or have you wasted your time with novels, magazines, television, too much sport?

Have you mastered your will with the spirit of sacrifice, self-denial, and charity?

Have you been the master of your heart, your feelings and your thoughts?

Employers

Have you treated your employees and servants in a harsh or tyrannical manner? Have you overburdened them with work, or obliged them to do unnecessary work on Sundays or Holy Days of Obligation? Have you kept them from Mass on those days?

Have you always given them proper and sufficient food and treated them kindly in sickness? Have you dismissed them unjustly before the time agreed on? Have you refused them their just dues, neglected to pay them, or taken advantage of their poverty or simplicity to engage them on hard or unjust terms?

Have you failed to encourage and exhort them to keep out of sin and dangerous occasions, to go regularly to Mass, to frequent the Sacraments? Have you been in any way an occasion of sin to them?

Have you failed to watch over their morals? Have you suffered them to keep improper company or late hours?

Employees

Have you failed to serve your employers diligently and faithfully? Have they suffered any harm or loss through your fault, neglect, theft or wastefulness?

Have you retained part of what they gave you to make purchases, or taken anything under pretense that your wages were too low? How much?

Have you revealed unnecessarily the faults of your employers, sowed discord at work or in their families, or been the cause, by false or malicious complaints, of other employees being discharged?

Are you in a situation where your Faith and morals are endangered, or where you have not the opportunity of fulfilling your religious duties?

Have you connived or aided your employers in their crimes? Have you printed, bound, or sold books or papers against faith or morals?

Magistrates and Public Officers

Have you failed to faithfully discharge the duties of your office?

Have you through weakness, human respect, desire of popularity or eagerness for office and personal advantage, betrayed the public interest, or sacrificed the rights of any individual, or suffered crime to go unchecked and unpunished? In what way?

Have you directly or indirectly received bribes, or allowed yourself to be influenced, by promises or presents, in the administration of justice, or in your official conduct?

Have you embezzled public funds, or used them to your own advantage? Have you enriched yourself or your friends at the expense of the public by means of unjust contracts? In what way and how much?

Have you abused your official power to gratify revenge, to favor your friends, or to shield or aid the wicked?

Have you neglected the cause of the poor, the innocent, the helpless and the oppressed?

Have you given scandal by open neglect and disregard of your holy religion and your Catholic duties?

Lawyers, Notaries and Clerks of Court

Have you advocated unjust claims or sustained an unjust cause? Did you obtain an unjust decision? Have you knowingly prosecuted an innocent person?

Have you injured the cause of your client by treachery, gross ignorance, or neglect?

Have you given treacherous, doubtful, or dishonest advice? Have you unjustly flattered the hopes of your client, or otherwise encouraged useless litigation?

Have you been guilty of fraud, bribery or other injustices? Have you procured false testimony, or encouraged others to commit perjury?

Have you been guilty of fraud in drawing up legal documents, or made them ambiguous, or contrary to the intentions of the persons concerned?

Have you falsified, destroyed, or substituted documents? Have you made out false bills of cost, demanded unlawful or exorbitant fees, or charged anyone for services not rendered? How much have you cheated in this manner?

Physicians and Surgeons

Have you undertaken the care of the sick without sufficient science or experience? Have you been negligent in the treatment of serious or extraordinary cases? Have you endangered persons by dangerous remedies or made merciless experiments on patients in hospitals or on the poor?

Have you failed to consult other physicians when necessary, or have you made choice of such as would connive with your mistakes?

Have you caused needless expenses by unnecessary consultations, useless remedies, etc...?

Have you followed the opinions of others contrary to the laws of God, or sanctioned an improper course of treatment? What injury and injustice have you caused thereby?

Have you undertaken surgical operations beyond your science or skill, or conducted them recklessly?

Have you willfully taken the life of a child? Have you directly or indirectly procured, permitted or encouraged abortion or sinful birth control?

Have you taught or encouraged others to hinder conception or to practice onanism?

Have you taught or encouraged the use, or abuse of drugs, liquors, etc...?

Have you hastened anyone's death, at his own request, or the request of his relatives? Have you failed to warn those in danger of death, so that they could receive the sacraments in time?

Have you suffered a child to die without baptism?

Druggists

Have you sold medicine or any other object to destroy life, to hinder conception, or to excite the passions?

Have you sold liquor to drunkards? Have you sold drugs to those who abuse drugs?

Those Having a Hotel, Bar, or Public House

Have you overcharged your guest, or adulterated your liquors? To what amounts, and how often? Have you served alcohol to drunkards, or to those partially drunk, or allowed anyone to drink to excess in your house or place?

Have you taken money from those whom you knew to be ruining their family by wasting their money?

Have you made your house a place of dissipation on Sundays and even during Mass? Have you allowed gambling in your establishment, or tolerated blasphemy, obscenity or quarrels?

Have you allowed persons to visit or lodge for immoral purposes? Have you made it a place of scandalous liaisons, sinful amusements, immodest dances or other sinful abuses?

Have you kept immodest pictures and papers in your house? Have you shown immodest movies? Is your business an occasion of sin to your neighbor, or injury to your family and a hindrance to your own salvation?

Though the above examination of conscience is quite extensive, there may be other sins that spring to mind. If you decide to make a general confession during this second phase of the preparation, you could write out your sins, or photocopy the pages containing the examination of conscience and highlight the relevant sins. In both cases, destroy the papers after having confessed, which apart from preserving secrecy, will also be symbolic of the sins being "destroyed" in the sight of God.

Do not spend all of your time just examining your conscience, but also try to spend a considerable amount of time with view to increasing your sorrow for the sins you have committed. The remainder of the week could be thus used, until you make your confession. Remember that the degree of contrition can also, if intense, not only take away the guilt of sin, but also remit all temporal punishment due to those sins (St. Thomas Aquinas, *Summa Theologica*, Supplement, Q.5, A.3).

It is not absolutely necessary to go to confession at this point in the preparation, as St. Louis states that it can be made on the day of consecration itself. However, since the first two weeks of the preparation deal with a rejection of the spirit of the world, which is manifested through sin, and a thorough knowledge of self—which implies an examination of conscience—then perhaps this week would be more suitable for confession and would relieve the soul of the unnecessary burden of carrying the remembrance, and perhaps the guilt, of one's own sins for the next three weeks.

WEEK 2, DAY 2–THOUGHTS ON CONFESSION

Based on Fr. Eugene Boylan's book,
This Tremendous Lover, Chapter 9

Hope and Confidence in God

Sometimes, the sight of our many sins can induce despondency, or even despair. That is not the work of God, but of the devil. God loves the sinner, but hates the sin. If you can arrive at that same hatred of sin, then there is nothing to worry about—no matter how great or frequent those sins may have been! Our Lord Himself said:

> For the Son of man is come to seek and to save that which was lost (Lk. 19:10; Mt. 18:11).

> But the Pharisees and scribes murmured, saying to his disciples: Why do you eat and drink with publicans and sinners? And Jesus answering, said to them: They that are whole need not the physician, but they that are sick. I came not to call the just, but sinners to penance. (Lk. 5:30-32).

There is no sin that cannot be forgiven.

> If your sins be as scarlet, they shall be made as white as snow: and if they be red as crimson, they shall be white as wool (Is. 1:18). All God wants is repentance and sorrow for past sin. "If the wicked do penance for all his sins which he hath committed, and keep all my commandments, and do judgment and justice, living he shall live and shall not die. I will not remember all his iniquities that he hath done: in his justice which he hath wrought, he shall live. Is it my will that a sinner should die, saith the Lord God, and not that he should be converted from his ways, and live?...Because he considereth and turneth away himself from all his iniquities which he hath wrought, he shall surely live, and not die....Be converted, and do penance for all your iniquities: and iniquity shall not be your ruin. Cast away from you all your transgressions, by which you have transgressed, and make to yourselves a new heart and a new spirit (Ezek. 18:21-31).

Rise to a New Life

The Sacrament of Confession casts away our transgressions and gives us a new heart and a new spirit. It is a spiritual resurrection. We enter the "tomb" of the confessional and leave our sins and guilt there, emerging as a new person, having put off the "old man" and put on the new—as St. Paul says: "To put off...the old man, who is corrupted according to the desire of error, and be renewed in spirit of your mind: and put on the new man..." (Eph. 4:22-23).

Perfect Contrition

The Sacrament of Confession was instituted for the remission of all sins committed after Baptism. These sins must be remitted, either through a perfect sorrow, or, normally, through the Sacrament of Penance. Where there is question of mortal sins, they can only be remitted outside of confession by sorrow when that sorrow attains what we call "perfect contrition"— which arises out of the love of God, not a love of ourselves and our own interests, nor from a servile fear of God and His punishments. Added to this "perfect contrition" must be a desire of going to Confession. St. Thomas Aquinas says: "The entire punishment may be remitted by contrition, yet confession and satisfaction are still necessary" (St. Thomas Aquinas, *Summa Theologica,* Supplement., Q.1, A.1, ad 3).

Attrition

In addition to "perfect contrition," mortal sins are more usually remitted in the confessional, where an imperfect sorrow called "attrition" suffices; such a sorrow, rather than being based on a profound love of God, would merely have as its root an imperfect motive of sorrow such as the fear of losing heaven, or the fear of hell. St. Thomas puts it thus: "Attrition signifies a certain, but not perfect, displeasure for sins committed, whereas contrition denotes perfect displeasure" (*idem*, Q.1, A.2, ad 2).

"A man cannot be sure that his contrition suffices for the remission of both punishment and guilt: wherefore he is bound to confess and make satisfaction, especially since his contrition would not be true contrition, unless he had the purpose of confessing..." (*idem*, Q.5, A.2, ad 1).

Sorrow and Feelings

Since sorrow is an act of the will, it will not always be felt. It is exceptional to find those who sincerely shed tears over their sins, or who feel the loss of God so much, that it is a greater pain than any other pain. Most souls, even very holy souls, would feel more emotional sorrow at the loss of someone dear to them—a parent or close friend—than they would feel for their sins. Yet that does not lessen the value of their sorrow for sin. Feelings have nothing to do with it. The real measure and test of the depth of sorrow is the will and decision to avoid sin in the future. It is the displeasure shown towards the sins that one used to commit. When a person offends us, all the tears and protestations of sorrow matter little if, within a very short space of time, he does it again. His words were insincere. Yet, if he avoids offending you again, that has proved the depth of his sorrow to be true.

The Mercies of God Are Above all His Works

It is of capital importance that we never ever let our past sins—no matter how great or filthy they may have been—come between God and ourselves, or make us in any way doubt God's love, friendship and mercy. As the Psalmist says: "The Lord is gracious and merciful: patient and plenteous in mercy. The Lord is sweet to all: and his tender mercies are over all his works" (Ps.144:8-9). God does not do things by halves. When He forgives sins, He forgives completely. Their guilt is blotted out entirely and He will not reproach us with them again.

Yet, His generosity goes even further. When a soul falls into mortal sin, all the merits from its past life are lost. If, however, the soul repents and obtains pardon, these merits revive again. Such is God's generosity and love.

This is a point of great importance. There is always a great temptation to discouragement and distrust, even after our sins have been forgiven. We feel that God still holds our sins against us; that His providence will be less favorable to us in the future; we feel that He no longer trusts us and that He will be reserved and sparing in His granting of graces. We imagine, too, that no matter how great our progress may be in the future, the ultimate result will always be spoiled by that unfortunate past. There is a certain height, which we could have formerly reached before falling into sin, which we now imagine to be beyond our reach.

All that is natural—but it is also quite wrong! It is based upon a wrong notion of God. God loves to bring good out of evil. He did so with St. Paul, with Mary Magdalen, with St. Augustine, with St. John of God, with St. Matthew Talbot and many, many more. It is our lack of confidence that places obstacles in the way. To quote Cardinal Billot: "The penitent can recover something greater, in so far as one who gave himself to heroic works after sin, is more loved by God than one who, though never stained by mortal sin, is remiss in the exercise of virtues" (*De Poen.* Q.89; *Summa Theologica,* IIIa, Q.89, A.2).

Many sins were forgiven Mary Magdalen, because she loved much. If we love Him as she did, our sins will be forgiven us; and we can be *more* pleasing to God by a life of ardent love *after* our sin, than the lukewarm life of our previous innocence. Truly God can bring good out of evil!

Pay Now, or Pay Later

When a sinner has made a good confession, his mortal sins are forgiven; the eternal punishment they earned is remitted. Yet this does not mean that the temporal punishment is automatically remitted in the bargain. Even though the eternal penalty is removed, the temporal penalty still has to be paid.

If I crash into your car and sincerely beg your forgiveness, you will undoubtedly forgive me my wrongdoing. Yet, when you say "I forgive you" it merely means that you will not forever hold it against me and that we are still friends. However, there is still the problem of the damage to your car. It has to be repaired—and I, or my insurance, have to pay for that damage.

Similarly with sin. God forgives and restores us to His friendship, but the damage of sin requires satisfaction. We either satisfy in this life, or in Purgatory. However, satisfaction in this life is "interest-free" whereas satisfaction in Purgatory incurs a very, very high rate of interest! Hence "Prayer and Penance." In talking to

God, we should continually protest our displeasure at having committed so many sins in the past and that compunction must be seen to be sincere, which it will be if backed up with acts of penance and satisfaction. Actions speak louder than words!

Satisfaction for Sin

The "penance" that the priest imposes on us, in confession, has a very special efficacy for making satisfaction for our sins. However, the "Three *Hail Marys*" or whatever he may impose, does not necessarily pay the entire debt of temporal punishment that we have incurred. In most cases, it should be only looked upon as a "down-payment" on the temporal debt that we still owe. The reason he gives so little penance is that our charity is so lukewarm, and he fears that we might not fulfill heavier penances. If you feel you could do more penance than that which the priest gives you, then tell him so and ask for additional penance.

All our good works and all that we willingly suffer, can be used to make satisfaction for our sins and we can even invoke the merits of Christ, those of His Mother and all the saints, on our behalf. It is important to realize that there is a great difference between making satisfaction for our sins in Purgatory and doing so here on earth. In Purgatory the sufferings are much greater and we cannot gain any merit from them. Here on earth, we make satisfaction with far less suffering, and every act we perform, for that end, can be meritorious.

Sins Forgotten, Sins Forgiven?

Sometimes we cannot recall all our sins—especially if we have sinned much and over a long period of time. What happens then? St. Thomas says: "A man...is bound to have contrition for each individual mortal sin. If he is unable to discover [remember] it, after having applied himself with due care, it is enough that he be contrite for it according to the manner in which it stands in his knowledge and he should not only grieve for the sin, but also for having forgotten it, because this is due to his neglect. If, however, the sin has altogether escaped his memory, then he is excused from his duty through being unable to fulfill it, and it is enough

that he be contrite in general for everything wherein he has offended God. But when the sin is recalled to memory, then he is
bound to have contrition for that sin in particular" (St. Thomas
Aquinas, *SummaTheologica,* Supplement., Q.1, A.3, ad 2).

WEEK 2: DAY 3–FIRST MEDITATION

Based on the *Imitation of Christ,* Book 2, Chapter 5

Knowing Oneself

We cannot trust too much in ourselves, because we often
lack grace and understanding. There is only little enlightenment
in us and this we quickly lose through negligence. Often we are
unaware of how blind we are interiorly.

We often do wrong, and then do worse by trying to excuse
ourselves. At times we are moved by our passions and we mistake
it for zeal. We blame little things in others, but pass over great
things in ourselves. We are quick enough at perceiving and weighing what we suffer from others, but we care little if we have made
others suffer.

If you would carefully examine and weigh your own shortcomings, then you would have little time to judge others so harshly.

Interior persons prefer to look after themselves before worrying about other matters; and he that diligently attends to himself,
is easily silent with regard to others. You will never be an interior
and devout person, unless you pass over the concerns of others in
silence, so as to better look after yourself. If you pay attention to
your own way of life and to God, then you will hardly be concerned and agitated at what goes on around you.

What does it profit a man if he gains the whole world, yet
loses his own soul? What are you doing if you are not looking
after your own soul? What good is it to know all things, if you do
not know yourself?

If you wish to have true peace of soul and union with God,
then you must set everything else aside and turn your gaze upon
yourself, not others. Then, being free of all temporal care, curios-

ity and anxiety, you will make great progress. But if you attach yourself to temporal things and concerns, then you will fail greatly.

Esteem nothing to be as great, as pleasant, as agreeable to you as God and God alone. Look upon all comfort and consolation, that you might receive from other creatures, as vain. A soul that truly loves God, despises all things that are less than God, preferring God to them all. For God alone, eternal and incomprehensible, can bring true comfort to the soul and true joy to the heart.

Acknowledging Our Unworthiness in the Sight of God
Based on the *Imitation of Christ*, Book 3, Chapter 8

I, who am but dust and ashes, will speak to the Lord. If I think myself to be anything great, Thou O Lord, stand against me and my sins point out the truth of the matter. But if I humble myself and acknowledge my nothingness, casting away all false self-esteem, realizing myself to be only dust and ashes—then Thy grace will favor me and enlighten my heart, plunging all false self-esteem to the depths of my nothingness.

It is in the depths of my nothingness that Thou show me to myself—what I am, what I have been and what I am to come to—for I am nothing and I never realized this. Left to myself, I am nothing and weak; but if Thou graciously look upon me, then I feel strong and am filled with joy.

What a wonder it is, that I, who am always sinking so low in my ways, should be picked-up and embraced by Thee. Thy love brings this about, freely guiding and assisting me in so many needs, preserving me from so many dangers and delivering me from so many evils.

It is said that we must love ourselves, but my love of self was misguided. Instead of pursuing what would have been good for my soul, I filled it with evil, thinking it to be good. In seeking and loving this evil, I lost Thee my only good and myself. Yet now, in seeking and loving Thee, I have found good and myself.

Blessed be Thou, O my God, for though I am unworthy of all good, Thy generosity and infinite goodness never ceases to do good to the ungrateful and those who have turned away from Thee. Bring us back to Thee, that we may be thankful, humble and devout—because Thou art our salvation, our power and our strength.

WEEK 2: DAY 3–SECOND MEDITATION

Based on the *Imitation of Christ*, Book 1, Chapter 24

On the Judgment and Punishment of Sinners

In all things look to your end! (Eccles. 7:40). Look to the day when you will have to stand before your strict Judge, from Whom nothing was hidden, Who takes no bribes, nor accepts excuses, but will judge in a just and correct manner.

O most miserable and foolish sinner! You are at times afraid of the anger of mere men! What will you say to God, Who knows all the evil you have done?

Why not do something to prepare for that day of judgment, when excuses will not be accepted and where there will be nobody to defend you, for everyone will be a sufficient burden to themselves? Now, while you are still alive and in health, can your penance be fruitful, your tears cleanse and your groans for mercy be heard!

The patient man has a great and healthy source of spiritual cleansing, when he learns to suffer wrongs, more grieved about the sin of the other than the harm done to him. The patient man prays gladly for his enemies, wholeheartedly forgives their faults, is not slow to ask forgiveness when he has done wrong. The patient man is more quickly moved to pity than anger. He often mortifies his own desires and subjects the flesh to the spirit. In doing all this, he lives out his purgatory upon earth. It is better to purge our sins and prune our vices in this life, than to have it done in the next. For if we nurture an excessive love of the flesh, then we truly deceive ourselves!

What else will the fires of purgatory or hell devour except your sins? The more you spare yourself and take things easy, in following the desires of the flesh, the more fuel you store up for the fires of purgatory or hell. In those things in which you have sinned the most, in those will you be most grievously punished.

There will be no vice without its appropriate punishment and torment. The proud will be humbled and filled with confusion. The covetous will be crushed by the greatest need and want. The glutton will be tormented with enormous hunger and thirst. The wanton and the pleasure-lovers will be drenched with blazing tar and stinking sulphur. The envious will howl in pain like rabid dogs. The lazy will be pricked by burning goads.

There, one hour in punishment will be more grievous than a hundred years of the bitterest penance on earth. Here, despite our labors, we can sometimes find rest from labor and the enjoyment and consolation of friends. There, you will find no friends, no rest, no consolation, no comfort.

Therefore, now is the time to be anxious and in sorrow for your sins, so that, in the day of judgment, you may be safe and blessed. For then the just shall stand with great constancy against those that have afflicted and oppressed them. Then shall he, who has humbly submitted himself to the judgments of men, stand up to judge. Then shall the poor and humble have great confidence and the proud shall fear on every side.

Then he who has learned to be a fool and despised for Christ, will suddenly be seen to have been wise in this world. Then tribulation, patiently borne, will seem pleasing, and all wickedness shall close its mouth (Ps. 106:42).

Then every devout man shall rejoice and the profane shall mourn. Then shall the mortified body appear more beautiful than the body pampered by all kinds of earthly delights. Then shall poor garments be esteemed and the fine clothes look contemptible.

Then the poor humble dwelling will be praised more than the over-decorated mansion. Then will virtue shine more brightly than the jewels that we adorned ourselves with.

Then will charity outweigh our precious gold. Then shall the acquisition of patience be treasured more than the acquisition of power. Then will humble obedience overshadow the pride of the clever ones, who always knew how to do things better.

Then shall the pure conscience delight more than the learned man. Then contempt of riches shall outweigh all the treasures of the earth. Then you will take more pleasure in having listened to the word of God, rather than that of gossip.

Then shall you find more consolation for receiving Communion, than having feasted at many banquets. Then holy deeds shall be worth more than holy words. Then shall a life of penance and discipline be more pleasing than any earthly delight.

Learn now how to suffer small things, so as to be able to accept great sufferings. Try out here first, what you may be able to endure hereafter. If you can endure so little now, how will you be able to endure eternal torments? If a little suffering makes you so impatient today, what will hell be like tomorrow?

You cannot serve two masters—you cannot delight yourself in this world and reign with Christ in the next! If all your life has been one of honor and pleasure, what good will it do you if you die tomorrow? Therefore all things are vain, except to love God and to serve Him alone.

For he who loves God with his whole heart, fears neither death, nor punishment, nor judgment, nor hell. For perfect love leads a soul straight to God. Yet for one who delights in sin, it is little wonder that he fears death and judgment. But if you cannot avoid sin and hell out of a love of God, then at lest avoid it out of a fear of hell. For once we lose the fear of God, it is only a little while before we lose our fear of sin and we quickly fall into the devil's hands.

WEEK 2: DAY 3–THIRD MEDITATION

Based on the *Imitation of Christ*, Book 1, Chapter 25

On the Ardent Amendment of Our Whole Life

Be watchful and diligent in the service of God, often reflecting: "Why have I come here? And why have I abandoned the world? Was it not that I might live for God and become a spiritual man?" Therefore be ardent for progress, because you will soon receive the reward for your labors and then neither fear nor sorrow shall come within your borders any more. You will labor a little now and you will find great rest and everlasting joy. And if you remain ardent and faithful in what you do, God, beyond doubt, will be faithful in rewarding you. You must hold on to the hope that you will attain the crown, but you must not be over-confident, in case you grow negligent and proud.

When a certain anxious person wavered often between fear and hope, on one occasion, overwhelmed with sadness, he threw himself down in a church before an altar, saying, as he turned these matters in his mind: "O, if I only knew that I should still persevere!" — immediately he heard God's reply in his heart: "And if you knew this, what would you do? Do now what you would do then and you will be perfectly safe." Immediately comforted and strengthened, he committed himself to God's will and his anxious wavering ceased. He no longer curiously searched to know what would happen to him, but studied rather to learn what God's well-pleasing and perfect will might be for the beginning and perfecting of every good work.

There is one thing that keeps many back from progress and heart-felt amendment: dread of the difficulty or the toil of the struggle. Whoever manfully strives to overcome those things which they find more troublesome or contrary to them, they will, more than all others, advance in virtue. There a man profits most and merits more abundant grace, wherever he overcomes himself and mortifies the spirit.

But all people have not equally as much to overcome and mortify. Yet a zealous imitator will make more valiant progress, though he have more passions, than another who has fewer passions, but is less ardent in the pursuit of virtues. Two things especially conduce to great amendment: these are, forcibly to withdraw from that to which nature is viciously inclined, and to press earnestly towards the good which we lack the most. Strive, also, to guard against and overcome those things which displease you most in others. Seek to advance on all fronts, so that, if you hear or see good examples, you may be inspired to imitate them. Yet, if you have thought anything blameworthy, take care not to do the same; or, if at times you have done so, be zealous in quickly correcting yourself. For as you observe others, so too are you observed by them. How pleasant and how sweet it is to see brethren, ardent and devout, well-mannered and disciplined! How sad and grievous to see them walk disorderly, not practicing those things to which they were called! How hurtful it is to neglect the purpose of their calling and to turn the heart to that which is not their business!

Be mindful of the purpose of which you have laid hold, and set before you the image of the crucified. You should be truly ashamed whenever you look upon the life of Jesus Christ, because you have shown so little zeal in imitating Him, even though you spent many years in the service of God. The religious man who exercises himself intensely and devotedly in the most holy life and passion of the Lord, will find there an abundance of useful and necessary things. Nor is there need to seek anything better outside Jesus. O, if Jesus crucified would only come into our heart, how quickly and adequately would we learn!

The fervent religious man receives and bears well all things which are commanded him. The negligent and lukewarm religious man has tribulation upon tribulation and suffers anguish on every side, because he lacks inner consolation and is forbidden to seek consolation in external and material things. The religious man who lives an indisciplined life, is exposed to grievous ruin. He who seeks things that are easier and less restrained, will always be in trouble, because one thing or the other will always displease him.

What do so many other religious men do, who live under the discipline of a cloistered life? They seldom go out, they live apart, they eat in the poorest fashion, dress roughly, labor much, speak little, keep long vigils, rise early, prolong prayer, read much, and keep themselves in all discipline. Consider the Carthusians, the Cistercians, and the monks and nuns of other religious orders: how they rise each night to sing praises to the Lord. What a base thing it would be for you to grow slothful in such holy work, when such a host of religious people are beginning to sing praise to God.

O, if only we had nothing else to do, but to praise the Lord our God with our whole heart and voice! O, if only we would never need to eat, or drink or sleep, but could always praise God and be free for spiritual exercises alone! Then you would be much more happy than now, when you are bound to serve the flesh and every sort of need. If only those needs did not exist, but only the spiritual refreshments of the soul, which, alas, we savor rarely enough.

When a man reaches the point where he seeks his consolation from no created thing, then he begins to find perfect contentment in God; then, too, will he be content with the outcome of all events. Then he will neither rejoice over great things, nor be sorrowful over little things, but will commit himself wholly and trustingly to God, Who is to him all in all; to Whom, assuredly, nothing is lost or perishes, but all things live for Him and at His command instantly obey.

Always remember the end and that time lost does not return. Without care and diligence, you will never acquire virtues. If you begin to grow lukewarm, you will begin to deteriorate. But if you give yourself to zeal, you will find great peace, and your labors for the grace of God and virtue will feel light. A fervent and diligent man is ready for everything. It is harder to resist vices and passions, than to sweat at bodily labors. He who does not shun small faults, gradually slips into greater. You will always rejoice in the evening, if you spend the day fruitfully. Watch over yourself. You will only progress in the same proportion as to the violence that you exert against yourself.

WEEK 2: DAY 4–FIRST MEDITATION

Based on the *Imitation of Christ*, Book 3, Chapter 20

Confession of Our Weaknesses and the Trials of this Life

I will confess my sin before you. I will confess to Thee, Lord, my weakness. Often it is a small thing that casts me down and saddens me. I resolve to act bravely, but when a small temptation comes along, then I find myself in great difficulty.

Thus by not rejecting this little temptation, I let it grow into a monster. Then when I think I am safe and sound, I find myself knocked down by the smallest of temptations. See, Lord, how great is my great weakness and how many my reasons to be humble. Be merciful and snatch me from the swamp of sin, before I sink below the surface.

I am often driven back and confounded in Thy presence, because I am so weak in resisting my passions and so prone to falling into sin. I do not do the good I want to do, and I end up by doing the evil I don't want to do; and this wearies me so! Although I do not always consent, the assault troubles me and I find it hard to live in the midst of this constant battle. Lord, look upon my labor and toil and help me achieve what I have undertaken to do. Fortify me with heavenly strength, in case the old man of my wretched sinful past, starts to dominate me again.

Neither is there a lack of afflictions and miseries. For when one temptation is overcome, another one attacks. At times many come at once. How can men love a sinful life that is so full of danger to the soul, a life that only brings bitterness, miseries and calamities? How can a sinful life be called life, when it brings with it so much suffering and even death? Yet it is loved and many seek their delights in it, and many attach themselves to it, ignoring a better and greater life in the time to come. The fool of this world thinks that there are pleasures under the nettles, because he has not tasted the sweetness of God and the inner beauty of virtue. Yet for the wise, who try to live a life of discipline, out of love for God, they clearly see how far the world has gone astray and how much it deceives itself.

WEEK 2: DAY 4–SECOND MEDITATION

Based on the *Imitation of Christ*, Book 3, Chapter 47

On Bearing Burdens to Win Eternal Life

Dearest soul, do not let the labors, which you have taken up for Me, break you, nor let tribulations in any way cast you down; but let these words of Mine strengthen you in every situation. I will repay you beyond all measure. You will not labor long, nor will you suffer forever. Wait a while and you shall see all your evils disappear.

Do all that you have to do, well. Toil faithfully in my vineyard. I will see to your reward. Write, read, sing, sigh, weep, be silent, pray, carry your cross manfully—eternal life is worth all of these and even greater combats.

If you could only see the everlasting crowns of the saints in heaven and the joy with which they now exult, you would not grieve so much over your difficulties. They were once held in contempt by the world and considered unworthy of life itself. Now the tables have been turned and they reign in heaven.

This should make you want to humble yourself even to the dust, and to strive to subject yourself to all, rather than be set over a single person. Realizing the crown that God has in store for you, you would not covet the pleasures of this world, but would rejoice to suffer tribulation for God and consider it a great gain to be thought of as nothing among men.

If these things really tasted sweet to you, then you would not complain like you do. What good would it do you if you gained the whole world but lost heaven? To lose or gain the kingdom of God is no small matter.

Therefore, lift your face heavenward. Look to the unimaginable reward that awaits all those who fought bravely and suffered courageously. The joy, comfort, rest and eternal glory they now enjoy is yours to enjoy too, one day.

Let not your past sins discourage you, let not the fear of the future nor the taunts and lies, suggested by the evil one, turn you from the path to sanctity that God has mapped out before you. God wishes your sanctity and salvation more than you desire it yourself. Yet the devil wishes your damnation. Turn away from the evil one, turn away from sin and turn towards Him who has overcome both the devil and the world.

WEEK 2: DAY 4–THIRD MEDITATION

Based on the *Imitation of Christ*, Book 3, Chapter 13

Obedience of the Humble Person After Christ's Example

Son, he who strives to withdraw himself from obedience, withdraws himself from grace; and he who seeks things for himself, loses those which are common to all. He who does not willingly and freely subject himself to one above him, shows that his flesh does not yet perfectly obey him, but keeps on fighting back and protesting.

Learn, therefore, quickly to submit yourself to one above you, if you wish to bring your own flesh into subjection. For the enemy without is more quickly conquered, if the inner man has not been laid waste.

There is no more troublesome or worse enemy, to your soul, than you are to yourself, if you are not in harmony with the spirit. You must altogether assume a true contempt of yourself, if you wish to prevail against flesh and blood. Because, as yet, you love yourself beyond due measure, therefore you shrink from giving yourself over to the will of others.

But what great thing is it, if you, who are dust and nothingness, submit to man for God's sake, when I, omnipotent and most high, Who have created everything out of nothing, subjected Myself humbly to man for your sake?

I became the most humble and lowly of all men, so that you, by My humility, might vanquish your pride. Learn to obey, dust. Learn to humble yourself, earth and mud, and bend beneath the feet of all. Learn to break your will in all its movements and to give yourself to all subjection.

Be angry with yourself, suffer not the swelling pride to live in you, but show yourself so subject and utterly small, that all can walk over you and tread on you like the mud of the streets. What have you, worthless man, to complain about? What, vile sinner, can you say in answer to those who upbraid you, who have so often offended God, and many a time deserved hell?

But My eye has spared you, because your soul was precious

in My sight, that you might know My love and live always thankful for My benefits, and might continually give yourself to true subjection and humility, and patiently bear self-contempt.

WEEK 2: DAY 5–FIRST MEDITATION

Based on the *Imitation of Christ*, Book 3, Chapter 7

On Grace and Humility

My son, it is more salutary and safe for you to hide the grace of devotion and not to exalt yourself, nor speak much about it, nor to give much weight to it, but rather to despise yourself, and fear that this grace has been given to one unworthy of it. Do not depend too much upon this grace of devotion, for it can quickly be changed into its opposite.

Reflect, in a state of grace, how wretched and helpless you tend to be without it. Nor does progress in the spiritual life consist in the grace of consolation, but rather in the humility, self-abnegation and patience with which you endure its withdrawal; when you refuse to grow dull in zeal for prayer, not abandoning your customary good works, but to willingly continue in those holy things despite the dryness and anguish of mind which you feel once the grace of devotion has been withdrawn.

For there are many, when things have not gone well with them, who became impatient or slothful. For a man's way is not always in his control, but it is God's part to give and to control, when He wills, as much as He wills, and to whom He wills, as it shall please Him and no more.

Many, presumptuous because of the grace of devotion, have destroyed themselves, because they have wished to do more then they were able, not considering the measure of their own littleness, following the heart's impulse rather than the judgment of reason.

Since they have gone beyond God's pleasure, they have quickly lost grace. They have been made poor and abandoned as worthless for having built a nest in heaven for themselves; so that made humble and impoverished, they should learn to fly, not on their own wings, but to hide themselves beneath Mine. Those who are new and inexperienced in the Lord's way, unless they rule themselves by the counsel of the wise, can easily be deceived and overthrown.

But if they wish to follow their feelings, rather than trust others with experience, their future will be full of dangers—unless they draw back from their own conceit. Rarely do those, who are wise in their own eyes, suffer humbly to be ruled by others. It is better to have little knowledge with humility, than to have great stores of varied knowledge along with pride. It is better for you to have little rather than much of that which can make you proud.

A man shows a lack of discretion by over-rejoicing when he has the grace of devotion, forgetting his former helplessness and his fear of the Lord. He should rather dread losing such a great grace. Neither is he wise when he becomes too despondent and loses confidence in Me in times of adversity or any kind of trouble.

He who wishes to be too secure in time of peace, is often found, in time of war, to be too cast down and full of fear. If you knew how to stay always humble and little in your own eyes, and to keep your spirit in order and subjection, then you would not be so easily offended, nor would fall into so many dangers.

It is good advice, when you have the grace of devotion, to think deeply on what it will be like when the light is gone. When this happens, consider that the light can come back again, for I have withdrawn it, for a time, as a warning to you and for My Own glory.

Often, such a trial is more profitable for you than if things always went your way. For progress and merit are not counted by the number of visions and consolations you may have, nor by your knowledge of the Scriptures, nor by the rank you hold. But your progress and merit is seen if you are grounded in true humility, and if, filled with God's love, you seek the honor of God, thinking nothing of yourself, but, in truth, despising yourself and even rejoicing more over being despised and humiliated, than being honored.

WEEK 2: DAY 5–SECOND MEDITATION

Based on the *Imitation of Christ*, Book 2, Chapter 10

On Gratitude for God's Grace

Why do you seek rest when you are born to labor? Prepare yourself more for patience, rather than comforts; and for carrying the cross rather than for joy. Even worldly persons would gladly receive consolation and spiritual joys, if they could always obtain it?

For spiritual consolations excel all the delights of the world and the pleasures of the flesh. For all worldly delights are either empty or shameful; but spiritual delights alone are pleasant and honorable. They spring from virtues and are poured by God into pure minds. But no one can enjoy such heavenly consolations all the time, nor whenever they so wish, for temptation does not cease for long.

But what opposes these divine consolations and graces is a false liberty of mind and an excessive confidence in oneself. God does well in giving us the grace of consolation, but man acts badly in not returning it all to God by giving thanks. For that reason the gifts of grace cannot flow in those who are ungrateful to their author, and do not pour back everything to the spring from which it came. For grace always comes to him who worthily returns thanks, and what is commonly given to the humble, is taken away from the proud.

I desire no consolation which takes from me the sting of conscience; nor do I seek consolation which leads to pride. For all that is high is not holy, nor every sweet thing good, nor every longing pure, nor everything that is dear pleasing to God.

I will gladly accept grace which makes me more humble and fearful, and more ready to abandon self. One taught by the gift of grace and made wise by the shock of its withdrawal, will not dare to attribute any good thing to himself, but rather will confess himself poor and naked.

Give to God what belongs to God, and ascribe to yourself what is yours; that is: render to God gratitude for grace, but to yourself alone, your sins and the punishment they merit.

Always put yourself in the lowest place and the highest place shall be given you, for the highest cannot be without the lowest, as a tall building cannot be without deep foundations. The highest saints of God are the least in their own eyes; and the more glorious they are in heaven, the more humble they are in themselves. For truth and humility are the two sides of the same coin. A humble man is a truthful man; and a truthful man is humble. Full of truth and heavenly glory, they are not desirous of vain glory. Rooted in God, they are not able to be proud.

Those who ascribe to God whatever good they have received, "seek not glory from one another, but desire the glory of God alone" (Jn. 5:44), and wish that God in Himself and in all His saints be praised above all, and always strive for that end.

Be grateful, therefore, for the smallest thing and you will be worthy of receiving greater. Let the least be, in your eyes, as good as the greatest, and the most inconsiderable as good as a special gift. Look to the Giver and not to the gift. If the dignity of the Giver be kept in mind, no gift will seem small or cheap, for nothing is small or cheap which comes from God most high.

Even if He has given chastisements and blows, we must be grateful, because He always acts with our salvation in mind—whatever He allows to happen to us. If you wish to keep grace of God, then be grateful for grace given and patient when it is taken away. Then let him pray that it returns; let him be wary and humble in case he loses it again.

WEEK 2: DAY 5–THIRD MEDITATION

Based on the *Imitation of Christ*, Book 3, Chapter 9

How Everything Must Return to God as its Final End

My son, I must be your highest and final end, if you truly wish to be happy. By having this intention, your affections will be purified, which more often than not, are wrongly bent towards yourself and created things. For if you seek yourself in anything, you will only encounter failure and become spiritually dry.

Refer, therefore, all things principally to Me, because I am the One Who has given you all things. Look upon everything as flowing from Me, and therefore it is that all things must be returned to Me, as to their source.

Out of Me, both little and great, rich and poor, draw living water as from a living fountain, and those who, of their own will, freely serve Me, will receive grace for grace. But he who will glory in anything outside of Me, or take delight in any private good, will not find true joy in his heart, but in very many ways will meet with perplexities and anguish.

You must, therefore, ascribe no good to yourself, nor attribute virtue to any man, but ascribe all to God, without Whom man has nothing. I gave all, I wish to repossess all—and I strictly require thanks for all I give.

This is truth, by which the emptiness of boasting is put to flight and, if heavenly grace and true love have entered in, there will be no envy or narrowing of the heart, nor will self-love lay hold of you. For divine charity conquers all things and enlarges all the powers of the soul, because there is no one good save God alone, Who is to be praised above all things and in all things blessed.

WEEK 2: DAY 6–FIRST MEDITATION

Based on the *Imitation of Christ*, Book 3, Chapter 53

God's Grace Is not Given to the Worldly Minded

Son, My grace is precious and does not suffer itself to be mixed with alien things, nor earthly consolations. You must therefore throw away any obstacles to grace, if you desire to receive it. Look for a hidden place, love to abide there alone, seek comfort from no one, but rather pour out devout prayer to God, that you may keep a contrite mind and a pure conscience.

Count the whole world nothing. Set time alone with God before all passing things. For you cannot have free time for Me and equally take delight in things that pass away. One must be separated from acquaintances and loved ones, and keep the mind away from all temporal comfort. So begs the blessed Apostle Peter, that Christ's faithful keep themselves as strangers and pilgrims in this world (I Pet. 2:11).

O, what great confidence shall he have at the hour of his death, whom no worldly affection holds back. But a sick soul is not yet capable of having a heart so detached from everything, nor does the natural man understand the liberty of the spiritual man (I Cor. 2:14). And yet, if he truly wishes to be spiritual, he must cut himself off from things far and near, and be afraid of no one more than his own self.

If you completely overcome yourself, you will easily bring all else into subjection. The perfect victory is to triumph over one's own self. For he who holds his own self in subjection, so that his sensual self obeys reason, and reason in all matters obeys Me, he is truly victor over self and master of the world.

If you ardently desire to climb this summit, you must manfully begin by taking an axe to the root (Mt. 3:11), so as to tear out and destroy the hidden and extravagant leanings towards yourself, and towards all personal and material goods.

This vice, by which a man inordinately loves himself, is at the bottom of all those evils which must be rooted out and overcome in you. Once this evil is conquered and truly subdued, a great peace and tranquillity will not be long in coming.

But since few fully strive to die completely to themselves and to rise above themselves, they remain entangled in themselves and cannot, in spirit, rise above themselves. He who longs freely to walk with Me, must put to death all his wicked and indisciplined affections, and not cling with desire, in selfish love, to any thing created.

WEEK 2: DAY 6–SECOND MEDITATION

Based on the *Imitation of Christ*, Book 3, Chapter 30

Seeking God's Help and the
Certainty of Regaining Grace

Son, I am the God Who comforts in the day of trouble (Nah. 1:7). Come to Me, when it is not well with you. This is what chiefly hinders heavenly comfort, that you are too slow in turning to prayer. For before you ask Me urgently, you meanwhile seek many comforts and delights in external things.

And so it comes about that these things are of no avail, until you see that it is I Who deliver those who trust in Me. Nor is there outside of Me, any real help, nor profitable counsel, nor lasting remedy. But now, with your spirit revived after the tempest, grow strong again in the light of My mercies, for I am at hand to repair all things, not only as they were, but abundantly and in fuller measure.

Is there anything at all difficult to Me? Or am I like one who promises, but does not do? (Jer. 32:27; Num. 23:19). Where is your faith? Stand firm and carry on! Be long-suffering—and a strong consolation will come to you in due time. Wait for Me, wait—I will come and heal you.

It is temptation which harasses you and nothing but empty fears which terrify. What does anxiety about the future bring you, except sadness upon sadness. Sufficient to the day is its own evil (Mt. 6:34). It is a vain and useless thing to be disturbed or pleased about future things, which may never come to pass.

But it is typical of man to be deceived by such imaginations, and it is the mark of a mind that is still weak, when it allows itself to be so easily drawn to the suggestions of the enemy. For he does not care whether it be by things true or false that he deceives and abuses you, or whether he overthrows you with a love for earthly things or by a fear of things to come. "Let not your heart be troubled, nor let it be afraid" (Jn.14:27).

Believe in Me and trust in My mercy. It is when you think that I am far from you, that I am often nearer. When you think that all is nearly lost, often greater gain of merit is at hand. All is not lost when things do not turn out as you would like. You should not judge according to what you feel at the moment, nor be troubled about some grief that befalls you, as if all hope of rising above it had been taken away from you.

Do not think that you have been utterly abandoned if, for the moment, I may have sent some tribulation upon you, or withdrawn some cherished consolation, for this is the way to the kingdom of heaven. Without doubt, this is more to your advantage, that you should be trained by adversity, rather than having everything as you would like it.

I know your hidden thoughts, and that it is of great advantage for your salvation that, at times, you should be left without consolation, in case you become puffed-up by much success, and so take vain pleasure in yourself, thinking yourself to be that which you are not. That which I have given, I can also justly take away and once again restore, when it shall please me.

When I shall have given, it is mine; when I shall have taken it away, I have not taken what is yours, for mine is every perfect gift (Jas. 1:17). If I shall have sent you grief, or any form of opposition, do not be angry, nor let your heart be cast down; I can quickly uplift, and transform every burden into joy. Nevertheless, I am just and much to be praised when I do this with you.

If you think rightly and observe truthfully, you should never be dejected and troubled by adversity, but rather rejoice and give thanks. You can even take a special joy in this, that by afflicting you with sorrows, I do not spare you (Job 6:10).

I said to my beloved disciples, just as the Father loved Me, so I love you. I most certainly did not send them forth to earthly joys, but to great conflicts; not to honors, but to much contempt; not to leisure but to toil; not to rest, but to bear much fruit in patience. These words, My son, remember.

WEEK 2: DAY 6–THIRD MEDITATION

Based on the *Imitation of Christ*, Book 3, Chapter 8

Acknowledging Our Unworthiness in the Sight of God

Shall I speak to my Lord, whereas I am but dust and ashes? (Gen. 18:27). If I think much of myself, Thou stand against me; and my sins bear witness to the truth and I cannot contradict it.

But if I shall humble myself and acknowledge my own unworthiness, and cast away all self-esteem, and make myself the dust I am, then Thy grace will be favorable to me, and Thy light will draw near to my heart, and all vain self-esteem, however little it may be, will be drowned in the valley of my nothingness and will perish for ever.

There Thou dost show me to myself, what I am, what I was, and what I am come to—"I am brought to nothing and I knew it not" (Ps. 72:22). If I am left to myself, then I am nothing and total weakness; but if suddenly Thou look upon me, immediately I am made strong and filled with new joy. It is wonderful to be suddenly lifted up and lovingly embraced by Thee, I, who by my own weight, am always sinking to the depths.

This is what Thy love does, freely guiding and assisting me in so many needs; guarding me from grave dangers and from innumerable evils. For, by an evil love of myself, I lost myself, and by seeking Thee alone, and purely loving Thee, I found both myself and Thee, and, by this love, I have profoundly annihilated myself. For, Thou Lord, deal with me beyond all merit and beyond what I dare to hope or ask.

May Thou be blessed, my God, because, though I am unworthy of any good, Thy excellence and boundless kindness never cease to do good to the ungrateful and to those who have turned far away from Thee. Turn us to Thyself that we may be thankful, because Thou art our salvation, our courage and our strength.

WEEK 2: DAY 7–FIRST MEDITATION

Based on the *Imitation of Christ*, Book 3, Chapter 52

We are More Worthy of Chastisement than Comfort

Lord, I am not worthy of Thy consolation, nor of any spiritual visitation; and therefore, Thou dealest justly with me when Thou leavest me without resource and desolate. For if I could shed tears like the sea, still I should not be worthy of Thy comfort. Therefore, I deserve nothing except to be scourged and punished, for I have often grievously offended Thee and sinned greatly in many ways. Therefore, if true account be taken, I am not worthy of the smallest consolation.

But Thou, gracious and merciful God, because Thou dost not wish Thy works to perish, to show the richness of Thy goodness towards the vessels of mercy (Rom. 9:23), but wish, even beyond our merit, to console Thy servants above all human measure. For Thy consolations are not like the consolations of men.

What have I done, Lord, that Thou shouldst confer any heavenly consolation on me? I recall that I have done nothing good, but have always been inclined to evil and so slow to mend my ways. It is true and I cannot deny it. If I should say otherwise, Thou wouldst stand against me and there would be none to defend me. What have I deserved for my sins but hell and eternal fire? In truth, I confess that I am worthy of all scorn and contempt, and neither is it fitting that I should be named among Thy devout servants. Though I find this hard to bear, I will, for truth's sake, accuse myself of my sins before Thee, that the more easily I may deserve to win Thy mercy.

What shall I say, being guilty and full of confusion? I cannot say anything but this: "I have sinned, Lord, I have sinned; have mercy on me, pardon me." "Suffer me, therefore, that I may lament my sorrow a little: Before I go, and return no more, to a land that is dark and covered with the mist of death" (Job 10:20-21). What else is required of a guilty and wretched sinner, except that he truly repent and humble himself for his sins?

Through this true contrition and humility of heart, there is born the hope of pardon; the troubled conscience is reconciled;

lost grace recovered; man is preserved from the wrath to come and God and the penitent soul meet each other with a kiss of peace. The humble contrition of sinners is acceptable to Thee, O Lord, a sacrifice more sweetly scented than the incense of myrrh. This is the pleasant ointment which Thou didst wish to be poured upon Thy holy feet, because a contrite and humbled heart is never despised (Ps. 50:19). Here is a sure place of refuge from the face and wrath of the enemy. Here, we wash away whatever we have contracted through our defilement.

WEEK 2: DAY 7–SECOND MEDITATION

Taken from St. Louis de Montfort's
True Devotion to Mary, §78 ff.

We Must Rid Ourselves of All that Is Bad in Us

Our best actions are ordinarily stained and corrupted by our corrupt nature. When we put clean, clear water into a vessel which has a foul and evil smell, or wine into a cask the inside of which has been tainted by another wine which has been in it, the clear water and the good wine are spoilt, and readily take on the bad odor. In like manner, when God puts into the vessel of our soul, spoilt by original and actual sin, His graces and heavenly dew, or the delicious wine of His love, His gifts are ordinarily spoilt and corrupted by the bad leaven and the evil which sin has left within us. Our actions, even the most sublime and virtuous, feel the effects of it. It is therefore of great importance in the acquiring of perfection—which, it must be remembered, is only acquired by union with Jesus Christ—to rid ourselves of everything that is bad within us; otherwise Our Lord, who is infinitely pure and hates infinitely the least stain upon our souls, will not unite Himself to us, and will cast us out from His presence.

To Rid Ourselves of Self We Must...

Thoroughly recognize, by the light of the Holy Ghost, our inward corruption, our incapacity for every good thing useful for salvation, our weakness in all things, our inconstancy at all times, our unworthiness of every grace, and our iniquity in every position. The sin of our first father has spoilt us all, soured us, puffed us up and corrupted us, as the leaven sours, puffs up and corrupts the dough into which it is put. The actual sins which we have committed, whether mortal or venial, pardoned though they may be, have nevertheless increased our concupiscence, our weakness, our inconstancy and our corruption, and have left evil remains in our souls.

Our bodies are so corrupted that they are called by the Holy Ghost bodies of sin (Rom. 6:6), conceived in sin (Ps. 50:7), nourished in sin, and capable of all sin—bodies subject to thousands of maladies, which go on corrupting from day to day, and which engender nothing but disease, vermin and corruption.

Our soul, united to our body, has become so carnal that it is called flesh: "All flesh having corrupted its way" (Gen. 6:12). We have nothing for our portion but pride and blindness of spirit, hardness of heart, weakness and inconstancy of soul, concupiscence, revolted passions, and sicknesses in the body. We are naturally prouder than peacocks, more groveling than toads, more vile than unclean animals, more envious than serpents, more gluttonous than hogs, more furious than tigers, lazier than tortoises, weaker than reeds, and more capricious than weathercocks. We have within ourselves nothing but nothingness and sin, and we deserve nothing but the anger of God and everlasting hell.

After this, ought we to be astonished if Our Lord has said that whoever wishes to follow Him must renounce himself and hate his own life, and that whosoever shall love his own life shall lose it, and whosoever shall hate it, shall save it? (Jn. 12:25). He who is infinite Wisdom does not give commandments without reason, and He has commanded us to hate ourselves only because we so richly deserve to be hated. Nothing is worthier of love than God, and nothing is worthier of hatred than ourselves.

WEEK 2: DAY 7–THIRD MEDITATION

Taken from St. Louis de Montfort's
True Devotion to Mary, § 81 ff

We Must Die to Ourselves Daily

In order to rid ourselves of self, we must die to ourselves daily. That is to say, we must renounce the operations of the powers of our soul and of the senses of our body. We must see as if we saw not, understand as if we understood not, and make use of the things of this world as if we made no use of them at all (I Cor. 7:29-31). This is what St. Paul calls dying daily (I Cor. 15:31). "Unless the grain of wheat falling into the ground die, itself remaineth alone," and bringeth forth no good fruit (Jn. 12:24-25). If we do not die to ourselves and if our holiest devotions do not incline us to this necessary and useful death, we shall bring forth no fruit worth anything, and our devotions will become useless. All our good works will be stained by self-love and our own will; and this will cause God to hold in abomination the greatest sacrifices we can make and the best actions we can do, so that at our death we shall find our hands empty of virtues and of merits and we shall not have one spark of pure love, which is only communicated to souls dead to themselves, souls whose life is hidden with Jesus Christ in God (Col. 3:3).

Choose that Marian Devotion that Helps Us Die to Self

We must choose, therefore, among all the devotions to the Blessed Virgin, the one which draws us most toward this death to ourselves, inasmuch as it will be the best and the most sanctifying. For we must not think that all that shines is gold, that all that tastes sweet is honey, or that all that is easy to do, and is done by the greatest number, is the most sanctifying. As there are secrets of nature, by which natural operations are performed more easily, in a short time and at little cost, so also are there secrets in the order of grace, by which supernatural operations, such as ridding ourselves of self, filling ourselves with God, and becoming perfect, are performed more easily.

WEEK 2: DAY 7–FOURTH MEDITATION

Taken from *Three Ages of the Interior Life*, Introduction and Chapter 2, by Rev. Fr. Garrigou-Lagrange, O.P.

As everyone can easily understand, the interior life is an elevated form of intimate conversation which everyone has with themselves as soon as they are alone, even amongst the noise of a great city. From the moment a man ceases to converse with others, he begins to converse interiorly with himself about what preoccupies him the most. This conversation varies greatly according to the different ages of life; that of an old man is not the same as that of a youth. It also varies greatly depending upon whether the man is good or bad.

If we are young, we often think of what we shall do in the future; if we are old, we often think of the past and our happy or unhappy experiences lead us to judge persons and events in a variety of favorable or unfavorable ways. If we are self-centered persons, then our intimate conversation with ourselves will be inspired by thoughts of pride or sensuality, where there is a very inferior true knowledge of self, mixed with large doses of self-love and indulgence.

We tend to be more acquainted with the part of the soul that we have in common with animals, rather than the higher part that we hold in common with the angels. Therefore, we are more concerned with sense related joys and sorrows—whether the weather is pleasant or unpleasant; whether we win or lose money; whether we are in full health or are suffering from some ailment. Similarly, when we are opposed by others, we easily become irritable, impatient and angry—all of which is prompted by our excessive self-love.

Yet, as regards the part of our soul which is common to both man and angels, we know little or nothing about it. We neither seek to increase our knowledge of this part of our soul, nor do we love it sufficiently. Our thoughts always come back down to the inferior and more base aspect of our soul—in other words we seek more the inferior pleasures of life, rather than the higher supernatural goods. It has been said that, if life is not raised to the level of thought, then thought ends by descending to the level of life. All declines and one's highest convictions gradually grow weaker.

Thus, the intimate interior conversation of the egoist leads, not to an interior life, but to death. His self-love leads him to wish that he was the center of everything, drawing everything to himself, both persons and things. Since this is impossible, he frequently ends in disillusionment and disgust; he becomes unbearable to himself and to others and ends by hating himself, because he wished to love himself excessively.

As soon as a man seriously seeks truth and goodness, this intimate conversation with himself tends to become conversation with God. He converses with himself about what he should do to live a good life. This at times preoccupies himself greatly; he recognizes and feels his weakness and the need for placing his confidence , not in himself, but in God. Little by little, instead of seeking himself in everything, instead of tending more or less consciously to make himself a center, man tends to seek God in everything and, as a substitute for his own egoism, he focuses more on God and neighbor.

While still in a state of mortal sin, this man may have Christian faith and hope, which subsists in us even after the loss of charity, as long as we have not sinned mortally by disbelief, despair or presumption. When this is so, this man's intimate interior conversation with himself is occasionally illumined by the supernatural light of faith; now and then he thinks of eternal life and desires it, although this desire remains weak. He is sometimes led by a special inspiration to enter a church to pray.

Finally, if this man has attrition for his sins, confesses them and receives absolution for them, he receives the state of grace and charity, the love of God and neighbor. Thenceforth, when he is alone, his intimate interior conversation with himself changes. He begins to love himself in a holy manner, not for himself, but for God, and to love his neighbor for God's sake. He begins to understand that he must pardon his enemies and love them, and to wish eternal life for them as he does for himself.

Often, however, the intimate interior conversation of a man in the state of grace continues to be tainted with egoism, self-love, sensuality and pride. These sins are no longer mortal in him, they are venial; but if they are repeated, they incline him to fall into a serious sin, that is, back into spiritual death. Should this happen, this man tends again to flee from himself, because what he finds in himself is no longer life but death. Instead of making a salutary reflection on this subject, he may hurl himself back farther into death, by casting himself into pleasure and into the satisfactions of sensuality or of pride.

In a man's hours of solitude, this intimate conversation begins again, in spite of everything, as if to prove to him that it cannot stop. He would like to interrupt it and end it, but he cannot do so. The center of the soul has an irrestrainable need which demands satisfaction. In reality, God alone can answer this need and the only solution is to immediately take the road leading to Him. The soul must converse with someone other than itself. Why? Because it is not its own last end; because its end is the living God, and it cannot rest entirely except in Him. As St. Augustine puts it: "Our heart is restless, until it reposes in Thee."

WEEK THREE

INTRODUCTION TO WEEK THREE: KNOWING MARY

We now enter the third of our five week preparation for St. Louis de Montfort's *True Devotion Consecration to Mary*. The first two weeks dealt with the *Spirit of the World* and *Knowledge of Self*, with the aim of emptying ourselves of worldliness and cultivating a disgust for our past sinfulness, excessive self-love and pride. Yet, just as nature abhors a vacuum, so too must we replace the bad spirit—of which we seek to rid ourselves—with something else. This means acquiring the good spirit of Jesus and Mary. Therefore, in this third period of preparation, we must start to realize, appreciate and grow in the appreciation of the role that Mary has in our salvation and daily spiritual life. She is our Sovereign...our Mother...our Mediatrix...our Benefactress and our Mistress. Mary is a perfect mold of sanctity in which we must mold ourselves, in order to become perfect imitations of her Son. To be truly devoted to Mary, we must make *her* intentions *our* intentions, *her* dispositions *our* dispositions, *her* guiding spirit must become *our* guiding spirit.

The past week, with its knowledge of self, if well done, was most probably a very depressing one. We will have focused upon our faults and past failings: our pride, worldliness, avarice, lack of charity, gossiping, back-biting, complaining, laziness, lukewarmness, *etc.* Hopefully, we experienced a revulsion at the sight of our past (or even present) state. So much so that we want to flee from it, leaving it far behind. Confession may be the first thing required, to empty our souls of the filth of sin. However, since nature abhors a vacuum, we must replace our sins and past failings with something else—that something else is Mary with her graces and virtues—and she really *is* "something else!"

Getting to Know Mary

This week is devoted to meditating upon Mary and humbly asking God to grant us the grace to know Mary better. We are about to attempt a difficult and serious thing. We are to penetrate into a secret and hidden world of beauty, to discover its wondrous charms, so as to love it and dwell in it—just like God, Who finds in it joy, contentment and where He reigns with all power and majesty.

We shall seek to know Mary. We, the sin-stained wretches of the earth, the rebels of creation, we shall seek to know her whom the angels do not sufficiently know. We shall seek to uncover the secret that Mary is—a secret only fully known by God. For He alone knows Mary and delights in Mary. If we wish to know Mary, then we must earnestly beg Him for this grace and privilege and, besides praying for it, we should also perform some penance, make some pilgrimage or go to visit some church named after her.

We must offer up some little acts of mortification, denial of our own will, our desires and tastes, *etc.* We must use every means possible to induce God to look favorably upon us and to grant our request. We will turn to the angels and seek their intercession. We will beg the saints to plead with God for us. We will pray for the souls in purgatory and ask them, in return, to pray to God that He might share His secret with us.

When we have done all this, when we have confessed our unworthiness, and heard or said Mass and received our Divine Lord in her honor, we will then ask Him to grant this special favor of which we are so unworthy. We will say:

Lord, look upon our unworthiness and show us Thy mercy. Pour into our minds but one single ray of Thy Holy Spirit and make us know Mary. Let Thy glory and mercy shine by stooping to speak to us—as you once stooped down and became man for us. Thou hast hidden these things from the wise and prudent, but revealed them to little ones—please reveal to us the greatness, power, majesty, beauty and mercy of Mary, our Mother.

Mary Our Mother

This will be the first thought in our minds that Mary, though a virgin, is also a Mother—the Mother of God and our Mother too. We will imprint upon our minds the fact that Mary loves us more, far more, than our natural mothers could possibly love us—even more than we could love ourselves. A mother's love is the most practical thing in existence. It is never satisfied with words, but is always pouring itself out on someone. Motherly love is also capable of the greatest sacrifices; it is born in suffering, and time serves only to increase its generosity and service.

If this is true of the motherly love we have all experienced, what must be said of her, who became the Mother of Sorrows and the Queen of Martyrs for love of us? When we see her with the sword of Simeon plunged deeply into her heart, how can we ever doubt that her love for mankind is as practical as that of her Divine Son?

Since she became the Mother of Men, she has never stopped showing herself a Mother to all who have gone to her for help. He who is mighty has done great things to her; and she in turn, who is mighty through the power of her divine motherhood, has done great things for those who have sought her intercession. She has been and will continue to be the cause of our joy until the end of time.

Devotion Takes Time to Grow

True Devotion must grow through several stages—just like a seed, once planted, must go through different stages of growth until it finally matures and brings forth much fruit. Do not imagine that the moment you make the True Devotion Consecration, you will become a saint! You will have planted the *seed* of True Devotion, which will grow, over the future months and years, into the mature *Tree of Life* that Mary is. Prior to the Consecration, we will make use of the externals that help interior devotion—we will pray to Mary, we will read about Mary, we will have ourselves enrolled in, and wear, the Brown Scapular and also the Miraculous Medal, we will regularly pray the Rosary, we will place images or statues of Mary in our homes. This will be to the True Devotion what the sun, rain and minerals are to the seed. Without these helps, the seed will die. By a correct use of these externals of Marian devotion, we shall see Mary increasingly influence and permeate the whole of our daily life. Our True Devotion will grow like the *Tree of Life*, which it is.

That is what the word *devotion* implicitly demands! For it comes from the Latin verb *devovere,* meaning *to avow oneself to*, or *to give oneself entirely* to a deity or cause of some kind. Thus devotion to Mary implicitly requires this total consecration of ourselves to her, and through her to God.

To do this, we must imitate the interior life of Mary...her virtues...her actions...her supernatural way of seeing things...her participation in the salvation of souls...her union with God. Always remembering that *"Where Mary is, there also is God!"* However, before we can imitate anyone, we must first carefully observe and study that person. Consequently, we will study the Blessed Mother in order to imitate her virtues and absorb the spirit that animates her.

A wonderful source for meditating upon her virtues is the Litany of the Blessed Virgin, which is like a mirror into which we can gaze to see how much we resemble Mary. Just as a child takes on the characteristics of its parents by observing them, so too we should imitate Our Lady's virtues by meditating upon those listed in her litany.

The general exercises of this week, in addition to the prayers and meditation listed below, are:

1. Make acts professing your love and affection towards Mary.

2. Make acts full of faith in Mary's power and her desire to help you.

3. Make acts full of trust and confidence in Mary and, with her help, try to imitate her.

4. Thank God for all the graces and privileges that He has given to Mary and also to you, because of her intercession.

However we cannot love, trust, rely upon or imitate someone whom we do not know—all these things are consequences of
knowledge. Therefore, we must first grow in knowledge of Mary
and, then, seeing who and what she really is, we will find that
love, confidence, trust and reliance—thus the desire to imitate
her will be a natural consequence of getting to know her. Mary is
the masterpiece of God Almighty. She is His greatest creation.
She is the most loving and caring of all mothers. She is the most
merciful of all judges. She is the most generous of all benefactors.
She is the most lovable of all creatures. The reason she is so little
loved, is that she is so little known.

RECOMMENDED PRAYERS FOR WEEK THREE

Litany of the Holy Ghost

Litany of the Blessed Virgin Mary

Ave Maris Stella

Recitation of the Holy Rosary

Prayer to Mary by St. Louis de Montfort

(Each prayer need not be said daily.)

Litany of the Holy Ghost

Lord, have mercy on us,
Christ, have mercy on us
Lord, have mercy on us
Father, all powerful,
Have mercy on us.
Jesus, Eternal Son of the Father,
Redeemer of the world, *Save us.*
Spirit of the Father and the Son, boundless life of both,
Sanctify us.
Holy Trinity, *Hear us.*
Holy Ghost, Who proceedest
from the Father and the Son, *Enter our hearts.*
Holy Ghost, Who art equal to the Father and the Son,
Enter our hearts.
Promise of God the Father, *Have mercy on us.*
Ray of heavenly light,
Author of all good,
Source of heavenly water,
Consuming fire,
Ardent charity,
Spiritual unction,
Spirit of love and truth,
Spirit of wisdom and understanding,
Spirit of counsel and fortitude,
Spirit of knowledge and piety,
Spirit of the fear of the Lord,
Spirit of grace and prayer,
Spirit of peace and meekness,
Spirit of modesty and innocence,
Holy Ghost, the Comforter,
Holy Ghost, the Sanctifier,
Holy Ghost, Who governest the Church,
Gift of God, the Most High,
Spirit Who fillest the universe,
Spirit of the adoption of the children of God,

Holy Ghost, *inspire us with horror of sin.*
Holy Ghost, *come and renew the face of the earth.*
Holy Ghost, *shed Thy light in our souls.*
Holy Ghost, *engrave Thy law in our hearts.*
Holy Ghost, *inflame us with the flame of Thy love.*
Holy Ghost, *open to us the treasures of Thy graces.*
Holy Ghost, *teach us to pray well.*
Holy Ghost, *enlighten us with Thy heavenly inspirations.*
Holy Ghost, *lead us in the way of salvation.*
Holy Ghost, *grant us the only necessary knowledge.*
Holy Ghost, *inspire in us the practice of good.*
Holy Ghost, *grant us the merits of all virtues.*
Holy Ghost, *make us persevere in justice.*
Holy Ghost, *be Thou our everlasting reward.*

Lamb of God, Who takest away the sins of the world,
 Send us Thy Holy Ghost.
Lamb of God, Who takest away the sins of the world,
 Pour down into our souls the gifts of the Holy Ghost.
Lamb of God, Who takest away the sins of the world,
 Grant us the Spirit of wisdom and piety.

V. Come, Holy Ghost! Fill the hearts of Thy faithful.
R. And enkindle in them the fire of Thy Love.

Let us pray

Grant, O merciful Father, that Thy Divine Spirit enlighten, inflame and purify us, that He may penetrate us with His heavenly dew and make us fruitful in good works; through our Lord Jesus Christ, Thy Son, Who with Thee, in the unity of the same Spirit, liveth and reigneth forever and ever. *R. Amen.*

Litany of the Blessed Virgin Mary

Lord, have mercy on us.
Christ, have mercy on us.
Lord, have mercy on us.
Christ, hear us.
Christ, graciously hear us.
God the Father of heaven, *Have mercy on us.*
God the Son, Redeemer of the world,
God the Holy Ghost,
Holy Trinity, one God,
Holy Mary, *Pray for us.*
Holy Mother of God,
Holy Virgin of virgins,
Mother of Christ,
Mother of divine grace,
Mother most pure,
Mother most chaste,
Mother inviolate,
Mother undefiled,
Mother most amiable,
Mother most admirable,
Mother of good counsel,
Mother of our Creator,
Mother of our Savior,
Virgin most prudent,
Virgin most venerable,
Virgin most renowned,
Virgin most powerful,
Virgin most merciful,
Virgin most faithful,
Mirror of justice,
Seat of wisdom,
Cause of our joy,
Spiritual vessel,
Vessel of honor,
Singular vessel of devotion,
Mystical rose,

Tower of David,
Tower of ivory,
House of gold,
Ark of the covenant,
Gate of heaven,
Morning Star,
Health of the sick,
Refuge of sinners,
Comforter of the afflicted,
Help of Christians,
Queen of angels,
Queen of patriarchs,
Queen of prophets,
Queen of Apostles,
Queen of martyrs,
Queen of confessors,
Queen of virgins,
Queen of all saints,
Queen conceived without original sin,
Queen assumed into heaven,
Queen of the most holy Rosary,
Queen of peace,

Lamb of God, Who takes away the sins of the world,
 Spare us, O Lord.
Lamb of God, Who takes away the sins of the world,
 Graciously hear us, O Lord.
Lamb of God, Who takes away the sins of the world,
 Have mercy on us.

V. Pray for us, O holy Mother of God.
R. That we may be made worthy of the promises of Christ.

Let us pray

Grant unto us, Thy servants, we beseech Thee, O Lord God, at all times to enjoy health of soul and body; and by the glorious intercession of Blessed Mary, ever virgin, when freed from the sorrows of this present life, to enter into that joy which hath no end. Through Christ our Lord. *R. Amen.*

Ave Maris Stella

Hail, bright star of ocean,
God's own Mother blest,
Ever sinless Virgin,
Gate of heavenly rest.

Taking that sweet Ave
Which from Gabriel came,
Peace confirm within us,
Changing Eva's name.

Break the captives' fetters,
Light on blindness pour,
All our ills expelling,
Every bliss implore.

Show thyself a Mother;
May the Word Divine,
Born for us thy Infant,
Hear our prayers through thine.

Virgin all excelling,
Mildest of the mild,
Freed from guilt, preserve us,
Pure and undefiled.

Keep our life all spotless,
Make our way secure,
Till we find in Jesus
Joy forevermore.

Through the highest heaven
To the Almighty Three,
Father, Son and Spirit,
One same glory be. Amen.

St. Louis de Montfort's Prayer to Mary.

Hail Mary, beloved Daughter of the Eternal Father! *Hail Mary*, admirable Mother of the Son! *Hail Mary*, faithful Spouse of the Holy Ghost! *Hail Mary*, my dear Mother, my loving mistress, my powerful sovereign! Hail my joy, my glory, my heart and my soul! Thou art all mine by mercy, and I am all thine by justice. But I am not yet sufficiently thine. I now give myself wholly to thee without keeping anything back for myself or others. If thou still seest in me anything which does not belong to thee, I beseech thee to take it and to make thyself the absolute mistress of all that is mine. Destroy in me all that may be displeasing to God, root it up and bring it to nought; place and cultivate in me everything that is pleasing to thee.

May the light of thy faith dispel the darkness of my mind; may thy profound humility take the place of my pride; may thy sublime contemplation check the distractions of my wandering imagination; may thy continuous sight of God fill my memory with His presence; may the burning love of thy heart inflame the lukewarmness of mine; may thy virtues take the place of my sins; may thy merits be my only adornment in the sight of God and make up for all that is wanting in me. Finally, dearly beloved Mother, grant, if it be possible, that I may have no other spirit but thine to know Jesus and His divine will; that I may have no other soul but thine to praise and glorify the Lord; that I may have no other heart but thine to love God with a love as pure and ardent as thine. I do not ask thee for visions, revelations, sensible devotion or spiritual pleasures. It is thy privilege to see God clearly; it is thy privilege to enjoy heavenly bliss; it is thy privilege to triumph gloriously in heaven at the right hand of thy Son and to hold absolute sway over angels, men and demons; it is thy privilege to dispose of all the gifts of God, just as thou willest.

Such is, O heavenly Mary, "the best part" which the Lord has given thee and which shall never be taken away from thee—and this thought fills my heart with joy. As for my part here below, I wish for no other than that which was thine: to believe sincerely without spiritual pleasures; to suffer joyfully without human consolation; to die continually to myself without respite; and to work zealously and unselfishly for thee until death as the humblest of thy servants. The only grace I beg thee to obtain for me is that every day and every moment of my life I may say: Amen—so be it, to all that thou didst do while on earth; Amen—so be it, to all that thou art now doing in heaven; Amen—so be it, to all that thou art doing in my soul, so that thou alone mayest fully glorify Jesus in me for time and eternity. Amen.

DAILY MEDITATIONS TO HELP US GROW IN THE KNOWLEDGE OF OUR LADY

WEEK 3: DAY 1–FIRST MEDITATION

Taken from St. Louis de Montfort's
True Devotion to Mary, §1 ff.

It was through the most holy Virgin Mary that Jesus came into the world, and it is also through her that He has to reign in the world....Mary is the excellent masterpiece of the Most High, the knowledge and possession of which He has reserved to Himself....Mary is the admirable Mother of the Son...the faithful spouse of the Holy Ghost....Mary is the sanctuary and the repose of the Holy Trinity, where God dwells more magnificently and more divinely than in any other place in the universe, not excepting His dwelling between the Cherubim and Seraphim. Nor is any creature, no matter how pure, allowed to enter into that sanctuary except by a great and special privilege.

I say with the saints, the divine Mary is the terrestrial paradise of the New Adam, where He was made flesh by the operation of the Holy Ghost, in order to work there incomprehensible marvels. She is the grand and divine world of God, where there are beauties and treasures unspeakable. She is the magnificence of the Most High, where He hid, as in her bosom, His only Son, and in Him all that is most excellent and most precious. Oh, what grand and hidden things that mighty God has wrought in this admirable creature, as she herself had to acknowledge, in spite of her profound humility: "He that is mighty hath done great things to me." (Lk. 1:49). The world knows them not, because it is both incapable and unworthy of such knowledge.

The saints have said admirable things of this holy city of God; and, as they themselves avow, they were never more eloquent and more content than when they spoke of her. Yet, after all they have said, they cry out that the height of her merits cannot be fully seen....The whole earth is full of her glory, especially among Christians, by whom she is taken as the protectress of many kingdoms, provinces, dioceses and cities. Many cathedrals are consecrated to God under her name. There is not a church without an altar in her honor, not a country, nor a canton, where there are not some miraculous images where all sorts of evils are cured and all sorts of good gifts obtained. Who can count the confraternities and congregations in her honor? How many religious orders have been founded in her name and under her protection? How many members are in these confraternities and how many religious men and women in all these orders, who publish her praises and confess her mercies! There is not a little child who, as it lisps the *Hail Mary*, does not praise her. There is scarcely a sinner who, even in his obduracy, has not some spark of confidence in her. Nay, the very devils in hell respect her while they fear her.

After that, we must cry out with the saints: *De Maria numquam satis—Of Mary there is never enough.* We have not yet praised, exalted, honored, loved and served Mary as we ought. She deserves still more praise, still more respect, still more love, and still more service. After that, we must cry out with the Apostle, "Eye has not seen, nor ear heard, nor man's heart comprehended" (I Cor. 2:9) the beauties, the grandeurs, the excellence of Mary— the miracle of the miracles of grace, of nature and of glory. "If you wish to comprehend the Mother," says a saint, "comprehend the Son; for she is the worthy Mother of God." "Here let every tongue be mute." It is with a particular joy that my heart has dictated what I have just written, in order to show that the divine Mary has been, up to this time, unknown and that this is one of the reasons that Jesus Christ is not known as He ought to be. If then, as is certain, the knowledge and the kingdom of Jesus Christ are to come into the world, they will be but a necessary consequence of the knowledge and the kingdom of the most holy Virgin Mary, who brought Him into the world for the first time and will make His second Advent full of splendor.

WEEK 3: DAY 1–SECOND MEDITATION

Taken from St. Louis de Montfort's
True Devotion to Mary, §14 ff.

I avow, with all the Church, that Mary, being a mere creature that has come from the hands of the Most High, is in comparison with His Infinite Majesty less than an atom; or rather, she is nothing at all, because only He is *"He Who is"* (Exod. 3:14); consequently that grand Lord, always independent and sufficient to Himself, never had, and has not now, any absolute need of the holy Virgin for the accomplishment of His will and for the manifestation of His glory. He has but to will in order to do everything.

Nevertheless, I say that, things being as they are now—that is, God having willed to commence and to complete His greatest works by the most holy Virgin ever since He created her—we may well think He will not change His conduct in the eternal ages; for He is God and He changes not, either in His sentiments or in His conduct.

It was only through Mary that God the Father gave His Only begotten to the world. Whatever sighs the patriarchs may have sent forth, whatever prayers the prophets and the saints of the Old Law may have offered up to obtain this treasure for full four thousand years, it was only Mary who merited it and found grace before God by the force of her prayers and the eminence of her virtues. The world was unworthy, says St. Augustine, to receive the Son of God directly from the Father's hands. He gave Him to Mary in order that the world might receive Him through her. The Son of God became man for our salvation; but it was in Mary and by Mary. God the Holy Ghost formed Jesus Christ in Mary; but it was only after having asked her consent by one of the first ministers of His court (the Angel Gabriel).

God the Son descended into her virginal womb as the New Adam into His terrestrial paradise....God made Man found His liberty in seeing Himself imprisoned in her womb....He glorified His independence and His majesty in depending on that sweet

Virgin in His conception, in His birth, in His presentation in the temple, in His hidden life of thirty years, and even in His death, where she was to be present, in order that He might make, with her, but one same sacrifice and be immolated to the Eternal Father by her consent, just as Isaac of old was offered by Abraham's consent to the will of God. It is she who nourished Him, supported Him, brought Him up and then sacrificed Him for us.

Oh, admirable and incomprehensible dependence of God...Jesus Christ gave more glory to God the Father by submission to His Mother during those thirty years than He would have given Him in converting the whole world by the working of the most stupendous miracles. Oh, how highly we glorify God when, to please Him, we submit ourselves to Mary, after the example of Jesus Christ, our sole Exemplar!

WEEK 3: DAY 1–THIRD MEDITATION

Taken from St. Louis de Montfort's
True Devotion to Mary, §62 ff.

Devotion to Mary Means Devotion to Jesus

If, then, we establish solid devotion to our Blessed Lady, it is only to establish more perfectly devotion to Jesus Christ and to provide an easy and secure means for finding Jesus Christ. If devotion to Our Lady removed us from Jesus Christ, we should have to reject it as an illusion of the devil; but far from this being the case, devotion to Our Lady, on the contrary, is necessary for us—as I have already shown, and will show still further hereafter—as a means of finding Jesus Christ perfectly, of loving Him tenderly and of serving Him faithfully.

I here turn for one moment to Thee, O sweet Jesus, to complain lovingly to Thy Divine Majesty that the greater part of Christians, even the most learned, do not know the necessary union there is between Thee and Thy holy Mother. Thou, Lord, art always with Mary and Mary is always with Thee, and she cannot be without Thee, else she would cease to be what she is.

She is so transformed into Thee by grace, that she lives no more—she is as though she were not. It is Thee, my Jesus, who livest and reignest in her, more perfectly than in all the angels and the blessed. Ah! If we knew the glory and the love which Thou receivest from this admirable creature, we should have very different thoughts both of Thee and her, from what we have now. She is so intimately united with Thee, that it were easier to separate the light from the sun, the heat from the fire; nay, it were easier to separate from Thee all the angels and the saints than the divine Mary, because she loves Thee more ardently and glorifies Thee more perfectly than all the other creatures put together.

Furthermore, after Mary has heaped her favors upon her children and faithful servants, and has obtained for them the blessing of the heavenly Father and union with Jesus Christ, she preserves them in Jesus and Jesus in them. She takes care of them, watches over them always, for fear they should lose the grace of God and fall into the snares of their enemies. "*She retains the saints in their fullness,*" and makes them persevere to the end, as we have seen. This is the interpretation of the story of Jacob and Esau, that great and ancient figure of predestination and reprobation, so unknown and so full of mysteries.

Turn Away from Mary and You Turn Away from Jesus

After that, my sweet Master, is it not an astonishingly pitiable thing to see the ignorance and the darkness of all men here below in regard to Thy holy Mother? I speak not so much of idolaters and pagans, who, knowing Thee not, care not to know her. I speak not even of heretics and schismatics, who care not to be devout to Thy holy Mother, being separated as they are from Thee and Thy holy Church; but I speak of Catholic Christians, and even of doctors among Catholics, who make profession of teaching truths to others, and yet know not Thee nor Thy holy Mother, except in a speculative, dry, barren and indifferent manner.

These gentlemen speak but rarely of Thy holy Mother and of the devotion we ought to have to her, because they fear, so they say, lest we should abuse it and do some injury to Thee in honoring Thy holy Mother too much. If they hear or see anyone devout to our Blessed Lady, speaking often of his devotion to that good Mother in a tender, strong and persuasive way, and as a secure means without delusion, as a short road without danger, as an immaculate way without imperfection, and as a wonderful secret for finding and loving Thee perfectly—they cry out against him and give him a thousand false reasons by way of proving to him that he ought not to talk so much of our Blessed Lady; that there are great abuses in that devotion; and that we must direct our energies to destroy these abuses; and to speak of Thee, rather than to incline the people to devotion to our Blessed Lady, whom they already love sufficiently.

We hear them sometimes speak of devotion to our Blessed Lady, not for the purpose of establishing it and persuading men to embrace it, but to destroy the abuses which are made of it; and all the while these teachers are without piety or tender devotion toward Thyself, simply because they have none for Mary. They regard the Rosary and the Scapular as devotions proper for weak and ignorant minds, without which men can save themselves; and if there falls into their hands any poor client of Our Lady who says his Rosary, or has any other practice of devotion toward her, they soon change his spirit and his heart. Instead of the Rosary, they counsel him the seven Penitential Psalms. Instead of devotion to the holy Virgin, they counsel him devotion to Jesus Christ.

O my sweet Jesus, do these people have Thy spirit? Do they please Thee in acting thus? Does it please Thee when, for fear of displeasing Thee, we neglect doing our utmost to please Thy Mother? Does devotion to Thy holy Mother hinder devotion to Thyself? Does she attribute to herself the honor we pay her? Does she head a faction of her own? Is she a stranger who has no connection with Thee? Does it displease Thee that we should try to please her? Do we separate or alienate ourselves from Thy love by giving ourselves to her and honoring her?

Yet, my sweet Master, the greater part of the learned could not discourage devotion to Thy holy Mother more, and could not show more indifference to it, even if all that I have just said

were true. Thus have they been punished for their pride! Keep
me, Lord, keep me from their sentiments and their practices, and
give me some share of the sentiments of gratitude, esteem, respect and love, which Thou hast in regard to Thy holy Mother, so
that the more I imitate and follow her, the more I may love and
glorify Thee.

WEEK 3: DAY 1–FOURTH MEDITATION

Taken from St. Louis de Montfort's
True Devotion to Mary, §16 ff.

Jesus and Mary Are Inseparable

It was only through Mary that God the Father gave His Only
begotten to the world. He gave Him to Mary in order that the
world might receive Him through her. The Son of God became
man for our salvation; but it was in Mary and by Mary. God the
Son descended into her virginal womb as the New Adam into
His terrestrial paradise, to take His pleasure there, and to work in
secret marvels of grace.

God made Man found His liberty in seeing Himself imprisoned in her womb. He made His omnipotence shine forth in
letting Himself be carried by that humble maiden. He found His
glory and His Father's in hiding His splendors from all creatures
here below, and revealing them to Mary only.

He glorified His independence and His majesty in depending on that sweet Virgin in His conception, in His birth, in His
presentation in the temple, in His hidden life of thirty years, and
even in His death, where she was to be present, in order that He
might make, with her, but one same sacrifice and be immolated
to the Eternal Father by her consent, just as Isaac of old was offered by Abraham's consent to the will of God.

It is she who nourished Him, supported Him, brought Him
up and then sacrificed Him for us. Jesus Christ gave more glory
to God the Father by submission to His Mother, during those
thirty years, than He would have given Him in converting the
whole world, by the working of the most stupendous miracles.

God the Son wishes to form Himself and, so to speak, to incarnate Himself in His members, every day, by His dear Mother. "This man and that man is born in her" (Ps. 86:5), says the Holy Ghost through the Royal Psalmist. If Jesus Christ, the Head of men, is born in her, then the predestinate, who are the members of that Head, ought also to be born in her by a necessary consequence. One and the same mother does not bring forth into the world the head without the members, or the members without the head; for this would be a monster of nature.

So in like manner, in the order of grace, the head and the members are born of one and the same Mother; and if a member of the Mystical Body were born of any other mother than Mary, who has produced the Head, he would not be one of the predestinate, nor a member of Jesus Christ, but simply a monster in the order of grace. Inasmuch as grace perfects nature, and glory perfects grace, it is certain that Our Lord is still, in heaven, as much the Son of Mary as He was on earth; and that, consequently, He has retained the obedience and submission of the most perfect Child toward the best of all mothers.

But we must take great pains not to conceive this dependence as any abasement or imperfection in Jesus Christ. For Mary is infinitely below her Son, who is God, and therefore she does not command Him as a mother here below would command her child who is below her. Mary, being altogether transformed into God by grace and by the glory which transforms all the saints into Him, asks nothing, wishes nothing, does nothing contrary to the eternal and immutable will of God.

God the Son has communicated to His Mother all that He acquired by His life and His death, His infinite merits and His admirable virtues; and He has made her the treasurer of all that His Father gave Him for His inheritance. It is by her that He applies His merits to His members, and that He communicates His virtues and distributes His graces. She is His mysterious canal; she is His aqueduct, through which He makes His mercies flow gently and abundantly.

WEEK 3: DAY 1–FIFTH MEDITATION

Taken from the Gospel according to St. Luke, Chapter 1

26 And in the sixth month, the angel Gabriel was sent from God into a city of Galilee, called Nazareth.

27 To a virgin espoused to a man whose name was Joseph, of the house of David; and the virgin's name was Mary.

28 And the angel being come in, said unto her: Hail, full of grace, the Lord is with thee: blessed art thou among women.

29 Who having heard, was troubled at his saying, and thought with herself what manner of salutation this should be.

30 And the angel said to her: Fear not, Mary, for thou hast found grace with God.

31 Behold thou shalt conceive in thy womb, and shalt bring forth a son; and thou shalt call his name Jesus.

32 He shall be great, and shall be called the Son of the most High; and the Lord God shall give unto him the throne of David his father; and he shall reign in the house of Jacob for ever.

33 And of his kingdom there shall be no end.

34 And Mary said to the angel: How shall this be done, because I know not man?

35 And the angel answering, said to her: The Holy Ghost shall come upon thee and the power of the most High shall overshadow thee. And therefore also the Holy which shall be born of thee shall be called the Son of God.

36 And behold thy cousin Elizabeth, she also hath conceived a son in her old age; and this the sixth month with her that is called barren:

37 Because no word shall be impossible with God.

38 And Mary said: Behold the handmaid of the Lord; be it done to me according to thy word. And the angel departed from her.

Jesus Chooses to Work Through Mary

If we examine closely the rest of Our Blessed Lord's life, Mary's role will become clear. We shall see that it was His will to begin His miracles by Mary. He sanctified St. John in the womb of his mother, St. Elizabeth, but it was by Mary's word. As soon as she spoke, John was sanctified; and this was His first miracle of grace. At the marriage feast of Cana, He changed the water into wine, but it was at Mary's humble prayer; and this was His first miracle of nature. He began His miracles by Mary, and will continue them to the end of ages by Mary.

Taken from the Gospel according to St. Luke, Chapter 1

39 And Mary rising up in those days, went into the hill country with haste into a city of Juda.

40 And she entered into the house of Zachary, and saluted Elizabeth.

41 And it came to pass, that when Elizabeth heard the salutation of Mary, the infant leaped in her womb. And Elizabeth was filled with the Holy Ghost:

42 And she cried out with a loud voice, and said: Blessed art thou among women, and blessed is the fruit of thy womb.

43 And whence is this to me, that the mother of my Lord should come to me?

44 For behold as soon as the voice of thy salutation sounded in my ears, the infant in my womb leaped for joy.

45 And blessed art thou that hast believed, because those things shall be accomplished that were spoken to thee by the Lord.

46 And Mary said: My soul doth magnify the Lord.

47 And my spirit hath rejoiced in God my Savior.

48 Because he hath regarded the humility of his handmaid; for behold from henceforth all generations shall call me blessed.

49 Because he that is mighty, hath done great things to me; and holy is his name.

50 And his mercy is from generation unto generations, to them that fear him.

51 He hath showed might in his arm: he hath scattered the proud in the conceit of their heart.

52 He hath put down the mighty from their seat, and hath exalted the humble.

53 He hath filled the hungry with good things; and the rich he hath sent empty away.

54 He hath received Israel his servant, being mindful of his mercy:

55 As he spoke to our fathers, to Abraham and to his seed for ever.

56 And Mary abode with her about three months; and she returned to her own house.

WEEK 3: DAY 2–FIRST MEDITATION

Taken from St. Louis de Montfort's *The Secret of Mary*, §1-23

Here is a secret, chosen soul, which the most High God taught me and which I have not found in any book, ancient or modern. Inspired by the Holy Ghost, I am confiding it to you, with these conditions:

1. That you share it only with people who deserve to know it because they are prayerful, give alms to the poor, do penance, suffer persecution, are unworldly and work seriously for the salvation of souls;

2. That you use this secret to become holy and worthy of heaven, and the more you make use of it, the more benefit you will derive from it. Under no circumstances must you let this secret make you idle and inactive. It would then become harmful and lead to your ruin;

3. That you thank God every day of your life for the grace He has given you in letting you into a secret that you do not deserve to know.

As you go on using this secret in the ordinary actions of your life, you will come to understand its value and its excellent quality. At the beginning, however, your understanding of it will be clouded, because of the seriousness and number of your sins, and your unconscious love of self.

Chosen soul, living image of God and redeemed by the Precious Blood of Jesus Christ, God wants you to become holy like Him in this life, and glorious like Him in the next (Mt. 5:48).

It is certain that growth in the holiness of God is your vocation. All your thoughts, words, actions, everything you suffer or undertake, must lead you towards that end. Otherwise you are resisting God, in not doing the work for which He created you and for which He is even now keeping you in being.

Chosen soul, how will you bring this about? What steps will you take to reach the high level to which God is calling you? The means of holiness and salvation are known to everybody, since they are found in the Gospel; the masters of the spiritual life have explained them; the saints have practiced them and shown how essential they are, for those who wish to be saved and attain perfection. These means are: sincere humility, unceasing prayer, complete self-denial, abandonment to divine Providence, and obedience to the will of God.

The grace and help of God are absolutely necessary for us to practice all these, and we are sure that grace will be given to all, though not in the same measure. I say "not in the same measure," because God does not give His graces in equal measure to everyone (Rom. 12:6), although, in His infinite goodness, He always gives sufficient grace to each. It all comes to this, then: we must discover a simple means to obtain from God the grace needed to become holy. It is precisely this that I wish to teach you. My contention is that you must first discover Mary, if you would obtain this grace from God.

Since Mary produced the head of the elect, Jesus Christ, she must also produce the members of that head, that is, all true Christians. A mother does not conceive a head without members, nor members without a head. If anyone, then, wishes to become a member of Jesus Christ, he must be formed in Mary through the grace of Jesus Christ. The Holy Ghost espoused Mary and produced His greatest work, the incarnate Word, in her, by her and through her. He continues to produce every day, in a mysterious but very real manner, the souls of the elect in her and through her.

St. Augustine went so far as to say that, even in this world, all the elect are enclosed in the womb of Mary, and that their real birthday is when this good mother brings them forth to eternal life. Consequently, just as an infant draws all its nourishment from its mother, who gives according to its needs, so the elect draw all their spiritual nourishment and all their strength from Mary.

Mary is called by St. Augustine, and is indeed, the "living mold of God." In her alone the God-man was formed in His human nature without losing any feature of the Godhead. In her alone, by the grace of Jesus Christ, man is made godlike as far as human nature is capable of it.

A sculptor can make a statue or a life-like model in two ways: firstly, by using his skill, strength, experience and good tools to produce a statue out of a hard, shapeless matter; or, secondly, by making a cast of it in a mold. The first way is long and involved and open to all sorts of accidents. It only needs a faulty stroke of the chisel or hammer to ruin the whole work. The second is quick, easy, straightforward, almost effortless and inexpensive, but the mold must be perfect and true to life and the material must be easy to handle and offer no resistance.

Mary is the great mold of God. No godly feature is missing from this mold. Everyone who casts himself into it and allows himself to be molded, will acquire every feature of Jesus Christ. He will take on a faithful likeness to Jesus with no possibility of distortion.

Dear friend, what a difference there is between a soul brought up in the ordinary way to resemble Jesus Christ by people who, like sculptors, rely on their own skill and industry, and a soul thoroughly tractable, entirely detached, most ready to be molded in her, by the working of the Holy Ghost. What blemishes and defects, what shadows and distortions, what natural and human imperfections are found in the first soul, and what a faithful and divine likeness to Jesus is found in the second!

Let us not imagine, then, as some misguided teachers do, that Mary, being simply a creature, would be a hindrance to union with the Creator. Far from it, for it is no longer Mary who lives, but Jesus Christ himself, God alone, Who lives in her. Her transformation into God far surpasses that experienced by St. Paul (Gal. 2:20) and other saints, more than heaven surpasses the earth.

Mary was created only for God and she leads every soul straight to God and to union with Him. Mary is the wonderful echo of God. The more a person joins himself to her, the more effectively she unites him to God.

The saints tell us that when we have once found Mary—and through Mary, Jesus, and through Jesus, God the Father— then we have discovered every good. When we say "every good," we except nothing. This does not mean that one who has discovered Mary through a genuine devotion is exempt from crosses and sufferings. Far from it! One is tried even more than others, because Mary, as Mother of the living, gives to all her children splinters of the tree of life, which is the Cross of Jesus. But while meting out crosses to them, she gives the grace to bear them with patience, and even with joy.

The difficulty, then, is how to arrive at the true knowledge of the most holy Virgin and so find grace in abundance through her. God, as the absolute Master, can give directly what He ordinarily dispenses only through Mary, and it would be rash to deny that He sometimes does so. However, St. Thomas assures us that, following the order established by His divine Wisdom, God ordinarily imparts His graces to men through Mary. Therefore, if we wish to go to Him, seeking union with Him, we must use the same means which He used in coming down from heaven to assume our human nature and to impart His graces to us. That means was a complete dependence on Mary His Mother, which is true devotion to her.

WEEK 3: DAY 2–SECOND MEDITATION

Taken from St. Louis de Montfort's
The Secret of Mary, §24-40

There are indeed several true devotions to Our Lady. I do not intend treating of those which are false. The first consists in fulfilling the duties of our Christian state, avoiding all mortal sin, performing our actions for God, more through love than through fear, praying to Our Lady occasionally and honoring her as the Mother of God, but without our devotion to her being exceptional. The second consists in entertaining for Our Lady deeper feelings of esteem and love, of confidence and veneration. This devotion inspires us to join the Confraternities of the Holy Rosary and the Scapular, to say the five or fifteen decades of the Rosary, to venerate our Lady's pictures and shrines, to make her known to others, and to enroll in her sodalities. This devotion, in keeping us from sin, is good, holy and praiseworthy, but it is not as perfect as the third, nor as effective in detaching us from creatures, or in practicing that self-denial necessary for union with Jesus Christ.

The third devotion to Our Lady is one which is unknown to many and practiced by very few. This is the one I am about to present to you. This devotion consists in surrendering oneself in the manner of a slave to Mary, and to Jesus through her, and then performing all our actions with Mary, in Mary, through Mary, and for Mary. Let me explain this statement further.

We willingly and lovingly and under no constraint, consecrate and sacrifice to her unreservedly our body and soul. We give to her our material possessions, such as house, family, income, and even the inner possessions of our soul, namely, our merits, graces, virtues and atonements.

Notice that, in this devotion, we sacrifice to Jesus through Mary all that is most dear to us, that is, the right to dispose of ourselves, of the value of our prayers and alms, of our acts of self-denial and atonements. This is a sacrifice which no religious order would require of its members. We leave everything to the free disposal of Our Lady, for her to use as she wills for the greater glory of God, of which she alone is perfectly aware.

We leave to her the right to dispose of all the satisfactory and prayer value of our good deeds, so that, after having done so and without going so far as making a vow, we cease to be master over any good we do. Our Lady may use our good deeds, either to bring relief or deliverance to a soul in purgatory, or perhaps to bring a change of heart to a poor sinner.

By this devotion we place our merits in the hands of Our Lady, but only that she may preserve, increase and embellish them, since merit for increase of grace and glory cannot be handed over to any other person. But we give to her all our prayers and good works, inasmuch as they have intercessory and atonement value, for her to distribute and apply to whom she pleases. If, after having thus consecrated ourselves to Our Lady, we wish to help a soul in purgatory, rescue a sinner, or assist a friend by a prayer, an alms, an act of self-denial or an act of self-sacrifice, we must humbly request it of Our Lady, abiding always by her decision, which, of course, remains unknown to us.

I have said that this devotion consists in adopting the status of a slave with regard to Mary. We must remember that there are three kinds of slavery. There is, first, a slavery based on nature. All men, good and bad alike, are slaves of God in this sense. The second is a slavery of compulsion. The devils and the damned are slaves of God in this second sense. The third is a slavery of love and free choice. This is the kind chosen by one who consecrates himself to God through Mary, and this is the most perfect way for us human beings to give ourselves to God, our Creator.

In giving ourselves to Jesus through Mary's hands, we imitate God the Father, Who gave us His Son only through Mary, and Who imparts His graces to us only through Mary. Likewise, we imitate God the Son, Who by giving us His example for us to follow, inspires us to go to Him using the same means He used in coming to us, that is, through Mary. Again, we imitate the Holy Ghost, Who bestows His graces and gifts upon us only through Mary.

Consecrating ourselves in this way, to Jesus through Mary, implies placing our good deeds in Mary's hands. Now, although these deeds may appear good to us, they are often defective and not worthy to be considered and accepted by God, before Whom even the stars lack brightness.

Any good our soul could produce is of less value to God our Father, in winning His friendship and favor, than a worm-eaten apple would be in the sight of a king, when presented by a poor peasant to his royal master as payment for the rent of his farm. But what would the peasant do if he were wise and if he enjoyed the esteem of the queen? Would he not present his apple first to her and, would she not, out of kindness to the poor man and out of respect for the king, remove from the apple all that was maggoty and spoilt, place it on a golden dish and surround it with flowers? Could the king then refuse the apple? Would he not accept it most willingly from the hands of his queen, who showed such loving concern for that poor man? "If you wish to present something to God, no matter how small it may be," says St. Bernard, "Place it in the hands of Mary to ensure its certain acceptance."

Dear God, how everything we do comes to so very little! But let us adopt this devotion and place everything in Mary's hands. When we have given her all we possibly can, emptying ourselves completely to do her honor, she far surpasses our generosity and gives us very much for very little. She enriches us with her own merits and virtues. She places our gift on the golden dish of her charity and clothes us, as Rebecca clothed Jacob, in the beautiful garments of her first-born and only Son, Jesus Christ, which are His merits, and which are at her disposal.

Giving ourselves in this way to Our Lady is a practice of charity towards our neighbor of the highest possible degree, because in giving ourselves over to Mary, we give her all that we hold most dear and we let her dispose of it as she wishes, in favor of the living and the dead. In adopting this devotion, we put our graces, merits and virtues into safe keeping, by making Mary the depositary of them.

"When you follow Mary you will not go astray; when you pray to her, you will not despair; when your mind is on her, you will not wander; when she holds you up, you will not fall; when she protects you, you will have no fear; when she guides you, you will feel no fatigue; when she is on your side, you will arrive safely home" (St. Bernard). And again, "She keeps her Son from striking us; she prevents the devil from harming us; she preserves virtue in us; she prevents our merits from being lost and our graces from receding." These words of St. Bernard explain, in substance, all that I have said.

WEEK 3: DAY 2–THIRD MEDITATION

Taken from St. Louis de Montfort's
The Secret of Mary, §43-59

The Interior Constituents of
This Consecration and Its Spirit

I have already said that this devotion consists in performing all our actions with Mary, in Mary, through Mary, and for Mary. It is not enough to give ourselves, just once, as a slave to Jesus through Mary; nor is it enough to renew that consecration once a month or once a week. That alone would make it just a passing devotion and would not raise the soul to the level of holiness which it is capable of reaching.

It is easy to enroll in a confraternity; easy to undertake the devotion; easy to say every day the few vocal prayers prescribed. The chief difficulty is to enter into its spirit, which requires an interior dependence on Mary and, effectively, becoming her slave and the slave of Jesus through her. I have met many people who, with admirable zeal, have set about practicing exteriorly this holy slavery of Jesus and Mary, but I have met only a few who have caught its interior spirit, and fewer still who have persevered in it.

Act with Mary

The essential practice of this devotion is to perform all our actions with Mary. This means that we must take her as the accomplished model for all we have to do.

Before undertaking anything, we must forget self and abandon our own views. We must consider ourselves as a mere nothing before God, as being personally incapable of doing anything supernaturally worthwhile, or anything conducive to our salvation. We must have habitual recourse to Our Lady, becoming one with her and adopting her intentions, even though they are unknown to us. In this way, we pursue our interior life and make spiritual progress only in dependence on Mary.

Act in Mary

We must always act in Mary, that is to say, we must gradually acquire the habit of recollecting ourselves interiorly and, so, form within us an idea or a spiritual image of Mary. She must become, as it were, an Oratory for the soul, where we offer up our prayers to God, without fear of being ignored. Mary will be the only means we will use in going to God and she will become our intercessor for everything we need. When we pray, we will pray in Mary. When we receive Jesus in Holy Communion, we will place Him in Mary, for Him to take His delight in her. If we do anything at all, it will be in Mary and, in this way, Mary will help us to forget self—everywhere and in all things.

Act through Mary

We must never go to our Lord except through Mary, using her intercession and good standing with Him. We must never be without her when praying to Jesus.

Act for Mary

We must perform all our actions for Mary, which means that, as slaves of this noble Queen, we will work only for her, promoting her interests and her high renown; and making this the first aim in all our acts, while the glory of God will always be our final end. In everything we must renounce self-love, because more often than not, without our being aware of it, selfishness sets itself up as the end of all we work for. We should often repeat, from the depths of our heart: "Dear Mother, it is to please you that I go here or there, that I do this or that, that I suffer this pain or that injury."

Beware, chosen soul, of thinking that it is more perfect to direct your work and intention straight to Jesus or straight to God. Without Mary, your work and your intention will be of little value.

The Effects That This Devotion
Produces in a Faithful Soul

Experience will teach you much more about this devotion than I can tell you, but if you remain faithful to the little I have taught you, you will acquire a great richness of grace that will surprise you and fill you with delight. Let us set to work, then, dear soul, through perseverance in the living of this devotion, in order that Mary's soul may glorify the Lord in us and her spirit be within us to rejoice in God her Savior. This devotion, faithfully practiced, produces countless happy effects in the soul. The most important of them is that it establishes, even here on earth, Mary's life in the soul, so that it is no longer the soul that lives, but Mary who lives in it. In a manner of speaking, Mary's soul becomes identified with the soul of her servant. She is a great wonder-worker especially in the interior of souls.

But why dwell any longer on this? Experience alone will teach us the wonders wrought by Mary in the soul, wonders so great, that the wise and the proud and even a great number of devout people find it hard to credit them.

We are given reason to believe that, towards the end of time and perhaps sooner than we expect, God will raise up great men filled with the Holy Ghost and imbued with the spirit of Mary. Through them Mary, Queen most powerful, will work great wonders in the world, destroying sin and setting up the kingdom of Jesus her Son, upon the ruins of the corrupt kingdom of the world. These holy men will accomplish this by means of the devotion of which I only trace the main outlines and which suffers from my incompetence.

WEEK 3: DAY 2–FOURTH MEDITATION

Taken from St. Louis de Montfort's
True Devotion to Mary, §29 ff.

God the Father wishes to have children by Mary till the consummation of the world; and He speaks to her these words: "Dwell in Jacob" (Eccles. 24:13); that is to say: Make your dwelling and residence in My predestined children, prefigured by Jacob, and not in the reprobate children of the devil, prefigured by Esau. Just as in the natural and corporal generation of children there are a father and a mother, so in the supernatural and spiritual generation there are a Father, who is God, and a Mother, who is Mary. All the true children of God, the predestinate, have God for their Father and Mary for their Mother. He who has not Mary for his Mother, has not God for his Father.

This is the reason why the reprobate, such as heretics, schismatics and others, who hate our Blessed Lady, or regard her with contempt and indifference, have not God for their Father, however much they boast of it, simply because they have not Mary for their Mother. For if they had her for their Mother, they would love and honor her, as a true child naturally loves and honors the mother who has given him life.

The most infallible and indubitable sign by which we may distinguish a heretic, a man of bad doctrine, a reprobate, from one of the predestinate, is that the heretic and the reprobate have nothing but contempt and indifference for Our Lady, endeavoring by their words and examples to diminish the worship and love of her, openly or hiddenly, and sometimes by misrepresentation.

"This man and that man is born in her" (Ps. 86:5), says the Holy Ghost through the Psalms. According to the explanation of some of the Fathers, the first man that is born in Mary, is the Man-God, Jesus Christ; the second is a mere man, the child of God and Mary's by adoption. If Jesus Christ, the Head of men, is born in her, then the predestinate, who are the members of that Head, ought also to be born in her, by a necessary consequence.

One and the same mother does not bring forth into the world the head without the members, or the members without the head; for this would be a monster of nature. So in like manner, in the order of grace, the head and the members are born of one and the same Mother; and if a member of the Mystical Body of Jesus Christ—that is to say, one of the predestinate—were born of any other mother than Mary, who has produced the Head, he would not be one of the predestinate, nor a member of Jesus Christ, but simply a monster in the order of grace.

St. Augustine, surpassing himself, and going beyond all I have yet said, affirms that all the predestinate, in order to be conformed to the image of the Son of God, are in this world hidden in the womb of the most holy Virgin, where they are guarded, nourished, brought up and made to grow by that good Mother until she has brought them forth to glory after death, which is properly the day of their birth, as the Church calls the death of the just. O mystery of grace, unknown to the reprobate, and but little known even to the predestinate!

WEEK 3: DAY 3–FIRST MEDITATION

Taken from the Gospel according to St. Luke, Chapter 2

1 And it came to pass that in those days there went out a decree from Caesar Augustus, that the whole world should be enrolled.

2 This enrolling was first made by Cyrinus, the governor of Syria.

3 And all went to be enrolled, every one into his own city.

4 And Joseph also went up from Galilee, out of the city of Nazareth into Judea, to the city of David, which is called Bethlehem: because he was of the house and family of David,

5 To be enrolled with Mary his espoused wife, who was with child.

6 And it came to pass, that when they were there, her days were accomplished, that she should be delivered.

7 And she brought forth her firstborn son, and wrapped him up in swaddling clothes, and laid him in a manger; because there was no room for them in the inn.

8 And there were in the same country shepherds watching, and keeping the night watches over their flock.

9 And behold an angel of the Lord stood by them, and the brightness of God shone round about them; and they feared with a great fear.

10 And the angel said to them: Fear not; for, behold, I bring you good tidings of great joy, that shall be to all the people:

11 For, this day, is born to you a Savior, who is Christ the Lord, in the city of David.

12 And this shall be a sign unto you: you shall find the infant wrapped in swaddling clothes, and laid in a manger.

13 And suddenly there was with the angel a multitude of the heavenly army, praising God, and saying:

14 Glory to God in the highest; and on earth peace to men of good will.

15 And it came to pass, after the angels departed from them into heaven, the shepherds said one to another: Let us go over to Bethlehem, and let us see this word that is come to pass, which the Lord hath showed to us.

16 And they came with haste; and they found Mary and Joseph, and the infant lying in the manger.

17 And seeing, they understood of the word that had been spoken to them concerning this child.

18 And all that heard, wondered; and at those things that were told them by the shepherds.

19 But Mary kept all these words, pondering them in her heart.

20 And the shepherds returned, glorifying and praising God, for all the things they had heard and seen, as it was told unto them.

WEEK 3: DAY 3–SECOND MEDITATION

Taken from St. Louis de Montfort's
True Devotion to Mary, §36 ff.

When the Holy Ghost, her Spouse, has found Mary in a soul, He flies there. He enters there in His fullness; He communicates Himself to that soul abundantly and to the full extent to which it makes room for His spouse. Nay, one of the greatest reasons why the Holy Ghost does not now do startling wonders in our souls, is because He does not find there a sufficiently great union with His faithful and inseparable spouse.

When Mary has struck her roots in a soul, she produces there marvels of grace, which she alone can produce, because she alone is the fruitful Virgin who never has had and never will have, her equal in purity and in fruitfulness. Mary has produced, together with the Holy Ghost, the greatest thing which has been or ever will be—a God Man; and she will consequently produce the greatest saints that there will be in the end of time. The formation and the education of the great saints, who shall come at the end of the world, are reserved for her. For it is only that singular and miraculous Virgin who can produce, in union with the Holy Ghost, singular and extraordinary things.

I have said that this would come to pass, particularly at the end of the world and indeed presently, because the Most High with His holy Mother has to form for Himself great saints, who shall surpass most of the other saints in sanctity, as much as the cedars of Lebanon outgrow the little shrubs...

These great souls, full of grace and zeal, shall be chosen to match themselves against the enemies of God, who shall rage on all sides; and they shall be singularly devout to our Blessed Lady, illuminated by her light, strengthened with her nourishment, led by her spirit, supported by her arm and sheltered under her protection, so that they shall fight with one hand and build with the other.

With the one hand they shall fight, overthrow and crush the heretics with their heresies, the schismatics with their schisms, the idolaters with their idolatries and the sinners with their impieties. With the other hand they shall build the temple of the true Solomon and the mystical city of God, that is to say, the most holy Virgin, called by the Fathers the "Temple of Solomon" and the "City of God." By their words and their examples, they shall draw the whole world to true devotion to Mary. This shall bring upon them many enemies, but shall also bring many victories and much glory for God alone.

This is what God revealed to St. Vincent Ferrer, the great apostle of his age, as he has sufficiently noted in one of his works. This city, which men shall find at the end of the world to convert themselves in, and to satisfy the hunger they have for justice, is the most holy Virgin, who is called by the Holy Ghost the "City of God." (Ps. 86:3). It was through Mary that the salvation of the

world was begun, and it is through Mary that it must be consummated. Mary hardly appeared at all in the first coming of Jesus
Christ, in order that men, as yet but little instructed and enlightened on the Person of her Son, should not remove themselves
from Him in attaching themselves too strongly and too grossly to
her....But in the second coming of Jesus Christ, Mary has to be
made known and revealed by the Holy Ghost in order that,
through her, Jesus Christ may be known, loved and served. The
reasons which moved the Holy Ghost to hide His spouse during
her life and to reveal her but very little since the preaching of the
Gospel, subsist no longer.

WEEK 3: DAY 3–THIRD MEDITATION

Taken from the Gospel according to St. Luke, Chapter 1

This saving of the good wine till the end fits in well with the
birth of St. John the Baptist, the last and greatest of those who
prepared the way for the first coming of Christ. In these latter
times, there will similarly be many "St. John the Baptists" raised
up, like the best wine, saved for the end. St. Louis says: "....I have
said that this would come to pass, particularly at the end of the
world and indeed presently, because the Most High with His holy
Mother has to form for Himself great saints who shall surpass
most of the other saints in sanctity as much as the cedars of Lebanon outgrow the little shrubs..."

57 Now Elizabeth's full time of being delivered was come, and
she brought forth a son.

58 And her neighbors and kinsfolk heard that the Lord had
showed his great mercy towards her, and they congratulated with
her.

59 And it came to pass, that on the eighth day they came to
circumcise the child, and they called him by his father's name,
Zachary.

60 And his mother answering, said: Not so; but he shall be
called John.

61 And they said to her: There is none of thy kindred that is called by this name.

62 And they made signs to his father, how he would have him called.

63 And demanding a writing table, he wrote, saying: John is his name. And they all wondered.

64 And immediately his mouth was opened, and his tongue loosed, and he spoke, blessing God.

65 And fear came upon all their neighbors; and all these things were noised abroad over all the hill country of Judea.

66 And all they that had heard them laid them up in their heart, saying: What then, think ye, shall this child be? For the hand of the Lord was with him.

67 And Zachary his father was filled with the Holy Ghost; and he prophesied, saying:

68 Blessed be the Lord God of Israel; because he hath visited and wrought the redemption of his people:

69 And hath raised up an horn of salvation to us, in the house of David his servant:

70 As he spoke by the mouth of his holy prophets, who are from the beginning:

71 Salvation from our enemies, and from the hand of all that hate us:

72 To perform mercy to our fathers, and to remember his holy testament,

73 The oath, which he swore to Abraham our father, that he would grant to us,

74 That being delivered from the hand of our enemies, we may serve him without fear,

75 In holiness and justice before him, all our days.

76 And thou, child, shalt be called the prophet of the Highest: for thou shalt go before the face of the Lord to prepare his ways:

77 To give knowledge of salvation to his people, unto the remission of their sins:

78 Through the bowels of the mercy of our God, in which the Orient from on high hath visited us:

79 To enlighten them that sit in darkness, and in the shadow of death: to direct our feet into the way of peace.

80 And the child grew, and was strengthened in spirit; and was in the deserts until the day of his manifestation to Israel.

WEEK 3: DAY 3–FOURTH MEDITATION

Taken from St. Louis de Montfort's
True Devotion to Mary, §22 ff.

The conduct which the Three Persons of the Most Holy Trinity have deigned to pursue in the Incarnation and the first coming of Jesus Christ. They still pursue daily, in an invisible manner, throughout the whole Church; and They will still pursue it even to the consummation of ages in the last coming of Jesus Christ.

God the Son has communicated to His Mother all that He acquired by His life and His death, His infinite merits and His admirable virtues; and He has made her the treasurer of all that His Father gave Him for His inheritance. It is by her that He applies His merits to His members, and that He communicates His virtues, and distributes His graces. She is His mysterious canal; she is His aqueduct, through which He makes His mercies flow gently and abundantly....God the Holy Ghost has chosen her to be the dispenser of all He possesses, in such wise that she distributes to whom she wills, as much as she wills, as she wills and when she wills, all His gifts and graces.

The Holy Ghost gives no heavenly gift to men, which He does not have pass through her virginal hands. Such has been the will of God, Who has willed that we should have everything through Mary; so that she who was impoverished, humbled and who hid herself even unto the abyss of nothingness by her profound humility her whole life long, should now be enriched and exalted and honored by the Most High. Such are the sentiments of the Church and the holy Fathers.

Inasmuch as grace perfects nature, and glory perfects grace, it is certain that Our Lord is still, in heaven, as much the Son of

Mary as He was on earth; and that, consequently, He has retained the obedience and submission of the most perfect Child toward the best of all mothers....Mary is infinitely below her Son, who is God, and, therefore, she does not command Him as a mother here below would command her child, who is below her.

Mary asks nothing, wishes nothing, does nothing contrary to the eternal and immutable will of God. When we read then in the writings of Saints Bernard, Bernardine, Bonaventure and others that in heaven and on earth everything, even God Himself, is subject to the Blessed Virgin, they mean that the authority which God has been well pleased to give her is so great, that it seems as if she had the same power as God; and that her prayers and petitions are so powerful with God, that they always pass for commandments with His Majesty, who never resists the prayer of His dear Mother, because she is always humble and conformed to His will.

If Moses, by the force of his prayer, stayed the anger of God against the Israelites, in a manner so powerful that the most high and infinitely merciful Lord, being unable to resist him, told him to let Him alone that He might be angry with and punish that rebellious people, what must we not, with much greater reason, think of the prayer of the humble Mary, that worthy Mother of God, which is more powerful with His Majesty than the prayers and intercessions of all the angels and saints both in heaven and on earth?

WEEK 3: DAY 4–FIRST MEDITATION

Taken from the Gospel according to St. John, Chapter 2

1 And the third day, there was a marriage in Cana of Galilee: and the mother of Jesus was there.

2 And Jesus also was invited, and his disciples, to the marriage.

3 And the wine failing, the mother of Jesus saith to him: They have no wine.

4 And Jesus saith to her: Woman, what is that to me and to thee? My hour is not yet come.

5 His mother saith to the waiters: Whatsoever he shall say to you, do ye.

6 Now there were set there six waterpots of stone, according to the manner of the purifying of the Jews, containing two or three measures apiece.

7 Jesus saith to them: Fill the waterpots with water. And they filled them up to the brim.

8 And Jesus saith to them: Draw out now, and carry to the chief steward of the feast. And they carried it.

9 And when the chief steward had tasted the water made wine, and knew not whence it was, but the waiters knew who had drawn the water; the chief steward calleth the bridegroom,

10 And saith to him: Every man at first setteth forth good wine, and when men have well drunk, then that which is worse. But thou hast kept the good wine until now.

11 This beginning of miracles did Jesus in Cana of Galilee; and manifested his glory, and his disciples believed in him.

12 After this he went down to Capharnaum, he and his mother, and his brethren, and his disciples: and they remained there not many days.

Comments

The saving of the good wine, till the end, fits in well with that which St. Louis de Montfort says about the latter times: "According to the explanation of St. Bernard—all the rich among the people shall supplicate her face from age to age, and particularly at the end of the world; that is to say, the greatest saints, the souls richest in graces and virtues, shall be the most assiduous in praying to our Blessed Lady, and in having her always present as their perfect model for imitation and their powerful aid for help....I have said that this would come to pass, particularly at the end of the world and indeed presently, because the Most High with His holy Mother has to form for Himself great saints who shall surpass most of the other saints in sanctity as much as the cedars of Lebanon outgrow the little shrubs..."

WEEK 3: DAY 4–SECOND MEDITATION

Taken from St. Louis de Montfort's
True Devotion to Mary, §50 ff.

God, then, wishes to reveal and make known Mary, the masterpiece of His hands, in these latter times:

1. Because she hid herself in this world and put herself lower than the dust by her profound humility, having obtained from God and from His Apostles and Evangelists that she should not be made manifest.

2. Because, as she is the masterpiece of the hands of God, as well here below by grace as in heaven by glory, He wishes to be glorified and praised in her by those who are living upon the earth.

3. As she is the dawn which precedes and reveals the Sun of Justice, who is Jesus Christ, she must be seen and recognized in order that Jesus Christ may also be.

4. Being the way by which Jesus came to us the first time, she will also be the way by which He will come the second time, though not in the same manner.

5. Being the sure means and the straight and immaculate way to go to Jesus Christ and to find Him perfectly, it is by her that the souls, who are to shine forth especially in sanctity, have to find Our Lord.

He who shall find Mary shall find life (Prov. 8:35), that is, Jesus Christ, who is the Way, the Truth and the Life. (Jn. 14:6). But no one can find Mary who does not seek her; and no one can seek her who does not know her; for we cannot seek or desire an unknown object. It is necessary, then, for the greater knowledge and glory of the Most Holy Trinity, that Mary should be more than ever known.

6. Mary must shine forth more than ever in mercy, in might and in grace, in these latter times: in mercy, to bring back and lovingly receive the poor strayed sinners, who shall be converted and shall return to the Catholic Church; in might, against the enemies of God, idolaters, schismatics, Mahometans, Jews and souls hardened in impiety, who shall rise in terrible revolt against

God, to seduce all those who shall oppose them and to make them fall by promises and threats; and finally, she must shine forth in grace, in order to animate and sustain the valiant soldiers and faithful servants of Jesus Christ, who shall battle for His interests.

7. Lastly, Mary must be terrible to the devil and his crew, as an army ranged in battle, principally in these latter times, because the devil, knowing that he has but little time, and now less than ever, to destroy souls, will every day redouble his efforts and his combats. He will presently raise up cruel persecutions and will put terrible snares before the faithful servants and true children of Mary, whom it gives him more trouble to conquer than it does to conquer others.

WEEK 3: DAY 4–THIRD MEDITATION

Taken from St. Louis de Montfort's
True Devotion to Mary, §90 ff.

Today, more than ever, we must take pains in choosing true devotion to our Blessed Lady, because, more than ever before, there are false devotions to our Blessed Lady which are easily mistaken for true ones. The devil, like a false coiner and a subtle and experienced sharper, has already deceived and destroyed so many souls by a false devotion to the Blessed Virgin, that he makes a daily use of his diabolical experience to plunge many others, by this same way, into everlasting perdition; amusing them, lulling them to sleep in sin, under the pretext of some prayers badly said, or of some outward practices, which he inspires.

As a false coiner does not ordinarily counterfeit anything but gold or silver, and very rarely other metals, because they are not worth the trouble, so the evil spirit does not, for the most part, counterfeit other devotions, but only those to Jesus and Mary—devotion to Holy Communion and to our Blessed Lady—because they are among other devotions what gold and silver are among other metals.

It is then very important to recognize, first of all, false devotions to our Blessed Lady, in order to avoid them, and true devotion, in order to embrace it; secondly, which of the many practices of true devotion to our Blessed Lady is the most perfect, the most agreeable to her, the most glorious to God, and the most sanctifying for ourselves, so that we may adopt that one.

I find seven kinds of false devotees and false devotions to Our Lady, namely:

1. the critical devotees;
2. the scrupulous devotees;
3. the external devotees;
4. the presumptuous devotees;
5. the inconstant devotees;
6. the hypocritical devotees;
7. the interested devotees.

Critical Devotees: The critical devotees are, for the most part, proud scholars, rash and self-sufficient spirits, who have at heart some devotion to the holy Virgin, but who criticize nearly all the practices of devotion which simple people pay, simply and holily, to their good Mother, because these practices do not fall in with their own humor and fancy. They call in doubt all the miracles and pious stories recorded by authors worthy of faith, or drawn from the chronicles of religious orders: narratives which testify to us the mercies and the power of the most holy Virgin.

They cannot see, without uneasiness, simple and humble people on their knees before an altar or an image of Our Lady, sometimes at the corner of a street, in order to pray to God there; and they even accuse them of idolatry, as if they adored the wood or the stone. They say that they are not so credulous as to believe so many tales and stories that are told about Our Lady. These kinds of false devotees, proud and worldly people, are greatly to be feared. They do an infinite wrong to devotion to Our Lady; and they are but too successful in alienating people from it, under the pretext of destroying its abuses.

Scrupulous Devotees: The scrupulous devotees are those who fear to dishonor the Son by honoring the Mother, to abase the one in elevating the other. They cannot bear that we should attribute, to Our Lady, the most just praise which the holy Fathers have given her. It is all they can do to endure that there should be more people before the altar of the Blessed Virgin than before the Blessed Sacrament—as if the one were contrary to the other, as if those who prayed to our Blessed Lady did not pray to Jesus Christ through her. They are unwilling that we should speak, so often, of Our Lady and address her so frequently.

External Devotees: External devotees are persons who make all devotion to our Blessed Lady consist in outward practices. They have no taste except for the exterior of this devotion, because they have no interior spirit of their own. They will say quantities of Rosaries with the greatest speed; they will hear many Masses distractedly; they will go, without devotion, to processions; they will enroll themselves in all her confraternities—without amending their lives, without doing any violence to their passions, or without imitating the virtues of that most holy Virgin. They only love the sensible part of devotion, without having any relish for its solidity. If they have not sensible sweetness in their practices, they think they are doing nothing; they get all out of joint, throw everything up, or do everything at random. The world is full of these exterior devotees.

Presumptuous Devotees: Presumptuous devotees are sinners abandoned to their passions, or lovers of the world, who, under the fair name of Christians and clients of our Blessed Lady, conceal pride, avarice, impurity, drunkenness, anger, swearing, detraction, injustice or some other sin. They sleep in peace in the midst of their bad habits, without doing any violence to themselves to correct their faults, under the pretext that they are devout to the Blessed Virgin. They promise themselves that God will pardon them; that they will not be allowed to die without confession; and that they will not be lost eternally, because they say the Rosary, because they fast on Saturdays, because they belong to the Confraternity of the Holy Rosary, or wear the Scapular, or are enrolled in other congregations, or they wear the little habit or little chain of Our Lady.

They will not believe us when we tell them that their devotion is only an illusion of the devil and a pernicious presumption, likely to destroy their souls. They say that God is good and merciful; that He has not made us to condemn us everlastingly; that no man is without sin; that they shall not die without confession; that one good act of contrition at the hour of death is enough; that they are devout to Our Lady, wear the Scapular, say daily, without fail and without vanity, seven *Our Fathers* and seven *Hail Mary*'s in her honor; and that they sometimes say the Rosary and the Office of Our Lady, besides fasting and other things.

To give authority to all this, and to blind themselves still further, they quote certain stories which they have heard or read— it does not matter to them whether they be true or false—relating how people have died in mortal sin without confession, and then, because in their lifetime they sometimes said some prayers, or went through some practices of devotion to Our Lady, how they have been raised to life again, in order to go to confession; or their soul has been miraculously retained in their bodies till confession; or through the clemency of the Blessed Virgin, they have obtained from God, at the moment of death, contrition and pardon of their sins, and so have been saved; and that they themselves expect similar favors.

Nothing in Christianity is more detestable than this diabolical presumption. For how can we truly say that we love and honor our Blessed Lady when by our sins we are pitilessly piercing, wounding, crucifying and outraging Jesus Christ, her Son?

WEEK 3: DAY 4–FOURTH MEDITATION

Taken from St. Louis de Montfort's
True Devotion to Mary, §101 ff.

Inconstant Devotees: The inconstant devotees are those who are devout to our Blessed Lady by fits and starts. Sometimes they are fervent and sometimes lukewarm. Sometimes they seem ready to do anything for her, and then a little afterward, they are not like the same people. They begin by taking up all the devotions to her, and enrolling themselves in the confraternities; and then they do not practice the rules with fidelity. They change like the moon; and Mary puts them under her feet with the crescent, because they are changeable and unworthy to be reckoned among the servants of that faithful Virgin, who have, for their special graces, fidelity and constancy. It were better for such persons not to burden themselves with so many prayers and practices, but to choose a few and fulfill them with faithfulness and love, in spite of the world, the devil and the flesh.

Hypocritical Devotees: We have still to mention the false devotees to Our Blessed Lady, who are the hypocritical devotees, who cloak their sins and sinful habits with her mantle, in order to be taken by men for what they are not.

Interested Devotees: There are also the interested devotees, who have recourse to Our Lady only to gain some lawsuit, or to avoid some danger, or to be cured of some illness, or for some other similar necessity, without which they would forget her altogether. All these are false devotees, pleasing neither to God nor to His holy Mother.

WEEK 3: DAY 5–FIRST MEDITATION

Taken from St. Louis de Montfort's
True Devotion to Mary, §121 ff.

The Nature of True Devotion

This devotion consists, then, in giving ourselves entirely to Our Lady, in order to belong entirely to Jesus through her. We must give her *(1)* our body, with all its senses and its members; *(2)* our soul, with all its powers; *(3)* our exterior goods of fortune, whether present or to come; *(4)* our interior and spiritual goods, which are our merits and our virtues, and our good works, past, present and future.

In a word, we must give her all we have in the order of nature and in the order of grace, and all that may become ours in the future, in the orders of nature, grace and glory; and this we must do without the reserve of so much as one farthing, one hair, or one least good action; and we must do it also for all eternity; and we must do it, further, without pretending to, or hoping for, any other recompense for our offering and service except the honor of belonging to Jesus Christ through Mary and in Mary—as though that sweet Mistress were not (as she always is) the most generous and the most grateful of creatures.

Here we must note that there are two things in the good works we perform, namely, satisfaction and merit; in other words, their satisfactory or impetratory value, and their meritorious value. The satisfactory or impetratory value of a good action is that action inasmuch as it satisfies for the pain due to sin, or obtains some new grace; the meritorious value, or the merit, is the good action inasmuch as it merits grace now and eternal glory hereafter.

Now, in this consecration of ourselves to Our Lady, we give her all the satisfactory, impetratory and meritorious value of our actions; in other words, the satisfactions and the merits of all our good works. We give her all our merits, graces and virtues—not to communicate them to others, for our merits, graces and virtues are, properly speaking, incommunicable, and it is only Jesus

Christ who, in making Himself our surety with His Father, is able to communicate His merits—but we give her them to keep them, augment them and embellish them for us, as we shall explain by and by. Our satisfactions, however, we give her to communicate to whom she likes, and for the greatest glory of God.

WEEK 3: DAY 5–SECOND MEDITATION

Taken from St. Louis de Montfort's
True Devotion to Mary, §132 ff.

But some may object that this devotion, in making us give to Our Lord, by Our Lady's hands, the value of all our good works, prayers, mortifications and alms, puts us in a state of incapacity for assisting the souls of our parents, friends and benefactors.

I answer them as follows:

1. That it is not credible that our parents, friends and benefactors should suffer from the fact of our being devoted and consecrated, without exception, to the service of Our Lord and His holy Mother. To think this would be to think unworthily of the goodness and power of Jesus and Mary, who know well how to assist our parents, friends and benefactors, out of our own little spiritual revenue or by other ways.

2. This practice does not hinder us from praying for others, whether dead or living, although the application of our good works depends on the will of Our Blessed Lady. On the contrary, it is this very thing which will lead us to pray with more confidence; just as a rich person who has given all his wealth to his prince, in order to honor him the more, would beg the prince all the more confidently to give an alms to one of his friends who should ask for it. It would even be a source of pleasure to the prince to be given an occasion of proving his gratitude, toward a person who had stripped himself to clothe him, and impoverished himself to honor him. We must say the same of Our Blessed Lord and of Our Lady. They will never let themselves be outdone in gratitude.

Someone may perhaps say, "If I give to Our Blessed Lady all the value of my actions to apply to whom she wills, I may have to suffer a long time in Purgatory."

This objection, which comes from self-love and ignorance of the generosity of God and His holy Mother, refutes itself. A fervent and generous soul who gives God all he has, without reserve, so that he can do nothing more; who lives only for the glory and reign of Jesus Christ, through His holy Mother, and who makes an entire sacrifice of himself to bring it about—will this generous and liberal soul, I say, be more punished in the other world, because it has been more liberal and more disinterested than others? Far, indeed, will that be from the truth! Rather, it is toward that soul, as we shall see by what follows, that Our Lord and His holy Mother are the most liberal in this world and in the other, in the orders of nature, grace and glory.

WEEK 3: DAY 5–THIRD MEDITATION

Taken from St. Louis de Montfort's
True Devotion to Mary, §105 ff.

Characteristics of a True Devotion: After having laid bare and condemned the false devotions to the most holy Virgin, we must, in a few words, give the characteristics of true devotion. It must be:

1. interior
2. tender
3. holy
4. constant
5. disinterested

Interior: True devotion to Our Lady is interior; that is, it comes from the mind and the heart. It flows from the esteem we have for her, the high idea we have formed of her greatness, and the love which we have for her.

Tender: It is tender; that is, full of confidence in her, like a child's confidence in his loving mother. This confidence makes the soul have recourse to her in all its bodily and mental necessities, with much simplicity, trust and tenderness. It implores the aid of its good Mother at all times, in all places and above all things: in its doubts, that it may be enlightened; in its wanderings, that it may be brought into the right path; in its temptations, that it may be supported; in its weaknesses, that it may be strengthened; in its falls, that it may be lifted up; in its discouragements, that it may be cheered; in its scruples, that they may be taken away; in the crosses, toils and disappointments of life, that it may be consoled under them. In a word, in all the evils of body and mind, the soul ordinarily has recourse to Mary, without fear of annoying her or displeasing Jesus Christ.

Holy: True devotion to Our Lady is holy; that is to say, it leads the soul to avoid sin and to imitate the virtues of the Blessed Virgin, particularly her profound humility, her lively faith, her blind obedience, her continual prayer, her universal mortification, her divine purity, her ardent charity, her heroic patience, her angelic sweetness and her divine wisdom. These are the ten principal virtues of the most holy Virgin.

Constant: True devotion to Our Lady is constant. It confirms the soul in good and does not let it easily abandon its spiritual exercises. It makes it courageous in opposing the world in its fashions and maxims, the flesh in its weariness and passions, and the devil in his temptations; so that a person truly devout to Our Blessed Lady is neither changeable, irritable, scrupulous nor timid. It is not that such a person does not fall, or change sometimes in the sensible feeling of devotion. But when he falls, he rises again by stretching out his hand to his good Mother. When he loses the taste and relish of devotion, he does not become disturbed because of that; for the just and faithful client of Mary lives by the faith (Heb. 10:38) of Jesus and Mary, and not by natural sentiment.

Disinterested: Lastly, true devotion to Our Lady is disinterested; that is to say, it inspires the soul not to seek itself, but only God, and God in His holy Mother. A true client of Mary does not serve that august Queen from a spirit of lucre and interest, nor for his own good, whether temporal or eternal, corporal or spiritual, but exclusively because she deserves to be served and God alone in her. He does not love Mary just because she obtains favors for him, or because he hopes she will, but solely because she is so worthy of love. It is on this account that he loves and serves her as faithfully in his disgusts and dryness, as in his sweetness and sensible fervor. He loves her as much on Calvary as at the marriage of Cana.

Oh, how agreeable and precious in the eyes of God and of His holy Mother is such a client of our Blessed Lady, who has no self-seeking in his service of her! But, in these days, how rare is such a sight! It is that it may be less rare, that I have taken my pen in hand to put on paper what I have taught with good results, in public and in private, during my missions for many years.

WEEK 3: DAY 5–FOURTH MEDITATION

Taken from St. Louis de Montfort's
True Devotion to Mary, §116 ff.

Exterior Practices of the True Devotion

True devotion to Our Lady also has several exterior practices, of which the following are the principal ones:

1. to enroll ourselves in her confraternities and enter her congregations;
2. to join the religious orders instituted in her honor;
3. to proclaim her praises;
4. to give alms, to fast and to undergo outward and inward mortifications in her honor;
5. to wear her liveries, such as the Rosary, the Scapular or the little chain;
6. There are also many prayers that can be said, among them are the following:

To recite with attention, devotion and modesty the holy Rosary, composed of fifteen decades of *Hail Mary's* in honor of the fifteen principal mysteries of Jesus Christ; or five decades, which is one third of the Rosary, either in honor of the five Joyful Mysteries, which are the Annunciation, the Visitation, the Nativity of

Jesus Christ, the Purification, and the Finding of Our Lord in the Temple; or in honor of the five Sorrowful Mysteries, which are the Agony of Our Lord in the Garden of Olives, His Scourging, His Crowning with Thorns, His Carrying of the Cross, and His Crucifixion; or in honor of the five Glorious Mysteries, which are the Resurrection, the Ascension, the Descent of the Holy Ghost at Pentecost, the Assumption of our Blessed Lady, body and soul, into heaven, and her Coronation by the Three Persons of the Most Holy Trinity.

We may also say a chaplet of six or seven decades in honor of the years which we believe Our Lady lived on earth; or the Little Crown of the Blessed Virgin, composed of three *Our Father's* and twelve *Hail Mary's*, in honor of her crown of twelve stars or privileges; or the Office of Our Lady, so universally received and recited in the Church; or the little Psalter of the holy Virgin, which St. Bonaventure composed in her honor, and which is so tender and so devout that one cannot say it without being moved by it; or fourteen *Our Father's* and *Hail Mary's* in honor of her fourteen joys; or some other prayers, hymns and canticles of the Church, such as the *Salve Regina*, the *Alma*, the *Ave Regina Coelorum*, or the *Regina Coeli*, according to the different seasons; or the *Ave Maris Stella*, the *O Gloriosa Domina*, the *Magnificat*, or some other practices of devotion, of which books are full;

7. to sing, or have sung, spiritual canticles in her honor;
8. to make a number of genuflections or reverences, while saying, for example, every morning, sixty or a hundred times, *Ave Maria, Virgo Fidelis (Hail Mary, Faithful Virgin)*, to obtain from God through her the grace to be faithful to the graces of God during the day; and then again in the evening, *Ave Maria, Mater Misericordiae (Hail Mary, Mother of Mercy)* to ask pardon of God through her, for the sins that we have committed during the day;
9. to take care of her confraternities, to adorn her altars, to crown and ornament her images;
10. to carry her images, or to have them carried, in procession, and to carry a picture or an image of her about our own persons, as a mighty arm against the evil spirit;

11. to have copies of her name or picture made and placed in churches, or in houses, or on the gates and entrances into cities, churches and houses;

12. to consecrate ourselves to her in a special and solemn manner.

WEEK 3: DAY 6–FIRST MEDITATION

Taken from St. Louis de Montfort's
True Devotion to Mary, §117 ff.

Exterior Practices of the True Devotion (cont.)

There are numerous other practices of true devotion toward the Blessed Virgin which the Holy Ghost has inspired in saintly souls and which are very sanctifying; they can be read at length in the *Paradise Opened to Philagius* of Fr. Barry, the Jesuit, in which he has collected a great number of devotions which the saints have practiced in honor of Our Lady—devotions which serve marvelously to sanctify our souls, provided they are performed as they ought to be, that is to say,

1. with a good and pure intention to please God only, to unite ourselves to Jesus Christ as to our Last End, and to edify our neighbor;

2. with attention and without voluntary distraction;

3. with devotion, equally avoiding precipitation and negligence;

4. with modesty, and a respectful and edifying posture of the body.

But after all, I loudly protest that, having read nearly all the books which profess to treat of devotion to Our Lady, and having conversed familiarly with the best and wisest of men of these latter times, I have never known nor heard of any practice of devotion toward her at all equal to the one which I unfold; demanding from the soul, as it does, more sacrifices for God, ridding the soul more of itself and of its self-love, keeping it more faithfully in grace and grace more faithfully in it, uniting it more perfectly and more easily to Jesus Christ; and finally, being more glorious to God, more sanctifying to the soul and more useful to our neighbor than any other of the devotions to her.

WEEK 3: DAY 6–SECOND MEDITATION

Taken from St. Louis de Montfort's
True Devotion to Mary, §213 ff.

The Effects of the True Devotion

My dear friends, be sure that if you are faithful to the interior and exterior practices of this devotion which I will point out, the following effects will take place in your soul:

1. You will have a greater knowledge and contempt of yourself.
2. You will participate in Mary's faith.
3. You will be delivered from all scruples, cares and fears.
4. You will obtain a great confidence in God and Mary.
5. You will have communicated to you, the soul and spirit of Mary.
6. Your soul will be transformed into the likeness of Jesus Christ.
7. You will give great glory to God by the True Devotion.

1. By the light which the Holy Ghost will give you through His dear spouse, Mary, you will understand your own evil, your corruption and your incapacity for anything good. In consequence of this knowledge, you will despise yourself. You will think of yourself only with horror. In other words, the humble Mary will communicate to you a portion of her profound humility, which will make you despise yourself—despise nobody else, but love to be despised yourself.

2. Our Blessed Lady will give you also a portion of her faith, which was the greatest of all faiths that ever were on earth. Greater than the faith of all the patriarchs, prophets, apostles and saints put together....The more, then, that you gain the favor of that august Princess and faithful Virgin, the more will you act by pure faith; a pure faith which will make you care hardly at all about sensible consolations and extraordinary favors; a lively faith animated by charity, which will enable you to perform all your actions from the motive of pure love; a faith firm and immovable as a rock, through which you will rest quiet and constant in the midst of storms and hurricanes; a courageous faith, which will enable you to undertake and carry out without hesitation great things for God and for the salvation of souls; lastly, a faith which will be your blazing torch, your divine life, your hidden treasure of divine wisdom and your omnipotent arm; which you will use to enlighten those who are in the darkness of the shadow of death, to inflame those who are lukewarm and who have need of the heated gold of charity, to give life to those who are dead in sin, to touch and overthrow, by your meek and powerful words, the hearts of marble and the cedars of Lebanon; and finally, to resist the devil and all the enemies of salvation.

3. This Mother of fair love will take away from your heart all scruple and all disorder of servile fear. She will open and enlarge it to run the way of her Son's commandments (Ps. 118:32) with the holy liberty of the children of God. She will introduce, into it, pure love, of which she has the treasure, so that you shall no longer be guided by fear, as hitherto, in your dealings with the God of charity, but by love alone.

4. Our Blessed Lady will fill you with great confidence in God and in herself:

   (a) because you will not be approaching Jesus by yourself, but always by that good Mother;

   (b) because, as you have given her all your merits, graces and satisfactions to dispose of at her will, she will communicate to you her virtues and will clothe you in her merits,

   (c) because, as you have given yourself entirely to her, body and soul, she, who is generous with the generous, and even more generous, will in return give herself to you in a marvelous but real manner....What will still further increase your confidence in her is that you will have less confidence in yourself.

5. The soul of Our Blessed Lady will communicate itself to you, to glorify the Lord. Her spirit will enter into the place of yours, to rejoice in God her salvation, provided only that you are faithful to the practices of this devotion. When will souls breathe Mary as the body breathes air? When that time comes, wonderful things will happen in those lowly places, where the Holy Ghost, finding His dear spouse, as it were, reproduced in souls, shall come in with abundance and fill them to overflowing with His gifts, and particularly with the gift of wisdom, to work miracles of grace....That time will not come until men shall know and practice this devotion which I am teaching. "That Thy reign may come, let the reign of Mary come."

6. If Mary, who is the tree of life, is well cultivated in our soul by fidelity to the practices of this devotion, she will bear her fruit in her own time, and her fruit is none other than Jesus Christ. Take notice, if you please, that I say the saints are molded in Mary. There is a great difference between making a figure in relief by blows of hammer and chisel, and making a figure by throwing it into a mold. Statuaries and sculptors labor much to make figures in the first manner; but to make them in the second manner, they work little and do their work quickly.

St. Augustine calls our Blessed Lady "the mold of God"—the mold fit to cast and mold gods. He who is cast in this mold is presently formed and molded in Jesus Christ, and Jesus Christ in him. At a slight expense and in a short time he will become God, because he has been cast in the same mold which has formed a God.

7. By this practice, faithfully observed, you will give Jesus more glory in a month than by any other practice, however difficult, in many years; and I give the following reasons for it:

(a) Because, doing your actions by our Blessed Lady, as this practice teaches you, you abandon your own intentions and operations, although good and known, to lose yourself, so to speak, in the intentions of the Blessed Virgin, although they are unknown.

(b) Because the soul in this practice counts as nothing whatever it thinks or does of itself, and puts its trust and takes its pleasures only in the dispositions of Mary, when it approaches Jesus or even speaks to Him. Thus it prac-

tices humility far more than the souls who act of themselves.

(c) Because Our Blessed Lady, being pleased, out of great
charity, to receive the present of our actions in her virginal hands, gives them an admirable beauty and splendor. Moreover, she offers them herself to Jesus Christ,
and it is evident that Our Lord is thus more glorified by
them, than if we offered them by our own criminal hands.

WEEK 3: DAY 6–THIRD MEDITATION

Taken from St. Louis de Montfort's
True Devotion to Mary, §51 ff.

The struggle against Satan. In these cruel persecutions of
the devil, which shall go on increasing daily till the reign of Anti-
christ, we ought to understand that first and celebrated predic-
tion and curse of God pronounced in the terrestrial paradise
against the serpent. It is to our purpose to explain this here for
the glory of the most holy Virgin, for the salvation of her children and for the confusion of the devil: "I will put enmities between thee and the woman and thy seed and her seed; she shall
crush thy head, and thou shalt lie in wait for her heel" (Gen.
3:15).

God has never made and formed but one enmity; but it is an
irreconcilable one, which shall endure and grow even to the end.
It is between Mary, His worthy Mother, and the devil—between
the children and the servants of the Blessed Virgin, and the children and tools of Lucifer. The most terrible of all the enemies,
which God has set up against the devil, is His holy Mother Mary.
He has inspired her, even since the days of the earthly paradise—
though she existed then only in His idea—with so much hatred
against that cursed enemy of God, with so much ingenuity in
unveiling the malice of that ancient serpent, with so much power
to conquer, to overthrow and to crush that proud, impious rebel,
that he fears her not only more than all angels and men, but in a
sense more than God Himself.

Not that the anger, the hatred and the power of God are not infinitely greater than those of the Blessed Virgin, for the perfections of Mary are limited; but first, because Satan, being proud, suffers infinitely more from being beaten and punished by a little and humble handmaid of God, and her humility humbles him more than the divine power; and secondly, because God has given Mary such great power against the devils that—as they have often been obliged to confess, in spite of themselves, by the mouths of the possessed—they fear one of her sighs for a soul more than the prayers of all the saints, and one of her threats against them more than all other torments.

WEEK 3: DAY 6–FOURTH MEDITATION

Taken from the Gospel according to St. Luke, Chapter 2

21 And after eight days were accomplished, that the child should be circumcised, his name was called Jesus, which was called by the angel, before he was conceived in the womb.

22 And after the days of her purification, according to the law of Moses, were accomplished, they carried him to Jerusalem, to present him to the Lord:

23 As it is written in the law of the Lord: Every male opening the womb shall be called holy to the Lord:

24 And to offer a sacrifice, according as it is written in the law of the Lord, a pair of turtledoves, or two young pigeons:

25 And behold there was a man in Jerusalem named Simeon, and this man was just and devout, waiting for the consolation of Israel; and the Holy Ghost was in him.

26 And he had received an answer from the Holy Ghost, that he should not see death, before he had seen the Christ of the Lord.

27 And he came by the Spirit into the temple. And when his parents brought in the child Jesus, to do for him according to the custom of the law,

28 He also took him into his arms, and blessed God, and said:

29 Now thou dost dismiss thy servant, O Lord, according to thy word in peace;

30 Because my eyes have seen thy salvation,

31 Which thou hast prepared before the face of all peoples:

32 A light to the revelation of the Gentiles, and the glory of thy people Israel.

33 And his father and mother were wondering at those things which were spoken concerning him.

34 And Simeon blessed them, and said to Mary his mother: Behold this child is set for the fall, and for the resurrection of many in Israel, and for a sign which shall be contradicted;

35 And thy own soul a sword shall pierce, that, out of many hearts, thoughts may be revealed.

36 And there was one Anna, a prophetess, the daughter of Phanuel, of the tribe of Aser; she was far advanced in years, and had lived with her husband seven years from her virginity.

37 And she was a widow until fourscore and four years; who departed not from the temple, by fasting and prayers serving night and day.

38 Now she, at the same hour, coming in, confessed to the Lord; and spoke of him to all that looked for the redemption of Israel.

39 And after they had performed all things according to the law of the Lord, they returned into Galilee, to their city Nazareth.

40 And the child grew, and waxed strong, full of wisdom; and the grace of God was in him.

WEEK 3: DAY 7–FIRST MEDITATION

Taken from the Gospel according to St. John, Chapter 2

13 And the pasch of the Jews was at hand, and Jesus went up to Jerusalem.

14 And he found in the temple them that sold oxen and sheep and doves, and the changers of money sitting.

15 And when he had made, as it were, a scourge of little cords, he drove them all out of the temple, the sheep also and the oxen, and the money of the changers he poured out, and the tables he overthrew.

16 And to them that sold doves he said: Take these things hence, and make not the house of my Father a house of traffic.

17 And his disciples remembered, that it was written: The zeal of thy house hath eaten me up.

18 The Jews, therefore, answered, and said to him: What sign dost thou show unto us seeing thou dost these things?

19 Jesus answered, and said to them: Destroy this temple, and in three days I will raise it up.

20 The Jews then said: Six and forty years was this temple in building; and wilt thou raise it up in three days?

21 But he spoke of the temple of his body.

22 When therefore he was risen again from the dead, his disciples remembered that he had said this, and they believed the scripture, and the word that Jesus had said.

23 Now when he was at Jerusalem, at the pasch, upon the festival day, many believed in his name, seeing his signs which he did.

24 But Jesus did not trust himself unto them, for that he knew all men,

25 And because he needed not that any should give testimony of man: for he knew what was in man.

WEEK 3: DAY 7–SECOND MEDITATION

Taken from St. Louis de Montfort's
True Devotion to Mary, §53 ff.

What Lucifer has lost by pride, Mary has gained by humility. What Eve has damned and lost by disobedience, Mary has saved by obedience. Eve, in obeying the serpent, has destroyed all her children together with herself, and has delivered them to him; Mary, in being perfectly faithful to God, has saved all her children and servants together with herself, and has consecrated them to His Majesty.

God has not only set an enmity, but enmities, not simply between Mary and the devil, but between the race of the holy Virgin and the race of the devil; that is to say, God has set enmities, antipathies and secret hatreds between the true children and servants of Mary and the children and slaves of the devil. They have no love for each other. They have no sympathy for each other. The children of Belial, the slaves of Satan, the friends of the world (for it is the same thing), have always, up to this time, persecuted those who belong to Our Blessed Lady and will, in the future, persecute them more than ever; just as Cain, of old, persecuted his brother Abel, and Esau his brother Jacob, who are the figures of the reprobate and the predestinate.

But the humble Mary will always have the victory over that proud spirit, and so great a victory that she will go so far as to crush his head, where his pride dwells. She will always discover the malice of the serpent. She will always lay bare his infernal plots and dissipate his diabolical councils, and even to the end of time will guard her faithful servants from his cruel claw.

But the power of Mary over all the devils will especially shine forth in the latter times, when Satan will lay his snares against her heel: that is to say, her humble slaves and her poor children, whom she will raise up to make war against him. They shall be little and poor in the world's esteem, and abased before all like the heel, trodden underfoot and persecuted, as the heel is by the other members of the body. But in return for this they shall be rich in the grace of God, which Mary shall distribute to them abundantly. They shall be great and exalted before God in sanctity, superior to all other creatures by their lively zeal, and so well sustained with God's assistance that, with the humility of their heel, in union with Mary, they shall crush the head of the devil and cause Jesus Christ to triumph.

WEEK 3: DAY 7–THIRD MEDITATION

Taken from St. Louis de Montfort's
True Devotion to Mary, §55 ff.

The formation of the apostles of the latter times. In a word, God wishes that His holy Mother should be at present more known, more loved, more honored than she has ever been. This, no doubt, will take place if the predestinate enter, with the grace and light of the Holy Ghost, into the interior and perfect practice which I will disclose to them shortly. Then they will see clearly, as far as faith allows, that beautiful Star of the Sea. They will arrive happily in harbor, following its guidance, in spite of the tempests and the pirates. They will consecrate themselves entirely to her service as subjects and slaves of love. They will experience her sweetness and her maternal goodness, and they will love her tenderly like well beloved children. They will know the mercies of which she is full, and the need they have of her help; and they will have recourse to her in all things, as to their dear advocate and Mediatrix with Jesus Christ. They will know what is the surest, the easiest, the shortest and the most perfect means of going to Jesus Christ; and they will give themselves to Mary, body and soul, without reserve, that they may thus belong entirely to Jesus Christ.

But who shall those servants, slaves and children of Mary be? They shall be the ministers of the Lord who, like a burning fire, shall kindle the fire of divine love everywhere. They shall be "like sharp arrows in the hand of the powerful" Mary to pierce her enemies. (Ps. 126:4). They shall be the sons of Levi, well purified by the fire of great tribulation, and closely adhering to God (I

Cor. 6:17), who shall carry the gold of love in their heart, the incense of prayer in their spirit, and the myrrh of mortification in their body. They shall be everywhere the good odor of Jesus Christ to the poor and to the little, while at the same time, they shall be an odor of death to the great, to the rich and to the proud worldlings.

They shall be clouds thundering and flying through the air at the least breath of the Holy Ghost; who, detaching themselves from everything and troubling themselves about nothing, shall shower forth the rain of the Word of God and of life eternal. They shall thunder against sin; they shall storm against the world; they shall strike the devil and his crew; and they shall pierce through and through, for life or for death, with their two-edged sword of the Word of God (Eph. 6:17), all those to whom they shall be sent on the part of the Most High.

WEEK 3: DAY 7–FOURTH MEDITATION

Taken from St. Louis de Montfort's
True Devotion to Mary, §58 ff.

They shall be the true apostles of the latter times, to whom the Lord of Hosts shall give the word and the might to work marvels and to carry off with glory the spoils of His enemies. They shall sleep without gold or silver and, what is more, without care, in the midst of the other priests, ecclesiastics and clerics (Ps. 67:14); and yet they shall have the silvered wings of the dove to go, with the pure intention of the glory of God and the salvation of souls, wheresoever the Holy Ghost shall call them. Nor shall they leave behind them, in the places where they have preached, anything but the gold of charity, which is the fulfillment of the whole law (Rom. 13:10).

In a word, we know that they shall be true disciples of Jesus Christ, walking in the footsteps of His poverty, humility, contempt of the world, charity; teaching the narrow way of God in pure truth, according to the holy Gospel, and not according to the maxims of the world; troubling themselves about nothing;

not accepting persons; sparing, fearing and listening to no mortal, however influential he may be. They shall have in their mouths the two-edged sword of the Word of God. They shall carry on their shoulders the bloody standard of the Cross, the Crucifix in their right hand and the Rosary in their left, the sacred Names of Jesus and Mary in their hearts, and the modesty and mortification of Jesus Christ in their own behavior.

These are the great men who are to come; but Mary is the one who, by order of the Most High, shall fashion them for the purpose of extending His empire over that of the impious, the idolaters and the Mahometans. But when and how shall this be? God alone knows. As for us, we have but to hold our tongues, to pray, to sigh and to wait: "With expectation I have waited" (Ps. 39:2).

THE MOST HOLY ROSARY

Many great things have been said of the Holy Rosary by saints, popes, theologians and even devils. Padre Pio used to call the Rosary "*the* weapon." Pope Pius IX said: "I could conquer the world if I had an army to say the Rosary" (*Legion of Mary Handbook*, chap.14). Pope Pius XI adds: "The Rosary is a powerful weapon to put the demons to flight and to keep oneself from sin....It serves admirably to overcome the enemies of God and of religion....If you desire peace in your hearts, in your homes, and in your country, assemble each evening to recite the Rosary. Let not even one day pass without saying it, no matter how burdened you may be with many cares and labors." Pope Leo XIII speaks along the same lines, saying: "The Rosary is the most excellent form of prayer and the most efficacious means of attaining eternal life. It is the remedy for all our evils, the root of all our blessings. There is no more excellent way of praying." Pope Pius IX testifies that: "Among all the devotions approved by the Church, none has been so favored by so many miracles as the Rosary devotion."

St. Louis de Montfort speaks of the "true disciples of Jesus Christ, walking...according to the holy Gospel and not according to the maxims of the world....They shall carry on their shoulders the bloody standard of the Cross, the Crucifix in their right hand and the Rosary in their left, the sacred Names of Jesus and Mary in their hearts..." (*True Devotion*, §59). That is why Our Lady, in this *Age of Mary*, has insisted upon the Rosary so much. We include the following passages in order to help you better understand, appreciate and pray the Rosary.

There is no need to meditate the following texts, just read them, since we hope that you will return to them week after week, as you grow in your understanding of and devotion to the Most Holy Rosary. We recommend that you read a passage before praying your daily Rosary—if circumstances allow for this. This will almost certainly improve the way in which you will pray your Rosaries.

The Fifteen Promises of Mary
to Those Who Recite the Holy Rosary

1. Whoever shall faithfully serve me by the recitation of the Rosary, shall receive signal graces.

2. I promise my special protection and the greatest graces to all those who shall recite the Rosary.

3. The Rosary shall be a powerful armor against hell, it will destroy vice, decrease sin and defeat heresies.

4. It will cause virtue and good works to flourish; it will obtain for souls the abundant mercy of God; it will withdraw the hearts of men from the love of the world and its vanities, and will lift them to the desire of eternal things. Oh, if only souls would sanctify themselves by this means.

5. The soul which recommends itself to me by the recitation of the Rosary, shall not perish.

6. Whoever shall recite the Rosary devoutly, applying himself to the consideration of its sacred mysteries, shall never be conquered by misfortune. God will not chastise him in His justice and he shall not perish by an unprovided death; if he be just, he shall remain in the grace of God and become worthy of eternal life.

7. Whoever shall have a true devotion for the Rosary shall not die without the sacraments of the Church.

8. Those who are faithful in reciting the Rosary shall have, during their life and at their death, the light of God and the plenitude of His graces; at the moment of death they shall participate in the merits of the saints in paradise.

9. I shall deliver from purgatory those who have been devoted to the Rosary.

10. The faithful children of the Rosary shall merit a high degree of glory in heaven.

11. You shall obtain all you ask of me by the recitation of the Rosary.

12. All those who propagate the holy Rosary shall be aided by me in their necessities.

13. I have obtained from my Divine Son that all the advocates

of the Rosary shall have for intercessors the entire celestial court during their life and at the hour of death.

14. All who recite the Rosary are my sons and brothers of my only son Jesus Christ.

15. Devotion of my Rosary is a great sign of predestination. (*Given to St. Dominic and Blessed Alan de la Roche*)

EXTRACTS FROM ST. LOUIS DE MONTFORT'S BOOK *THE SECRET OF THE ROSARY*

The Rosary is a veritable school of Christian life. It is a reminder of the Gospels, a guidebook to virtue and a source of grace. For St. Louis de Montfort, the Rosary was not simply a method of prayer: it was his most effective tool and weapon in his apostolic work. Fittingly has the Church called him an "*extraordinary preacher of the Rosary*." He preached it in season and out of season; established it in every parish where he gave a mission. There was no limit to the power of the Rosary and to it he attributed much of his success with sinners. "Let me but place my rosary around a sinner's neck," he used to say, "and he will not escape me."

A White Rose—For Priests

Dear Ministers of the Most High, you my fellow priests who preach the truth of God, let me give you this little book as a white rose that I would like you to keep. The truths, contained in it, are set forth in a very simple and straightforward manner as you will see. Please keep them in your heart, so that you yourselves may make a practice of the Holy Rosary and taste its fruit; and please have them always on your lips, too, so that you will always preach the Rosary and thus convert others by teaching them the excellence of this holy devotion.

I beg of you to beware of thinking of the Rosary as something of little importance—as do ignorant people and even several great, but proud, scholars. Far from being insignificant, the Rosary is a priceless treasure which is inspired by God.

When the Holy Spirit has revealed this secret to a priest and director of souls, how blessed is that priest! For the vast majority of people fail to know this secret, or else only know it superficially. If such a priest really understands this secret, he will say the Rosary every day and will encourage others to say it. God and His Blessed Mother will pour abundant grace into his soul, so that he may become God's instrument for His glory—and his word, though simple, will do more good in one month than that of other preachers in several years.

Therefore, my dear brethren and fellow priests, it will not be enough for us to preach this devotion to others; we must practise it ourselves. Even if we firmly believed in the importance of the Holy Rosary, but never said it ourselves, people could hardly be expected to act upon our advice, for no one can give what he does not have: "Jesus began to do and to teach" (Acts 1:1). We ought to pattern ourselves on Our Blessed Lord, Who began by practising what He preached. We ought to emulate St. Paul, who knew and preached nothing but Jesus Crucified. This is really and truly what you will be doing if you preach the Holy Rosary. It is not just a conglomeration of *Our Fathers* and *Hail Marys*, but, on the contrary, it is a divine summary of the mysteries of the life, passion, death and glory of Jesus and Mary.

A Red Rose—For Sinners

Poor men and women who are sinners, I, a greater sinner than you, wish to give to you this rose—a crimson one, because the Precious Blood of Our Lord has fallen upon it. Every day unbelievers and unrepentant sinners cry: "Let us crown ourselves with roses" (Wis. 2:8). But our cry should be: "Let us crown ourselves with roses of the Most Holy Rosary."

How different are theirs from ours! Their roses are pleasures of the flesh, worldly honors and passing riches, which wilt and decay in no time, but ours—the *Our Father* and *Hail Mary*, which we have said devoutly over and over again and to which we have added good penitential acts—will never wilt or die and they will be just as exquisite thousands of years from now, as they are today.

On the contrary, sinners' roses only look like roses, while in point of fact they are cruel thorns, which prick them during life by giving them pangs of conscience; at their death they pierce them with bitter regret and, still worse, in eternity, they turn to burning shafts of anger and despair. But if our roses have thorns, they are the thorns of Jesus Christ Who changes them into roses. If our roses prick us, it is only for a short time—and only in order to cure the illness of sin and to save our souls.

So, by all means, we should eagerly crown ourselves with these roses from heaven and recite the entire Rosary every day, that is to say three Rosaries, each of five decades, which are like three little wreaths, or crowns, of flowers.

If you say the Rosary faithfully until death, I do assure you that, in spite of the gravity of your sins "you shall receive a never fading crown of glory" (I Pet. 5:4). Even if you are on the brink of damnation, even if you have one foot in hell, even if you have sold your soul to the devil as sorcerers do, who practise black magic, and even if you are a heretic as obstinate as a devil, sooner or later you will be converted and will amend your life and save your soul, if—and mark well what I say—if you say the Holy Rosary devoutly every day, until death, for the purpose of know-ing the truth and obtaining contrition and pardon for your sins.

First Rose—The Prayers of the Rosary

The Rosary is made up of two things: mental prayer and vocal prayer. In the Holy Rosary, mental prayer is none other than meditation of the chief mysteries of the life, death and glory of Jesus Christ and of His Blessed Mother. Vocal prayer consists in saying fifteen decades while, at the same time, meditating on and contemplating the fifteen principal virtues which Jesus and Mary practised in the fifteen mysteries of the Holy Rosary. So the Rosary is a blessed blending of mental and vocal prayer by which we honor and learn to imitate the mysteries and the virtues of the life, death, passion and glory of Jesus and Mary.

Fourth Rose—Blessed Alan de la Roche

All things, even the holiest, are subject to change, especially when they are dependent on man's free will. It is hardly to be wondered at, then, that the Confraternity of the Holy Rosary only retained its first fervor for one century after it was instituted by St. Dominic. After this, it was like a thing buried and forgotten.

Doubtless, too, the wicked scheming and jealousy of the devil were largely responsible for getting people to neglect the Holy Rosary, and thus block the flow of God's grace which it had drawn down upon the world. Thus, in 1349, God punished the whole of Europe and sent the most terrible plague that had ever been known into every land. This scourge of God was quickly followed by two others: the heresy of the Flagellantes and a tragic schism in 1376.

Later on, when these trials were over, thanks to the mercy of God, Our Lady told Blessed Alan to revive the ancient Confraternity of the Most Holy Rosary. Blessed Alan was one of the Dominican Fathers from the monastery at Dinan, in Brittany. He was an eminent theologian and was famous for his sermons. Our Lady chose him because, since the Confraternity had originally been started in this province, it was most fitting that a Dominican, from the very same province, should have the honor of re-establishing it. Blessed Alan began this great work in 1460 after a special warning from Our Lord. This is how he received His urgent message, as he tells it himself:

One day when he was saying Mass, Our Lord, Who wished to spur him on to preach the Holy Rosary, spoke to him in the Sacred Host, saying: "How can you crucify Me again so soon?" "What did You say, Lord?" asked Blessed Alan, horrified. "You crucified Me once before by your sins," answered Jesus, "and I would willingly be crucified again rather than have My Father offended by the sins you used to commit. You are crucifying Me again now, because you have all the learning and understanding that you need to preach My Mother's Rosary, and you are not doing so. If you only did this, you could teach many souls the right path and lead them away from sin—but you are not doing

it and so you yourself are guilty of the sins that they commit."
This terrible reproach made Blessed Alan solemnly resolve to
preach the Rosary unceasingly.

Our Lady too spoke to him one day to inspire him to preach
the Holy Rosary more and more: "You were a great sinner in your
youth," she said, "but I obtained the grace of your conversion
from my Son. Had such a thing been possible I would have liked
to have gone through all kinds of suffering to save you, because
converted sinners are a glory to me. And I would have done this
also to make you worthy of preaching my Rosary far and wide."

St. Dominic appeared to Blessed Alan, as well, and told him
of the great results of his ministry: he had preached the Holy
Rosary unceasingly, his sermons had borne great fruit and many
people had been converted during his missions. He said to Blessed
Alan: "See the wonderful results I have had through preaching
the Holy Rosary! You and all those who love Our Lady ought to
do the same so that, by means of this holy practice of Rosary, you
may draw all people to the real science of virtues."

Eighth Rose—Marvels of the Rosary

It would hardly be possible for me to put into words, how
much Our Lady thinks of the Holy Rosary and of how she vastly
prefers it to all other devotions. Neither can I sufficiently express
how highly she rewards those who work to preach the devotion,
to establish it and spread it, nor on the other hand how firmly she
punishes those who work against it.

All during life, St. Dominic had nothing more at heart than
to praise Our Lady, to preach her greatness and to inspire everybody to honor her by saying her Rosary. As a reward he received
countless graces from her. She crowned his labors with many
miracles and prodigies. Almighty God always granted him what
he asked through Our Lady. The greatest honor of all was that
she helped him crush the Albigensian heresy and made him the
founder and patriarch of a great religious order.

As for Blessed Alan de la Roche, who restored the devotion
to the Rosary, he received many privileges from Our Lady; she

graciously appeared to him several times to teach him how to work out his salvation, to become a good priest and perfect religious, and how to pattern himself on Our Lord.

He used to be horribly tempted and persecuted by devils, and then deep sadness would fall upon him and, sometimes, he used to be near to despair—but Our Lady always comforted him by her presence, which banished the clouds of darkness from his soul.

Blessed Thomas of St. John was well known for his sermons on the Most Holy Rosary, and the devil, jealous of the success he had with souls, tortured him so much, that he fell ill and was sick so long, that the doctors gave him up.

Our Lady blesses ,not only those who preach her Rosary, but she highly rewards all those who get others to say it by their example. Alphonsus, King of Leon and Galicia, very much wanted all his servants to honor the Blessed Virgin by saying the Rosary. So he used to hang a large Rosary on his belt and always wore it, but, unfortunately never said it himself. Nevertheless, his wearing it encouraged his courtiers to say the Rosary very devoutly.

One day, the King fell seriously ill and, when he was given up for dead, he found himself, in a vision, before the judgment seat of Our Lord. Many devils were there accusing him of all the sins he had committed and Our Lord, as Sovereign Judge, was just about to condemn him to hell, when Our Lady appeared to intercede for him. She called for a pair of scales and had his sins placed in one of the balances, whereas she put the Rosary, that he had always worn, on the other scale, together with all the Rosaries that had been said because of his example. It was found that the Rosaries weighed more than his sins.

Looking at him with great kindness Our Lady said: "As a reward for this little honor that you paid me in wearing my Rosary, I have obtained a great grace for you from my Son. Your life will be spared for a few more years. See that you spend these years wisely and do penance"

When the King regained consciousness be cried out: "Blessed be the Rosary of the Most Holy Virgin Mary, by which I have been delivered from eternal damnation!" After he had recovered

his health he spent the rest of his life in spreading devotion to the
Holy Rosary and said it faithfully every day.

Eleventh Rose—The Creed

The Creed, or the Symbol of the Apostles, which is said on
the crucifix of the Rosary, is a holy summary of all Christian
truths. It is a prayer that has great merit, because faith is the root,
foundation and beginning of all Christian virtues, of all eternal
virtues and also of all prayers that are pleasing to Almighty God.
"He that cometh to God, must believe" (I Cor. 13:7; Heb.
11:6)....Whosoever wishes to come to God, must first of all believe and the greater his faith, the more merit his prayer will have,
the more powerful it will be, and the more it will glorify God.

I shall not take time here to explain the Creed word for word,
but I cannot resist saying that the first few words "I believe in
God" are marvelously effective as a means of sanctifying our souls
and of putting devils to rout, because these three words contain
the acts of the three theological virtues of faith, hope and charity.

It was by saying *I believe in God* that the saints overcame
temptations, especially those against faith, hope or charity, whether
they came during their lifetime or at their death. They were also
the last words of St. Peter, Martyr; a heretic had cleft his head in
two by a cruel blow of his sword and St. Peter was almost at his
last gasp, but he somehow managed to trace these words in the
sand with his finger before he died [St. Peter of Verona, O.P.,
1206-1253, was a Dominican priest who fought heresy courageously and zealously. In doing this he gave his life for the Faith].

The Holy Rosary contains many mysteries of Jesus and Mary
and since faith is the only key which opens up these mysteries for
us, we must begin the Rosary by saying the Creed very devoutly
and, the stronger our faith, the more merit our Rosary will have.

This faith must be lively and informed by charity. In other
words, to recite properly the Rosary, it is necessary to be in God's
grace, or at least in quest of it. This faith must be strong and
constant, that is, one must not be looking for sensible devotion
and spiritual consolation in the recitation of the Rosary; nor should

one give it up because his mind is flooded with countless involuntary distractions, or because one experiences a strange distaste in the soul and an almost continual and oppressive fatigue in the body. Neither feeling, nor consolation, nor highs, nor transports, nor the continual attention of the imagination are needed; faith and good intentions are quite enough. "Faith alone suffices" (words from the hymn *Pange Lingua*).

Twelfth Rose: Part I—The *Our Father*

The *Our Father*, or Lord's Prayer, has great value—above all because of its Author, Who is neither a man, nor an angel, but the King of angels and men, Our Lord and Savior Jesus Christ. St. Cyprian says that it was fitting that our Savior, by Whom we were reborn into the life of grace, should also be our heavenly Master and should teach us how to pray.

The beautiful order, the tender forcefulness and the clarity of this divine prayer, pay tribute to our divine Master's wisdom. It is a short prayer, but can teach us so very much and it is well within the grasp of uneducated people, while scholars find it a continual source of meditation on the mysteries of our Faith.

The *Our Father* contains all the duties we owe to God, the acts of all the virtues and the petitions for all our spiritual and corporal needs. Tertullian says that the *Our Father* is a summary of the New Testament. Thomas à Kempis says that it surpasses all the desires of all the saints; that it is a condensation of all the beautiful sayings of all the Psalms and Canticles; that in it we ask God for everything that we need; that by it we praise Him in the very best way; that we lift up our souls from earth to heaven and unite them with God.

St. John Chrysostom says that we cannot be our Master's disciples unless we pray as He did and in the way that He showed us. Moreover God the Father listens more willingly to the prayer that we have learned from His Son, rather than those of our own making, which have all our human limitations. We should say the *Our Father* with the certitude that the eternal Father will hear it, because it is the prayer of His Son, Whom He always hears, and we are His members. God will surely grant our petitions, made through the Lord's Prayer, because it is impossible to imagine that such a good Father could refuse a request couched in the language of so worthy a Son, reinforced by His merits, and made at His behest.

St. Augustine says that whenever we say the *Our Father* devoutly, our venial sins are forgiven. The just man falls seven times a day, but in the Lord's Prayer he will find seven petitions, which will both help him to avoid downfalls and will protect him from his spiritual enemies. Our Lord, knowing how weak and helpless we are and how many difficulties we get into, made His Prayer short and easy to say, so that if we say it devoutly and often, we can be sure that Almighty God will quickly come to our aid.

I have a word for you, devout souls, who pay little attention to the prayer that the Son of God gave us Himself and asked us to say: It is high time for you to change your way of thinking. You only like prayers that men have written—as though anybody, even the most inspired man in the whole world, could possibly know more about how we ought to pray than Jesus Christ Himself! You look for prayers in books, written by other men, almost as though you were ashamed of saying the prayer that Our Lord told us to say.

You have managed to convince yourself that the prayers in these books are for scholars and for rich people of the upper classes, whereas the Rosary is only for women and children and the lower classes. As if the prayers and praises, which you have been reading, were more beautiful and more pleasing to God than those which are to be found in the Lord's Prayer! It is a very dangerous temptation to lose interest in the prayer that Our Lord gave us and to take up prayers that men have written instead.

Not that I disapprove of prayers that the saints have written, so as to encourage the faithful to praise God, but it is not to be endured that they should prefer the latter to the Prayer which was uttered by Wisdom Incarnate. If they ignore this Prayer, it is just as though they pass up the spring to go after the brook and, refusing the clear water, drink dirty water instead. The Rosary, made up of the Lord's Prayer and the Angelic Salutation, is this clear and ever flowing water which comes from the Fountain of Grace;

whereas other prayers, which they look for in books, are nothing but tiny streams, which spring from this fount.

When we say this wonderful prayer we touch God's heart at the very outset by calling Him by the sweet name of Father—Our Father. He is the dearest of fathers: all-powerful in His creation, wonderful in the way He maintains the world, completely lovable in His Divine Providence, always good and infinitely so in the Redemption. We have God for our Father, so we are all brothers—and heaven is our homeland and our heritage. This should be more than enough to teach us to love God and our neighbor and to be detached from the things of this world.

Twelfth Rose: Part II—The *Our Father* (cont.)

So we ought to love our Heavenly Father and should say to Him over and over again:

Our Father Who art in heaven...
Thou Who dost fill heaven and earth
With the immensity of Thy Being,
Thou Who art present everywhere.
Thou Who art in the saints—by Thy glory,
In the damned—by Thy Justice,
In the good—by Thy grace;
And even in sinners—by the patience with which Thou dost
  tolerate them.
Grant, we beseech Thee, that we may always remember that
  we come from Thee;
Grant that we may live as Thy true children ought to live;
Grant that we may set our course towards Thee and never
  swerve;
Grant that we may use our every power, our hearts and souls
  and strength to tend towards Thee and Thee alone.
Hallowed be Thy name...
King David the prophet said that the name of the Lord is
  holy and awe-inspiring, and Isaias that heaven is always
  echoing with the praises of the Seraphim, who unceasingly
  praise the holiness of the Lord God of Hosts.

We ask here that all the world may learn to know and adore the attributes of our God, Who is so great and so holy. We ask that He may be known, loved and adored by pagans, Turks, Jews, barbarians and by all infidels—that all men may serve and glorify Him by a living faith, a staunch hope, a burning charity and by renouncing all erroneous beliefs. This all adds up to say that we pray that all men may be holy, because our God Himself is all-holy.

> *Thy Kingdom come:*
> Do Thou reign in our souls—by Thy grace;
> So that after death—we may be found meet to reign with
>   Thee
> In Thy Kingdom—in perfect and unending bliss.
> Oh Lord we firmly believe—in this happiness to come;
> We hope for and we expect it, because God the Father has
>   promised it in His great goodness;
> It was purchased for us by the merits of God the Son and
>   God the Holy Spirit—
> He Who is the Light has made it known to us.

> *Thy will be done on earth as it is in heaven...*
> As Tertullian says, this sentence does not, in the least, mean that we are afraid of people thwarting God's designs, because nothing whatsoever can happen without Divine Providence having foreseen it and having made it fit into His plans beforehand. No obstruction in the whole world can possibly prevent the will of God from being carried out.

> Rather, when we say *Thy will be done,* we ask God to make us humbly resigned to all that He has seen fit to send us in this life. We also ask Him to help us to do, in all things and at all times, His holy will, made known to us by the commandments, promptly, lovingly and faithfully, as the saints and angels do it in heaven.

Give us this day our daily bread...

Our Lord taught us to ask God for everything that we need whether in the spiritual or temporal order. By asking for our *daily bread* we humbly admit our own poverty and insufficiency and pay tribute to our God, knowing that all temporal goods come from His Divine Providence.

When we say *bread,* we ask for that which is just necessary to live; and, of course, this does not include luxuries.

We ask for this bread today *this day* which means that we are concerned only for the present, leaving the morrow in the hands of Providence.

And when we ask for our *daily bread* we recognize that we need God's help every day and that we are entirely dependent upon Him for His help and protection.

Forgive us our trespasses as we forgive those who trespass against us...

Every sin, say St. Augustine and Tertullian, is a debt which we contract towards Almighty God and His justice demands payment down to the very last farthing. Unfortunately, we all have these sad debts.

No matter how many they may be, we should go to God in all confidence and with true sorrow for our sins, saying "Our Father Who art in heaven, forgive us our sins of thought and those of speech, forgive us our sins of commission and omission, which make us infinitely guilty in the eyes of Thy Divine Justice.

"We dare to ask this, because Thou art our loving and merciful Father and because we have forgotten those who have offended us, out of obedience to Thee and out of charity.

"Do not permit us, in spite of our infidelity to Thy graces, to give in to the temptations of the world, the devil and the flesh."

But deliver us from evil...

The evil of sin and temporal punishment and everlasting punishment which we know that we have rightly deserved.

Amen (So be it)...

This word at the end of *Our Father* is very consoling and St.
Jerome says that it is a sort of seal of approbation, that
Almighty God puts at the end of our petitions, to assure
us that He will grant our requests—very much as though
He Himself were answering: "Amen! May it be as you have
asked, for verily you have obtained what you asked for."
This is what is meant by the word "Amen."

Thirteenth Rose—The *Our Father* (cont.)

Each word of the Lord's Prayer is a tribute we pay to the
perfections of God.

Our Father—this means that He is the Father of mankind
because He has created us and continues to sustain us, and because He has redeemed us. He is also the merciful Father of sinners, the Father Who is the friend of the just and the glorious
Father of the blessed in heaven.

When we say *Who art*, by these words we pay tribute to the
infinity and immensity and fullness of God's essence. God is rightly
called "He Who is" (Exod. 3:14); that is to say, He exists of necessity, essentially, and eternally, because He is the Being of beings
and the Cause of all beings. He possesses within Himself, in a
supereminent degree, the perfections of all beings and He is in all
of them by His essence, by His presence and by His power, but
without being bounded by their limitations. We honor His sub-
limity and His glory and His majesty by the words *Who art in
heaven,* that is to say, "Who is seated as on a throne, holding sway
over all men by Thy justice."

When we say *hallowed be Thy name* we worship God's holiness; and we give obedience to His Kingship and bow to the justice of His laws by the words *Thy Kingdom come*, praying that
men will obey Him on earth as the angels do in heaven.

We show our trust in His Providence by asking for our *daily
bread,* and we appeal to His mercy when we ask for the forgiveness of our sins.

We look to His great power when we beg Him *not to lead us into temptation,* and we show our faith in His goodness by our hope that He will *deliver us from evil.*

The Son of God has always glorified His Father by His works and He came into the world to teach men to give glory to Him. He showed men how to praise Him by this prayer which He taught us with His own lips. It is our duty, therefore, to say it often—we should say it reverently and attentively and in the spirit in which Our Lord taught it.

Fourteenth Rose—The *Our Father* (cont.)

We make as many acts of the noblest Christian virtues as we pronounce words, when we recite attentively this divine prayer.

In saying *"Our Father Who art in heaven,"* we make acts of faith, adoration and humility. When we ask that *His name be hallowed* and glorified we show a burning zeal for His glory, and when we ask for the spread of His Kingdom we make an act of hope; by the wish that *His will he done an earth as it is in heaven,* we show a spirit of perfect obedience.

In asking for our *daily bread* we practice poverty of spirit and detachment from worldly goods. When we beg Him to *forgive us our sins* we make an act of sorrow for them. By *forgiving those who have trespassed against us* we give proof of the virtue of mercy in its highest degree.

Through asking God's *help in all our temptations,* we make acts of humility, prudence and fortitude. As we wait for Him *to deliver us from evil* we exercise the virtue of patience.

Finally, while asking for all these things—not for ourselves alone but also for our neighbor and for all members of the Church—we are carrying out our duty as true children of God, we are imitating Him in His love, which embraces all men and we are keeping the commandment of love of neighbor.

If we sincerely ask God that our neighbor may have the very same blessings that we ourselves stand in need of, it goes without saying that we will give up all hatred, quarreling and jealousy. And of course if we ask God each day for our daily bread we shall learn to hate gluttony and lasciviousness, which thrive in rich surroundings.

While sincerely asking God to *forgive us as we forgive those who trespass against us*, we no longer give way to anger and thoughts of getting even; instead, we return good for evil and really love our enemies.

To ask God to *save us from falling into sin* when we are tempted is to give proof that we are fighting laziness and that we are genuinely seeking means to root out vicious habits and to work out our salvation.

To pray God to *deliver us from evil* is to fear His justice and this will give us true happiness. For since the fear of God is the beginning of wisdom, it is through the virtue of the fear of God that men avoid sin.

Fifteenth Rose—The *Hail Mary*

The Angelic Salutation is so heavenly and so beyond us in its depth of meaning that Blessed Alan de la Roche held that no mere creature could ever possibly understand it, and that only Our Lord and Savior Jesus Christ, Who was born of the Blessed Virgin Mary, can really explain it.

Its enormous value is due, first of all to Our Lady, to whom it was addressed; to the purpose of the Incarnation of the Word, for which reason this prayer was brought from heaven; and also to the Archangel Gabriel, who was the first ever to say it.

The Angelic Salutation is a most concise summary of all that Catholic theology teaches about the Blessed Virgin. It is divided into two parts, that of praise and petition: the first shows all that goes to make up Mary's greatness and the second, all that we need to ask her for and all that we may expect to receive through her goodness.

The Most Blessed Trinity revealed the first part of it to us and the latter part was added by St. Elizabeth, who was inspired by the Holy Spirit. Holy Mother Church gave us the conclusion in the year 430, when she condemned the Nestorian heresy, at the council of Ephesus, and defined that the Blessed Virgin is truly the Mother of God. At this time she ordered us to pray to Our Lady under this glorious title by saying: "*Holy Mary, Mother of God, pray for us sinners, now, and at the hour of our death.*"

The greatest event in the whole history of the world was the Incarnation of the Eternal Word, by Whom the world was redeemed and peace was restored between God and men. Our Lady was chosen as His instrument for this tremendous event and it was put into effect when she was greeted with the Angelic Salutation. The Archangel Gabriel, one of the leading princes of the heavenly court, was chosen as ambassador to bear these glad tidings.

By the Angelic Salutation God became man, a virgin became the Mother of God, the souls of the just were delivered from Limbo, the empty thrones in heaven filled. In addition sin was forgiven, grace was given to us, sick people were made well, the dead were brought back to life, exiles were brought home, and the anger of the Most Blessed Trinity was appeased and men obtained eternal life.

Sixteenth Rose—The *Hail Mary*: Its Beauty

Even though there is nothing so great as the majesty of God and nothing so low as man insofar as he is a sinner, Almighty God does not despise our poor prayers. On the contrary, He is pleased when we sing His praises.

St. Gabriel's greeting to Our Lady is one of the most beautiful hymns which we can possibly sing to the glory of the Most High. "I will sing a new song to you" (Ps.143:9). This new hymn, which David foretold was to be sung at the coming of the Messias, is none other than the Angelic Salutation.

There is an old hymn and a new hymn: the first is that which the Jews sang out of gratitude to God—for creating them and maintaining them in existence—for delivering them from captivity and leading them safely through the Red Sea—for giving them manna to eat and for all His other blessings.

The new hymn is that which Christians sing in thanksgiving for the graces of the Incarnation and the Redemption. As these marvels were brought about by the Angelic Salutation, so also do we repeat the same salutation, to thank the Most Blessed Trinity for His immeasurable goodness to us.

When we praise and bless Our Lady by saying the Angelic Salutation, she always passes on these praises to Almighty God in the same way as she did when she was praised by St. Elizabeth. The latter blessed her in her most elevated dignity as Mother of God and Our Lady immediately returned these praises to God by her beautiful *Magnificat*.

Just as the Angelic Salutation gives glory to the Blessed Trinity, it is also the very highest praise that we can give Our Lady.

One day, when St. Mechtilde was praying and was trying to think of some way in which she could express her love of the Blessed Mother better than she had done before, she fell into ecstasy. Our Lady appeared to her with the Angelic Salutation in flaming letters of gold upon her bosom, and said to her:

> My daughter, I want you to know that no one can please me more than by saying the salutation which the Most Adorable Trinity sent to me and by which He raised me to the dignity of Mother of God.

> By the word *Ave* (which is the name Eve, *Eva*), I learned that in His infinite power God had preserved me from all sin and its attendant misery which the first woman had been subject to.

> The name *Mary*, which means "lady of light," shows that God has filled me with wisdom and light, like a shining star, to light up heaven and earth.

> The words *full of grace* remind me that the Holy Spirit has showered so many graces upon me, that I am able to give these graces in abundance to those who ask for them through me as Mediatrix.

> When people say *The Lord is with thee*, they renew the indescribable joy that was mine when the Eternal Word became incarnate in my womb.

> When you say to me *blessed art thou among women*, I praise Almighty God's divine mercy which lifted me to this exalted plane of happiness.

And at the words *blessed is the fruit of thy womb, Jesus,* the whole of heaven rejoices with me to see my Son, Jesus Christ, adored and glorified for having saved mankind.

Seventeenth Rose—The *Hail Mary*: Its Fruits

Blessed Alan De La Roche, who was so deeply devoted to the Blessed Virgin, had many revelations from her and we know that he confirmed the truth of these revelations by a solemn oath. Three of them stand out with special emphasis: the first, that if people fail to say the *Hail Mary* out of carelessness, or because they are lukewarm, or because they hate it, this is a sign that they will probably, and indeed shortly, be condemned to eternal punishment.

The second truth is that those who love this divine salutation bear the very special stamp of predestination.

The third is that those to whom God has given the signal grace of loving Our Lady and of serving her out of love, must take very great care to continue to love and serve her until the time when she shall have had them placed in heaven by her divine Son, in the degree of glory which they have earned (Blessed Alan, chapter XI, paragraph 2).

The heretics, all of whom are children of the devil and clearly bear the sign of God's reprobation, have a horror of the *Hail Mary*. They still say the *Our Father*, but never the *Hail Mary*; they would rather wear a poisonous snake around their necks than wear a Scapular or carry a Rosary.

Among Catholics those who bear the mark of God's reprobation think but little of the Rosary (whether that of five decades or fifteen). They either fail to say it, or only say it very quickly and in a lukewarm manner.

Even if I did not believe that which has been revealed to Blessed Alan de la Roche, even then my own experience would be enough to convince me of this terrible, but consoling truth. I do not know, nor do I see clearly, how it can be that a devotion which seems to be so small, can be the infallible sign of eternal salvation and how its absence can be the sign of God's eternal displeasure; nevertheless, nothing could possibly be more true.

My *Hail Mary*, my Rosary of fifteen or of five decades, is the prayer and the infallible touchstone by which I can tell those who are led by the Spirit of God from those who are deceived by the devil. I have known souls who seemed to soar like eagles to the heights by their sublime contemplation and yet, who were pitifully led astray by the devil. I only found out how wrong they were when I learned that they scorned the *Hail Mary* and the Rosary, which they considered as being far beneath them.

The more the garden of the soul is watered by this prayer the more enlightened one's intellect becomes, the more zealous his heart, and the stronger his armor against his spiritual enemies.

The *Hail Mary* is a sharp and flaming shaft which, joined to the Word of God, gives the preacher the strength to pierce, move and convert the most hardened hearts—even if he has little or no natural gift for preaching.

Eighteenth Rose—The *Hail Mary*: Its Blessings

This heavenly salutation draws down upon us the blessings of Jesus and Mary in abundance, for it is an infallible truth that Jesus and Mary reward, in a marvelous way, those who glorify them. They repay us a hundredfold for the praises that we give them. "I love them that love me...that I may enrich them that love me and fill their treasures" (Prov. 8:17-21).

Now, if we say the *Hail Mary* properly, is not this a way to love, bless and glorify Jesus and Mary? In each *Hail Mary* we bless both Jesus and Mary: "Blessed art thou among women, and blessed is the fruit of thy womb, Jesus." By each *Hail Mary* we give Our Lady the same honor that God gave her when He sent the Archangel Gabriel to greet her for Him. How could anyone possibly think that Jesus and Mary, who often do good to those that curse them, could ever curse those that bless and honor them by the *Hail Mary*?

Both St. Bernard and St. Bonaventure say that the Queen of Heaven is certainly no less grateful and conscientious than the gracious and well-mannered people of this world. Just as she excels in all other perfections, so she surpasses us all in the virtue of gratitude; therefore she would never let us honor her with love and respect without repaying us one hundredfold. St. Bonaventure says that Mary will greet us with grace if we greet her with the *Hail Mary*.

Nineteenth Rose—Happy Exchange

It is written: "Give and it shall be given unto you" (Lk. 6:38). To take Blessed Alan's illustration of this: "Supposing each day I give you one hundred and fifty diamonds, even if you were my enemy, would you not forgive me?" "He that honoreth his mother (the Blessed Virgin) is as one that layeth up a treasure" (Eccles. 3:5). So every day do give her at least fifty *Hail Marys*—for each one is worth fifteen precious stones and they please Our Lady far more than all the riches of this world put together.

And you can expect such great things from her generosity! She is our Mother and our friend. This is really so, for the charity of the Blessed Virgin far surpasses the natural love of all mankind and even of all the angels, as St. Augustine says.

One day St. Gertrude had a vision of Our Lord counting gold coins. She summoned the courage to ask Him what He was doing. He answered: "I am counting the *Hail Marys* that you have said; this is the money with which you can pay your way to heaven."

The holy and learned Jesuit, Suarez, was so deeply aware of the value of the Angelic Salutation that he said that he would gladly give all his learning for the price of one *Hail Mary* that had been said properly.

Twentieth Rose—The *Hail Mary*: An Explanation

Are you in the miserable state of sin? Then call on the divine Mary and say to her: *Ave*, which means "I salute thee with the most profound respect, thou who art without sin" and she will deliver you from the evil of your sins.

Are you groping in the darkness of ignorance and error? Go to Mary and say to her: *Hail Mary;* which means "Hail thou, who art bathed in the light of the Sun of Justice" and she will give you some of her light.

Have you strayed from the path leading to heaven? Then call on Mary, for her name means "Star of the Sea, the North Star which guides the ships of our souls during the voyage of this life," and she will guide you to the harbor of eternal salvation.

Are you in sorrow? Turn to Mary, for her name means also "Sea of Bitterness which has been filled with sharp pain in this world, but which is now turned into a Sea of the Purest Joy in heaven," and she will turn your sorrow to joy and your afflictions into consolation.

Have you lost the state of grace? Praise and honor the numberless graces with which God has filled the Blessed Virgin and say to her: *Thou art full of grace* and filled with all the gifts of the Holy Spirit, and she will give you some of these graces.

Are you all alone, having lost God's protection? Pray to Mary, and say: *"The Lord is with thee*—and this union is far nobler and more intimate than that which He has with the saints and the just—because thou art one with Him."

Have you become an outcast and have you been accursed by God? Then say to Our Lady: *"Blessed art thou above all women* and above all nations, by thy purity and fertility; thou hast turned God's maledictions into blessings for us," and she will bless you.

Twentieth Rose—The *Hail Mary*: Explanation (cont.)

Then, at the end of your prayer, pray thus with Holy Mother Church:
Holy Mary...
Holy in body and in soul;
Holy because of thy incomparable and eternal devotion to the service of God;
Holy in thy great rank of Mother of God;
Who has endowed thee with eminent holiness;
A worthy attribute of this great dignity.

Mother of God...
And our Mother;
Our Advocate and Mediatrix;
Thou who art the Treasurer of God's graces,
And who dost dispense them as thou seest fit.
Oh, we beg of thee, obtain for us soon the forgiveness of our
    sins;
And grant that we may be reconciled with God's infinite
    Majesty.

Pray for us, sinners...
Thou who art always filled with compassion for those in need;
Thou who wilt never despise sinners or turn them away;
For, but for them, thou wouldst never have been Mother of
    the Redeemer,
Pray for us

Now...
During this short life
So fraught with sorrow and uncertainty.
Pray for us now, now—because we can be sure of nothing
    except the present moment.
Pray for us now—that we are being attacked night and day
    by powerful and ruthless enemies ...

And at the hour of our death...
So terrible and full of danger,
When our strength is waning and our spirits are sinking;
And our souls and bodies are worn out with fear and pain;

Pray for us then at the hour of our death
When the devil is working with might and main,
To ensnare us and cast us into perdition.
Pray for us at the turning point,
When the die will be cast once and for all,
And our lot, for ever and ever, will be heaven or hell.
Come to the help of thy poor children, O Mother of pity:

And, oh, Advocate and Refuge of Sinners,
Protect us at the hour of our death
And drive far from us our bitter enemies,
The devils our accusers, those with frightful presence, fill us
    with dread.
Light our Path through the valley of the shadow of death.

Please, Mother
Lead us to thy Son's Judgment Seat
And do not forsake us there.
Intercede for us and ask thy Son to forgive us
And let us into the ranks of the blessed, Thy elect
In the realm of everlasting glory.
Amen. So be it.

No one could help admiring the beauty of the Holy Rosary
which is made up of two heavenly things: the Lord's Prayer and
the Angelic Salutation. How could there possibly be any prayers
more pleasing to Almighty God and the Blessed Virgin, or any
that are easier, more precious or more helpful than these two
prayers? We should always have them in our hearts and on our
lips to honor the Most Blessed Trinity, Jesus Christ our Savior,
and His Most Holy Mother.

Twenty-First Rose—The Fifteen Mysteries

A mystery is a sacred thing which is difficult to understand.
The works of Our Lord and of His Blessed Mother can be rightly
called mysteries, because they are so full of wonders and all kinds
of perfections and deep and sublime truths—which the Holy Spirit
reveals to the humble and simple souls who honor these mysteries.

The works of Jesus and Mary can also be called wonderful
flowers; but their perfume and beauty can only be appreciated by
those who study them carefully—and who open them and drink
in their scent by diligent and sincere meditation.

St. Dominic has divided up the lives of Our Lord and Our
Lady into fifteen mysteries which stand for their virtues and their

most important actions. These are the fifteen pictures whose every detail must rule and inspire our lives. They are fifteen flaming torches to guide our steps throughout this earthly life. They are fifteen shining mirrors which help us to know Jesus and Mary and to know ourselves as well. They will also help light the fire of their love in our hearts. They are fifteen fiery furnaces which can consume us completely in their heavenly fires.

Our Lady taught St. Dominic this excellent method of praying and ordered him to preach it far and wide, so as to reawaken the fervor of Christians and to revive in their hearts a love for Our Blessed Lord.

She also taught it to Blessed Alan de la Roche and said to him in a vision: "When people say one hundred and fifty Angelic Salutations this prayer is very helpful to them and is a very pleasing tribute to me. But they will do better still and will please me even more if they say these salutations while meditating on the life, death and passion of Jesus Christ—for this meditation is the soul of this prayer."

For, in reality, the Rosary said without meditating on the sacred mysteries of our salvation would be almost like a body without a soul: excellent *matter* but without the *form* which is meditation—this latter being that which sets it apart from all other devotions.

Twenty-Second Rose—Likens to Christ

The chief concern of a Christian soul should be to tend to perfection. St. Paul tells us: "Be ye followers of God, as most dear children" (Eph. 5:1). This obligation is included in the eternal decree of our predestination, as the one and only means prescribed by God to attain everlasting glory.

St. Gregory of Nyssa makes a delightful comparison when he says that we are all artists and that our souls are blank canvases, which we have to fill in. The colors which we must use are the Christian virtues; and our Model is Jesus Christ, the perfect Living Image of God the Father. Just as a portrait painter, who wants to do a good job, places himself before his model and glances at him before making each stroke, so the Christian must always have the life and virtues of Jesus Christ before his eyes, so that he may never say, think or do the least thing, which is not in harmony with his Model.

It was because Our Lady wanted to help us in the great task of working out our salvation, that she ordered St. Dominic to teach the faithful to meditate upon the sacred mysteries of the life of Jesus Christ. She did this, not only that they might adore and glorify Him, but chiefly that they might pattern their lives and actions upon His virtues.

Children copy their parents through watching them and talking to them; and they learn their own language through hearing them speak. An apprentice learns his trade through watching his master at work; in the very same way the faithful members of the Confraternity of the Holy Rosary can become like their divine Master if they reverently study and imitate the virtues of Jesus Christ, which are shown in the fifteen mysteries of His life. They can do this with the help of His grace and through the intercession of His Blessed Mother.

Twenty-Third Rose—A Memorial

A Christian who does not meditate on the mysteries of the Rosary is very ungrateful to Our Lord and shows how little he cares for all that our Divine Savior has suffered to save the world. This attitude seems to show that he knows little or nothing of the life of Jesus Christ, and that he has never taken the trouble to find out about Him—what He did and what He went through in order to save us.

A Christian, of this kind ought to fear that, having never known Jesus Christ or having put Him out of his mind and heart, He will disown him at the Day of Judgment and will say reproachfully: "Amen I say to you, I know you not" (Mt. 25:12).

Let us, then, meditate on the life and sufferings of Our Lord by means of the Holy Rosary; let us learn to know Him well and to be grateful for all His blessings so that, at the Day of Judgment, He may number us among His children and His friends.

Twenty-Fourth Rose—Means of Perfection

The saints always made Our Lord's life the principal object of their study; they meditated on His virtues and sufferings and in this way they arrived at Christian perfection. Once St. Bernard began this meditation he always continued it. "At the very beginning of my conversion," he said, "I made a bouquet of myrrh made up of the sorrows of my Savior. I placed this bouquet upon my heart, thinking of the stripes, the thorns and the nails of His passion. I used all my mental strength to meditate on these mysteries every day."

This, too, was a practice of the Holy Martyrs; we know how admirably they triumphed over the most cruel sufferings. St. Bernard says that the martyrs' wonderful constancy could have only sprung from one source—their constant meditation on the wounds of Jesus Christ. The martyrs were Christ's athletes, His champions; while their blood gushed forth and their bodies were wracked with cruel torments, their generous souls were hidden in the wounds of Our Lord. These wounds made them invincible.

It is a great mistake to think that only priests and religious, and those who have withdrawn from the turmoil of the world, are supposed to meditate upon the truths of our Faith and the mysteries of the life of Jesus Christ. If priests and religious have an obligation to meditate on the great truths of our holy religion, in order to live up to their vocation worthily, the same obligation, then, is just as much incumbent upon the laity—because of the fact that every day they meet with spiritual dangers which might make them lose their souls.

Therefore, they should arm themselves with the frequent meditation on the life, virtues and sufferings of Our Blessed Lord—which are so beautifully contained in the fifteen mysteries of the Holy Rosary.

Twenty-Fifth Rose—Wealth of Sanctification

Never will anyone really be able to understand the marvelous riches of sanctification which are contained in the prayers and mysteries of the Holy Rosary. This meditation on the mysteries of the life and death of Our Lord is the source of the most wonderful fruits for those who use it.

Today people want things that strike and move and that leave deep impressions on the soul. Nor has there ever been, in the whole history of the world, anything more moving than the wonderful story of the life, death and glory of Our Savior which is contained in the Holy Rosary. In the fifteen *tableaux*, the chief scenes or mysteries of His life unfold before our eyes. How could there ever be any prayers more wonderful and sublime than the Lord's Prayer and the Salutation of the angel? All our desires and all our needs are found expressed in these two prayers.

The meditation on the mysteries and the prayers of the Rosary is the easiest of all prayers, because the diversity of the virtues of Our Lord Jesus Christ, and the different stages of His life which we study, refresh and fortify our mind in a wonderful way and help us to avoid distractions.

For learned people, these mysteries are the source of the most profound doctrine, but simple people find in them a means of instruction well within their reach.

We must learn this easy form of meditation before progressing to the highest state of contemplation. This is the view of St. Thomas Aquinas and the advice that he gives, when he says that, first of all, one must practice on a battlefield, as it were, by acquiring all the virtues which the Holy Rosary gives us to imitate.

To think that it is possible to say prayers that are finer and more beautiful than the *Our Father* and the *Hail Mary*, is to fall prey to a strange illusion of the devil. These heavenly prayers are the support, the strength and the safeguard of our souls—but I must admit that it is not always necessary to say them as vocal prayers. It is quite true that, in a sense, mental prayer is more perfect than vocal prayer, but, believe me, it is really dangerous, not to say fatal, to give up saying the Rosary of your own accord, under the excuse of seeking a more perfect union with God.

Sometimes a soul that is proud in a subtle way and who may have done everything that he can do, to interiorly rise to the sublime heights of contemplation that the saints have reached, may be deluded by the noon-day devil into giving up his former devotions, because he thinks that he has found a greater good. He then looks upon his erstwhile practices as inferior and only fit for ordinary and mediocre souls.

Believe me, if you genuinely wish to reach a high level of prayer in all honesty, and without falling into the traps that the devil sets for those who pray, say your whole Rosary every day, or at least five decades of it.

If, by the grace of God, you have already reached a high level of prayer, keep up the practice of saying the Holy Rosary if you wish to remain in that state and if you hope, through it, to grow in humility. For never will anyone, who says his Rosary every day, become a formal heretic or be led astray by the devil. This is a statement that I would gladly sign with my blood.

On the other hand, if Almighty God, in His infinite mercy, draws you to Him as forcibly as He did some of the saints while saying the Rosary, make yourself passive in His hands and let yourself be drawn towards Him. Let God work and pray in you, and let Him say your Rosary in His way and this will be enough for the day.

Far from making you lose ground in mental prayer, or stunting your spiritual growth, it will be the most tremendous help to you. You will find that it will be a real Jacob's ladder, with fifteen rungs and by each one of these you will go from virtue to virtue and from light to light.

Twenty-Sixth Rose—Sublime Prayer

The example of St. Francis de Sales, the great spiritual director of his time, should spur you on to join the holy Confraternity of the Rosary, since, great Saint that he was, he bound himself by oath to say the whole Rosary every single day, as long as he lived.

St. Charles Borromeo also said it every day and strongly recommended the devotion to his priests, to the ecclesiastics in the seminaries and also to all his people.

St. Pius V, one of the greatest Popes who have ever ruled the Church, said the Rosary every day. St. Thomas of Villanova, Archbishop of Valence, St. Ignatius, St. Francis Xavier, St. Francis Borgia, St. Theresa and St. Phillip Neri, as well as many other great men whom I have not mentioned, were deeply devoted to the Holy Rosary.

Follow their example; your spiritual directors will be pleased and, if they are aware of the benefit that you can derive from this devotion, they will be the very first to urge you to adopt it.

Twenty-Seventh Rose: Part I—Benefits

I should like to give you even more reasons for embracing this devotion, which so many great souls have practiced; the Rosary recited, with meditation on the mysteries, brings about the following marvelous results:

1. it gradually gives us a perfect knowledge of Jesus Christ;
2. it purifies our souls, washing away sin;
3. it gives us victory over all our enemies;
4. it makes it easy for us to practice virtue;
5. it sets us on fire with love of Our Blessed Lord;
6. it enriches us with graces and merits;
7. it supplies us with what is needed to pay all our debts to God and to our fellow men, and finally, it obtains all kinds of graces for us from Almighty God.

Twenty-Seventh Rose: Part II—Benefits

If, by chance, your conscience is burdened with sin, take your Rosary and say at least part of it, honoring some of the mysteries of the life, passion or glory of Our Lord Jesus Christ, and be sure that, while you are meditating upon these mysteries and honoring them, He will show His sacred wounds to His Father in heaven. He will plead for you and will obtain for you contrition and the forgiveness of your sins.

One day Our Lord said to Blessed Alan: "If only these poor wretched sinners would say My Rosary, they would share in the merits of My passion and I would be their Advocate and would appease My Father's Justice."

This life is nothing but warfare and a series of temptations;

we do not have to contend with enemies of flesh and blood, but with the very powers of hell. What better weapons could we possibly use to combat them, than the Prayer which our great Captain taught us, and the Angelic Salutation which has chased away devils, destroyed sin and renewed the world? What better weapon could we use than meditation on the life and passion of Our Lord and Savior Jesus Christ? For, as St. Peter says, it is with this thought we must arm ourselves in order to defend ourselves against the very same enemies which he conquered and which molest us every day (Cf. I Pet 4:1).

"Put you on the armor of God" (Eph. 6:11). So arm yourselves with the arms of God—with the Holy Rosary—and you will crush the devil's head and you will stand firm in the face of all his temptations. This is why, even the material Rosary itself, is such a terrible thing for the devil and why the saints have used it to enchain devils and to chase them out of the bodies of people who were possessed. Such happenings are reported in more than one authentic record.

Blessed Alan said that a man he knew of had desperately tried all kinds of devotions to rid himself of the evil spirit, who possessed him, but without success. Finally, he thought of wearing his Rosary around his neck, which eased him considerably. He discovered that whenever he took it off, the devil tormented him cruelly, so he resolved to wear it night and day. This drove the evil spirit away forever, because he could not bear such a terrible chain. Blessed Alan also testified that he had delivered a large number of people, who were possessed, by putting the Rosary around their necks.

Twenty-Eighth Rose—Salutary Effects

St. Augustine says quite emphatically that there is no spiritual exercise more fruitful, or more useful to our salvation, than continually turning our thoughts to the sufferings of Our Savior. St. Albert the Great, who had St. Thomas Aquinas as his disciple, learned, in a revelation, that by simply thinking of, or meditating on, the passion of Our Lord Jesus Christ, a Christian gains more merit than if he had fasted on bread and water every Friday for a whole year, or had beaten himself with his discipline once a week until the blood flowed, or had recited the whole Book of Psalms every day. If this is so, then how great must be the merit that we can gain by the Holy Rosary, which commemorates the whole life and passion of Our Savior!

One day, Our Lady revealed to Blessed Alan that, after the Holy Sacrifice of the Mass, which is the most important, as well as the living, memorial of Our Blessed Lord's passion, there could not possibly be a finer devotion, or one of greater merit than that of the Holy Rosary, which is like a second memorial and representation of the life and passion of Our Lord Jesus Christ.

Fr. Dorland says that, in 1481, Our Lady appeared to Venerable Dominic, the Carthusian, who lived at Treves, and said to him: "Whenever one of the faithful, who is in a state of grace, says the Rosary while meditating on the mysteries of the life and passion of Jesus Christ, he obtains full and entire remission of all his sins."

St. Dominic was so convinced of the efficacy of the Holy Rosary and of its great value that, when he heard confessions, he hardly ever gave any other penance. You have seen an example of this already in the story that I told you of the lady in Rome to whom he gave one single Rosary for her penance.

St. Dominic was a great saint and other confessors should be sure to walk in his footsteps, by asking their penitents to say the Rosary, together with meditation on the sacred mysteries, rather than giving them other penances which are less meritorious, less pleasing to God, less likely to help them advance in virtue and not as efficacious as the Rosary for helping them avoid falling into sin. Let us turn, then, to the Holy Rosary in all our needs and we shall infallibly obtain the graces we ask of God to save our souls.

Twenty-Ninth Rose—Means of Salvation

St. Denis said that there is nothing more noble and more pleasing to God than to cooperate in the work of saving souls and to frustrate the devil's plans for ruining them. The Son of God came down to earth for no other reason than to save souls.

He upset Satan's empire by founding the Church, but the former rallied his strength and wreaked cruel violence on souls by the Albigensian heresy, by the hatred, dissensions and abominable vices, which he spread throughout the world in the XIth, XIIth and XIIIth centuries.

Only stringent measures could possibly cure such terrible disorders and repel Satan's forces. The Blessed Virgin, Protectress of the Church, has given us a most powerful means for appeasing her Son's anger, uprooting heresy and reforming Christian morals, in the Confraternity of the Holy Rosary. It has proved its worth, for it has brought back charity and frequent reception of the Sacraments, which flourished in the first golden centuries of the Church, and it has reformed Christian morals.

Pope Leo X said, in his Bull, that this Confraternity had been founded in honor of God and of the Blessed Virgin, as a wall, to hold back the evils that were going to break upon the Church.

Gregory XIII said that the Rosary was given us from heaven, as a means of appeasing God's anger and of imploring Our Lady's intercession.

Jules III said that the Rosary was inspired by God, in order that heaven might be more easily opened to us, through the favors of Our Lady.

Paul III and St. Pius V stated that the Rosary was given to the faithful in order that they might have spiritual peace and consolation more easily. Surely everyone will want to join a Confraternity which was founded for such noble purposes.

Fr. Dominic, the Carthusian, who was deeply devoted to the Holy Rosary, had this vision: heaven was opened for him to see and the whole heavenly Court was assembled in magnificent array. He heard them sing the Rosary in an enchanting melody and each decade was in honor of a mystery of the life, passion or glory of our Lord Jesus Christ and of His Blessed Mother.

It must not be thought that the Rosary is only for women and for simple and ignorant people; it is also for men and for the greatest of men. As soon as St. Dominic acquainted Pope Innocent III with the fact that he had received a command, from heaven, to establish the Confraternity of the Most Holy Rosary, the Holy Father gave it his full approval, urged St. Dominic to preach it and said that he wished to become a member himself. Members of the Confraternity have always been from all walks of life: dukes, princes, kings, as well as prelates, cardinals and Sovereign Pontiffs; it would take too long to give all their names in this little book, which is but a summary.

Thirty-Seventh Rose—A Monastery Reformed

A nobleman, who had several daughters, entered one of them in a lax monastery, where the nuns were very proud and thought of nothing else but worldly pleasures. The nuns' confessor, on the other hand, was a zealous priest and had a great love for the Holy Rosary. Wishing to guide this nun into a better way of life, he ordered her to say the Rosary every day in honor of the Blessed Virgin, while meditating on the life, passion and glory of Jesus Christ.

She joyously undertook to say the Rosary and, little by little, she grew to have a repugnance for the wayward habits of her sisters in religion. She developed a love for silence and prayer—and this in spite of the fact that the others despised and ridiculed her and called her a fanatic.

It was at this time that a holy priest, who was making the visitation of the convent, had a strange vision while he was making his meditation: he saw a nun in her room, rapt in prayer, kneeling in front of a Lady of breathless beauty who was surrounded by angels. The latter had flaming spears, with which they repelled a crowd of devils, who wanted to come in. These evil spirits then fled to the other nuns' rooms, under the guise of vile animals.

By this vision the priest became aware of the lamentable state the monastery was in and he was so upset that he thought he might almost die of grief. He immediately sent for the young religious and exhorted her to persevere.

As he pondered on the value of the Rosary, he decided to try to reform the sisters by means of it. He bought a supply of beautiful Rosaries and gave one to each nun, imploring them to say the Rosary every day, even going so far as to promise them that, if they would only say it faithfully, he would not try to force them to alter their lives. Wonderful and strange as it may seem, the nuns agreed to this pact and were glad to be given the Rosaries and promised to say them.

Little by little they began to give up their empty and worldly pursuits, letting silence and recollection come into their lives. In less than a year they all asked that the monastery be reformed.

So the Holy Rosary worked more changes in their hearts than the priest could have worked by exhorting and commanding them.

Thirty-Ninth Rose—Parish Transformed

A Danish priest used to love to tell how the very same improvement had occurred in his own parish. He always told his story with great rejoicing of soul because it gave such glory to Almighty God. He said:

> I had preached as compellingly as I could, touching on many aspects of our Holy Faith, and using every argument I could possibly think of, to get the people to amend their way of life. But in spite of all my efforts they went unconcernedly about their way as before; and it was then that I decided to preach the Holy Rosary.
>
> I told my congregations how precious it is and I taught them how to say it. I kept on preaching the Holy Rosary and the devotion took root in the parish. Six months later I was overjoyed to see that people had really changed for the better. How true it is, that this God-given prayer has divine power—the power to touch our hearts and to fill them with horror of sin and the love of virtue!

One day Our Lady said to Blessed Alan:

> Just as Almighty God chose the Angelic Salutation to bring about the Incarnation of His Word and the Redemption of mankind, in the same way, those who want to bring about moral reforms and who want people reborn in Jesus Christ, must honor me and greet me with the same salutation. I am the channel by which God came to men, and so, next to my Son Jesus Christ, it is through me that men must obtain grace and virtue.

I, who write this, have learned from my own experience that the Rosary has the power to convert even the most hardened hearts. I have known people who have gone to missions and who have heard sermons on the most terrifying subjects, without being in the least moved; and yet, after they had, on my advice, started to say the Rosary every day, they eventually became converted and gave themselves completely to God.

When I have gone back again to visit parishes, where I have given missions, I have seen a tremendous difference in them; in those parishes where people had given up the Rosary, they had generally fallen back into their sinful ways again, whereas in places where the Rosary was said faithfully, I found the people were persevering in the grace of God and were advancing each day in virtue.

Fortieth Rose—Admirable Effects

Blessed Alan De La Roche, Fr. Jean Dumont, Fr. Thomas, the chronicles of St. Dominic and other writers, who have seen these things with their own eyes, speak of the marvelous conversions that are brought about by the Holy Rosary. Great sinners— both men and women—have been converted after twenty, thirty, or even forty years of sin and unspeakable vice, because they persevered in saying the Holy Rosary. And these have been people who, beforehand, had been deaf to all pleading! I shall not tell you about those wonderful conversions here, because I do not want to make this book too long. And I am not even going to refer to those which I have seen with my very own eyes.

Dear reader, I promise you, that if you practice this devotion and help to spread it, you will learn more from the Rosary than from any spiritual book. And what is more, you will have the happiness of being rewarded by Our Lady in accordance with the promises that she made to St. Dominic, to Blessed Alan de la Roche and to all those who practice and encourage this devotion which is so dear to her. For the Holy Rosary teaches people about the virtues of Jesus and Mary, and leads them to mental prayer and to imitate Our Lord and Savior Jesus Christ. It teaches them to approach the Sacraments often, to genuinely strive after Christian virtues and to do all kinds of good works, as well as interesting them in the many wonderful indulgences which can be gained through the Rosary.

People are often quite unaware of how rich the Rosary is in indulgences. This is because many priests, when preaching on the Rosary, hardly ever mention indulgences and give rather a flowery and popular sermon which excites admiration, but scarcely teaches anything.

Be that as it may I shall say no more than to assure you, in the words of Blessed Alan de la Roche, that the Holy Rosary is the root and the storehouse of countless blessings. For through the Holy Rosary:

1. Sinners are forgiven;
2. Souls that thirst are refreshed;
3. Those who are fettered have their bonds broken;
4. Those who weep find happiness;
5. Those who are tempted find peace;
6. The poor find help;
7. Religious are reformed;
8. Those who are ignorant are instructed;
9. The living learn to overcome pride;
10. The dead (the Holy Souls) have their pains eased by suffrages.

One day, Our Lady said to Blessed Alan: "I want people, who have a devotion to my Rosary, to have my Son's grace and blessing during their lifetime and at their death, and, after their death, I want them to be freed from all slavery, so that they will be like kings wearing crowns and with scepters in their hands and enjoying eternal glory." Amen. So be it.

THE BROWN SCAPULAR

Our Lady once said to St. Dominic: "One day, through the Rosary and the Scapular, I will save the world." At Fatima, in 1917, when Our Lady made her final apparition on October 13, she was seen clothed in the habit of the Order of Our Lady of Mount Carmel—and Lucy, one of the seers, added that never was Our Lady as beautiful as she was then. Lucy also goes on to say that: "The Rosary and the Scapular are inseparable!" In one sense, we can look at the Rosary as being our spiritual sword and the Brown Scapular as our spiritual shield in our daily battle with the devil and the world. The following passages on the history, significance and role of the Brown Scapular are taken from *The Scapular of Carmel*, by the Prior General of the Carmelites, Most Rev. E.K. Lynch (1955).

1. THE HISTORY OF THE BROWN SCAPULAR

It's no exaggeration to say that the Scapular devotion is as universal as the Church. It would be difficult to find a Catholic who has not at least heard of it for, as Pius XII says, it is in the "first rank" of popular devotions to the Blessed Mother. And yet how many there are who know little or nothing about the origin of the Scapular.

Like many good and holy things that have come down to us from the past, the Scapular, to be understood properly, has to be seen in the light of its historical setting; to take it away from the century of its origin, is to deprive it of a great deal of its significance and to rob it of its value as a religious symbol.

Since the rise of monasticism a Scapular, consisting of two pieces of cloth joined at the shoulders and hanging down back and breast, has been a part of the monastic Habit. The fact that it hung from the shoulders, immediately suggested a spiritual meaning, for Christ spoke of the faith in terms of a burden to be carried— "My yoke," He said, "is sweet and my burden light." As the monk rose in the morning to begin a new day, the putting on of the Scapular reminded him that he had taken the sweet burden of divine service upon him and that the day ahead was to be all for God.

Medieval Origins

Coming as it did in the 13th century, the Friar Movement was bound to be affected by the feudal system which was then at its height. The Friars were, by profession if not by origin, poor men who identified themselves with the poorer classes and worked among them. Their Habit, even though similar to that of the monk, was that of the common folk. It was inevitable that the relation of vassal to lord, that dominated the whole economic, social and political life of the Middle Ages, would affect their religious outlook and that the timeless relation of creature to Creator would also be expressed in terms of it.

Living as we do in an age very different from that of the Middle Ages, in an age of growing independence, we find it hard to visualize the dependence of the vassal upon his lord. While Feudalism held sway, it was a matter of life and death to belong to a lord. The vassal's act of homage to the lord gave him the right of protection by the lord—something as important then as it is now.

Knowing how faith and actual living were one in the Middle Ages, one can see how feudal ideas influenced religious ideas and practices. We can also see how the Habit, of which the Scapular is the principal part, took on a new meaning. Being a man of God, the Friar was keenly aware that God is our one and only Master. Following the custom of the time, he presented himself before his Divine Master as the vassal presented himself before his lord — "to pay his homage" and to receive the investiture from his hands. The Scapular, hanging from the shoulders, was an outward sign that the friar was "God's man," that he belonged entirely to Him and that he would pay Him the homage of his whole life.

If we would only remember this symbolism each time we place the Scapular on our shoulders! One can easily see how the wearing of a Scapular could be a strong incentive to give a faithful and generous service in the vineyard of the Master. Even the sight of it could be a reminder of a promise made, but easily forgotten by the ordinary person.

Carmelites in Exile

As a result of the Saracen invasion, the Carmelites finally decided to leave Mount Carmel. Fortunately, they found staunch friends among the Crusaders, and accompanied them on their return journey to Europe. Some Carmelites settled in Cyprus, others in Italy, while others continued their journey to France and England. The English group found a benefactor in Lord de Grey, who gave them Aylesford in Kent.

Although the Carmelites found many favorably disposed to them in the West, they also encountered much opposition, so much so that, about the middle of the 13th century, it seemed as if their days were numbered as an Order. However, in 1246, at a Chapter held in Aylesford, they elected St. Simon Stock, an Englishman, as their Superior General.

Scapular Vision

As Simon saw the waves of opposition mounting higher and higher, he realized that Our Lady was his only hope. The Habit he wore spoke for itself for it was in her honor he had taken it. It had always reminded him that he was hers, and the long years of his life were an act of homage to her. He went to her as the vassal would to his lord and asked her for protection. Saluting her as the Flower of Carmel and the Star of the Sea he asked her for the *privilegium*—the protection a lord would give his vassals. In answer to his fervent prayer she appeared to him and, giving him the Scapular of his Order, she said: "This shall be a sign to you and to all Carmelites: whosoever dies wearing this shall not suffer eternal fire." The Promise Mary attached to the Scapular went far beyond Simon's expectations. It saved the Order, confirmed its Marian character and made Mary more a Mother than a Queen to it.

The Scapular Devotion is based on this spiritual Motherhood of Mary. The total dedication of the Order to her, made the Brown Scapular a sign of consecration to her. What more fitting sign could one find of her spiritual motherhood than a garment. When she brought forth her Firstborn, she wrapped Him up in swaddling clothes and it was she who wove the seamless garment by which He was known.

In a comparatively short time the wearing of the Brown Scapular spread to the whole Church and became the unmistakable mark of the good Catholic. Popes, kings, princes, nobles and humble folk alike lived and died in the hope of the promise made to St. Simon, and the Scapular devotion grew to be one of the leading devotions to the Mother of God. As a Marian devotion, it has stood the test of time and the seven centuries that have elapsed since the Vision, have served to reveal its beauty. It has kept generation after generation aware of its duty to call Mary blessed, and in the homage paid to her. Countless saints have come to realize that, to find her is to find life in her Son and to draw salvation from Him.

2. THE SPIRITUAL SIGNIFICANCE OF THE BROWN SCAPULAR

Millions are enrolled in it and wear it, without ever knowing what it should mean to them in their daily lives. It is evident that the Blessed Mother wishes to call our attention to the Brown Scapular, for Lucy, now Sister Mary of the Immaculate Heart, assures us that when Our Lady appeared to her at Fatima, she wore, on one occasion, the Carmelite Habit and held the Brown Scapular in her hand. Sister Mary of the Immaculate Heart also tells us that Mary was never so beautiful as she was on that occasion. This latest expression of love, for the Habit of Carmel, should focus the attention of the faithful upon it and bring all true lovers of Mary to wear it worthily.

God and Symbolism

From the beginning, God has been pleased to accommodate Himself to our ways of thinking and acting. The voice of nature is the language of heaven, and the invisible things of God are made known to us through the things we see, hear, taste, touch and smell. In all His dealings with us, we find God making use of a beautiful symbolism. In His dealings with us, God shows a preference for the simple things of life. What could be simpler than the manger of rough straw, in which His life here below began! That same simplicity went with Him to the grave. He instituted a sacramental system, in which seven simple elements became the efficient signs of divine grace. Since the natural function of water is to wash, He chose it to show us what His grace does for the soul stained by Original Sin. Since bread is the staff of life, He chose it to reveal how the grace of the Eucharist nourishes our souls. The symbolism of the whole sacramental system is designed to lead us into the knowledge of what divine grace is doing in the hidden depths of our souls.

The spiritual significance of a simple garment is perhaps as old as human society itself. A garment has always signified something more important than itself. After the Fall God clothed our first parents—and the garments He gave them were the sign of His forgiveness. Jacob made a coat of divers colors for his favorite son, Joseph, and Anna also made a coat for her son, Samuel. St. Paul does not hesitate to call the human nature of Christ a Habit. Our Lord compared grace to a wedding-garment, and St. Paul loved to use the same metaphor of a garment when exhorting us to put on Christ and to clothe ourselves with his virtues.

Spiritual Clothing

The garment, perhaps, that has the greatest significance for us is the one made by the Blessed Mother for the Infant Jesus. We can easily imagine our Blessed Mother making the swaddling clothes in preparation for the birth of her Son; and when she set out for Bethlehem she made sure to bring them with her, that she might wrap Him up and lay Him in the manger. Later, at Nazareth, she prepared the seamless garment He wore to Calvary. Our Blessed Lady's motherhood extends to all the redeemed. She is the Mother of the "*whole Christ*," that is, of the whole Mystical Body of Christ.

The Scapular is a sign of our special adoption by the Mother of God. The first and the greatest privilege it brings is that it envelops us in the special love of our Blessed Mother. It makes us "hers" in a very special way. She repeats to us the words of the prophet Ezechiel: "And I passed by thee and saw thee: and behold thy time was the time of lovers: and I spread my garment over thee and covered thy ignominy. And I swore to thee, and I entered into a covenant with thee...and thou becamest mine" (Ezek. 16:10).

A mother's love is the most practical thing in existence. It is never satisfied with words, but is always pouring itself out on someone. Mother love is also capable of the greatest sacrifices. It is born in suffering and time serves only to increase its generosity and service. If this is true of the mother love we have all experienced, what must be said of the love of her who became the Mother of Sorrows and the Queen of Martyrs for love of us? When we see her with the sword of Simeon plunged deeply into her heart, how can we ever doubt that her love for mankind is as practical as that of her Divine Son?

Mary's Protection

Through the alliance of the Scapular our Lady has called us the "sons of her choice," that our souls may live and we may be well used for her sake. The dazzling splendor of her holiness makes her the terror of demons. She is "terrible as an army in battle array" against all the forces of evil that would molest us or attempt to snatch us from under the mantle of her maternal protection. As the Queen of Angels, she can summon legions of heavenly hosts to our defense.

As long as we live our lives and finish our course under the sweet protection of her mantle, we have nothing to fear. Our path to heaven is made easy by her who crushed the serpent's head and shared the glorious victory of her risen Son. Our Lady is the Gate of Heaven, particularly to those whom she has clothed in the garments of her love: "Whithersoever thou shalt go, I will go; and where thou shalt dwell I also will dwell" (Ruth 1:16). The ever-vigilant eye of our Blessed Mother is always upon those who wear her Habit, and where her eye is there also is the love of her Heart to save and defend us. The might of her love follows us and whithersoever we go and wherever we dwell it is about us.

3. A PLEDGE OF EVERLASTING SALVATION

It is the teaching of our Holy Faith that no one can merit the gift of final perseverance. We have no lease upon the state of grace, no insurance against its loss. It does not follow that, because we are in the state of grace today, tomorrow will find us the friends of God and heirs to His Kingdom. We carry our treasure of divine grace in the earthen vessel of a fallen human nature, which is so easily broken. To continue the metaphor, one might say that it has been broken ever since the Fall and that our personal sins have weakened its powers of resistance.

The Danger of Losing Grace

Even though the Good Samaritan has left us His medicinal grace to heal the wounds left by sin, He has not taken away the tendencies and temptations that are a legacy of Original Sin. In our redeemed human nature, there is an inherent weakness which places sanctifying grace in constant danger of being lost. This moral weakness has led to the formation of bad habits and inclinations to sin which have their roots deep in our nature. Bad habits are not easily rooted out and, while they remain, the state of grace is in peril.

Another factor that enters into final perseverance is that of the time of our death. We could never merit that death will come when we are in the state of grace. This depends upon Divine Providence and lies outside the order of merit. Strictly speaking, a person could live for years in the state of grace and have the misfortune to fall into grievous sin. If death overtook him before he had a chance to go to confession, or to make an act of perfect contrition, he would be lost.

The Means of Final Perseverance

This doctrine of the Church disturbs our complacency and

brings us to throw ourselves—more and more—upon the mercy of God. He Who made us knows what is in man; He knows the clay of which we are formed and has promised that, if we rely upon Him, we shall not be tempted above our strength. Moreover, He has given His word that, if we use the means of salvation which He has left us, the crowning grace of final perseverance will be ours.

One of the greatest means of final perseverance we have is devotion to our Blessed Mother. It is the constant teaching of the Church that devotion to God's Mother is not only a means, but a pledge of eternal salvation. She is our life, our sweetness and our hope. She loves us with the same love she has for her Firstborn. She was made to be the Mother of Mercy, and her mission on earth and in heaven is not to judge, but to show mercy and to open her pierced Heart wider and wider to the poor banished children of Eve who cry to her for help. As St. Bernard says:

> She is impetuous in mercy; she is resistless in mercy. The duration of her mercy is unto the end of the sinner's life. The broadness of her mercy is unto the limits of the earth. The height of her mercy is unto heaven. The depth of her mercy is unto the lowest abyss of sin and sorrow. She is always merciful. She is only merciful. She is our Mother of mercy.

Mother of Mercy

If it is the property of God to be merciful and to spare, then, surely, it is also the very nature of the Mother of Mercy to pour forth her mercy even where there are no merits. The quality of her mercy is never strained; and the devil, into whose heart a ray of hope can never shine, is the only one excluded from her love. She sees in every soul, even in that of the most wretched, the image of her Son, and, if necessary, she would become again the Queen of Martyrs to save the least of her children.

Our Blessed Mother holds such a place in the economy of our redemption, that some do not hesitate to state that devotion to her is a necessary condition of salvation. "They who are not thy servants, O Mary," says St. Albert the Great, "shall perish." St. Bonaventure repeats the same thought when he says: "They

who neglect the service of Mary shall die in their sins." And again:
"For them from whom Mary turns away her face, there is not
even a hope of salvation." St. Ignatius of Antioch, a martyr of the
second century, writes: "A sinner can be saved only through the
holy Virgin who, by her merciful prayers, obtains salvation for so
many who, according to strict justice, would be lost."

Sign of Predestination

If a lack of devotion to her is a mark of eternal reprobation, a
constant love for her must be a sign of eternal salvation. Many
spiritual writers state that devotion to Mary is a sign of predestination. St. Alphonsus Liguori says: "It is impossible that a servant
of Mary be damned, provided he serves Her faithfully and commends himself to her maternal protection." St. Anselm writes:
"He who turns to Thee and is regarded by Thee cannot be lost."
St. Antonine is of the same opinion, saying: "As it is impossible
for them from whom Mary turns away her eyes of mercy to be
saved, so it is necessary that they, to whom She turns her eyes of
mercy and for whom She intercedes, be saved and glorified."

From the moment we are enrolled in the Scapular, we are
dedicated to her in a special way and have a special claim upon
her protection and intercession. The Scapular is her garment of
salvation. Her pursuing love will follow us to the end of life, en-
abling us to live and die in the state of grace. In virtue of the
alliance she has entered into with those who wear the Scapular,
she will never cease to do them good until they need her help no
longer.

God Is Not Mocked

Let us not conclude, however, that the Scapular is endowed
with some kind of supernatural power, which will save us no matter
what we do, or how much we sin. We might apply here what St.
Alphonsus says about devotion to Mary in general:

> When we declare that it is impossible for a servant of Mary to
> be lost, we do not mean those who by their devotion to Mary
> think themselves warranted to sin freely. We state that these reck-
> less people, because of their presumption, deserve to be treated

with rigor and not with kindness. We speak here of the servants of Mary who, to the fidelity with which they honor and invoke Her, join the desire to amend their lives. I hold it morally impossible that these be lost.

It is clear, from the words of St. Alphonsus, that a certain measure of fidelity is required on the part of those who wish to gain the special love and protection of Our Lady. The very wearing of the Scapular is, in itself, an act of devotion and when it is done faithfully, it renders habitual homage to its Queen. "Other pious practices," writes Fr. Chaignon, S.J., "are attached to certain times and to certain places, but the devotion to the Scapular belongs to all times and places. Thanks to my little Habit, wherever I am, whatever I am doing, Mary never sees me without seeing, on my body, an evidence of my devotion to her. Always and everywhere my Scapular pleads for me, recommends me to her tenderness, tells her that I love her and that I confide all my interests to her maternal care."

The constant, daily practice of wearing the Scapular is, therefore, an act of faithful homage to our Lady, but, as St. Alphonsus adds, the desire to amend one's life is also necessary, before we can be morally certain that she will be the cause of our eternal salvation. However, we should be careful not to place limits upon the mercy of her, who is the refuge of sinners and the Mother of mercy. In this age of measurement, we should beware of attempting to reduce our Blessed Mother's love for sinners to fixed formulas. If the father of the prodigal loved his wayward son so much, that he aroused the jealousy of the faithful one, why cannot our Blessed Mother love and save where others would hate and condemn? If she is a Mother for the sake of sinners, why can she not obtain from her Son that strong grace which compels even the rebellious will and bends it at the last towards God?

St. Alphonsus addresses her in the following words: "Thou canst relieve the most wretched and save the most abandoned." And St. Hilary says: "Even though one has been a sinner, if he has been devoted to Mary, he shall not perish for ever." Spiritual writers tell us that it was the intercession of Mary that brought about the conversion of the good thief. Up to his last moments he lived in crime and sin. What brought about his conversion? The prayer of Our Lady, standing at the foot of the Cross, won for him not only forgiveness, but a place in heaven that very day. During the course of history, the miracle of Calvary has been repeated over and over again. Sinners, in whom scarcely a glimmer of faith remained, have been saved through the "suppliant omnipotence" of that same Mother, who lives to save even the most wretched.

"God's love," says St. Augustine, "never deserts us." If this be true of the love of God for the sinner, it is, in a sense, even more true of the love of Mary, for her love is that of a Mother. Even though we may desert her, she will never desert us. The Scapular will always catch her eye of mercy and bring to her lips, from her compassionate heart, a prayer for our return. Of one thing we may be certain: her eyes of mercy will be upon those who wear her Scapular and she will admit defeat only at the gate of hell. Since the beauty of life is in her, she will do all in her power to put life where she finds death, strength where she finds weakness, and beauty of virtue where she finds the ugliness of sin. The one thing we should fear most is to forget to call upon her and to remind her of her promise to save us from hell.

Another point to remember is that enrollment in the Scapular brings us into the Order of Carmel to share its good things and to participate in its spiritual treasure of Masses, prayers and good works. In one of her letters to a friend, Celina Maudelonde, who had asked her for prayers for the return of her husband to the practice of his religion, the Little Flower, St. Therese, writes: "I am glad you have been enrolled in the holy Scapular. It is a sure sign of predestination; and moreover will it not unite you more intimately still with your little sisters of Carmel?" When the story of our salvation is known, perhaps it will be found that we have been granted the grace of a happy death through the prayers of our brothers and sisters in Carmel.

"There is a second reason," says Fr. Schultz, C.SS.R., "why those who wear the Scapular will save their souls: they will never be without the help of prayer." The Mother of God showed a vision of hell to the three little children of Fatima and said to them: "Pray for sinners: remember that many souls are lost because they have nobody to pray for them." The sinner who wears the Scapular has a whole world-wide Confraternity praying for him.

4. THE SIGN OF OUR PERFECT CONSECRATION TO MARY

"May it be to them a sign of their Consecration to the Most Sacred Heart of the Immaculate Virgin" wrote Pius XII in a letter to the Superior General of the Carmelites, on the occasion of the Seventh Centenary of the Brown Scapular. So, too, is our Scapular a sign of our True Devotion Consecration to the Blessed Virgin.

Devotion—Old and New

Devotion to the Mother of God is as old as the Church. One might say that it began when Christ called her by the name of Mother. Her own prophecy, that all generations would call her blessed, has been fulfilled to the letter—for the long history of the Church is full of praises and devotion towards her.

Like everything that comes from the heart, devotion varies from age to age. Love is always restless, moving and for ever seeking new ways of expression. This is, of course, as it should be for where there is life there is always renewal and variety.

The history of devotion to Mary reveals great variety. Every age has sought to honor her in its own way and, what is true of ages, is also true of peoples and countries. East and West are still one in love for her. Devotion to her reminds one of a great unfinished symphony directed by the Holy Ghost.

Consecration to Mary

The modern form of devotion to Mary is Consecration. Pius XII consecrated the entire world to her Immaculate Heart and, by word and example, he has encouraged this form of devotion to her. In his letter commemorating the Seventh Centenary of the Brown Scapular, he asked all the branches of the Carmelite Order to see in it a sign of their Consecration to Mary.

Strictly speaking, it is not correct to say that this form of Marian devotion is new, except in the sense that emphasis has been put on it in our day. As a matter of fact, devotion in the old and true sense of the term always meant Consecration, that is complete surrender of oneself. When the Holy Father asked all who wear the Scapular to see in it a sign of their Consecration to Mary, he simply focused attention upon the old and historical significance of the Carmelite Habit or Scapular. From the early days of Carmel its Habit has been a medium of Consecration to the Mother of God. Its oldest formula of profession was to God and to the Blessed Virgin Mary of Mount Carmel. The hermits on the Mount engaged in contemplation to honor her and the avowed purpose of their life was to imitate her. She was their Sister and Model. They imitated her and kept the word of God in their hearts and pondered upon it.

One might ask: what does Consecration mean? For our present purpose it simply means making a thing sacred by surrendering it to God. The man becomes a priest by being taken from among men and dedicated to the service of God; the cup becomes the chalice by being withdrawn from profane use and given over exclusively to the service of the altar; the place is made sacred by being reserved for divine worship. From the moment of Consecration the person, thing or place belongs to God in a special way. As St. Louis de Montfort puts it: "The most perfect Consecration to Jesus is nothing else but a perfect and entire Consecration of ourselves to the Blessed Virgin."

Consecration, however, should mean more than a formula that is soon forgotten. What we pledge to Mary is not just the moment, or even the day of our Consecration, but our whole life. We give her all that we are and all that we have in time and in eternity to become her property, if one could use the word. Consecration is total surrender, a complete giving up of oneself to her. That is what our True Devotion Consecration should achieve—a total surrender of oneself to Mary and her cause, which is none other than the cause of Jesus Christ.

The Scapular should be a constant reminder that we belong to her at all times and in all places and that she has a right to all our service. This is so easy to forget that we need to be constantly reminded of what we are and of the change that has taken place in our lives as a result of our Consecration. We are not different from the people of old, to whom God commanded Moses to say: "Tell them to make to themselves fringes in the corners of their garments, putting in them bands of blue that when they shall see them they shall remember all the commandments of the Lord and not follow their own thoughts and eyes, going astray after divers things" (Num. 15:38). We, too, could forget—but the fringes of the brown Scapular are there, around our necks, to make us always mindful of the sweet yoke of Mary that we have taken upon ourselves.

Consecration, therefore, is more than outward conformity to certain practices of devotion; it involves the whole of our life, more especially the mind and the heart. When one thinks of a consecrated life, the glorious example of Christ and of His Blessed Mother comes to mind. Christ's whole life was spent for the glory of his Father. He came not to do His own will, but the will of God the Father who sent Him. Even when His human nature recoiled in horror, from the bitter chalice of the Garden, His prayer was: "…not My will, but Thine be done." When the evening of his life came, He turned to His Father in heaven and confessed that He had sought only His glory upon the earth. The life, that began in the crib and ended on the cross, was a life of one totally consecrated to the Heavenly Father.

Mary the Perfect Imitation of Christ

The life of the Blessed Mother was a perfect replica of that of her Son. Her *fiat*, made to the Archangel, gives us the key to her entire life. She was always and everywhere the handmaid of the Lord and she lived to do His will. She kept every word that was spoken to her in her heart and made her life the incarnation of the Divine Will, as much as she knew it. When she told the waiters at the wedding feast to do what her Son would tell them, she revealed the secret of her own life and taught all of us the true meaning of the consecrated life.

Let us not think for one moment that a consecrated life after the example of Christ and his Holy Mother is too much to ask of us. Each one of us may say with St. Paul: "He loved me and He gave Himself up for me." As St. Bernard puts it: "He bought the whole of me with the whole of Himself." Since His Mother was a helper like Himself in the work of the redemption, can we not say of her, also, that she bought each and every one of us with the whole of herself? She was all things to all men, for she lived only to magnify the Lord and to rejoice always in Him. When she asks us, therefore, to give all we are and all we have to God through her, she is just asking us to follow her example.

Consecration to Mary brings an added burden to our shoulders; but where there is true love, it is a glorious privilege to serve. The proud boast of St. Paul was that he was the servant of Jesus Christ; and he challenged any power to separate him from the love of God that is in Christ Jesus. Our proud boast should be that we belong in a special way to Mary and that the service of our entire life is all too small a return for what she has done for us.

Slaves of Sin? Slaves of Mary?

What keeps us back, sometimes, from making a complete surrender of ourselves, is our ignorance of the true purpose of life. We were not made for ourselves, but for God and we can achieve true greatness and nobility only by living for God. Experience shows that human life must be given to someone, or to something, and that if we do not offer it to God, it becomes the slave of some low passion. "The men of the world," says St. Ambrose, "have as many masters as they have passions. Immodesty comes and says to them, you are mine, because you covet sensual pleasures. Covetousness says, you are mine; for the gold and silver you possess are the price of your liberty. All the vices come and say, you are mine." Every man born into this world serves some master and offers his life on some altar. And if our master is not God, it is bound to be some low passion that makes us its slave. It is better, therefore, to be a slave of the Blessed Virgin and heaven, than to be enslaved to our passions, the world and, ultimately, hell.

How uplifting it is for us to know that Mary, the Queen of heaven, has said to each of us: thou art mine. The special adoption that is ours through the Consecration of the Scapular may be expressed in the words of Ezechiel: "I passed by thee and saw thee...and I spread my garment about thee, and I entered into a covenant with thee...and thou becamest mine " (Ezek. 16:8).

Acquiring the Spirit of Mary

To become "hers" in deed as well as in name, we must first of all strive to cultivate her spirit, for it is the spirit and not the letter that vivifies and gives meaning to our life. "If any man," says St. Paul, "have not the spirit of Christ, he is not His" (Rom. 8:9). The same applies to Mary: if we have not her spirit in us, we have no part with her and our Consecration to her loses its meaning. We should all take to heart the counsel of the Venerable Michael of St. Augustine: "May Mary's spirit be in us all, that by that spirit we may live."

There is no need to say that the spirit is the deepest force in us; for not only is it rooted in the soul, but it bends all the powers of the soul in a certain direction and makes them means to an end. It governs mind and heart and, through them, becomes life and action.

If, therefore, the spirit of Mary is in us, it gives a new meaning to life and converts all we do into the service of her and of her Divine Son. It lifts us above the passing things of time, lending vision, beauty and eternal value to even the smallest actions. It gives light to our minds and makes her ways ours. The spirit that rejoiced only in God, is sure to transform our heart, bringing us to love what she loved and to hate what she hated.

Consecration puts a seal upon the heart, but if the spirit of Mary is not in it, then it is not clean and the seal will soon be broken. The clean, unspotted heart is the only one that is worthy of the Immaculate: it is created in us by living in her spirit day by day. That is what we are seeking to achieve by the True Devotion Consecration.

However, let us not think that we can obtain her spirit by the flick of a switch. Her spirit is something that we progressively acquire, like a child that gradually learns more and more from its parents by simply being in their presence—year after year.

If we are to cultivate the mind and heart of Mary, we must be faithful to the dying command of her Son to behold her. She is "the mirror of fashion and the mold of form" for every soul that is consecrated to her, and if we do not look into that mirror and mold our life accordingly, we are certain to lose sight of our ideal. Every wearer of the Scapular should follow the counsel of the great Carmelite, Bostius: "May the loving memory of Mary accompany you day and night, wherever you are, wherever you go, in whatever you do. May it be part of your conversation, your recreation, your sorrow and your rest....You are indeed my heart and my soul, O Virgin Mother."

Obligations towards Mary

If Consecration to Mary is to be a power for good in our daily lives, it must show itself in a sense of filial piety which will keep her in our minds and hearts. As her chosen sons, our attitude towards her should be that of her First-born who lived with her, obeyed her, leaned upon her and grew up in wisdom and grace under her motherly guidance and protection. It is an abiding sense of being "hers" that will enable us to live our Consecration to her.

The Scapular should be a constant reminder of the obligations we have taken upon ourselves. Its wearer is doubly clothed; for at Baptism he is clothed with the white robe of baptismal innocence, which he is commanded to carry unspotted to the white Throne of God, and, at the time of his investiture in the Scapular, he receives the brown robe of Mary, which reminds him of his obligation to clothe himself with the virtues of the Blessed Mother.

If Christ, says St. Bernard, is our garment, He should be visible in our person. And if Mary is our garment, she too should be visible in our person and we should reveal her virtues in our conduct. No one should ever see the Scapular without seeing something of Our Lady in its wearer. The consecrated life should always bear the good fruit of love, charity, kindness, meekness, gentleness and prayerfulness; it should be the bearer of Christ to others. "Mary gave us Christ," says Bossuet, "and we should see to it that, in giving ourselves to her, we give her back another Christ." When Christ lives again in us and is visible in our daily lives, then our Consecration to Mary, His Mother, is all it should be.

The saintly monk of our own time, Dom Marmion, was deeply devoted to Mary and after Holy Communion, while Christ was present in his soul, he would re-consecrate himself to her by simply saying: "Mother, behold thy son." It is when Christ lives in us and abides with us that we are the sons of His Mother. It is the living image of Christ that makes the consecrated life. And there is no better place to find it than in the life of his Mother.

How beautifully all we have written about Consecration to Mary may be expressed in the words of Ecclesiasticus: "Put thy feet into her fetters and thy neck into her chains. Bow down thy shoulder and be not grieved with her bands. Come to her with all thy mind, and keep her ways with all thy power. Search for her and she shall be made known to thee and when thou hast gotten her, let her not go: for in the latter end thou shalt find rest in her, and she shall be turned to thy joy. Then shall her fetters be a strong defense for thee, and a firm foundation, and her chain a robe of glory. For in her is the beauty of life and her bands are a healthful binding. Thou shalt put her on as a robe of glory and thou shalt set her upon thee as a crown of joy" (Eccles. 6:25-32).

5. OUR AFFILIATION TO THE ORDER OF MOUNT CARMEL

"I have brought you into the land of Carmel to eat the fruit thereof, and the best things thereof" (Jer. 2:7).

When we think of the many pitfalls along the way to heaven and remember our own blindness and weakness, it is consoling to know that we may travel the lonely path, enveloped in the special love of God's Blessed Mother. Wherever her Scapular is, there is her watchful eye to guide our faltering footsteps. It turns her eyes of mercy towards us and drives our hellish foes far from us, and in the strength of the grace her love obtains, we press forward to the gate of heaven.

Mary's special protection in life, in death and after death is not the only spiritual value the Scapular possesses. Both the Order and the Church have opened their spiritual treasures to endow it. From the time of our enrollment in the Scapular, we share in all the Masses, prayers and good works of the entire Order—the Church has made it her great sacramental.

It is interesting to recall how the Scapular, which is the habit of the Religious of Mount Carmel, found its way outside the Order to carry its spiritual benefits to those who live in the world. The century in which the Carmelite Order came to the West was the age of medieval splendor. It was an age in which the great Religious Orders rendered outstanding service to the Church by preaching their particular devotions. The Dominicans preached the Rosary; the Franciscans, penance; and the Carmelites, their devotion to Our Lady of the Scapular. These devotions soon became popular and, in the course of time, they formed a bond of unity with the Orders, which was responsible for the rise of Confraternities and Third Orders. Those who wished to be affiliated with the Dominican Order were devoted to the Rosary; those who wished to be identified with the Franciscan Order wore the cord of St. Francis and practiced penance; and those who preferred the Carmelite Order wore the Habit in miniature form and had a special devotion to our Lady of Mount Carmel.

The Third Order and the Confraternity

The letters of affiliation, which these men and women received from the Order, entitled them to a share in its Masses, prayers and good works and, in some cases, gave them the right to be buried in the Habit. Soon they came to be known as brothers and sisters of the Brothers of Our Lady.

The Third Order came into existence later, although we do not know the exact date of its inception. The Bull of John XXII, dated July 8, 1318, proves that it was in existence before this date.

One might ask what the difference is between the Confraternity and the Third Order. If members of both organizations share the same promise and are affiliated to the same Order, what difference could there be? In his little work on the Third Order, Fr. O'Shea, O. Carm., explains the difference very clearly:

> The purpose of the Third Order,, he writes, is something very definitely in advance of the aim of the Confraternity. The Confraternity admits to participation in the privileges of the Order by what may be called affiliation. The person, so admitted, is not and cannot be called a member of the Order. He shares in its spiritual life and privileges, but he does not in any sense live the life of a Carmelite, neither is he bound to the observance of the counsels of perfection, nor of those other means which we must make use of, who are called by God to the interior life of the Order.

> The Carmelite Order is, for the members of the Confraternity, a great external aid to salvation by helping them with its prayers and good works and by affording participation in the indulgences and spiritual privileges granted to it by the successors of St. Peter. It regards them as its children, who are especially beloved by our Blessed Lady. On the other hand, the Third Order, as the name indicates, gives an actual membership of the Order and carries with it the obligation of living according to a rule, which involves, to a certain extent, the practice of the evangelical counsels.

> What membership of the Third Order does imply, therefore, is that it places one in a better and more secure way of serving God and of attaining to eternal salvation. This is the great outstanding advantage of membership of the Third Order; it gives the whole reason for its existence, which is to enable people living in the world, to follow in a degree suitable to their state in life the Carmelite Rule of St. Albert.

There are two forms of the Confraternity: the organized Confraternity, which is attached to a Church and has officers and members just like any other parish organization; and the unorganized Confraternity, to which all who are enrolled in the Brown Scapular belong.

Few wearers of the Scapular realize what their association with the Order, through membership in the Third Order or the Confraternity, means in terms of spiritual benefits. The Carmelite Order is the spiritual family of Our Blessed Mother. It is made up of the First, Second and Third Orders.

Sharing in a Spiritual Treasure

As an Order that has given countless saints to heaven it has, to speak humanly, a certain standing in the sight of God, and the long centuries of existence have left it with a spiritual treasury of merits, that must be pleasing in the sight of God. Membership, in even the unorganized Confraternity, makes us a part of that great family of Mary and entitles us to share in all the Masses, prayers and good works of its members.

This is something the world cannot understand; its policy is "an eye for an eye and a tooth for a tooth," and all that it has is too little for itself. But since love is the bond that binds all together in Carmel, charity is the guiding principle of its life. For hundreds of years, the Brothers of Our Lady have persevered in prayer with her, for all who wear her holy Habit; love for her has led them to bear each other's burdens, to support each other on the way to heaven.

Never Without Help

This thought, that we have a spiritual family behind us, to sustain us by its never-ceasing prayer, is one of the great, strong props of our spiritual life. What a mighty volume of prayer it is that goes up to the throne of God from Carmel! Long, indeed, is the litany of Carmel's saints; and those, who have joined their Queen in Heaven, cannot forget those here on earth, whom they see wearing the same Habit and living in the same faith as they did.

The Little Flower promised to spend her heaven doing good upon earth; the roses of her love are bound to fall in the greatest profusion upon those who belong to her beloved Carmel. She is just one among the many Carmelite saints who are spending their heaven praying for the wearers of the Scapular. The united prayers and good works of the whole Order, here below, must also speak most eloquently on our behalf. The prayers of St. Teresa and her nuns retarded the Protestant Reformation and saved the faith for millions of souls.

This is just a single instance of how powerful the prayer of Carmel is to move heaven. Hands lifted up in prayer are the most powerful hands outside heaven: they succeed when all else fails.

When we feel the need of moral and spiritual support, we often ask our friends to say a prayer for our intention. When we belong to even the Confraternity, we have thousands and thousands of brothers and sisters in Carmel praying for us always; and when we are dead and forgotten by our nearest and dearest, they will continue to intercede for us until we reach the, gate of heaven and the arms of our Blessed Mother.

What profound charity there is in the prayer which the Order offers for those who have put on the Habit:

> Look, O Lord, on this tiny flock which, having cast aside the world and the desires of the flesh, finds refuge in its humility under the wing of thy protection. Shield these devout souls with the sign of thy invincible Cross and fill them with the interior virtue of our holy Order that they may be adorned by faith, strengthened by hope, and inflamed by charity. Inasmuch as they have renounced Satan and sought Thee as their only Spouse and true Father, pour over them the dew of Thy blessings. Pardon all their sins, strengthen their hearts in the hour of temptation and keep their minds free from sinful desires, so that, stripped of all unlawful longings, they may seek after the Cross alone. May they flee the world like Magdalen and live a heavenly life here below that, one day, with thy saints they may enter into the enjoyment of the things the eye has not seen, nor the ear heard, nor the heart longed for. Through the same Christ...(Reception: Carmelite Ritual).

Special Privileges

In order to promote the Scapular devotion and bring as many as possible under the mantle of Mary's special protection, Popes Clement VII and Clement X decreed that all, who wear the Scapular, participate in a special manner in the fruits, not only the spiritual works of the Carmelites, to whom they are united as a Confraternity, but, also, in all the good done throughout the whole Church. Pope Sixtus IV opened to them the spiritual treasures of the Dominican and Franciscan Orders by granting them all the privileges, indulgences and favors which are granted to the cord of St. Francis, to the Rosary of Our Blessed Lady, or to any Confraternity whatsoever, so that "they enjoy them as much as if they were really members of these Sodalities."

There are many "good things," which Carmel shares with those who wear its Habit, and we can well understand why Blessed Claude states that the Scapular devotion "is the most favored of all Marian devotions." How badly we need the help of Carmel! No matter how poor we may be—our spiritual wants far exceed our material ones—we can all say with the Psalmist: "I am needy and poor" (Ps. 69:6). When we reflect upon our spiritual poverty and remember how unworthy we are to plead our cause before God, it helps to know that we have the support of so many Masses, prayers and good works. Many a poor sinner is saved through the prayers of a good mother or kind friend. St. Monica's persevering prayer converted her prodigal son and the only return she asked, for so many years of prayer, was a remembrance at the altar. Carmel is a prayerful Mother that never forgets her children, and eternity, alone, will tell how many have gained heaven through her never-failing intercession for those who wear the Habit of her Queen.

6. REFLECTING MARY—THE IMAGE OF CHRIST

> May they all see in this keepsake of the Virgin Herself (Scapular) a mirror of humility and purity; may they read in the very simplicity of the Garment a concise lesson in modesty and simplicity (Pope Pius XII).

When God wanted Moses to build the Ark, He called him to the Mountain, showed him a plan and commanded him to follow it accurately. Our vocation summons us to another Mount—Carmel—where we are shown the pattern of life that Our Lady of Mount Carmel wishes us to follow. She is the living pattern of all who live in Carmel with Her.

Prototype of the Perfect Christian

As we enter her blessed Land of Carmel to eat the fruits and the good things thereof, she addresses us in the words of Ecclesiasticus: "I am the mother of fair love, and of fear, and of knowledge, and of holy hope. In me is all grace of the way and of the truth: in me is all hope of life and of virtue. Come over to me all ye that desire me; and be filled with my fruits. For my spirit is sweet above honey: and my inheritance above honey and the honeycomb."

Addressing Christ, John of St. Samson said to Him:

> Nothing brings before our eyes in a better way thy humanity and divinity than that which Mary has done outwardly and inwardly by deeds, words and the conduct of her whole life. She is a most life-like representation of Thee, a copy of Thee to the extent that when we understand her perfections we understand Thee; we behold thy goodness in hers, thy love in hers just as we behold her goodness and love in thine. We must, therefore, contemplate her in her exterior and interior goodness, as we do Thee, and in *a way that exceeds all natural speculation, no matter how pure, simple, exalted and fruitful it may be. But if that which one sees in her, transcends all understanding and comprehension, how much less can one understand what is hidden in her! Such things must be admired, revered and contemplated in the delightful quiet of an unspeakable, profound and secret silence. To gaze on them is to be ravished and spell-bound because in her we behold the deepest revelation of Thyself.*

Mary is all this and more. She is the living image of Christ, the deepest and most beautiful revelation of Him to the poor banished children of Eve. She is the first fruit of the Redemption, the first and greatest of the Redeemed in whom one finds God's original design for human living in all the splendor of original justice. She is the prototype of the perfect Christian and of the Church. It was surely with her in mind that John compared the Church to a woman clothed with the sun, the moon under her feet and a crown of twelve stars about her head. In the words of Chesterton: "She sums up all the Church has to say to humanity." Centuries ago, Origen stated that no one can understand the Gospel of John, who has not leaned on the breast of Christ and taken Mary for his Mother.

Carmel took Her for its Mother and its first rule is to behold Her in the radiance and splendor of her virtues. Since she is the Mother of all and the world's first love, all are devoted to her and call her by the sweet name of Mother.

Immaculate Purity

The spotless purity of Mary became the pearl of great price which she hid in the Land of Carmel and which every generation of Carmelites has lived to find. Her immaculate purity led her to consecrate all her love to God and it gave her life a singleness of purpose that made her soul the living image of Christ. It became fruitful in every virtue and she has become the joyful Mother of many.

Mary has inspired all generations of Carmelites to offer God the sacrifice of the clean heart. Their holy ambition was not simply to avoid sin but to purify their hearts of every attachment to creatures. They knew that a divided love is unworthy of God and it was their desire to love Him with their whole hearts that urged them to cleanse themselves from every attachment. Since this purification of soul must be accomplished before one can enter heaven, one can see why the Scapular Devotion is intimately bound up with release from Purgatory.

In this sex-ridden age when the virtues of purity, chastity and modesty are not only neglected but despised, one wonders what the future holds for society. It was devotion to Mary that refined the ways and manners of men, sanctified the home and exalted these virtues. The crude materialism, of the present, rejects them and pagan vice is finding its way back into the lives of men.

Mary's spotless purity made her soul the living image of the holiness of God and of the Church, the Spouse of Christ. Souls that follow her example reflect this heavenly splendor and prepare themselves for union with God. They see God even in this life and will see Him face to face in the next.

The Scapular should be a constant reminder of the absolute purity of Mary and of our duty to imitate her. It should separate us from all that is not holy and inspire us to greater and greater purification of our lives. Blessed, indeed, are the clean of heart for they shall see God.

Mary and the Word of God

St. Luke records how Mary "kept all the things that were said to Her pondering them in her heart." She made her heart the living library of every word that came to her from God; so much so that one may call her the Mother of the contemplative soul.

St. Thomas calls Scripture "the Heart of Christ"—for it reveals His Heart. Mary saw God in every sacred word that reached her. The same Holy Spirit that overshadowed her, also formed Christ in the body of Holy Scripture. In the word, she found life and unbroken union with God.

The word of God was like a seed, planted in her soul, which grew like the grain of mustard seed, to be the greatest of all living things; and when the time came for her to say "be it done unto me according to thy word," she had already conceived the word in her heart. Her Immaculate Heart became the mirror of that of her Son: she was the one most like Him. "Behold," cried Dante, "the face most like Christ's; its brightness alone can prepare you to see Him."

The burning desire of her soul is to form her Son in us, whom grace has made His brothers. How easy it should be to find Him in her. As the moon reflects the blazing light of the sun, so does she reflect His light. As Pope St. Pius X says: "This copy of Christ, the closest human nature can produce, is more suitable to our stature."

All for God and God Alone

The way to become all God wants us to be, is Mary's way. Virtue can grow from no seed that is not the word of God planted in our souls, covered with the warm love of our hearts and watered by the living water of divine grace. If we want to grow into Christ and live in Him, we must read and meditate upon His word and thereby be transfigured into new creatures.

Mary was so intent upon the word, that it opened the depths of her soul to God and immolated her whole being to His will. Her words—"behold the handmaid of the Lord; be it done unto me according to Thy word"—reveal how she lived in God's will. Since she kept nothing back, God gave her everything and the handmaid became the Queen of Heaven. Sanctity invaded her whole being and He, who is Holy, did great things for her.

Here again she is the model of total surrender to God. It is not enough to keep our hearts clean: they must be given to God that He may possess them. We die to self, so that we may live to Him, and the life that is lived in His Will is bound to become holy.

The Consecration of the Scapular has no other meaning than this. Carmel's Habit is a symbol of surrender, of service and devotion. When it is received we are reminded that it is a symbol of the yoke of Christ and of the burden that is light when carried with Mary's help. It makes us Mary's and the command she gives us is "whatsoever He shall say to you, do ye." We cast aside the world and the desires of the flesh and live to clothe ourselves with the new man, who was created according to God in justice and holiness of life.

Mary's Way—the Easiest, Shortest and Most Perfect

To live as Mary did seems to ask too much of weak, human nature and when we are tempted to think this way, we should recall the simplicity of her life. The Little Flower reminds us that her own life was "wholly commonplace" and she could not listen to the sermon that put her above the power of imitation of the ordinary person. She did the simple things, of what we would call a primitive household, in such an ordinary way that she attracted no attention. The whole value of her work lay in the spirit of consecration to God's will that motivated it. The Scapular is a symbol of this true instinct of simplicity and ordinariness. It is the life that we live, day in and day out, that glorifies Him and our love for Him should be so great, that it cannot be expressed any other way. If we offer our life, as it is, to God, to do as He wills, then His holiness is sure to invade it, influence it and change it.

Lover of the Eucharist

Mary's life was centered in the Eucharist and she was a very intimate part of it—both as a Sacrifice and a Sacrament. It was due to her that Christ was able to give us His flesh to eat and His blood to drink. Knowing that He was both Priest and Victim, she prepared Him for Calvary and, when the day of sacrifice arrived, she offered herself in union with Him. Did She receive Him in Holy Communion? It could well be that she was in the room of the Last Supper, for it was a custom that the Mother should light the lamp that marked the beginning of the Passover. She also lived in John's house and since the Beloved Disciple surely did as Christ commanded, when He said "Do this in commemoration of Me," one may take it for granted that she received her God and her Son in the Blessed Sacrament.

The Living Bread transformed her life and drew her to Himself. If Paul could say "I live, now not I, but Christ liveth in me," then how must Christ have lived in the Mother He loved so much! The great Lover of the Eucharist, the Little Flower, cried out "O Host sacred and divine, O Bread of exiles, it is not I that lives— my life comes all from Thee." After the death of her Son, Mary was the great exile of heaven and it was the Host, sacred and divine, that transfigured her whole being. True devotion to Mary will also show itself in love for the Eucharist.

The Eucharist is the sacrament of our union with Christ. In the words of Elizabeth of the Trinity, He wants us to be another humanity in which He may renew the whole mystery of his life here below. He wishes us to abide in Him as Mary did that He may draw us to Himself for ever.

The Scapular, which originated as an apron, should remind us that we are here to serve. Christ said that He came to serve, not to be served, and Mary declared herself the handmaid. We, her children, should live to serve others. Mary was a woman of action as well as of prayer; she crushed the serpent's head and is like "an army in battle array" against all the enemies of her Son. We must join forces with her. Her arms were all spiritual. Hands lifted up in prayer are more powerful than the hands that strike in battle; lives patterned on hers are more eloquent than words and the deeds we do in union with her are full of redemptive power. As we rise, morning after morning, let us ask her to use us today.

WEEK FOUR

INTRODUCTION TO WEEK FOUR: KNOWING JESUS

In this fourth period of preparation, we approach the goal or real purpose of St. Louis Marie de Montfort's *True Devotion to Mary*. This devotion is simply the shortest, safest and quickest way of knowing, loving and serving Our Lord Jesus Christ—which is also the ultimate purpose of our existence. Yet, as St. Therese of the Child Jesus used to bewail: "Jesus *is so little loved, because He is so little known!*"

Here on earth, two of the principal ways in which we can come to know and love Jesus are the Cross and Communion. If we were to try and simplify it still further, then the Sacrifice of the Mass would say it all. For the Mass is both a Sacrifice (the Cross) and a Sacrament (Communion). If we want to find Jesus, then we will find Him in the Holy Sacrifice of the Mass. We arrive at an ever deeper knowledge and understanding of Christ by entering more and more into the spirit of the Mass, which is none other than the spirit of Jesus. It is through the Mass that we accomplish our principal duties towards God—adoration, propitiation, petition and thanksgiving. In the Mass, through the Gospel readings, we continually dwell upon the life and spirit of Jesus; His spirit is also handed down to us through the writings of His immediate disciples; the Mass imparts to us the sacrificial spirit of Christ that led Him to work tirelessly for the salvation of sinners. It is in the Mass, during Holy Communion, that we enter into a most intimate union with Our Lord Jesus Christ. It is

by a fruitful reception of that Sacrament, that we are sanctified
and transformed into other "Christs" and receive the graces and
the strength to continue Christ's salvific work, as His instruments,
in the world around us.

St. Louis de Montfort's recommended meditations should
certainly help us grow in this knowledge of Our Lord, and, hopefully, once we know more about Him, we will also grow in our
love of Him and in our desire to do something for Him. The
most effective way of showing our love of Him and furthering
the growth of His kingdom, is by taking up our crosses and carrying them out of love of God. Our Lord Himself said:

If you want to be my disciple, take up your cross and follow
me.

If the Head of the Mystical Body—Who is the Way, the Truth
and the Life—passed by the way of the cross, then it would be
spiritual suicide for the Mystical Body to go in an opposite direction to Its Head. In the Cross is salvation; in the Cross is satisfaction for sin; in the Cross is peace; in the Cross is the power of
conversion; in the Cross is our merit and our glory. Let us boast,
with St. Paul, in nothing else but the Cross of Our Lord Jesus
Christ—a Cross we have the honor of sharing. Thus, this week
we will speak of the Cross.

Though St. Louis Marie De Montfort did not recommend
his own work, *Letter to the Friends of the Cross,* as part of the
preparations, we have, nevertheless, included it among the meditations. The most obvious reason for St. Louis failing to recommend the *Letter,* is the fact that it was not at that time a published
work, and therefore inaccessible to the vast majority of people.

However, Our Lord is not only found in the Cross, He is also
present—Body, Blood, Soul and Divinity—in the Holy Eucharist. The Eucharist is both a Sacrifice (of the Cross) and a Sacrament that communicates Our Lord and His graces to us. The
Eucharist strengthens us and makes light the burden of the Cross.
Our Lord Himself says: "Come to me, all you that labor and are
burdened, and I will refresh you. Take up my yoke upon you and
learn of me, because I am meek and humble of heart: and you

shall find rest for your souls. For my yoke is sweet and my burden light!" (Mt. 11:28-30).

To know Jesus, we must first find Him and where on earth will we find Him, but in the Eucharist? If we ignore Him there, then we seek Him in vain elsewhere—for that is where He primarily wanted to be found, known and adored. It is when we receive Him in Holy Communion that it can truly be said: "The kingdom of God is within you!"

Our Lord could and would do so much more for us, if we would only enter into that intimate union that can be ours in Holy Communion. Yet, today, the world increasingly ignores, neglects and even disbelieves Our Lord's Real Presence among men.

The *Imitation of Christ* so rightly says:

Alas, how little is what I do! What a short time I spend when I am preparing myself for Communion! Rarely am I recollected, rarely free from all distraction! Surely, in the saving presence of Thy Godhead, no unbecoming thought should arise, nor any created thing lay hold of me—for it is not an angel, but the Lord of Angels, Whom I am about to receive as my guest!...Why then am I not more on fire before Thy awesome presence? Why do I not prepare myself, with greater care, to take up Thy holy things?...How great ought to be the reverence and devotion which I and all Christian people should have in the presence of this Sacrament!...Many rush to various places to visit the relics of the saints and are astonished to hear of their wonderful works; they look upon the vast buildings of their shrines and kiss their bones enwrapped in silks and gold....Often, in seeing such things, there is no more than a curiosity of men and the novelty of what they look upon, but with no real repentance and little fruit of better living being carried home. But here, in the Sacrament of the Altar, Thou art wholly present and where the abundant fruit of salvation is fully received....In this Sacrament, spiritual grace is conferred; and lost virtue made good in the soul; and beauty, marred by sin, returns....It must be a matter for grief and great pity that, lukewarm and negligent, we are not drawn, with greater affection, to receive Christ.... It is to be greatly lamented that many show such little esteem for this saving Mystery, which makes heaven glad and preserves the whole world. O, the blindness and hardness of heart that does not more highly prize so unspeakable a gift; and from daily custom, slides away into a disregard of it (*Imitation of Christ* Bk. 4, ch. 1).

By a much more fervent participation in the Sacrifice of the Mass and a more fruitful reception of the Sacrament of the Eucharist, our understanding and appreciation of the Cross of Jesus will greatly increase, not to mention our growth in the true spirit of Christ, whereby we will be able to say with St. Paul: "...with Christ I am nailed to the cross. And I live, now not I: but Christ liveth in me" (Gal. 2:19-20).

RECOMMENDED PRAYERS FOR WEEK FOUR

Litany to the Holy Ghost
Litany of the Sacred Heart of Jesus
Litany of the Holy Name of Jesus
St. Louis de Montfort's "Prayer to Jesus"
O Jesus Living in Mary
Ave Maris Stella
(*Each prayer need not be said daily.*)

Litany of the Holy Ghost

Lord, have mercy on us,
Christ, have mercy on us
Lord, have mercy on us
Father, all powerful,
Have mercy on us.
Jesus, Eternal Son of the Father,
Redeemer of the world, *Save us.*
Spirit of the Father and the Son, boundless life of both,
Sanctify us.
Holy Trinity, *Hear us.*
Holy Ghost, Who proceedest
from the Father and the Son, *Enter our hearts.*
Holy Ghost, Who art equal to the Father and the Son,
Enter our hearts.
Promise of God the Father, *Have mercy on us.*
Ray of heavenly light,
Author of all good,
Source of heavenly water,
Consuming fire,
Ardent charity,
Spiritual unction,
Spirit of love and truth,
Spirit of wisdom and understanding,
Spirit of counsel and fortitude,
Spirit of knowledge and piety,
Spirit of the fear of the Lord,
Spirit of grace and prayer,
Spirit of peace and meekness,
Spirit of modesty and innocence,
Holy Ghost, the Comforter,
Holy Ghost, the Sanctifier,
Holy Ghost, Who governest the Church,
Gift of God, the Most High,
Spirit Who fillest the universe,
Spirit of the adoption of the children of God,
Holy Ghost, *inspire us with horror of sin.*

Holy Ghost, *come and renew the face of the earth.*
Holy Ghost, *shed Thy light in our souls.*
Holy Ghost, *engrave Thy law in our hearts.*
Holy Ghost, *inflame us with the flame of Thy love.*
Holy Ghost, *open to us the treasures of Thy graces.*
Holy Ghost, *teach us to pray well.*
Holy Ghost, *enlighten us with Thy heavenly inspirations.*
Holy Ghost, *lead us in the way of salvation.*
Holy Ghost, *grant us the only necessary knowledge.*
Holy Ghost, *inspire in us the practice of good.*
Holy Ghost, *grant us the merits of all virtues.*
Holy Ghost, *make us persevere in justice.*
Holy Ghost, *be Thou our everlasting reward.*

Lamb of God, Who takest away the sins of the world,
 Send us Thy Holy Ghost.
Lamb of God, Who takest away the sins of the world,
 Pour down into our souls the gifts of the Holy Ghost.
Lamb of God, Who takest away the sins of the world,
 Grant us the Spirit of wisdom and piety.

V. Come, Holy Ghost! Fill the hearts of Thy faithful.
R. And enkindle in them the fire of Thy Love.

Let us pray

Grant, O merciful Father, that Thy Divine Spirit enlighten, inflame and purify us, that He may penetrate us with His heavenly dew and make us fruitful in good works; through our Lord Jesus Christ, Thy Son, Who with Thee, in the unity of the same Spirit, liveth and reigneth forever and ever. *R. Amen.*

Litany of the Sacred Heart

Lord, have mercy on us.
Christ, have mercy on us.
Lord, have mercy on us.
Christ, hear us.
Christ, graciously hear us
God the Father of heaven, *Have mercy on us.*
God the Son, Redeemer of the world,
God, the Holy Ghost,
Holy Trinity, one God,
Heart of Jesus, Son of the eternal Father,
Heart of Jesus, formed by the Holy Ghost in the Virgin
Mother's womb,
Heart of Jesus, substantially united to the Word of God,
Heart of Jesus, of infinite Majesty,
Heart of Jesus, holy Temple of God,
Heart of Jesus, tabernacle of the Most High,
Heart of Jesus, house of God and gate of Heaven,
Heart of Jesus, glowing furnace of charity,
Heart of Jesus, vessel of justice and love,
Heart of Jesus, full of goodness and love,
Heart of Jesus, abyss of all virtues,
Heart of Jesus, most worthy of all praise,
Heart of Jesus, King and center of all hearts,
Heart of Jesus, wherein are all the treasures of wisdom and
knowledge,
Heart of Jesus, wherein dwelleth all the fullness of the Godhead,
Heart of Jesus, in Whom the Father is well pleased,
Heart of Jesus, of Whose fullness we have all received,
Heart of Jesus, desire of the everlasting hills,
Heart of Jesus, patient and rich in mercy,
Heart of Jesus, rich unto all who call upon Thee,
Heart of Jesus, fount of life and holiness,
Heart of Jesus, propitiation for our offenses,
Heart of Jesus, overwhelmed with reproaches,
Heart of Jesus, bruised for our iniquities,
Heart of Jesus, obedient even unto death,

Heart of Jesus, pierced with a lance,
Heart of Jesus, source of all consolation,
Heart of Jesus, our life and resurrection,
Heart of Jesus, our peace and reconciliation,
Heart of Jesus, victim for our sins,
Heart of Jesus, salvation of those who hope in Thee,
Heart of Jesus, hope of those who die in Thee,
Heart of Jesus, delight of all the Saints,
Lamb of God, Who takest away the sins of the world,
          Spare us, O Lord.
Lamb of God, Who takest away the sins of the world,
          Graciously hear us, O Lord.
Lamb of God, Who takest away the sins of the world,
          Have mercy on us.

V. Jesus, meek and humble of Heart,
R. Make our hearts like unto Thine.

Let us pray
      Almighty and everlasting God, look upon the Heart of Thy
well beloved Son and upon the praise and satisfaction which He
offers unto Thee in the name of sinners; and do Thou, of Thy
great goodness, grant them pardon when they seek Thy mercy, in
the name of the same Jesus Christ, Thy Son, who liveth and
reigneth with Thee for ever and ever. *R. Amen.*

Litany of the Holy Name of Jesus

Lord, have mercy on us.
Christ, have mercy on us.
Lord, have mercy on us.
Jesus, hear us.
Jesus, graciously hear us.
God the Father of heaven, *Have mercy on us.*
God the Son, Redeemer of the world,
God the Holy Ghost,
Holy Trinity, one God,
Jesus, Son of the living God,
Jesus, splendor of the Father,
Jesus, brightness of eternal light,
Jesus, King of glory,
Jesus, sun of justice,
Jesus, Son of the Virgin Mary,
Jesus, most amiable,
Jesus, most admirable,
Jesus, mighty God,
Jesus, Father of the world to come,
Jesus, angel of the great counsel,
Jesus, most powerful,
Jesus, most patient,
Jesus, most obedient,
Jesus, meek and humble of heart,
Jesus, lover of chastity,
Jesus, lover of us,
Jesus, God of peace,
Jesus, author of life,
Jesus, model of virtues,
Jesus, lover of souls,
Jesus, our God,
Jesus, our refuge,
Jesus, Father of the poor,
Jesus, treasure of the faithful,
Jesus, Good shepherd,
Jesus, true light,

Jesus, eternal wisdom,
Jesus, infinite goodness,
Jesus, our way and our life,
Jesus, joy of angels,
Jesus, King of patriarchs,
Jesus, master of Apostles,
Jesus, teacher of Evangelists,
Jesus, strength of martyrs,
Jesus, light of confessors,
Jesus, purity of virgins,
Jesus, crown of all saints,
Be merciful, *spare us, O Jesus.*
Be merciful, *graciously hear us, O Jesus.*
From all evil, *Deliver us O Jesus*
From all sin,
From Thy wrath,
From the snares of the devil,
From the spirit of fornication,
From everlasting death,
From the neglect of Thine inspirations,
Through the mystery of Thy holy Incarnation,
Through Thy nativity,
Through Thine infancy,
Through Thy most divine life,
Through Thy labors,
Through Thine agony and Passion,
Through Thy cross and dereliction,
Through Thy sufferings,
Through Thy death and burial,
Through Thy Resurrection,
Through Thine Ascension,
Through Thine institution of the most Holy Eucharist,
Through Thy joys,
Through Thy glory,
Lamb of God, Who takest away the sins of the world,
	Spare us, O Jesus.

Lamb of God, Who takest away the sins of the world,
Graciously hear us, O Jesus.
Lamb of God, Who takest away the sins of the world,
Have mercy on us, O Jesus.

V. Jesus, hear us.
R. Jesus, graciously hear us.

Let us pray:

O Lord Jesus Christ, Who hast said: Ask and ye shall receive; seek and ye shall find; knock and it shall be opened unto you; grant, we beseech Thee, to us who ask the gift of Thy divine love, that we may ever love Thee with all our hearts, and in all our words and actions, and never cease praising Thee.

Grant us, O Lord, a perpetual fear and love of Thy holy Name; for Thou never failest to govern those whom Thou dost solidly establish in Thy love. Who livest and reignest world without end. *R. Amen.*

St. Louis De Montfort's Prayer to Jesus

O most loving Jesus, deign to let me pour forth my gratitude before Thee, for the grace Thou hast bestowed upon me in giving me to Thy holy Mother through the devotion of Holy Bondage, that she may be my advocate in the presence of Thy majesty and my support in my extreme misery. Alas, O Lord! I am so wretched that without this dear Mother I should be certainly lost.

Yes, Mary is necessary for me at Thy side and everywhere: that she may appease Thy just wrath, because I have so often offended Thee; that she may save me from the eternal punishment of Thy justice, which I deserve; that she may contemplate Thee, speak to Thee, pray to Thee, approach Thee and please Thee; that she may help me to save my soul and the souls of others; in short, Mary is necessary for me that I may always do Thy holy will and seek Thy greater glory in all things.

Ah, would that I could proclaim throughout the whole world the mercy that Thou hast shown to me! Would that everyone might know I should be already damned, were it not for Mary! Would that I might offer worthy thanksgiving for so great a blessing! Mary is in me. Oh, what a treasure! Oh, what a consolation! And shall I not be entirely hers? Oh, what ingratitude! My dear Savior, send me death rather than such a calamity, for I would rather die than live without belonging entirely to Mary.

With St. John the Evangelist at the foot of the Cross, I have taken her a thousand times for my own and as many times have given myself to her but if I have not yet done it as Thou, dear Jesus, dost wish, I now renew this offering as Thou desire me to renew it. And if Thou seest in my soul or my body anything that does not belong to this august Princess, I pray Thee to take it and cast it far from me, for whatever in me does not belong to Mary is unworthy of Thee.

O Holy Spirit, grant me all these graces. Plant in my soul the Tree of true Life, which is Mary; cultivate it and tend it so that it may grow and blossom and bring forth the fruit of life in abundance. O Holy Spirit, give me great devotion to Mary, Thy faithful spouse; give me great confidence in her maternal heart and an abiding refuge in her mercy, so that by her Thou mayest truly

form in me Jesus Christ, great and mighty, unto the fullness of
His perfect age. Amen.

O Jesus Living In Mary

O Jesus living in Mary
Come and live in Thy servants;
In the spirit of Thy holiness,
In the fullness of Thy might,
In the truth of Thy virtues,
In the perfection of Thy ways,
In the communion of Thy mysteries,
Subdue every hostile power,
In Thy spirit, for the glory of the Father. Amen.

Ave Maris Stella

Hail, bright star of ocean,
God's own Mother blest,
Ever sinless Virgin,
Gate of heavenly rest.

Show thyself a Mother;
May the Word Divine,
Born for us thy Infant,
Hear our prayers through thine.

Taking that sweet Ave
Which from Gabriel came,
Peace confirm within us,
Changing Eva's name.

Virgin all excelling,
Mildest of the mild,
Freed from guilt, preserve us,
Pure and undefiled.

Break the captives' fetters,
Light on blindness pour,
All our ills expelling,
Every bliss implore.

Keep our life all spotless,
Make our way secure,
Till we find in Jesus
Joy forevermore.

Through the highest heaven
To the Almighty Three,
Father, Son and Spirit,
One same glory be. Amen.

DAILY MEDITATIONS TO HELP US GROW
IN THE KNOWLEDGE OF OUR LORD

WEEK 4: DAY 1–FIRST MEDITATION

Taken from St. Louis de Montfort's
True Devotion to Mary, §60 ff.

Jesus Christ—the Beginning and End of All Things

Having spoken thus far of the necessity of devotion to the most holy Virgin, I must now show in what this devotion consists. This I will do, with God's help, after I shall have first laid down some fundamental truths which shall throw light on that grand and solid devotion which I desire to disclose.

Jesus Christ our Savior, true God and true Man, ought to be the last end of all our other devotions, else they are false and delusive. Jesus Christ is the Alpha and the Omega, the beginning and the end, of all things. We labor, as the Apostle says, to render every man perfect in Jesus Christ; because it is in Him alone that the whole plenitude of the Divinity dwells together with all the other plenitudes of graces, virtues and perfections.

It is in Him alone that we have been blessed with all spiritual benediction; and He is our only Master, Who has to teach us; our only Lord on Whom we ought to depend; our only Head to Whom we must be united; our only Model to Whom we should conform ourselves; our only Physician Who can heal us; our only Shepherd Who can feed us; our only Way Who can lead us; our only Truth Whom we must believe; our only Life Who can animate us; and our only All in all things Who can satisfy us.

There has been no other name given under heaven, except the name of Jesus, by which we can be saved. God has laid no other foundation of our salvation, our perfection or our glory, than Jesus Christ. Every building which is not built on that firm Rock, is founded upon the moving sand, and sooner or later will infallibly fall. Every one of the faithful who is not united to Him, as a branch to the stock of the vine, shall fall, shall wither and shall be fit only to be cast into the fire. Outside of Him there exists nothing but error, falsehood, iniquity, futility, death and damnation.

But if we are in Jesus Christ and Jesus Christ is in us, we have no condemnation to fear. Neither the angels of heaven, nor the men of earth, nor the devils of hell, nor any other creature can injure us; because they cannot separate us from the love of God, which is in Jesus Christ. By Jesus Christ, with Jesus Christ, in Jesus Christ, we can do all things; we can render all honor and glory to the Father in the unity of the Holy Ghost; we can become perfect ourselves, and be to our neighbor a good odor of eternal life.

WEEK 4: DAY 1–SECOND MEDITATION

Taken from St. Louis de Montfort's
True Devotion to Mary, §68 ff.

Through Mary, We Belong to Jesus

We must conclude that we do not belong to ourselves but are entirely His, as His members and His slaves, whom He has bought at an infinitely dear price, the price of all His Blood. Before Baptism we belonged to the devil, as his slaves; but Baptism has made us true slaves of Jesus Christ, who have no right to live, to work or to die, except to bring forth fruit for that God-Man (Rom. 7:4); to glorify Him in our bodies and to let Him reign in our souls, because we are His conquest, His acquired people and His inheritance.

It is for the same reason that the Holy Ghost compares us: *(1)* to trees planted along the waters of grace, in the field of the Church, who ought to bring forth their fruit in their seasons; *(2)* to the branches of a vine of which Jesus Christ is the stock and which must yield good grapes; *(3)* to a flock of which Jesus Christ is the Shepherd and which is to multiply and give milk; *(4)* to a good land of which God is the Husbandman, in which the seed multiplies itself and brings forth thirtyfold, sixtyfold and a hundredfold. (Ps. 1:3; Jn.15:2; 10:11; Mt.13:8). Jesus Christ cursed the unfruitful fig tree (Mt. 21:19), and pronounced sentence against the useless servant who had not made any profit on his talent. (Mt. 25:24-30). All this proves to us that Jesus Christ wishes to receive some fruits from our wretched selves, namely our good works, because those works belong to Him alone.

I say that we ought to belong to Jesus Christ, and to serve Him not only as mercenary servants, but as loving slaves who, as a result of their great love, give themselves up to serve Him in the quality of slaves simply for the honor of belonging to Him. Before Baptism we were the slaves of the devil. Baptism has made us the slaves of Jesus Christ: Christians must needs be either the slaves of the devil or the slaves of Jesus Christ. What I say absolutely of Jesus Christ, I say relatively of Our Lady. Since Jesus Christ chose her for the inseparable companion of His life, of His death, of His glory and of His power in heaven and upon earth, He gave her by grace, relatively to His Majesty, all the same rights and privileges which He possesses by nature. "All that is fitting to God by nature is fitting to Mary by grace," say the saints; so that, according to them, Mary and Jesus, having but the same will and the same power, have also the same subjects, servants and slaves.

WEEK 4: DAY 1–THIRD MEDITATION

Taken from St. Louis de Montfort's
True Devotion to Mary, §80 ff.

Whoever Shall Love His Own Life Shall Lose it

Our Lord has said that whoever wishes to follow Him, must renounce himself and hate his own life, and that whosoever shall love his own life shall lose it, and whosoever shall hate it, shall save it (Jn. 12:25). He Who is infinite Wisdom does not give commandments without reason, and He has commanded us to hate ourselves, only because we so richly deserve to be hated. Nothing is worthier of love than God and nothing is worthier of hatred than ourselves.

In order to rid ourselves of self, we must die to ourselves daily. That is to say, we must renounce the operations of the powers of our soul and of the senses of our body. We must see as if we saw not, understand as if we understood not, and make use of the things of this world as if we made no use of them at all. (I Cor. 7:29-31).

This is what St. Paul calls dying daily. (I Cor. 15:31). "Unless the grain of wheat falling into the ground die, itself remaineth alone," and bringeth forth no good fruit. (Jn. 12:24-25). If we do not die to ourselves and if our holiest devotions do not incline us to this necessary and useful death, we shall bring forth no fruit worth anything, and our devotions will become useless. All our good works will be stained by self-love and our own will; and this will cause God to hold in abomination the greatest sacrifices we can make and the best actions we can do; so that at our death we shall find our hands empty of virtues and of merits and we shall not have one spark of pure love, which is only communicated to souls dead to themselves, souls whose life is hidden with Jesus Christ in God.

Taken from St. Louis de Montfort's *Friends of the Cross*, §2 ff.

We are a group of crusaders united to fight against the world, not like those religious men and women, who leave the world for fear of being overcome, but like brave, intrepid warriors on the battlefront, refusing to retreat or even to yield an inch. Let us be brave. Let us fight with all our might.

Let us bind ourselves together in that strong union of heart and mind which is far superior, far more terrifying to the world and hell than the armed forces of a well-organized kingdom are to its enemies. Demons are united for our destruction, but we are united for their overthrow; the avaricious are united to barter and hoard up gold and silver. Let us combine our efforts in the pursuit of the eternal treasures hidden in the Cross. Reprobates unite to make merry, but we unite to suffer.

We have been chosen by God from among the tens of thousands who have only reason and sense for their only guide. We, who are raised above reason and thoroughly opposed to the things of sense, live in the light of true faith and burn with love for the

Cross.

Such a Friend of the Cross is a mighty king, a hero who triumphs over the devil, the world and the flesh and their threefold concupiscence. He overthrows the pride of Satan by his love for humiliation, he triumphs over the world's greed by his love for poverty and he restrains the sensuality of the flesh by his love for suffering.

Such a Friend of the Cross is a holy man, separated from visible things. His heart is lifted high above all that is frail and perishable; "his conversation is in heaven" (Phil. 3:20); he journeys here below like a stranger and pilgrim. He keeps his heart free from the world, looks upon it with an unconcerned glance of his left eye and disdainfully tramples it under foot.

A Friend of the Cross is a trophy which the crucified Christ won on Calvary in union with His Blessed Mother. Conceived in the sorrowful heart of Christ, he comes into this world through the gash in the Savior's right side and is all empurpled in His blood.

True to this heritage, he breathes forth only crosses and blood, death to the world, the flesh and sin and hides himself here below with Jesus Christ in God (Col. 3:3). Thus, a perfect Friend of the Cross is a true Christ-bearer, or rather another Christ, so much so that he can say with truth: "I live now not I, but Christ liveth in me" (Gal. 2:20).

WEEK 4: DAY 1–FOURTH MEDITATION

Taken from St. Louis de Montfort's
True Devotion to Mary, §84

To Jesus Through Mary

Our Lord is our advocate and Mediator of redemption with God the Father. It is through Him that we ought to pray, in union with the whole Church, Triumphant and Militant. It is through Him that we have access to the Majesty of the Father, before Whom we ought never to appear except sustained and clothed with the merits of His Son.

But have we not need of a mediator with the Mediator Himself? Is our purity great enough to unite us directly to Him, and by ourselves? Is He not God, in all things equal to His Father, and consequently as worthy of respect as His Father? If through His infinite charity He has made Himself our bail and our Mediator with God His Father, are we on that account, to have less respect and less fear for His Majesty and His Sanctity? Let us say boldly with St. Bernard, that we have need of a mediator with the Mediator Himself, and that it is the divine Mary who is the most capable of filling that charitable office. It was through her that Jesus Christ came to us, and it is through her that we must go to Him. If we fear to go directly to Jesus Christ, our God, whether because of His infinite greatness or because of our vileness or because of our sins, let us boldly implore the aid and intercession of Mary, our Mother.

All this is taken from St. Bernard and St. Bonaventure, so that according to them, we have three steps to mount to go to God: the first, which is nearest to us and the most suited to our capacity, is Mary; the second is Jesus Christ; and the third is God the Father. To go to Jesus, we must go to Mary; she is our mediatrix of intercession. To go to God the Father, we must go to Jesus; for He is our Mediator of redemption. Now the devotion, that I propose, observes this order perfectly.

WEEK 4: DAY 2–FIRST MEDITATION

The Passion of Our Lord by St. Matthew, Chapter 26.

1 And it came to pass, when Jesus had ended all these words, he said to his disciples:

2 You know that after two days there will be the pasch, and the son of man shall be delivered up to be crucified:

3 Then were gathered together the chief priests and ancients of the people into the court of the high priest, who was called Caiphas:

4 And they consulted together, that by subtlety they might apprehend Jesus, and put him to death.

5 But they said: "Not on the festival day, lest perhaps there should be a tumult among the people"....

14 ....Then one of the twelve, who was called Judas Iscariot, went to the chief priests,

15 And said to them: What will you give me, and I will deliver him unto you? But they appointed him thirty pieces of silver.

16 And from thenceforth he sought an opportunity to betray him....

21 ....And whilst they were eating, he said: Amen I say to you, one of you is about to betray me.

22 And they, being very much troubled, began every one to say: Is it I, Lord?

23 But he answering, said: He that dips his hand with me in the dish, he shall betray me.

24 The Son of man indeed goes, as it is written of him: but woe to that man by whom the Son of man shall be betrayed: it were better for him, if that man had not been born.

25 And Judas, that betrayed him, answering, said: Is it I, Rabbi? He saith to him: Thou hast said it.

WEEK 4: DAY 2–SECOND MEDITATION

The Passion of Our Lord by St. Matthew, Chapter 26

30 And a hymn being said, they went out to mount Olivet....

36 ....Then Jesus came with them into a country place which is called Gethsemane; and he said to his disciples: Sit you here till I go yonder and pray.

37 And taking with him Peter and the two sons of Zebedee, he began to grow sorrowful and to be sad.

38 Then he saith to them: My soul is sorrowful even unto death: stay you here, and watch with me.

39 And going a little further, he fell upon his face, praying, and saying: My Father, if it be possible, let this chalice pass from me. Nevertheless not as I will but as thou wilt.

40 And he cometh to his disciples, and findeth them asleep, and he saith to Peter: Could you not watch one hour with me?

41 Watch ye, and pray that ye enter not into temptation. The spirit indeed is willing, but the flesh weak.

42 Again the second time, he went and prayed, saying: My Father, if this chalice may not pass away, but I must drink it, thy will be done.

43 And he cometh again, and findeth them sleeping: for their eyes were heavy.

44 And leaving them, he went again: and he prayed the third time, saying the selfsame words.

45 Then he cometh to his disciples, and saith to them: Sleep ye now and take your rest; behold the hour is at hand, and the Son of man shall be betrayed into the hands of sinners.

46 Rise, let us go: behold he is at hand that will betray me.

47 As he yet spoke, behold Judas, one of the twelve, came, and with him a great multitude with swords and clubs, sent from the chief priests and the ancients of the people.

48 And he that betrayed him, gave them a sign, saying: Whomsoever I shall kiss, that is he, hold him fast.

49 And forthwith coming to Jesus, he said: Hail, Rabbi. And he kissed him.

50 And Jesus said to him: Friend, whereto art thou come? Then they came up, and laid hands on Jesus, and held him.

WEEK 4: DAY 2–THIRD MEDITATION

The Passion of Our Lord by St. Matthew, Chapter 26

51 And behold one of them that were with Jesus, stretching forth his hand, drew out his sword: and striking the servant of the high priest, cut off his ear.

52 Then Jesus saith to him: Put up again thy sword into its place: for all that take the sword shall perish with the sword.

53 Thinkest thou that I cannot ask my Father, and he will give me presently more than twelve legions of angels?

54 How then shall the scriptures be fulfilled, that so it must be done?

55 In that same hour Jesus said to the multitudes: You are come out as it were to a robber with swords and clubs to apprehend me. I sat daily with you, teaching in the temple, and you laid not hands on me.

56 Now all this was done, that the scriptures of the prophets might be fulfilled. Then the disciples all leaving him, fled.

57 But they holding Jesus led him to Caiphas the high priest, where the scribes and the ancients were assembled.

58 And Peter followed him afar off, even to the court of the high priest. And going in, he sat with the servants, that he might see the end.

59 And the chief priests and the whole council sought false witness against Jesus, that they might put him to death:

60 And they found not, whereas many false witnesses had come in. And last of all there came two false witnesses:

61 And they said: This man said, I am able to destroy the temple of God, and after three days to rebuild it.

62 And the high priest rising up, said to him: Answerest thou nothing to the things which these men witness against thee?

63 But Jesus held his peace. And the high priest said to him: I adjure thee by the living God, that thou tell us if thou be the Christ the Son of God.

64 Jesus saith to him: Thou hast said it. Nevertheless I say to you, hereafter you shall see the Son of man sitting on the right hand of the power of God, and coming in the clouds of heaven.

65 Then the high priest rent his garments saying: He hath blasphemed; what further need have we of witnesses? Behold, now you have heard the blasphemy:

66 What think you? But they answering said: He is guilty of death.

67 Then did they spit in his face, and buffeted him: and others struck his face with the palms of their hands,

68 Saying: Prophesy unto us, O Christ, who is he that struck thee?

69 But Peter sat without in the court: and there came to him a servant maid, saying: Thou also wast with Jesus the Galilean.

70 But he denied before them all, saying: I know not what thou

sayest.

71 And as he went out of the gate, another maid saw him and she saith to them that were there: This man also was with Jesus of Nazareth.

72 And again he denied with an oath: I know not the man.

73 And after a little while they came that stood by, and said to Peter: Surely thou also art one of them; for even thy speech doth discover thee.

74 Then he began to curse and to swear that he knew not the man. And immediately the cock crew.

75 And Peter remembered the word of Jesus which he had said: Before the cock crow, thou wilt deny me thrice. And going forth, he wept bitterly.

WEEK 4: DAY 3–FIRST MEDITATION

The Passion of Our Lord by St. Matthew, Chapter 27

1 And when morning was come, all the chief priests and ancients of the people took counsel against Jesus, that they might put him to death.

2 And they brought him bound, and delivered him to Pontius Pilate the governor.

3 Then Judas, who betrayed him, seeing that he was condemned, repenting himself, brought back the thirty pieces of silver to the chief priests and ancients,

4 Saying: I have sinned in betraying innocent blood. But they said: What is that to us? Look thou to it.

5 And casting down the pieces of silver in the temple, he departed: and went and hanged himself with a halter.

6 But the chief priests having taken the pieces of silver, said: It is not lawful to put them into the treasury, because it is the price of blood.

7 And after they had consulted together: they bought with them the potter's field, to be a burying place for strangers.

8 For this cause that field was called Haceldama, that is, The field of blood, even to this day.

9 Then was fulfilled that which was spoken by Jeremias the prophet, saying: And they took the thirty pieces of silver, the price of him that was prized, whom they prized of the children of Israel.....

11 ....And Jesus stood before the governor, and the governor asked him, saying: Art thou the king of the Jews? Jesus saith to him: Thou sayest it.

12 And when he was accused by the chief priests and ancients, he answered nothing.

13 Then Pilate saith to him: Dost not thou hear how great testimonies they allege against thee?

14 And he answered him never a word; so that the governor wondered exceedingly.

15 Now upon the solemn day the governor was accustomed to release to the people one prisoner, whom they would.

16 And he had then a notorious prisoner, that was called Barabbas.

17 They therefore being gathered together, Pilate said: Whom will you that I release to you, Barabbas, or Jesus that is called Christ?

18 For he knew that for envy they had delivered him.

19 And as he was sitting in the place of judgment, his wife sent to him, saying: Have thou nothing to do with that just man; for I have suffered many things this day in a dream because of him.

20 But the chief priests and ancients persuaded the people, that they should ask for Barabbas, and make Jesus away.

21 And the governor answering, said to them: Whether will you of the two to be released unto you? But they said, Barabbas.

22 Pilate saith to them: What shall I do then with Jesus that is called Christ? They say all: Let him be crucified!

23 The governor said to them: Why, what evil hath he done? But they cried out the more, saying: Let him be crucified!

24 And Pilate seeing that he prevailed nothing, but that rather a tumult was made; taking water washed his hands before the people, saying: I am innocent of the blood of this just man; look you to it.

25 And the whole people answering, said: His blood be upon us and upon our children.

26 Then he released to them Barabbas, and having scourged Jesus, delivered him unto them to be crucified.

WEEK 4: DAY 3–SECOND MEDITATION

The Passion of Our Lord by St. Matthew, Chapter 27

27 Then the soldiers of the governor taking Jesus into the hall, gathered together unto him the whole band;

28 And stripping him, they put a scarlet cloak about him.

29 And plating a crown of thorns, they put it upon his head, and a reed in his right hand. And bowing the knee before him, they mocked him, saying: Hail, king of the Jews.

30 And spitting upon him, they took the reed and struck his head.

31 And after they had mocked him, they took off the cloak from him, and put on him his own garments, and led him away to crucify him.

32 And going out, they found a man of Cyrene, named Simon: him they forced to take up his cross.

33 And they came to the place that is called Golgotha, which is the place of Calvary.

34 And they gave him wine to drink mingled with gall. And when he had tasted, he would not drink.

35 And after they had crucified him, they divided his garments, casting lots; that it might be fulfilled which was spoken by the prophet saying: They divided my garments among them; and upon my vesture they cast lots.

36 And they sat and watched him.

37 And they put over his head his cause written: This is Jesus, King of the Jews.

38 Then were crucified with him two thieves: one on the right hand, and one on the left.

39 And they that passed by, blasphemed him, wagging their heads,

40 And saying: Vah, thou that destroyest the temple of God, and in three days dost rebuild it: save thy own self, if thou be the Son of God, come down from the cross.

41 In like manner also the chief priests, with the scribes and ancients, mocking, said:

42 He saved others; himself he cannot save. If he be the king of Israel, let him now come down from the cross, and we will believe him.

43 He trusted in God; let him now deliver him if he will have him; for he said: I am the Son of God.

44 And the selfsame thing the thieves also, that were crucified with him, reproached him with.

45 Now from the sixth hour there was darkness over the whole earth, until the ninth hour.

46 And about the ninth hour Jesus cried with a loud voice, saying: Eli, Eli, lamma sabacthani? That is, My God, my God, why hast thou forsaken me?

47 And some that stood there and heard, said: This man calleth Elias.

48 And immediately one of them running took a sponge, and filled it with vinegar; and put it on a reed, and gave him to drink.

49 And the others said: Let him be, let us see whether Elias will come to deliver him.

50 And Jesus again crying with a loud voice, yielded up the ghost.

51 And behold the veil of the temple was rent in two from the top even to the bottom, and the earth quaked, and the rocks were rent.

52 And the graves were opened: and many bodies of the saints that had slept arose,

53 And coming out of the tombs after his resurrection, came into the holy city, and appeared to many.

54 Now the centurion and they that were with him watching Jesus, having seen the earthquake, and the things that were done, were sore afraid, saying: Indeed this was the Son of God.

WEEK 4: DAY 3–THIRD MEDITATION

Based on the *Imitation of Christ*, Book 2, Chapter 8

On Close Friendship with Jesus

When Jesus is with you, the going seems easy and nothing seems difficult. When Jesus is not there everything is hard. When Jesus does not speak in our hearts, all human consolation is worthless, but if Jesus speaks but one word, great consolation is felt—even if we receive no human consolation. Did not Mary Magdalen immediately rise from the place where she sat weeping when Martha said: "The Master is here and is calling you?" Happy hour, when Jesus calls you from bitter tears to joyfulness of soul! How dry and hard and miserable you are without Jesus! How stupid and vain, if you desire anything outside Jesus! Is not this greater loss than if you should lose the whole world?

What can the world give you without Jesus? To be without Jesus is grievous hell, and to be with Jesus sweet paradise. If Jesus is with you, no enemy will be able to harm you. He who finds Jesus, finds a great treasure, greater than any good. And he who loses Jesus, loses everything, and more than the whole world. Whoever lives without Jesus is miserable. He who lives with Him, is the richest of men and all goes well with him.

It is an art to know how to live with Jesus, and great wisdom to know how to hold on to Him. Be humble and a man of peace, and Jesus will be with you. Be devout and still, and Jesus will remain with you. You can quickly send Jesus away and lose His grace, if you wish to turn aside to external things. And if you have driven Him away and lost Him, to whom will you fly, and whom then will you seek as friend? We cannot live without friends, and if Jesus is not your greatest friend, you will be truly sad and desolate. You do foolishly, therefore, if you trust or find joy in any other. It is better to have the whole world against you than to have Jesus offended by you. Therefore, of all things dear and precious, let Jesus alone be your special love.

All other things must be loved for Jesus' sake, but Jesus loved for Himself. Jesus Christ is to be loved apart from all others, He who only is found to be wholly good and faithful beyond all friends. For His sake and in Him, let both your friends and foes be dear to you. And pray for all these , that all may know and love him.

Never desire to be praised or loved above others, because this kind of praise and love belongs to God alone, Who has no other like Himself. Nor wish that anyone, in his heart, should be enamored with you, nor that you should be enamored with the love of anyone; but let Jesus be in you and in every good man.

Be pure and free of heart without being attached or entangled with any created thing. You must be stripped of earthly love and carry a pure heart to God, if you wish to be free, and to see how sweet the Lord is. You will not attain this unless you be led and drawn on by His grace, that, with all else cast off and dismissed, you are alone and one with God alone.

For when the grace of God comes to a man, then he is equipped for all things, and when it leaves him, then he will be poor and weak, as if abandoned to shipwreck and failure. In these things you are not to be cast down or filled with despair, but, calm in mind, stand by the will of God, and endure all things which come upon you, praising Jesus Christ, because after winter, summer comes, after night the day returns, and a great calm after the storm.

We Shall Now Enter the Way of the Cross

In the following meditations we shall embark upon the Royal Road of the Cross. If we seek to really know Jesus, then we must seek to know and understand the Cross. The Cross lies at the heart of history. In the Cross is the salvation of mankind. In the Cross we find our key to heaven. In the Cross we find a medicine for our ills. In the Cross we find the treasure with which to pay the debt of past sin. In the Cross we can prove our love for God. In the Cross we find Christ. Through the Cross we know Christ. For to know Jesus is to know Jesus crucified. He Himself said that it was for this that He had come into the world. Throw away the Cross, and you will throw away Christ and your key to heaven.

Due to this great importance of the Cross in both the history of mankind and in our own personal lives, we must now enter a quite extensive range of meditations that focus on the Cross alone. This is to help us to appreciate the purpose behind the Cross and to help us carry our own daily crosses. For if we want to find Jesus, we will only find Him amongst those crosses. For Jesus Himself said: "If any man will come after Me, let him deny himself, and take up his cross and follow Me!"

The following meditations will both, help us to carry the Cross, and uncover the Spirit of Jesus while doing so. Some may question why so much importance and space has been granted to the Cross, the answer is quite simply that without the Cross, there is no salvation.

WEEK 4: DAY 4–FIRST MEDITATION

Taken from St. Louis de Montfort's *Friends of the Cross,* §5 ff.

What Route Are We Following?

My dear Friends of the Cross, does every act of yours justify what the eminent name you bear implies? Or at least are you, with the grace of God, in the shadow of Calvary's Cross and of Our Lady of Pity, really eager and truly striving to attain this goal? Is the way you follow the one that leads to this goal? Is it the true way of life, the narrow way, the thorn-strewn way to Calvary? Or are you unconsciously traveling the world's broad road, the road to perdition? Do you realize that there is a highroad which to all appearances is straight and safe for man to travel, but which in reality leads to death?

Do you really know the voice of God and grace from the voice of the world and human nature? Do you distinctly hear the voice of God, our kind Father, pronouncing His threefold curse upon every one who follows the world in its concupiscence: "Woe, woe, woe to the inhabitants of the earth" (Apoc. 8: 13) and then appealing to you with outstretched arms: "Be separated, My chosen people (Is. 48:20, 52:11, Jer. 50:8, 51:6), beloved Friends of the Cross of My Son, be separated from those worldlings, for they are accursed by My Majesty, repudiated by My Son (Jn. 17:9) and condemned by My Holy Spirit (Jn.16:8-12).

Do not sit in their chair of pestilence, take no part in their gatherings; do not even step along their highways (Ps. 1:1). Hurry away from this great and infamous Babylon (Is. 48:20, Jer. 51:6); hearken only to the voice of My Beloved Son; follow only in His footprints; for He is the One I have given to be your Way, Truth, Life (Jn. 14:6) and Model: hear ye Him" (Mt. 17,5; Lk. 9:35; Mk. 9:6; 2 Pet. 1:17).

Is your ear attentive to the pleading of the lovable and Cross burdened Jesus, Come, follow Me, "He that followeth Me walketh not in darkness (Jn. 8:12) have confidence, I have conquered the world" (Jn. 16:33)?

WEEK 4: DAY 4–SECOND MEDITATION

Based on the *Imitation of Christ*, Book 2, Chapter 11

The Small Number of Those Who Love the Cross of Christ

Jesus has now many who love His heavenly kingdom, but few who carry His Cross. He has many who desire consolation, but few who desire tribulation. He finds more to share His table, but few His fasting. All wish to rejoice with Him, few want to bear anything for Him. Many follow Jesus to the breaking of bread, but few to drinking His chalice of suffering. Many revere the glory of His miracles, few follow the shame of His Cross. Many love Jesus so long as adversity does not befall them. Many praise and bless Him, as long as they receive some consolations from Him. But if Jesus should hide Himself and leave them for a little while, they start complaining or fall into deep dejection.

But those who love Jesus for Jesus' sake, and not for any consolation of their own, bless Him in all tribulation and anguish of heart, just as they do in the greatest consolation. And if it is His will never to give consolation, they would nevertheless always praise Him, and always be grateful to Him. Those who are always seeking consolations should be called mercenaries! They are not lovers of Christ, but of themselves, who are always thinking of their own advantages and gain? Where shall we find one who is willing to serve God for nothing?

Rarely is there found someone so spiritual that he is stripped of everything. For where shall we find someone truly poor in spirit and detached from every created thing? "His value is from afar, indeed from the uttermost shores." If a man has given all his possessions, it is still nothing; and if he has done great penance, it is still a small thing; and if he has grasped all knowledge, he is still far off; and if he has great virtue, and a great devotion, still much is lacking to him—one thing undoubtedly which is most needful to him. And what is that? That having given up all things, he give up himself, and go utterly out of himself and retain nothing of his self-love. And when he has done all that he knows should be done, that he should feel he has done nothing.

Let him not give great weight to what his life appears to be, but instead pronounce himself in truth an unprofitable servant, just as the Truth says: "When you have done all that has been bidden you, say: We are unprofitable servants." Then truly you will be poor and naked in spirit, and with the Prophet say: "I am poor and needy." Yet no one is richer, nor more potent, no one more free, than he who knows how to abandon self and reckon himself the lowliest.

WEEK 4: DAY 4–THIRD MEDITATION

Taken from St. Louis de Montfort's *Friends of the Cross,* §7 ff.

The Two Groups

Dear Brethren, these are the two groups that appear before you each day, the followers of Christ and the followers of the world. Our loving Savior's group is to the right, scaling a narrow path made all the narrower by the world's corruption. Our kind Master is in the lead, barefooted, thorn-crowned, robed in His blood and weighted with a heavy Cross. There is only a handful of people who follow Him, but they are the bravest of the brave. His gentle voice is not heard above the tumult of the world, or men do not have the courage to follow Him in poverty, suffering, humiliation and in the other crosses His servants must bear all the days of their life.

To the left is the world's group, the devil's in fact, which is far superior in number, and seemingly far more colorful and splendid in array. Fashionable folk are all in a hurry to enlist, the highways are overcrowded, although they are broad and ever broadening with the crowds that flow through in a torrent. These roads are strewn with flowers, bordered with all kinds of amusements and attractions and paved with gold and silver (Mt. 7:13-14).

To the right, the little flock that follows Jesus can speak only of tears, penance, prayer and contempt for worldly things. Sobbing in their grief, they can be heard repeating: "Let us suffer, let us weep, let us fast, let us pray, let us hide, let us humble ourselves, let us be poor, let us mortify ourselves, for he who has not the spirit of Christ, the spirit of the Cross, is none of Christ's. Those who are Christ's have crucified their flesh with its concupiscence. We must be conformed to the image of Jesus Christ or else be damned!"

"Be brave," they keep saying to each other, "be brave, for if God is for us, in us and leading us, who dare be against us? The One Who is dwelling within us is stronger than the one who is in the world, no servant is above his master; one moment of light tribulation worketh an eternal weight of glory; there are fewer elect than man may think; only the brave and daring take heaven by storm; the crown is given only to those who strive lawfully according to the Gospel, not according to the fashion of the world. Let us put all our strength into the fight, and run very fast to reach the goal and win the crown." Friends of the Cross spur each other on with such divine words.

Worldlings, on the contrary, rouse one another to persist in their unscrupulous depravity. "Enjoy life, peace and pleasure," they shout, "Enjoy life, peace and pleasure. Let us eat, let us drink, let us sing, let us dance, let us play. God is good, He did not make us to damn us, God does not forbid us to enjoy ourselves; we shall not be damned for that; away with scruples; we shall not die." And so they continue.

WEEK 4: DAY 4–FOURTH MEDITATION

Taken from St. Louis de Montfort's
Friends of the Cross, §13 ff.

The Obligation of Self-Denial and Imitating Christ
By the Way of the Cross

Christian perfection consists:

> In willing to be a saint: "If any man will come after Me";
> In self-denial: "Let him deny himself";
> In suffering: "Let him take up his cross";
> In doing: "Let him follow Me."

If *anyone,* not *many a one,* shows that the elect who are willing to be made conformable to the crucified Christ by carrying their cross are few in number. It would cause us to faint away from grief to learn how surprisingly small is their number.

It is so small that among ten thousand people there is scarcely one to be found, as was revealed to several saints, among whom St. Simon Stylita, referred to by the holy Abbot Nilus, followed by St. Basil, St. Ephrem and others. So small, indeed, that if God willed to gather them together, He would have to cry out as He did of yore through the voice of a prophet: "Come ye together one by one" (Is. 27:12), one from this province and one from that kingdom.

St. Louis de Montfort here speaks of that small group of saintly souls who carry their cross more perfectly. He does not, however, exclude from salvation that vast multitude of less perfect Christians which the mercy of God wills to save.

The Desire to Become a Saint

If anyone *wills:* if a person has a real and definite determination and is prompted not by natural feelings, habit, self-love, personal interest or human respect but by an all-masterful grace of the Holy Ghost which is not communicated indiscriminately: "It is not given to all men to understand this mystery" (Mt. 13:11). In fact, only a privileged number of men receive this practical knowledge of the mystery of the Cross. For that man who climbs up to Calvary and lets himself be nailed on the Cross with Jesus, in the heart of his own country, must be a brave man, a hero, a resolute man, one who is lifted up in God, who treats as dirt, both the world and hell, as well as his very body and his own will. He must be resolved to relinquish all things, to undertake anything and to suffer everything for Jesus.

Understand this, dear Friends of the Cross, should there be anyone among you who has not this firm resolve, he is just limping along on one foot, flying with one wing, and undeserving of your company, since he is not worthy to be called a Friend of the Cross, for we must love the Cross as Jesus Christ loved it "with a great heart and a willing mind" (II Mac. 1:3). That kind of half-hearted will is enough to spoil the whole flock, like a sheep with the scurvy. If any such one has slipped into your fold through the contaminated door of the world, then in the name of the crucified Christ, drive him out as you would a wolf from your sheep fold.

"If anyone will come after Me": for I have humbled Myself and reduced Myself to mere nothingness in such a way that I made Myself a worm rather than a man: "I am a worm and no man" (Ps. 21:7). After Me: for if I came into the world, it was only to espouse the Cross: "Behold I am come" (Ps. 39:8; Heb. 10:79); to set the cross in My heart of hearts: "In the midst of my heart" (Ps. 39:9), to love it from the days of my youth: "I have loved it from my youth" (Wis. 8:2) only to long for it all the days of my life: "how straitened I am" (Lk. 12:50); only to bear it with a joy I preferred even to the joys and delights that heaven and earth could offer: "Who, having joy set before Him, endured the cross" (Heb. 12:2); and, finally, not to be satisfied until I had expired in its divine embrace.

WEEK 4: DAY 5–FIRST MEDITATION

Taken from St. Louis de Montfort's
Friends of the Cross, §17 ff.

Self-Denial

Therefore, if anyone wants to come after Me, annihilated and crucified, he must glory as I did only in the poverty, humiliation and suffering of My Cross: "let him deny himself" (Mt.16:24).

Far be from the Company of the Friends of the Cross those who pride themselves in suffering, the worldly-wise elated geniuses and self-conceited individuals who are stubborn and puffed-up with their lights and talents. Far be they from us, those endless talkers who make plenty of noise, but bring forth no other fruit than vainglory. Far from us those high-browed devotees everywhere displaying the self-sufficient pride of Lucifer: "I am not like the rest!" (Lk.18:11). Far be from us those who must always justify themselves when blamed, resist when attacked and exalt themselves when humbled.

Be careful not to admit into your fellowship those frail, sensitive persons who are afraid of the slightest pin-prick, who sob and sigh when faced with the lightest suffering, who have never experienced a hair-shirt, a discipline or any other penitential instrument, and who, with their fashionable devotions, mingle the most artful delicacy and the most refined lack of mortification.

WEEK 4: DAY 5–SECOND MEDITATION

Taken from St. Louis de Montfort's
Friends of the Cross, §18 ff.

Suffering

Let him take up his cross, the one that is his. Let this man or this woman, rarely to be found and worth more than the entire world (Prov. 31:10-31), take up with joy, fervently clasp in his arms and bravely set upon his shoulders this cross that is his own and not that of another, his own cross, the one that My Wisdom designed for him in every detail of number, weight and measurement.

His own cross, whose four dimensions, its length, breadth, thickness and height (Eph. 3:18), I very accurately gauged with My own hands. His own cross, which all out of love for him I carved from a section of the very Cross I bore on Calvary, his cross, the grandest of all the gifts I have for My chosen ones on earth. His cross, made up in its thickness of temporal loss, humiliation, disdain, sorrow, illness and spiritual trial which My Providence will not fail to supply him with every day of his life.

His cross, made up in its length of a definite period of days or months when he will have to bear with slander or be helplessly stretched out on a bed of pain, or forced to beg, or else a prey to temptation, dryness, desolation and many another mental anguish; his cross, made up in its breadth of hard and bitter situations stirred up for him by his relatives, friends or servants. His cross, finally, made up in its depth of secret sufferings which I will have him endure nor will I allow him any comfort from created beings, for by My order they will turn from him too and even join Me in making him suffer.

Let him *carry* it, and not drag it, not shoulder it off, not lighten it, nor hide it. Let him hold it high in hand, without impatience or peevishness, without voluntary complaint or grumbling, without dividing or softening, without shame or human respect.

Let him place it on his forehead and say with St. Paul: "God forbid that I should glory save in the Cross of Our Lord Jesus Christ" (Gal. 6:14).

Let him carry it on his shoulders, after the example of Jesus Christ, and make it his weapon to victory and the scepter of his empire (Is. 9:16).

Let him root it in his heart and there change it into a fiery bush, burning day and night with the pure love of God, without being consumed.

The cross: it is the *cross* he must carry for there is nothing more necessary, more useful, more agreeable and more glorious than suffering for Jesus Christ. All of you are sinners and there is not a single one who is not deserving of hell; I myself deserve it the most. These sins of ours must be punished either here or hereafter. If they are punished in this world, they will not be punished in the world to come.

If we agree to God's punishing here below, this punishment will be dictated by love. For mercy, which holds sway in this world, will mete out the punishment, and not strict justice. This punishment will be light and momentary, blended with merit and sweetness and followed up with reward both in time and eternity.

But if the punishment due to our sins is held over for the next world, then God's avenging justice, which means fire and blood, will see to the punishing. What horrible punishment! How incomprehensible, how unspeakable! "Who knoweth the power of thy anger?" (Ps. 89:11).

Punishment devoid of mercy (Jas. 2:13), pity, mitigation or merit, without limit and without end. Yes, without end! That mortal sin of a moment that you committed, that deliberate evil thought which now escapes your memory, the word that is gone with the wind, that act of such short duration against God's law— they shall all be punished for an eternity, punished with the devils of hell, as long as God is God!

The God of vengeance will have no pity on your torments or your sobs and tears, violent enough to cleave the rocks. Suffering and still more suffering, without merit, without mercy and without end!

WEEK 4: DAY 5–THIRD MEDITATION

Taken from St. Louis de Montfort's
Friends of the Cross, §23 ff.

Cheerfulness and Courage Under the Cross

Do we think of this, my dear Brothers and Sisters, when we have some trial to undergo here below? Blessed indeed are we who have the privilege of exchanging an eternal and fruitless penalty for a temporary and meritorious suffering, just by patiently

carrying our cross. What debts we still have to pay! How many
sins we have committed which, despite a sincere confession and
heartfelt contrition, will have to be atoned for in Purgatory for
many a century, simply because in this world we were satisfied
with a few insignificant penances! Let us settle our debts with
good grace here below in cheerfully bearing our crosses, for in the
world to come everything must be expiated, even the idle word
(Mt. 12:36) and even to the last farthing.

If we could lay hands on the devil's death register in which he
has noted down all our sins and the penalty to be paid, what a
heavy debit we would find and how joyfully we would suffer many
years here on earth rather than a single day in the world to come.

Do you not flatter yourselves, Friends of the Cross, that you
are, or that you want to be the friends of God? Be firmly resolved
then to drink of the chalice which you must necessarily drink, if
you wish to enjoy the friendship of God.

"They drank the chalice of the Lord and became the friends
of God" (Common of Apostles, Lesson 7). The beloved Benjamin
had the chalice while his brothers had only the wheat (Gen. 44:14).
The disciple whom Jesus preferred had his Master's heart, went
up with Him to Calvary and drank of His chalice. "Can you
drink My chalice?" (Mt. 20:22).

To desire God's glory is good, indeed, but to desire it and
pray for it without being resolved to suffer all things is mere folly
and senseless asking. "You know not what you ask (Mt.
20:22)...you must undergo much suffering" (Acts 14:21): you
must, it is necessary, it is indispensable! We can enter the kingdom of heaven only at the price of many crosses and tribulations.

You take pride in being God's children and you do well; but
you should also rejoice in the lashes your good Father has given
you and in those He still means to give you; for He scourges
every one of His children (Prov. 3:11; Heb. 13:56; Apoc. 3:19).

If you are not of the household of His beloved sons, then—
how unfortunate! What a calamity! You are, as St. Augustine says,
listed with the reprobate. He also says: "The one that does not
mourn like a stranger and wayfarer in this world cannot rejoice in
the world to come as a citizen of heaven" (Sermon 31, 5 and 6).

If God the Father does not send you worthwhile crosses from time to time, that is because He no longer cares for you and is angry at you. He considers you a stranger, an outsider undeserving of His hospitality, or an unlawful child who has no right to share in his father's estate and no title to his father's supervision and discipline.

WEEK 4: DAY 5–FOURTH MEDITATION

Taken from St. Louis de Montfort's
Friends of the Cross, §26 ff.

Thorns or Roses? Jeers or Praise? Stones or Pillows?

Friends of the Cross, disciples of a crucified God, the mystery of the Cross is a mystery unknown to the Gentiles, repudiated by the Jews and spurned by both heretics and bad Catholics, yet it is the great mystery which you must learn to practice at the school of Jesus Christ and which you can learn only at His School. You would look in vain for any philosopher who taught it in the Academies of ancient times; you would ask in vain either the senses or reason to throw any light on it, for Jesus alone, through His triumphant grace, is able to teach you this mystery and make you relish it.

Become proficient, therefore, in this super-eminent branch of learning under such a skillful Master. Having this knowledge, you will be possessed of all other branches of learning, for it surpassingly comprises them all. The Cross is our natural as well as our supernatural philosophy. It is our divine and mysterious theology. It is our philosopher-stone which, by dint of patience, is able to transmute the grossest of metals into precious ones, the sharpest pain into delight, poverty into wealth and the deepest humiliation into glory. He amongst you who knows how to carry his cross, though he know not A from B, towers above all others in learning.

Listen to the great St. Paul, after his return from the third heaven where he was initiated into mysteries which even the angels had not learned. He proclaims that he knows nothing and wants to know nothing but Jesus Christ crucified (I Cor. 2:2). You can rejoice, then, if you happen to be a poor man without any schooling, or a poor woman deprived of intellectual attainments, for if you know how to suffer with joy, you are far more learned than a doctor of the Sorbonne, who is unable to suffer as you do.

You are members of Jesus Christ (I Cor. 6:15; 12:27; Eph. 5:30). What an honor! But, also, what need for suffering this entails! When the Head is crowned with thorns, should the members be wearing a laurel of roses? When the Head is jeered at and covered with mud from Calvary's road, should its members be enthroned and sprayed with perfume? When the Head has no pillow on which to rest, should its members be reclining on soft feathers? What an unheard of monster such a one would be!

No, no, dear companions of the Cross, make no mistake. The Christians you see around you, fashionably attired, supersensitive, excessively haughty and sedate, are neither true disciples, nor true members of the crucified Jesus. To think otherwise would be an insult to your thorn-crowned Head and His Gospel truth. My God! How many would-be Christians there are who imagine they are members of the Savior, when in reality they are His most insidious persecutors, for while blessing themselves with the sign of the Cross, they crucify Him in their hearts.

WEEK 4: DAY 5–FIFTH MEDITATION

Taken from St. Louis de Montfort's
Friends of the Cross, §27 ff.

Under the Chisel of God

If you are led by the spirit of Jesus and are living the same life with Him, your thorn-crowned Head, then you must look forward to nothing but thorns, nails and lashes, in a word, to nothing but a cross. A real disciple needs to be treated as his Master was, a member as its Head. And if the Head should offer you, as He offered St. Catherine of Sienna, the choice between a crown of thorns and a crown of roses, do as she did and grasp the crown of thorns, fastening it tightly to your brow in the likeness of Jesus.

You are aware of the fact that you are living temples of the Holy Spirit (I Cor. 6:19) and that, like living stones (I Pet. 2:5) you are to be placed by the God of love in the heavenly Jerusalem He is building. You must expect then to be shaped, cut and chiseled under the hammer of the Cross, otherwise you would remain unpolished stone, of no value at all, to be disregarded and cast aside.

Do not cause the hammer to recoil when it strikes you. Yield to the chisel that is carving you and the hand that is shaping you. It may be that this skillful and loving Architect wants to make you a cornerstone in His eternal edifice, one of His most faithful portraits in the heavenly kingdom. So let Him see to it. He loves you, He really loves you; He knows what He is doing, He has experience. Love is behind every one of His telling strokes; nor will a single stroke miscarry, unless your impatience deflects it.

At times the Holy Spirit compares the Cross to a winnowing that clears the good grain from the chaff and dust (Mt. 3:13; Lk. 3:17). Like grain in the winnowing then, let yourself be shaken up and tossed about without resistance, for the Father of the household is winnowing you and will soon have you in His harvest.

He also likens the Cross to a fire whose intense heat burns rust off iron. God is a devouring fire (Deut. 4:24, 9:3; Heb. 13:29) dwelling in our souls through His Cross, purifying them yet not consuming them, exemplified in the past in a burning bush (Ex. 3:23). He likens it at times to the crucible of a forge where gold is refined (Prov. 17:3; Eccli. 2:5) and dross vanishes in smoke, but, in the processing, the precious metal must be tried by fire, while the baser constituents go up in smoke and flame. So, too, in the crucible of tribulation and temptation, true Friends of the Cross are purified by their constancy in suffering while the enemies of the Cross vanish in smoke by their impatience and murmurings.

Consider the countless Apostles and Martyrs who were bathed in their own blood; the countless Virgins and Confessors who were impoverished, humiliated, exiled and cast aside. There at the side of Jesus consider Mary, who had never known either original or actual sin, yet whose tender, Immaculate Heart was pierced with a sharp sword even to its very depths. If I had time to dwell on the Passion of Jesus and Mary, I could prove that our sufferings are naught compared to theirs.

Who, then, would dare claim exemption from the Cross? Who would refuse to rush to the very place where he knows he will find a cross awaiting him? Who would refuse to borrow the words of the martyr, St. Ignatius: "Let fire and gallows, wild beasts and all the torments of the devil assail me, so that I may rejoice in the possession of Jesus Christ."

If you have not the patience to suffer and the generosity to bear your cross like the chosen ones of God, then you will have to trudge under its weight, grumbling and fretting like reprobates; like the two animals that dragged the Ark of the Covenant, lowing as they went (I Kgs. 6:12); like Simon the Cyrenaean who unwillingly put his hand to the very Cross of Christ (Mt. 7:32; Mk. 15:21) complaining while he carried it. You will be like the impenitent thief who from the summit of his cross plunged headlong into the depths of the abyss.

"Three crosses stand on Calvary's height. One must be chosen, so choose aright. Like a saint you must suffer, or a penitent thief, or like a reprobate, in endless grief."

WEEK 4: DAY 6–FIRST MEDITATION

Taken from St. Louis de Montfort's
Friends of the Cross, §33 ff.

Patience Under the Cross

This means that if you will not suffer gladly as Jesus did, or patiently like the penitent thief, then you must suffer despite yourself like the impenitent thief. You will have to drain the bitterest chalice even to the dregs, and with no hope of relief through grace. You will have to bear the entire weight of your cross, and without the powerful help of Jesus Christ.

Then, too, you will have that awful weight to bear which the devil will add to your cross, by means of the impatience the cross will cause you. After sharing the impenitent thief's unhappiness here on earth, you will meet him again in the fires of hell.

But if you suffer as you should, your cross will be a sweet yoke (Mt. 11:30), for Christ will share it with you. Your soul will be borne on it as on a pair of wings to the portals of heaven. It will be the mast on your ship, guiding you happily and easily to the harbor of salvation.

Carry your cross with patience: a cross patiently borne will be your light in spiritual darkness, for he knows naught who knows not how to suffer (Eccli. 34:9). Carry your cross with joy and you will be inflamed with divine love, for only in suffering can we dwell in the pure love of Christ.

Roses are only gathered from among thorns. As wood is fuel for the fire, so too is the Cross the only fuel for God's love. Remember that saying we read in the *Following of Christ*: "Inasmuch as you do violence to yourself," suffering patiently, "insofar do you advance" in divine love (Bk.1, Ch.15:11). Do not expect anything great from those fastidious, slothful souls who refuse the Cross when it approaches and who do not go in search of any, when discretion allows. What are they but untilled soil, which can produce only thorns, because it has not been turned up, harrowed and furrowed by a judicious laborer. They are like stagnant water which is unfit for either washing or drinking.

Carry your cross joyfully and none of your enemies will be able to resist its conquering strength (Lk. 21:15), while you yourself will enjoy its relish beyond compare. Yes, indeed, Brethren, remember that the real Paradise here on earth is to be found in suffering for Jesus. Ask the saints. They will tell you that they never tasted a banquet so delicious to the soul than when undergoing the severest torments. St. Ignatius the Martyr said: "Let all the torments of the devil come upon me!" "Either suffering or death!" said St. Theresa, and St. Magdalen de Pazzi: "Not death but suffering!" "May I suffer and be despised for Thy sake," said Blessed John of the Cross. In reading the lives of the saints we find many others speaking in the selfsame terms.

Be glad, therefore, and rejoice when God favors you with one of His choicest crosses, for without realizing it you are being blessed with the greatest gift that heaven has—the greatest gift of

God. Yes, the Cross is God's greatest gift. If you could only understand this, you would have Masses said; you would make novenas at the tombs of the saints; you would undertake long pilgrimages, as did the saints, to obtain this divine gift from heaven.

WEEK 4: DAY 6–SECOND MEDITATION

Taken from St. Louis de Montfort's
Friends of the Cross, §36 ff.

The Madness or the Glory of the Cross?

The world claims it is madness on your part, degrading and stupid, rash and reckless. Let the world in its blindness, say what it likes. This blindness which is responsible for a merely human and distorted view of the Cross is a source of glory for us. For every time they provide us with crosses by mocking and persecuting us, they are simply offering us jewels, setting us upon a throne and crowning us with laurels.

What I say is but little. Take all the wealth and honors and scepters and brilliant diadems of monarchs and princes, says St. John Chrysostom, they are all insignificant compared with the glory of the Cross, it is greater even than the glory of the Apostles and the Sacred Writers. Enlightened by the Holy Spirit, this saintly man goes as far as to say: If I were given the preference, I would gladly leave heaven to suffer for the God of heaven. I would prefer the darkness of a dungeon to the thrones of the highest heaven and the heaviest of crosses to the glory of the Seraphim. Suffering for me is of greater value than the gift of miracles, the power to command the infernal spirits, to master the physical universe, to stop the sun in its course and to raise the dead to life. Peter and Paul are far more glorious in the shackles of a dungeon than in being lifted to the third heaven and presented with the keys to Paradise.

In fact, was it not the Cross that gave Jesus Christ "a name which is above all names; that in the name of Jesus every knee should bow of those that are in heaven, on earth and under the earth" (Phil. 2:9-10). The glory of the one who knows how to suffer is so great that the radiance of his splendor rejoices heaven, angels and men and even the God of heaven. If the saints in heaven could still wish for something they would want to return to earth so as to have the privilege of bearing a cross.

If the Cross is covered with such glory on earth, how magnificent it must be in heaven. Who could ever understand and tell the eternal weight of glory we are given when, even for a single instant, we bear a cross as a cross should be borne (II Cor. 4:17)! Who could ever collate the glory that will be given in heaven for the crosses and sufferings we carried for a year, perhaps even for a lifetime.

Evidently, my dear Friends of the Cross, heaven is preparing something grand for you, as you are told by a great Saint, since the Holy Ghost has united you so intimately to an object which the whole world so carefully avoids. Evidently, God wishes to make of you as many saints as you are Friends of the Cross, if you are faithful to your calling and dutifully carry your cross as Jesus Christ has carried His.

But mere suffering is not enough. For even the devil and the world have their martyrs. We must suffer and bear our crosses in the footsteps of Jesus. *Let him follow Me*: this means that we must bear our crosses as Jesus bore His. To help you do this, I suggest the following rules:

WEEK 4: DAY 6–THIRD MEDITATION

Taken from St. Louis de Montfort's
Friends of the Cross, §42 ff.

14 Rules to Follow in the Carrying of the Cross

First. Do not, deliberately and through your own fault, procure crosses for yourself. You must not do evil in order to bring about good. You should never try to bring discredit upon yourself by doing things improperly, unless you have a special inspiration from on high. Strive rather to imitate Jesus Christ, Who did all things well (Mk. 7:37), not out of self-love or vainglory, but to please God and to win over His fellow men. Even though you do the best you can in the performance of your duty, you will still have to contend with contradiction, persecution and contempt which Divine Providence will send you against your will and without your choice.

Second. Should your neighbor be scandalized, although without reason, at any action of yours which in itself is neither good nor bad, then, for the sake of charity, refrain from it, to avoid the scandal of the weak. This heroic act of charity will be of much greater worth than the thing you were doing or intended to do.

If, however, you are doing some beneficial or necessary thing for others and were unreasonably disapproved by a hypocrite or prejudiced person, then refer the matter to a prudent adviser, letting him judge of its expedience and necessity. Should his decision be favorable, you have only to continue and let these others talk, provided they take no means to prevent you. Under such circumstances, you have our Lord's answer to His disciples when they informed Him that Scribes and Pharisees were scandalized at His words and deeds: *"Let them alone; they are blind"* (Mt. 15:14).

Third. Certain holy and distinguished persons have been asking for and seeking, or even, by eccentricities, bringing upon themselves, crosses, disdain and humiliation. Let us simply adore and admire the extraordinary workings of the Holy Spirit in these souls. Let us humble ourselves in the presence of this sublime virtue, without making any attempt to reach such heights, for compared with these racing eagles and roaring lions, we are simply fledglings and cubs.

Fourth. You can nevertheless and even should ask for the wisdom of the Cross, that sapid, experimental knowledge of the truth, which, in the light of faith, shows us the deepest mysteries, among others the mystery of the Cross. But this can be had only by dint of hard toil, profound humiliation and fervent prayer.

If you need that perfect spirit (Ps. 50:14) which enables us to bear the heaviest crosses with courage—that sweet, kindly spirit (Lk. 11:13) which enables us to relish in the higher part of the soul things that are bitter and repulsive—that wholesome, upright spirit (Ps. 50:12) which seeks God and God alone—that all-embracing knowledge of the Cross—briefly, that infinite treasure which gives the soul that knows how to make good use of it a share in the friendship of God (Wis. 7:14), ask for this wisdom; ask for it constantly, fervently, without hesitation or fear of not obtaining it. You will certainly obtain it and then see clearly, in the light of your own experience, how it is possible to desire, seek and relish the Cross.

Fifth. If, inadvertently, you blunder into a cross, or even if you do so through your own fault, forthwith humble yourself interiorly under the mighty hand of God (I Pet. 5:6), but do not worry over it. You might say to yourself: "*Lord, there is another trick of my trade.*" If the mistake you made was sinful, accept the humiliation you suffer as punishment. But if it was not sinful, then humbly accept it in expiation of your pride.

Often, actually very often, God allows His greatest servants, those who are far advanced in grace, to make the most humiliating mistakes. This humbles them in their own eyes and in the eyes of their fellow men. It prevents them from seeing and taking pride in the graces God bestows on them, or in the good deeds they do, so that, as the Holy Ghost declares: "*no flesh should glory in the sight of God*" (I Cor. 1:29).

Sixth. Be fully persuaded that through the sin of Adam and through our own actual sins, everything within ourselves is vitiated, not only the senses of the body, but even the powers of the soul. So much so that as soon as the mind, thus vitiated, takes delight in poring over some gift received from God, then the gift itself, or the act or the grace is tarnished and vitiated and God no longer favors it with His divine regard. Since looks and thoughts of the human mind can spoil man's best actions and God's choicest gifts, what about the acts which proceed from man's own will and which are more corrupt than the acts of the mind?

So we need not wonder, when God hides His own within the shadow of His countenance (Ps. 30:21), that they may not be defiled by the regards of their fellow men or by their own self-consciousness. What does not this jealous God allow and do to keep them hidden! How often He humiliates them! Into how many faults He permits them to fall! How often He allows them to be tempted as St. Paul was tempted! (II Cor. 12 :7) In what a state of uncertainty, perplexity and darkness he leaves them! How wonderful God is in His saints, and in the means He takes to lead them to humility and holiness!

Seventh. Be careful not to imitate proud self-centered zealots. Do not think that your crosses are tremendous, that they are tests of your fidelity to God and tokens of God's extraordinary love for you. This gesture has its source in spiritual pride. It is a snare quite subtle and beguiling, but full of venom. You ought to acknowledge...

First, that you are so proud and sensitive that you magnify straws into rafters, scratches into deep wounds, rats into elephants, a meaningless word, a mere nothing, in truth, into an outrageous, treasonable insult.

Second you should acknowledge that the crosses God sends you are really and truly loving punishments for your sins, and not special marks of God's benevolence.

Third, you must admit that He is infinitely lenient, when He sends you some cross or humiliation, in comparison with the number and atrocity of your sins. For these sins should be considered in the light of the holiness of a God Whom you have offended and Who can tolerate nothing that is defiled; in the light of a God dying and weighted down with sorrow at the sight of your sins; in the light of an everlasting hell which you have deserved a thousand times, perhaps a hundred thousand times.

Fourth, you should admit that the patience you put into suffering is more tinged than you think with natural human motives. You have only to note your little self-indulgences, your skillful seeking for sympathy, these confidences you so naturally make to friends, or perhaps to your spiritual director, your quick, clever excuses, the murmurings or rather the detractions so neatly worded, so charitably spoken against those who have injured you, the exquisite delight you take in dwelling on your misfortunes and that belief, so characteristic of Lucifer, that you are somebody (Acts 8:9), and so forth. Why, I should never finish if I were to point out all the ways and byways human nature takes, even in its sufferings.

Eighth. Take advantage of your sufferings, and more so of the small ones than of the great. God considers not so much what we suffer as how we suffer. To suffer much, yet badly, is to suffer like reprobates. To suffer much, even bravely, but for a wicked cause, is to suffer as a martyr of the devil. To suffer much or little for the sake of God is to suffer like saints.

If it be right to say that we can choose our crosses, this is particularly true of the little and obscure ones as compared with the huge, conspicuous ones, for proud human nature would likely ask and seek for the huge, conspicuous crosses even to the point of preferring them and embracing them. But to choose small, unnoticeable crosses and to carry them cheerfully requires the power of a special grace and unshakable fidelity to God.

Do then as the storekeeper does with his merchandise: make a profit on every article; suffer not the loss of the tiniest fragment of the true Cross. It may be only the sting of a fly or the point of a pin that annoys you, it may be the little eccentricities of a neighbor, some unintentional slight, the insignificant loss of a penny, some little restlessness of soul, a slight physical weakness, a light pain in your limbs.

Make a profit on every article as the grocer does, and you will soon become wealthy in God, as the grocer does in money, by adding penny to penny in his till. When you meet with the least contradiction, simply say: "*Blessed be God! My God I thank you.*" Then treasure up in the till of God's memory the cross which has just given you a profit. Think no more of it, except to say: "*Many thanks!*" or, "*Be merciful!*"

WEEK 4: DAY 6–FOURTH MEDITATION

Taken from St. Louis de Montfort's
Friends of the Cross, §50 ff.

14 Rules to Follow in the Carrying of the Cross (cont.)

Ninth. The love you are told to have for the Cross is not sensible love, for this would be impossible to human nature. It is important to note the three kinds of love: sensible love, rational love and love that is faithful and supreme; in other words, the love that springs from the lower part of man, the flesh; the love that springs from the superior part, his reason; and the love that springs from the supreme part of man, from the summit of his soul, which is the intellect enlightened by faith.

God does not ask you to love the Cross with the will of the flesh. Since the flesh is the subject of evil and corruption, all that proceeds from it is evil and it cannot, of itself, submit to the will of God and His crucifying law. It was this aspect of His human nature which Our Lord referred to when He cried out, in the Garden of Olives: "*Father,..not My will but Thine be done*" (Lk. 22:42).

If the lower powers of Our Lord's human nature, though holy, could not love the Cross without interruption, then with still greater reason, will our human nature, which is very much vitiated, repel it. At times, like many of the saints, we too may experience a feeling of even sensible joy in our sufferings, but that joy does not come from the flesh though it is in the flesh. It flows from our superior powers, so completely filled with the divine joy of the Holy Ghost, that it spreads to our lower powers. Thus a person, who is undergoing the most unbearable torture, is able to say: "*My heart and my flesh have rejoiced in the living God*" (Ps. 83:3).

There is another love for the Cross which I call rational, since it springs from the higher part of man, his reason. This love is wholly spiritual. Since it arises from the knowledge of the happiness there is in suffering for God, it can be and really is perceived by the soul. It also gives the soul inward strength and joy. Though this rational and perceptible joy is beneficial, even very beneficial, it is not an indispensable part of joyous, divine suffering.

This is why there is another love, which the masters of the spiritual life call the love of the summit and highest point of the soul, and which the philosophers call the love of the intellect.

When we possess this love, even though we experience no sensible joy or rational pleasure, we love and relish, in the light of pure faith, the cross we must bear, even though the lower part of our nature may often be in a state of warfare and alarm and may

moan and groan, weep and sigh for relief and thus we repeat with
Jesus Christ: "Father...not My will but Thine be done" (Lk. 2:42),
or with the Blessed Virgin: "Behold the handmaid of the Lord, be
it done to me according to Thy word" (Lk. 1:38). It is with one of
these two higher loves that we should accept and love our cross.

Tenth. Be resolved then, dear Friends of the Cross, to suffer
every kind of cross without excepting or choosing any: all poverty, all injustice, all temporal loss, all illness, all humiliation, all
contradiction, all calumny, all spiritual dryness, all desolation, all
interior and exterior trials. Keep saying: "My heart is ready, O
God, my heart is ready" (Ps. 56:8).

Be ready to be forsaken by men and angels and, seemingly,
by God Himself. Be ready to be persecuted, envied, betrayed,
calumniated, discredited and forsaken by everyone. Be ready to
undergo hunger, thirst, poverty, nakedness, exile, imprisonment,
the gallows and all kinds of torture, even though you are innocent of everything with which you may be charged.

What if you were cast out of your own home like Job and St.
Elizabeth of Hungary; thrown, like this saint, into the mire; or
dragged upon a manure pile like Job, malodorous and covered
with ulcers, without anyone to bandage your wounds, without a
morsel of bread, never refused to a horse or a dog? Add to these
dreadful misfortunes all the temptations with which God allows
the devil to prey upon you, without pouring into your soul the
least feeling of consolation. Firmly believe that this is the summit
of divine glory and real happiness for a true, perfect Friend of the
Cross.

Eleventh. For proper suffering, form the pious habit of considering four things: First, the Eye of God. God is like a great
king, who from the height of a tower observes with satisfaction
his soldier in the midst of the battle and praises his valor. What is
it on earth that attracts God's attention? Kings and emperors on
their thrones? He often looks at them with nothing but contempt.
Brilliant victories of a nation's armies, precious stones, any such
things that are great in the sight of men? "What is great to men, is
an abomination before God" (Lk. 16:15). What then does God
look upon with pleasure and delight? What is He asking the an-

gels about, and even the devils? It is about the man who is fighting for Him against riches, against the world, hell and himself, the man who is cheerfully carrying his cross. Hast thou not seen upon earth that great wonder which the heavens consider with admiration?— said the Lord to Satan; "hast thou considered My servant Job" (Job 2:3) who is suffering for Me?

Second, the Hand of God. Every disorder in nature, from the greatest to the smallest, is the work of His almighty Hand. The Hand that devastates an army of a hundred thousand (IV Kgs. 19:35) will make a leaf drop from a tree and a hair fall from your head (Lk. 21:18). The Hand that was laid so heavily upon Job is particularly light when it touches you with some little trial. This Hand fashions day and night, sun and darkness, good and evil. God permits the sin which provokes you; He is not the cause of its malice, although He does allow the act.

If anyone, then, treats you as Semei treated King David (II Kgs. 16:5-11), loading you with insults and casting stones at you, say to yourself: "I must not mind, I must not take revenge for this is an ordinance of God. I know that I have deserved every abuse and it is only right that God punish me. Desist, my hands, and strike not; desist, my tongue, and speak not; the person who injures me by word or deed is an ambassador, mercifully sent by God to punish me as His love alone knows how. Let us not incur His justice by assuming His right to vengeance. Let us not despise His mercy by resisting the affectionate strokes of His lash, lest, for His vengeance, He should remand us to the rigorous justice of eternity."

Consider how God bears you up with one Hand, of infinite power and wisdom, while with the other He chastises you. With the one He deals out death, while with the other He dispenses life. He humbles you and raises you up. With both arms, He reaches sweetly and mightily (Wis. 8:1) from the beginning of your life to its end. Sweetly: by not allowing you to be tempted or afflicted beyond your strength. Mightily: by favoring you with a powerful grace, proportioned to the vehemence and duration of your temptation or affliction. Mightily:—and the spirit of His Holy Church bears witness—"He is your stay on the brink of a

precipice, your guide along a misleading road, your shade in the
scorching heat, your raiment in the pouring rain or the biting
cold. He is your conveyance when you are utterly exhausted, your
help in adversity, your staff on the slippery way. He is your port
of refuge when, in the throes of a tempest, you are threatened
with ruin and shipwreck."

Third, consider the Wounds and Sorrows of our Crucified
Jesus. Hear what He Himself has to say: "All ye that pass along
the thorny and crucifying way I had to follow, look and see. Look
with the eyes of your body; look with the eye of contemplation,
and see if your poverty, nakedness, disgrace, sorrow, desolation
are like unto Mine. Behold Me, innocent as I am, then will you
complain, you who are guilty" (Lam. 1:12).

The Holy Ghost tells us, by the mouth of the Apostles, that
we should keep our eyes on Jesus Crucified (Gal. 3:1) and arm
ourselves with this thought of Him (I Pet. 4:1) which is our most
powerful and most penetrating weapon against all our enemies.
When you are assailed by poverty, disrepute, sorrow, temptation
or any other cross, arm yourselves with this shield, this breast-
plate, this helmet, this two-edged sword (Eph. 6:12-18), that is,
with the thought of Jesus crucified. There is the solution to your
every problem, the means you have to vanquish all your enemies.

Fourth, lift up your eyes, behold the beautiful crown that
awaits you in heaven if you carry your cross as you should. That
was the reward which kept Patriarchs and Prophets strong in faith
under persecution. It gave heart to the Apostles and martyrs in
their labors and torments.

Patriarchs used to say as Moses had said: "We would rather
be afflicted with the people of God," so as to enjoy eternal happiness with Him, "than to have the pleasure of sin for a short time
(Heb. 11:25-26). The prophets repeated David's words: "We suffer great persecutions on account of the reward" (Ps. 68:8,
118:112). The Apostles and martyrs voiced the sentiments of St.
Paul: "We are, as it were, men appointed to death: we are made a
spectacle to the world, and to angels, and to men," by our sufferings "being made the off-scouring of the world," (I Cor. 4:9-13),
"by reason of the exceeding and eternal weight of glory, which

this momentary and light tribulation worketh in us" (II Cor. 4:17).

Let us see and listen to the angels right above us: "Be careful not to forfeit the crown that is set aside for you if you bravely bear the cross that is given you. If you do not bear it well, someone will bear it in your stead and will take your crown. All the saints warn us: fight courageously, suffer patiently and you will be given an everlasting kingdom." Let us hear Jesus: "To him only will I give My reward who shall suffer and overcome through patience" (Apoc. 2:6, 11:17, 3:5, 21:7).

Let us lower our eyes and see the place we deserve: the place that awaits us in hell in the company of the wicked thief and the reprobate if we go through suffering as they did, resentful and bent on revenge. Let us exclaim after St. Augustine: "Burn, O Lord, cut, carve, divide in this world, in punishment for my sins, provided Thou pardon them in eternity."

Twelfth. Never murmur or deliberately complain about any created thing that God may use to afflict you. It is important to note the three kinds of complaints that may arise when misfortune assails you. The first is natural and involuntary. This happens when the human body moans and groans, sobs and sighs and weeps. If, as I said, the higher point of the soul submits to the will of God, there is no sin. The second is rational. Such is the case when we complain and disclose our hardship to some superior or physician, who is able to remedy it. This complaint may be an imperfection, if too eagerly made, but it is no sin. The third is sinful. This happens when a person complains of others either to rid himself of the suffering they cause him, or to take revenge. Or else when he wilfully complains about the sorrow, he must bear and shows signs of grief and impatience.

Thirteenth. Whenever you are given a cross, be sure to embrace it with humility and gratitude. If God, in His infinite goodness, favors you with a cross of some importance, be sure to thank Him in a special way and have others join you in thanking Him. Do as that poor woman did who, through an unjust lawsuit, lost everything she owned. She immediately offered the last few pennies she had, to have a Mass said in thanksgiving to Almighty God for the good fortune that had come to her.

Fourteenth. If you wish to be worthy of the best crosses, those that are not of your choice, then, with the help of a prudent director, take on some that are voluntary.

Suppose you have a piece of furniture that you do not need but prize. Give it to some poor person, and say to yourself: "Why should I have things I do not need, when Jesus is destitute?"

Do you dislike certain kinds of food, the practice of some particular virtue, or some offensive odor? Taste this food, practice this virtue, endure this odor, conquer yourself.

Is your affection for some person or thing too ardent and tender? Keep away, deprive yourself, break away from things that appeal to you.

Have you that natural tendency to see and be seen, to be doing things or going some place? Mind your eyes and hold your tongue, stop right where you are and keep to yourself.

Do you feel a natural aversion to some person or thing? Rise above self by keeping near them.

If you are truly Friends of the Cross, then, without your knowing it, love, which is always ingenious, will discover thousands of little crosses to enrich you. Then you need not fear self-conceit which often accompanies the patient endurance of conspicuous crosses and since you have been faithful in a few things, the Lord will keep His promise and set you over many things (Mt. 25:21-23): over many graces He will grant you; over many crosses He will send you; over much glory He will prepare for you....

WEEK 4: DAY 7–FIRST MEDITATION

Based on the *Imitation of Christ*, Book 3, Chapter 56

The Obligation of Self-Denial and Imitating Christ By Way of the Cross

Get out of yourself, and you will be able to pass into Me. I want you to learn complete self-abnegation in My will, without answering back or complaint. Follow Me—I am the Way, the Truth, and the Life. There is no journey without a route, no knowing without truth, no living without life.

I am the Way which you must follow, the Truth you must believe, the Life for which you must hope. I am the Way imperishable, the Truth infallible, the Life everlasting. I am the straightest Way, the highest Truth, the true Life, the blessed Life, the Life uncreated. If you remain in My Way you will know the truth, the truth will make you free, and you will lay hold of eternal life.

If you wish to enter into eternal life keep the commandments. If you wish to know the truth, believe Me. If you wish to be perfect, sell everything. If you wish to be My disciple renounce your very self. If you wish to possess the blessed life, despise the present life. If you wish to be exalted in heaven, humiliate yourself on earth. If you wish to reign with Me, carry your cross with Me. For only the Servants of the Cross will find the way of blessedness and true life.

Lord Jesus, since Thy way is narrow, and despised by the world, grant me to imitate Thee in despising the world. For the servant is not greater than his lord, nor the disciple above his master. Let Thy servant be occupied with Thy life, because there lies my salvation and true holiness. Whatever I read or hear outside of it, does not refresh me, nor fully delight me.

Come, let us march on, Jesus will be with us. For Jesus' sake we took up this cross. For Jesus' sake let us go on bearing it. He will be our helper, Who is our leader, and the One Who went before. Look, our King strides on ahead of us, and He will fight for us. Let us follow manfully, nor fear those things which terrify; let us be prepared to die bravely in battle, and let us not bring reproach against our honor by flying from the Cross.

WEEK 4: DAY 7–SECOND MEDITATION

Based on the *Imitation of Christ*, Book 4, Chapter 1

On the Sacrament of the Altar—On the Deep Reverence With Which Christ Must Be Received

The Voice of Christ
"Come to Me all who labor and are heavy-laden and I will refresh you," says the Lord. "The bread which I shall give is My Flesh, for the life of the world. Take it and eat, this is My Body, which is surrendered for you. Do this in memory of Me. He who eats My Flesh and drinks My blood, abides in Me and I in him. The words which I have spoken to you are spirit and life."

The Voice of the Disciple
These are Thy words, Christ, eternal Truth, although not said at one time, nor written together in one place. Therefore, because they are Thy words and true, all of them must be received by me with gratitude and trust. They are *Thy* words and Thou hast spoken them; they are also *my* words because Thou hast uttered them for my salvation. Gladly I receive them from Thy mouth, that they may be more firmly planted in my heart. Words of such great trustworthiness, full of sweetness and love, stir me, but my own sins terrify me, and my impure conscience beats me back from receiving mysteries so great. The sweetness of Thy words beckons me on, but the multitude of my sins weighs me down.

Thou bid me to approach Thee with confidence, if I wish to have a part in Thee, and that I may receive the nourishment of immortality, if I desire to win eternal life and glory. "Come," Thou sayest, "all you who labor and are heavy-laden, and I will refresh you." O, sweet and friendly word in a sinner's ear, that Thou, Lord God, invitest the needy and the poor to the communion of Thy most Holy Body! Who am I, Lord, that I should presume to approach Thee? Look, the heaven of heavens does not contain Thee, and Thou sayest: "Come to Me, all of you."

What does so friendly an invitation mean? How can I be so bold as to come, who am conscious of nothing good in myself?

How can I bring Thee into my house, who have so often affronted Thy most kindly face? Angels and Archangels stand in awe of Thee, the saintly, and the just fear Thee, and Thou sayest: "Come to me, all of you." Unless it were Thee, Lord, and unless it were Thy command, who would dare to draw near?

See how Noah, a just man, labored for a hundred years building the ark, that with a few he might be saved. How shall I, in one hour, be able to prepare myself to receive the Builder of the world? Moses, made an ark of imperishable wood, which he covered over with the purest gold, that he might store in it the tablets of the law. I, a loathsome creature, dare to take up so lightly the Founder of the law? Solomon, the wisest of Israel's kings, built, in seven years, a magnificent temple in praise of Thy name, and for eight days celebrated the ceremony of its dedication. I, who cannot spend a half-hour devoutly, how shall I dare bring Thee into my house?

O, my God, how much they tried to please Thee! Alas, how little is what I do! What a short time I spend when I am preparing myself for Holy Communion! Rarely am I quite composed, most rarely cleansed of all distraction. And surely in the saving presence of Thy Godhead, no unbecoming thought should arise, nor any created thing lay hold upon me, for it is not an angel, but the Lord of Angels, whom I am about to receive as my guest. There is a vast difference between the ark of the covenant with its relics, and Thy most pure Body with Its unspeakable virtues, between those sacrifices of the law which showed in symbol that which was to be, and the true sacrifice of Thy Body, the consummation of all the ancient sacrifices. How great should be my reverence for Thy most Holy Body!

WEEK 4: DAY 7–THIRD MEDITATION

On the Deep Reverence With Which Christ Must Be Received in the Eucharist (Part One)

Based on the *Imitation of Christ*, Book 4, Chapter 1

Why then am I not more on fire before Thy awesome presence? Why do I not prepare myself with greater care to take up Thy holy things, when those holy Patriarchs and Prophets of old, kings, too, and princes with the whole people, showed such heartfelt devotion towards the divine service?

The most devout King David danced before the ark of God with all his strength, remembering the benefits granted of old to his ancestors; he made musical instruments of varied sorts, and composed psalms, and appointed them to be sung with joy, and did so himself often with the harp, inspired with the Holy Spirit's grace; he taught the people of Israel to praise God with the whole heart, and with one voice of harmony each day to praise and to extol Him. If such devotion then was exercised, and such memorial of God's praise was manifest before the ark of witness, how great now, by me and all Christ's people, should reverence and devotion be shown in the presence of the Blessed Sacrament, and in taking up the most precious Body of Christ?

Many rush to different places to visit the relics of the saints, and wonder to hear the deeds they did; they look on the vast buildings of their shrines, and kiss their bones wrapped in silks and gold. And look, Thou art here, beside me on the altar, my God, saint of saints, Creator of men, and Lord of angels. Often in seeing such things, it is the curiosity of men, and the novelty of what they look upon, and small fruit of better living which is carried home, especially where there is much frivolous rushing about without real repentance. But here, in the Blessed Sacrament of the Altar, Thou art wholly present, my God, the man Christ Jesus, where also the abundant fruit of eternal salvation is fully received, as often as it is taken up worthily and devoutly. But any levity, curiosity or sensuality does not bring one to this, but strong faith, devout hope and sincere love.

WEEK 4: DAY 7–FOURTH MEDITATION

Based on the *Imitation of Christ*, Book 4, Chapter 1

On the Deep Reverence With Which Christ Must Be Received in the Eucharist (Part Two)

O God, unseen Creator of the world, how wondrously dost Thou deal with us, how sweetly and graciously dost Thou arrange things for Thy chosen ones, to whom Thou offer Thy own self for them to receive in the Blessed Sacrament! For this surpasses all reach of thought, this chiefly draws the heart of the devout and fires their love. For even Thy true faithful ones, who order their whole life for betterment, often receive from this most worthy Sacrament great grace of devotion, and love of virtue.

O, admirable and hidden grace of the Blessed Sacrament, which only Christ's faithful know, but which the faithless and the servants of sin cannot experience! In this Sacrament spiritual grace is conferred, and lost virtue made good in the soul, and beauty marred by sin returns. This grace is sometimes so great that, out of the fullness of devotion that it gives, even the feeble body feels ampler powers bestowed upon it.

It must nevertheless be a matter for grief and great pity that, lukewarm and negligent, we are not drawn with deeper feeling to receive Christ, in Whom stands the whole hope and merit of those who must be saved, for He is our sanctification and our redemption, the consolation of wayfarers, and the eternal fruitfulness of the saints. And so it is truly a matter for grief, that many attend so little to this health-giving mystery, which makes heaven glad, and preserves the whole wide world. Alas, the blindness and hardness of the human heart, not to attend the more to this gift so unutterable, and from daily custom to slide away to carelessness.

For if this most Holy Sacrament were to be celebrated in one place only, and consecrated by one priest only in the world, with what greater desire do you think would men be affected towards that place and such a priest of God, so that they might see the divine mysteries celebrated? But now many are made priests, and

Christ is offered up in many places, so that the grace and love of God towards man should appear so much the greater, as Holy Communion is more widely spread through all the world. Thanks to Thee, good Jesus, Eternal Pastor, Who deigned to refresh us poor exiles with Thy precious Body and Blood, and even with the speech of Thy own mouth to invite us to partake of these mysteries, saying: "Come to Me all you who labor and are heavy laden, and I will refresh you."

WEEK 4: DAY 7–FIFTH MEDITATION

On the Devout Soul's Yearning for Union with Christ in the Sacrament

The Voice of the Disciple

Who will grant me, Lord, to discover Thee alone, and open my whole heart to Thee, and enjoy Thee as my soul longs to do, and that no one may henceforth despise me, nor anything created move me or think upon me, but Thou alone should speak to me, and I to Thee, just as the lover is wont to speak to his beloved, and friend have fellowship with friend? This I pray, this I long for, that I may be wholly one with Thee, and withdraw my heart from all created things, and, through Holy Communion and its frequent reception, learn better to savor the heavenly and the eternal. Ah, Lord God, when shall I be wholly united and lost in Thee, and utterly forgetful of myself? "Thou in me and I in Thee"; so grant that thus we may abide together in one.

Truly, Thou art my Beloved, chosen from thousands, in whom it has pleased my soul to dwell all the days of its life. Truly Thou art my peacemaker, in Whom is perfect peace and true rest, and apart from Whom is toil and grief and misery unbounded. Thou art, in truth, a God Who hides Himself, and Thy counsel is not with the ungodly, but Thy speech is with the humble and sincere. O, how sweet, Lord, is Thy Spirit which, in order to show Thy sweetness towards Thy children, refreshes them with that Bread most sweet that comes down from heaven. Truly there is no other nation so great that has gods which draw close to it. Since Thou

O Lord, art always at the side of Thy faithful ones, to whom Thou givest Thyself to feed and delight them, to comfort them each day and lift their hearts heavenward.

For what other nation is there so renowned as the common people of Christ, or what created under heaven so beloved as the devout soul, whom God approaches that He may feed it with His glorious Flesh. O, grace unspeakable, O wondrous condescension, O love beyond measure, uniquely bestowed upon men! But what shall I return to the Lord for that grace, for love so excellent? There is nothing that I can give more acceptably than my heart in tribute totally to God for closest union with Him. Then all that is within me shall make glad, when my soul shall be made perfectly one with God. Then will He say to me: "If you will be with Me, I will be with thee." And I will reply to Him: "Deign, O Lord to abide with me, and I will gladly be with Thee. This is all my longing, that my heart be joined with Thine."

SUPPLEMENTARY MEDITATIONS

The following meditations are by no means obligatory, since the essence of their content has been covered in the preceding meditations of Week Four. If not used now, these supplementary meditations may be of use when renewing the Consecration in future years, or as sources of meditation in the weeks and months following the Consecration.

First Supplementary Meditation
Based on the *Imitation of Christ*, Book 2, Chapter 12

The Royal Way of the Holy Cross

This saying seems hard to many: "Deny yourself, take up your cross and follow Jesus." But much harder it will be to hear that final word: "Depart from Me, accursed ones, into eternal fire." For those who gladly hear now the word of the Cross and follow, shall have nothing then to fear from the hearing of eternal condemnation. This Sign of the Cross shall be in the heaven, when the Lord shall come to judgment. Then all the Servants of the Cross who have conformed in life to the Crucified, shall come to Christ the Judge with great confidence.

Why, therefore, do you fear to take up the Cross, through which is the road to the kingdom? In the Cross is salvation, in the Cross life, in the Cross protection from our foes; in the Cross is the inflow of heaven's sweetness, in the Cross strength of mind, in the Cross joy of the spirit; in the Cross is the height of virtue, in the Cross perfection of holiness. There is no salvation for the soul, nor hope of eternal life, except in the Cross.

Take up, therefore, your cross and follow Jesus, and you will go into eternal life. He went ahead of you bearing His own Cross, and died for you upon the Cross, that you, too, might bear your cross, and aspire to die upon the cross. For if you should have died with Him, equally, too, you shall live with Him; and if you have been a partner of His suffering, you will be a partner of His glory too.

Look and see! It all consists in the Cross, and it all lies in dying; and there is no other way to life and true peace within, save the way of the Holy Cross, and daily counting ourselves dead. Go where you wish, seek whatever you shall wish, and you will not find a higher way above, nor a safer way below, save the way of the Holy Cross. Dispose and order all things according to your own wishes and observations, and you will only find that, willingly or unwillingly, you must suffer something, and so you will ever find the Cross. For either you will feel pain of body, or you will endure tribulation of the soul within.

Sometimes you will be abandoned by God, sometimes you will be stirred up by your neighbor, and, what is more, often you will be a burden to your very self. Yet you will not be able to find release or alleviation in any remedy, but must endure while God so wills. For God wills that without consolation you should learn to suffer tribulation, and that you should utterly subject yourself to Him, and from tribulation become more humble. No one so feels Christ's suffering from the heart, like the one to whom it has befallen to suffer in the same way.

The Cross, therefore, is always ready and everywhere is waiting for you. You cannot escape it wherever you run, because, wherever you go, you carry yourself with you, and you will always find yourself. Turn above, turn below, turn without, turn within; and in all these places you will find the Cross, and everywhere you must maintain patience, if you wish to have peace within your soul and merit the eternal crown.

Second Supplementary Meditation
Based on the *Imitation of Christ*, Book 2, Chapter 12

The Royal Way of the Holy Cross

If you willingly carry the Cross, it will carry you and lead you to your desired haven, where assuredly you will see the end of suffering, although that will not be here on earth. If you carry it unwillingly, you make a burden for yourself, and load yourself all the more, and yet you will still have to carry it. If you cast away one cross, undoubtedly you will find another, and perhaps a heavier one. Do you think to escape what no mortal has been able to pass by? Who amongst the saints in the world was without a cross and tribulation? For Jesus Christ, Our Lord, was not one hour without the anguish of His suffering. "It behoved Christ to suffer," He said, "and to rise from the dead, and enter into His glory." And how do you seek another way than this royal way, which is the way of the Holy Cross?

The whole life of Christ was a cross and martyrdom; and do you seek for yourself quietness and joy? You are wrong, you are wrong, if you seek other than to suffer tribulations, because the whole life of man is full of miseries, and set about with crosses. And the higher one has progressed in spirit, so the heavier he will often find the crosses, because the pain of his exile grows from love. The grace of Christ, which so acts in frail flesh, gives such fervor of spirit, that the soul draws near to and loves what naturally it always loathes and flees.

It is not in the nature of man to bear the Cross, to love the Cross, to buffet the body and bring it into servitude, to bear insults willingly, to despise oneself and desire to be despised; to bear any adversities and losses, and to long for no prosperity in this world. If you count on yourself, you will not be able to do any of this; but if you trust in the Lord, you will be given strength from heaven, and the world and the flesh shall be subjected to your sway. You shall not even fear your enemy, the devil, if you have been armed by faith and marked by the Cross of Christ.

Set yourself therefore, like a good and faithful servant of Christ, to the manful carrying of the Cross of your Lord, crucified because of love for you. Prepare yourself to bear many adversities and various trials in this wretched life, because the Cross shall be with you wherever you shall be, and so in truth you will find it wherever you shall hide. So it must be, and there is no means of escaping evil's tribulation and sorrow, except by bearing them. Drink with love the Lord's chalice, if you desire to be His friend, and have part in Him. Leave consolations to God and set yourself to the bearing of tribulations, considering them to be the greatest consolations.

Third Supplementary Meditation
Based on the *Imitation of Christ*, Book 2, Chapter 12

The Royal Way of the Holy Cross

When you reach the point where tribulation is sweet and savory to you for Christ's sake, then consider it is well with you, because you have found paradise on earth. So long as suffering is a burden to you and you seek to escape, so long it will be ill with you, and tribulation will follow you everywhere. If you set yourself to what you should, namely, to suffer and to die, you will soon be made better, and will find peace. Though you had been snatched to the third heaven with Paul, you are not for that reason exempt from suffering evil. "I will show you," says Jesus, "what you must suffer for My name." Therefore, it remains to you to suffer, if it is your wish to love Jesus and serve Him for ever.

Would that you were worthy to suffer something for Jesus' name; what great glory would await you, what exaltation for all the saints of God, what encouragement also for your neighbor! For everyone commends patience, though few are willing to suffer. Surely, you should suffer a little for Christ, when many suffer more heavily for the world. Know for certain that you must live your life while dying. And as each one dies the more to self, so the more he begins to live for God. No man is fit for the understanding of heavenly things unless he has submitted himself to bearing adversities for Christ. Nothing is more acceptable to God, nothing more healthy for you in this world, than suffering willingly for Christ. And if you had to choose, you should rather pray to suffer adversity for Christ, than to be refreshed by many consolations, because you would be more like Christ, and more in conformity with all the saints. For our merit, and the advancement of your state, consists not in many delights and consolations, but in bearing great troubles and tribulations.

If, indeed, there had been anything better and more useful to man's salvation than to suffer, Christ would assuredly have shown it by word and deed. For both the disciples who follow Him, and all those desiring to follow Him, He clearly exhorts to carry the Cross, saying: "If anyone wishes to come after Me, let him deny himself, and take up his cross and follow Me." With all things, therefore, read and examined, let this be the last conclusion: "Through many tribulations we must enter the kingdom of God."

Fourth Supplementary Meditation
Based on the *Imitation of Christ*, Book 3, Chapter 5

The Wondrous Effect of God's Love

The one who loves flies, runs and is glad; he is free and not tied down. He gives all for all, and has all in all, because he rests in One Who is supreme above all things, from Whom every good thing flows and goes forth. It looks not to gifts, but turns to the Giver, above all good things. Love often knows no measure, but goes beyond all measure. Love feels no burden, thinks nothing of labors; it strives for more than it can do; it makes no complaint about impossibility, because it thinks all things are open and possible to it. It thinks it can do everything, and completes and brings to accomplishment many things, in which the one who does not love, fails and falls.

Love watches, and while sleeping does not sleep; wearied, is not tired; hemmed in, is not confined; fearful, is not disturbed;

but like a living flame and burning torch, it bursts upwards and securely passes through all. If anyone loves, he knows what this voice cries. A great city in the ears of God is the burning love of the soul which says: "Thou art wholly mine and I am wholly Thine."

Make me grow in love that I may learn to savor with the inner mouth of the heart, how sweet it is to love, and let me be melted down and swim in love. Let me be possessed by love, rising above myself by my strong fervor and ecstasy. Let me sing a song of love, let me follow my Beloved on high, let my soul faint in Thy praise, exalting in Thy love. Let me love Thee more than myself, and myself only because Thou dost love me, and let me love all men in Thee who truly love Thee, as the law of love, shining from Thee, bids.

Love is swift, sincere, pious, pleasant and beautiful, strong, patient, faithful, prudent, long-suffering, manly, and never seeks itself. For when anyone seeks himself, there he falls from love. Love is guarded, humble, upright, not soft, nor light, nor reaching for empty things, sober, chaste, steadfast, quiet, and self-controlled in all the senses. Love is subject and obedient to all in authority, vile and despised in its own eyes, devoted to God and thankful, trusting and hoping always in Him, even when God is not a sweet savor to him, because without sorrow there is no living in love.

He who is not prepared to suffer all things, and to stand by the will of the Beloved, is not worthy to be called a lover. The lover must willingly embrace all things hard and bitter for the Beloved's sake, and not to be turned away from Him by any adverse circumstances.

Fifth Supplementary Meditation
Based on the *Imitation of Christ*, Book 3, Chapter 6

The Proof of a True Lover

Son, you are not yet a strong and prudent lover. Why is that Lord? Because on account of a little opposition, you fall away from what you have begun and too greedily you seek consolation. A strong lover stands strong in temptations and does not believe the skillful persuasions of the enemy. As in prosperity I please him, so in adversity I do not displease him.

The prudent lover does not so much consider the lover's gift, as the love of the giver. He looks rather at the love than the value, and esteems all gifts below the giver. The noble lover does not dwell on the gift, but in Me above every gift. For that reason all is not lost, if at times you think less well of Me or of My saints than you might wish. That good and sweet affection of which you are sometimes conscious, is the effect of present grace, and a kind of foretaste of heaven. But do not desire such feelings, because they come and go. However, to fight against the evil movements of the mind that so often attack us, and to scorn the suggestion of the devil, is a mark of virtue and great merit.

Therefore, do not let strange fantasies disturb you, whatever source they come from. Bravely hold your ground and upright intention towards God. It is not illusion that sometimes you are suddenly snatched into rapture, and immediately return to the accustomed trifles of your heart. For you suffer them against your will, rather than invite them in; and so, as long as they displease you and you fight against them, it is merit and not loss.

Know that your old enemy strives to hinder your desire for good and to distract you from every holy exercise, such as the contemplation of the saints, from the remembrance of My passion, from the salutary remembrance of your sins, from weeding out your own heart and from the firm purpose of growing in virtue. He attacks you with many evil thoughts, that he may bring about weariness and terror in you, and call you back from prayer and holy reading. He hates humble Confession and, if he could, would make you cease from Communion. Do not believe him, nor take thought of him, even though he often lays out the set traps for you. Know that he is behind the many evil and unclean things that come to mind. Say to him: "Away, unclean spirit! Blush for shame miserable evil one! You are foul for bringing such matters to my ears. Depart from me, you accursed liar! I shall have no part to play with you! Jesus will be with me like a strong warrior, and you will put to shame, confusion and defeat! I would rather die and submit to any pain, than consent to you! Shut your mouth you accursed deceiver, I will not listen to you any more, even though you can cause more troubles for me!"

"The Lord is my light and my salvation, whom shall I fear. Though a host should camp against me, my heart shall not fear. The Lord is my helper and my redeemer."

Fight like a good soldier and if, sometimes, you collapse out of weakness, pick yourself up with greater strength than before, trusting in My more abundant grace and beware of empty confidence and pride. Because of this, many are led into error and sometimes almost slip into an incurable blindness. Let this ruin of the proud, who foolishly rely too much upon themselves, serve to warn you and keep you ever humble.

Supplementary Meditations on The Gospel of St John Chapters 13 to 21 inclusive

St. Louis de Montfort also recommends that we meditate upon the following passages from Scripture, which primarily deal with the Passion and Death of Our Lord. Spiritual writers are in agreement about the efficacy of meditating upon the Passion of Our Lord, saying that it is a means to overcoming temptations, a strength in our sufferings and an example of the virtues we need to practice in order to save our souls. That is why Holy Mother Church places them before us at that holiest of times—Holy Week—during which all four Evangelists give us an account of the events surrounding Our Lord's Passion. If such is the importance of these Gospel passages, then let us find time to dwell upon them.

Below, you will find supplementary passages from the Gospel of St. John. St. Louis de Montfort recommends that during this week of Knowledge of Jesus, we meditate upon chapters 13 to 21 of St. John's Gospel. These texts are so extensive that we felt it was not very practical to embody them in the main series of meditations featured during Week Four. This, however, does not lessen their importance in any way. Thus we have included them here in their entirety. It is not obligatory to meditate upon the following Scriptural passages, since the essence of their content has been covered in the preceding Scriptural meditations of Week Four. If not used now, these supplementary meditations may be of use when renewing the Consecration in future years, or as sources of meditation in the weeks and months following the Consecration.

Taken from the Gospel according to St. John, Chapter 13

1 Before this festival day of the pasch, Jesus knowing that his hour was come, that he should pass out of this world to the Father: having loved his own who were in the world, he loved them unto the end.

2 And when supper was done, (the devil having now put into the heart of Judas Iscariot, the son of Simon, to betray him,)

3 Knowing that the Father had given him all things into his hands, and that he came from God, and goeth to God;

4 He riseth from supper, and layeth aside his garments, and having taken a towel, girded himself.

5 After that, he putteth water into a basin, and began to wash the feet of the disciples, and to wipe them with the towel wherewith he was girded.

6 He cometh therefore to Simon Peter. And Peter saith to him: Lord, dost thou wash my feet?

7 Jesus answered, and said to him: What I do thou knowest not now; but thou shalt know hereafter.

8 Peter saith to him: Thou shalt never wash my feet. Jesus answered him: If I wash thee not, thou shalt have no part with me.

9 Simon Peter saith to him: Lord, not only my feet, but also my hands and my head.

10 Jesus saith to him: He that is washed, needeth not but to wash his feet, but is clean wholly. And you are clean, but not all.

11 For he knew who he was that would betray him; therefore he said: You are not all clean.

12 Then after he had washed their feet, and taken his garments, being sat down again, he said to them: Know you what I have done to you?

13 You call me Master, and Lord; and, you say well, for so I am.

14 If then I being your Lord and Master, have washed your feet; you also ought to wash one another's feet.

15 For I have given you an example, that as I have done to you, so you do also.

16 Amen, amen I say to you: The servant is not greater than his lord; neither is the apostle greater than he that sent him.

17 If you know these things, you shall be blessed if you do them.

18 I speak not of you all: I know whom I have chosen. But that the scripture may be fulfilled: He that eateth bread with me, shall lift up his heel against me.

19 At present I tell you, before it come to pass: that when it shall come to pass, you may believe that I am he.

20 Amen, amen I say to you, he that receiveth whomsoever I send, receiveth me; and he that receiveth me, receiveth him that sent me.

21 When Jesus had said these things, he was troubled in spirit; and he testified, and said: Amen, amen I say to you, one of you shall betray me.

22 The disciples therefore looked one upon another, doubting of whom he spoke.

23 Now there was leaning on Jesus' bosom one of his disciples, whom Jesus loved.

24 Simon Peter therefore beckoned to him, and said to him: Who is it of whom he speaketh?

25 He therefore, leaning on the breast of Jesus, saith to him: Lord, who is it?

26 Jesus answered: He it is to whom I shall reach bread dipped. And when he had dipped the bread, he gave it to Judas Iscariot, the son of Simon.

27 And after the morsel, Satan entered into him. And Jesus said to him: That which thou dost, do quickly.

28 Now no man at the table knew to what purpose he said this unto him.

29 For some thought, because Judas had the purse, that Jesus had said to him: Buy those things which we have need of for the

festival day: or that he should give something to the poor.

30 He therefore having received the morsel, went out immediately. And it was night.

31 When he, therefore, was gone out, Jesus said: Now is the Son of man glorified, and God is glorified in him.

32 If God be glorified in him, God also will glorify him in himself; and immediately will he glorify him.

33 Little children, yet a little while I am with you. You shall seek me; and as I said to the Jews: Whither I go you cannot come; so I say to you now.

34 A new commandment I give unto you: That you love one another, as I have loved you, that you also love one another.

35 By this shall all men know that you are my disciples, if you have love one for another.

36 Simon Peter saith to him: Lord, whither goest thou? Jesus answered: Whither I go, thou canst not follow me now; but thou shalt follow hereafter.

37 Peter saith to him: Why cannot I follow thee now? I will lay down my life for thee.

38 Jesus answered him: Wilt thou lay down thy life for me? Amen, amen I say to thee, the cock shall not crow, till thou deny me thrice.

Taken from the Gospel according to St. John, Chapter 14

1 Let not your heart be troubled. You believe in God, believe also in me.

2 In my Father's house there are many mansions. If not, I would have told you: because I go to prepare a place for you.

3 And if I shall go, and prepare a place for you, I will come again, and will take you to myself; that where I am, you also may be.

4 And whither I go you know, and the way you know.

5 Thomas saith to him: Lord, we know not whither thou goest; and how can we know the way?

6 Jesus saith to him: I am the way, and the truth, and the life. No man cometh to the Father, but by me.

7 If you had known me, you would without doubt have known my Father also: and from henceforth you shall know him, and you have seen him.

8 Philip saith to him: Lord, show us the Father, and it is enough for us.

9 Jesus saith to him: Have I been so long a time with you; and have you not known me? Philip, he that seeth me seeth the Father also. How sayest thou, Show us the Father?

10 Do you not believe, that I am in the Father, and the Father in me? The words that I speak to you, I speak not of myself. But the Father who abideth in me, he doth the works.

11 Believe you not that I am in the Father, and the Father in me?

12 Otherwise believe for the very works' sake. Amen, amen I say to you, he that believeth in me, the works that I do, he also shall do; and greater than these shall he do.

13 Because I go to the Father: and whatsoever you shall ask the Father in my name, that will I do: that the Father may be glorified in the Son.

14 If you shall ask me any thing in my name, that I will do.

15 If you love me, keep my commandments.

16 And I will ask the Father, and he shall give you another Paraclete, that he may abide with you for ever.

17 The spirit of truth, whom the world cannot receive, because it seeth him not, nor knoweth him: but you shall know him; because he shall abide with you, and shall be in you.

18 I will not leave you orphans, I will come to you.

19 Yet a little while: and the world seeth me no more. But you see because I live, and you shall live.

20 In that day you shall know, that I am in my Father, and you in me, and I in you.

21 He that hath my commandments, and keepeth them; he it is that loveth me. And he that loveth me, shall be loved of my Father: and I will love him, and will manifest myself to him.

22 Judas saith to him, not the Iscariot: Lord, how is it, that thou wilt manifest thyself to us, and not to the world?

23 Jesus answered, and said to him: if any one love me, he will

keep my word, and my Father will love him, and we will come to him, and will make our abode with him.

24 He that loveth me not, keepeth not my words. And the word which you have heard, is not mine; but the Father's who sent me.

25 These things have I spoken to you, abiding with you.

26 But the Paraclete, the Holy Ghost, whom the Father will send in my name, he will teach you all things, and bring all things to your mind, whatsoever I shall have said to you.

27 Peace I leave with you, my peace I give unto you: not as the world giveth, do I give unto you. Let not your heart be troubled, nor let it be afraid.

28 You have heard that I said to you: I go away, and I come unto you. If you loved me, you would indeed be glad, because I go to the Father: for the Father is greater than I.

29 And now I have told you before it came to pass: that when it shall come to pass, you may believe.

30 I will not now speak many things with you. For the prince of this world cometh, and in me he hath not any thing.

31 But he comes that the world may know, that I love the Father, and that I do as the Father has commanded me. Arise, let us go from here.

Taken from the Gospel according to St. John, Chapter 15

1 I am the true vine; and my Father is the husbandman.

2 Every branch in me, that beareth not fruit, he will take away: and every one that beareth fruit, he will purge it, that it may bring forth more fruit.

3 Now you are clean by reason of the word, which I have spoken to you.

4 Abide in me, and I in you. As the branch cannot bear fruit of itself, unless it abide in the vine, so neither can you, unless you abide in me.

5 I am the vine; you the branches: he that abideth in me, and I in him, the same beareth much fruit: for without me you can do nothing.

6 If any one abide not in me, he shall be cast forth as a branch, and shall wither, and they shall gather him up, and cast him into the fire, and he burneth.

7 If you abide in me, and my words abide in you, you shall ask whatever you will, and it shall be done unto you.

8 In this is my Father glorified; that you bring forth very much fruit, and become my disciples.

9 As the Father hath loved me, I also have loved you. Abide in my love.

10 If you keep my commandments, you shall abide in my love; as I also have kept my Father's commandments, and do abide in his love.

11 These things I have spoken to you, that my joy may be in you, and your joy may be filled.

12 This is my commandment, that you love one another, as I have loved you.

13 Greater love than this no man hath that a man lay down his life for his friends.

14 You are my friends, if you do the things that I command you.

15 I will not now call you servants: for the servant knoweth not what his lord doth. But I have called you friends: because all things whatsoever I have heard of my Father, I have made known to you

16 You have not chosen me: but I have chosen you and have appointed you, that you should go, and should bring forth fruit; and your fruit should remain that whatsoever you shall ask of the Father in my name, he may give it you

17 These things I command you, that you love one another.

18 If the world hate you, know ye, that it hath hated me before you.

19 If you had been of the world, the world would love its own: but because you are not of the world, but I have chosen you out of the world, therefore the world hateth you.

20 Remember my word that I said to you: The servant is not greater than his master. If they have persecuted me they will also persecute you: if they have kept my word, they will keep yours also.

21 But all these things they will do to you for my name's sake: because they know not him that sent me.

22 If I had not come, and spoken to them, they would not have sin; but now they have no excuse for their sin.

23 He that hateth me, hateth my Father also.

24 If I had not done among them the works that no other man hath done, they would not have sin; but now they have both seen and hated both me and my Father.

25 But that the word may be fulfilled which is written in their law: They hated me without cause.

26 But when the Paraclete cometh whom I will send you from the Father, the Spirit of truth, who proceedeth from the Father, he shall give testimony of me.

27 And you shall give testimony, because you are with me from the beginning.

Taken from the Gospel according to St. John, Chapter 16

1 These things have I spoken to you, that you may not be scandalized.

2 They will put you out of the synagogues: yea, the hour cometh, that whosoever killeth you, will think that he doth a service to God.

3 And these things will they do to you; because they have not known the Father, nor me.

4 But these things I have told you, that when the hour shall come, you may remember that I told you of them.

5 But I told you not these things from the beginning, because I was with you. And now I go to him that sent me, and none of you asketh me: Whither goest thou?

6 But because I have spoken these things to you, sorrow hath filled your heart.

7 But I tell you the truth: it is expedient to you that I go: for if I go not, the Paraclete will not come to you; but if I go, I will send him to you.

8 And when he is come, he will convince the world of sin, and of justice, and of judgment.

9 Of sin: because they believed not in me.

10 And of justice: because I go to the Father; and you shall see me no longer.

11 And of judgment: because the prince of this world is already judged.

12 I have yet many things to say to you: but you cannot bear them now.

13 But when he, the Spirit of truth, is come, he will teach you all truth. For he shall not speak of himself; but what things soever he shall hear, he shall speak: and the things that are to come, he shall show you.

14 He shall glorify me; because he shall receive of mine, and shall show it to you.

15 All things whatsoever the Father hath, are mine. Therefore I said, that he shall receive of mine, and show it to you.

16 A little while, and now you shall not see me; and again a little while, and you shall see me: because I go to the Father

17 Then some of his disciples said one to another: What is this that he saith to us:

A little while, and you shall not see me; and again a little while, and you shall see me, and, because I go to the Father?

18 They said therefore: What is this that he saith, A little while? We know not what he speaketh.

19 And Jesus knew that they had a mind to ask him; and he said to them: Of this do you inquire among yourselves, because I said: A little while, and you shall not see me; and again a little while, and you shall see me?

20 Amen, amen I say to you, that you shall lament and weep, but the world shall rejoice; and you shall be made sorrowful, but your sorrow shall be turned into joy.

21 A woman, when she is in labor, hath sorrow, because her hour is come; but when she hath brought forth the child, she remembereth no more the anguish, for joy that a man is born into the world.

22 So also you now indeed have sorrow; but I will see you again, and your heart shall rejoice; and your joy no man shall take from you.

23 And in that day you shall not ask me any thing. Amen, amen I say to you: if you ask the Father any thing in my name, he will give it you.

24 Hitherto you have not asked any thing in my name. Ask, and you shall receive; that your joy may be full.

25 These things I have spoken to you in proverbs. The hour cometh, when I will no more speak to you in proverbs, but will show you plainly of the Father.

26 In that day you shall ask in my name; and I say not to you, that I will ask the Father for you:

27 For the Father himself loveth you, because you have loved me, and have believed that I came out from God.

28 I came forth from the Father, and am come into the world: again I leave the world, and I go to the Father.

29 His disciples say to him: Behold, now thou speakest plainly, and speakest no proverb.

30 Now we know that thou knowest all things, and thou needest not that any man should ask thee. By this we believe that thou camest forth from God.

31 Jesus answered them: Do you now believe?

32 Behold, the hour cometh, and it is now come, that you shall be scattered every man to his own, and shall leave me alone; and yet I am not alone, because the Father is with me.

33 These things I have spoken to you, that in me you may have peace. In the world you shall have distress: but have confidence. I have overcome the world.

Taken from the Gospel according to St. John, Chapter 17

1 These things Jesus spoke, and lifting up his eyes to heaven, he said: Father, the hour is come, glorify thy son, that thy Son may glorify thee.

2 As thou hast given him power over all flesh, that he may give eternal life to all whom thou hast given him.

3 Now this is eternal life: That they may know thee, the only true God, and Jesus Christ, whom thou hast sent.

4 I have glorified thee on the earth; I have finished the work which thou gavest me to do.

5 And now glorify thou me, O Father, with thyself, with the glory which I had, before the world was, with thee.

6 I have manifested thy name to the men whom thou hast given me out of the world. Thine they were, and to me thou gavest them; and they have kept thy word.

7 Now they have known, that all things which thou hast given me, are from thee:

8 Because the words which thou gavest me, I have given to them; and they have received them, and have known in very deed that I came out from thee, and they have believed that thou didst send me.

9 I pray for them: I pray not for this world, but for them whom thou hast given me: because they are thine:

10 And all my things are thine, and thine are mine; and I am glorified in them.

11 And now I am not in the world, and these are in the world, and I come to thee. Holy Father, keep them in thy name whom thou hast given me; that they may be one, as we also are.

12 While I was with them, I kept them in thy name. Those whom thou gavest me have I kept; and none of them is lost, but the son of perdition, that the scripture may be fulfilled.

13 And now I come to thee; and these things I speak in the world, that they may have my joy filled in themselves.

14 I have given them thy word, and the world hath hated them, because they are not of the world; as I also am not of the world.

15 I pray not that thou shouldst take them out of the world, but that thou shouldst keep them from evil.

16 They are not of the world, as I also am not of the world.

17 Sanctify them in truth. Thy word is truth.

18 As thou hast sent me into the world, I also have sent them into the world.

19 And for them do I sanctify myself, that they also may be sanctified in truth

20 And not for them only do I pray, but for them also who through their word shall believe in me;

21 That they all may be one, as thou Father, in me, and I in thee; that they also may be one in us; that the world may believe that thou hast sent me.

22 And the glory which thou hast given me, I have given to them; that they may be one, as we also are one:

23 I in them, and thou in me; that they may be made perfect in one: and the world may know that thou hast sent me and hast loved them, as thou hast also loved me.

24 Father, I will that where I am, these also whom thou hast given me may be with me; that they may see my glory which thou hast given me, because thou hast loved me before the creation of the world.

25 Just Father, the world hath not known thee; but I have known thee and these have known that thou hast sent me.

26 And I have made known thy name to them, and will make it known; that the love wherewith thou hast loved me, may be in them, and I in them.

Taken from the Gospel according to St. John, Chapter 18

When Jesus had said these things he went forth with his disciples over the brook Cedron, where there was a garden, into which he entered with his disciples.

2 And Judas also, who betrayed him, knew the place; because Jesus had often resorted thither together with his disciples.

3 Judas therefore having received a band of soldiers and servants from the chief priests and the Pharisees, cometh thither with lanterns and torches and weapons.

4 Jesus therefore, knowing all things that should come upon him, went forth, and said to them: Whom seek ye?

5 They answered him: Jesus of Nazareth. Jesus saith to them: I am he. And Judas also, who betrayed him, stood with them.

6 As soon therefore as he had said to them: I am he; they went backward, and fell to the ground.

7 Again therefore he asked them: Whom seek ye? And they said, Jesus of Nazareth.

8 Jesus answered, I have told you that I am he. If therefore you seek me, let these go their way

9 That the word might be fulfilled which he said: Of them whom thou hast given me, I have not lost any one.

10 Then Simon Peter, having a sword, drew it, and struck the servant of the high priest, and cut off his right ear. And the name of the servant was Malchus.

11 Jesus therefore said to Peter: Put up thy sword into the scabbard. The chalice which my Father hath given me, shall I not drink it?

12 Then the band and the tribune, and the servants of the Jews, took Jesus, and bound him:

13 And they led him away to Annas first, for he was father-in-law to Caiphas, who was the high-priest of that year.

14 Now Caiphas was he who had given the counsel to the Jews: That it was expedient that one man should die for the people.

15 And Simon Peter followed Jesus, and so did another disciple. And that disciple was known to the high-priest, and went in with Jesus into the court of the high-priest.

16 But Peter stood at the door without. The other disciple therefore, who was known to the high-priest, went out, and spoke to the portress, and brought in Peter.

17 The maid therefore that was portress, saith to Peter: Art not thou also one of this man's disciples? He saith: I am not.

18 Now the servants and ministers stood at a fire of coals, because it was cold, and warmed themselves. And with them was Peter also, standing, and warming himself.

19 The high-priest therefore asked Jesus of his disciples, and of his doctrine.

20 Jesus answered him: I have spoken openly to the world: I have always taught in the synagogue, and in the temple, whither all the Jews resort; and in secret I have spoken nothing.

21 Why askest thou me? Ask them who have heard what I have spoken unto them: behold they know what things I have said.

22 And when he had said these things, one of the servants standing by, gave Jesus a blow, saying: Answerest thou the high-priest so?

23 Jesus answered him: If I have spoken evil, give testimony of the evil; but if well, why strikest thou me?

24 And Annas sent him bound to Caiphas the high-priest.

25 And Simon Peter was standing, and warming himself. They said therefore to him: Art not thou also one of his disciples? He denied it, and said: I am not.

26 One of the servants of the high-priest, a kinsman to him whose ear Peter cut off, saith to him: Did not I see thee in the garden with him?

27 Again therefore Peter denied; and immediately the cock crew.

28 Then they led Jesus from Caiphas to the governor's hall. And it was morning; and they went not into the hall, that they might not be defiled, but that they might eat the pasch.

29 Pilate therefore went out to them, and said: What accusation bring you against this man?

30 They answered, and said to him: If he were not a malefactor, we would not have delivered him up to thee.

31 Pilate therefore said to them: Take him you, and judge him according to your law. The Jews therefore said to him: It is not lawful for us to put any man to death;

32 That the word of Jesus might be fulfilled, which he said, signifying what death he should die.

33 Pilate therefore went into the hall again, and called Jesus, and said to him: Art thou the king of the Jews?

34 Jesus answered: Sayest thou this thing of thyself, or have others told it thee of me?

35 Pilate answered; Am I a Jew? Thy own nation, and the chief priests, delivered thee up to me: what hast thou done?

36 Jesus answered: My kingdom is not of this world. If my kingdom were of this world, my servants would certainly strive that I should not be delivered to the Jews: but now my kingdom is not from hence.

37 Pilate therefore said to him: Art thou a king then? Jesus answered: Thou sayest that I am a king. For this was I born, and for this came I into the world; that I should give testimony to the truth. Every one that is of the truth, heareth my voice.

38 Pilate saith to him: What is truth? And when he said this, he went out again to the Jews, and saith to them: I find no cause in him.

39 But you have a custom that I should release one unto you at the pasch: will you, therefore, that I release unto you the king of the Jews?

40 Then cried they all again, saying: Not this man, but Barabbas. Now Barabbas was a robber.

Taken from the Gospel according to St. John, Chapter 19

1 Then, therefore, Pilate took Jesus, and scourged him.

2 And the soldiers plaiting a crown of thorns, put it upon his head; and they put on him a purple garment.

3 And they came to him, and said: Hail, king of the Jews; and they gave him blows.

4 Pilate therefore went forth again, and saith to them: Behold, I bring him forth unto you, that you may know that I find no cause in him.

5 (Jesus therefore came forth, bearing the crown of thorns and the purple garment) And he saith to them: Behold the Man.

6 When the chief priests, therefore, and the servants, had seen him, they cried out, saying: Crucify him, crucify him. Pilate saith to them: Take him you, and crucify him: for I find no cause in him.

7 The Jews answered him: We have a law; and according to the law he ought to die, because he made himself the Son of God.

8 When Pilate therefore had heard this saying, he feared the more.

9 And he entered into the hall again and he said to Jesus: Whence art thou? But Jesus gave him no answer.

10 Pilate therefore saith to him: Speakest thou not to me? Knowest thou not that I have power to crucify thee and have power to release thee?

11 Jesus answered: Thou shouldst not have any power against me, unless it were given thee from above. Therefore, he that hath delivered me to thee, hath the greater sin.

12 And from henceforth Pilate sought to release him. But the Jews cried out, saying: If thou release this man, thou art not Caesar's friend. For whosoever maketh himself a king, speaketh against Caesar.

13 Now when Pilate had heard these words, he brought Jesus forth, and sat down in the judgment seat, in the place that is called Lithostrotos, and in Hebrew Gabbatha.

14 And it was the parasceve of the pasch, about the sixth hour, and he saith to the Jews: Behold your king.

15 But they cried out: Away with him; away with him; crucify him. Pilate saith to them: Shall I crucify your king? The chief priests answered: We have no king but Caesar.

16 Then therefore he delivered him to them to be crucified. And they took Jesus, and led him forth.

17 And bearing his own cross, he went forth to that place which is called Calvary, but in Hebrew Golgotha.

18 Where they crucified him, and with him two others, one on each side, and Jesus in the midst.

19 And Pilate wrote a title also, and he put it upon the cross. And the writing was: JESUS OF NAZARETH, THE KING OF THE JEWS.

20 This title therefore many of the Jews did read: because the place where Jesus was crucified was nigh to the city: and it was written in Hebrew, in Greek, and in Latin.

21 Then the chief priests of the Jews said to Pilate: Write not, The King of the Jews; but that he said, I am the King of the Jews.

22 Pilate answered: What I have written, I have written.

23 The soldiers therefore, when they had crucified him, took his garments, (and they made four parts, to every soldier a part,) and also his coat. Now the coat was without seam, woven from the top throughout.

24 They said then one to another: Let us not cut it, but let us cast lots for it, whose it shall be; that the scripture might be fulfilled, saying: They have parted my garments among them, and upon my vesture they have cast lot. And the soldiers indeed did these things.

25 Now there stood by the cross of Jesus, his mother, and his mother's sister, Mary of Cleophas, and Mary Magdalen.

26 When Jesus therefore had seen his mother and the disciple standing whom he loved, he saith to his mother: Woman, behold thy son.

27 After that, he saith to the disciple: Behold thy mother. And from that hour, the disciple took her to his own.

28 Afterwards, Jesus knowing that all things were now accomplished, that the scripture might be fulfilled, said: I thirst

29 Now there was a vessel set there full of vinegar. And they, putting a sponge full of vinegar about hyssop, put it to his mouth.

30 Jesus therefore, when he had taken the vinegar, said: It is consummated. And bowing his head, he gave up the ghost.

31 Then the Jews, (because it was the parasceve,) that the bodies might not remain upon the cross on the Sabbath day, (for that was a great Sabbath day,) besought Pilate that their legs might be broken, and that they might be taken away.

32 The soldiers therefore came; and they broke the legs of the first, and of the other that was crucified with him.

33 But after they were come to Jesus, when they saw that he was already dead, they did not break his legs.

34 But one of the soldiers with a spear opened his side, and immediately there came out blood and water.

35 And he that saw it, hath given testimony; and his testimony is true. And he knoweth that he saith true; that you also may believe.

36 For these things were done, that the scripture might be fulfilled: you shall not break a bone of him.

37 And again another scripture saith: They shall look on him, whom they pierced.

38 And after these things, Joseph of Arimathea (because he was a disciple of Jesus, but secretly for fear of the Jews) besought Pilate that he might take away the body of Jesus. And Pilate gave leave. He came therefore, and took away the body of Jesus.

39 And Nicodemus also came (he who at the first came to Jesus by night), bringing a mixture of myrrh and aloes, about an hundred pound weight.

40 They took therefore the body of Jesus, and bound it in linen cloths, with the spices, as the manner of the Jews is to bury.

41 Now there was in the place where he was crucified, a garden; and in the garden a new sepulchre, wherein no man yet had been laid.

42 There, therefore, because of the parasceve of the Jews, they laid Jesus, because the sepulchre was nigh at hand.

Taken from the Gospel according to St. John, Chapter 20

1 And on the first day of the week, Mary Magdalen cometh early, when it was yet dark, unto the sepulchre; and she saw the stone taken away from the sepulchre.

2 She ran, therefore, and cometh to Simon Peter, and to the other disciple whom Jesus loved, and saith to them: They have taken away the Lord out of the sepulchre, and we know not where they have laid him.

3 Peter therefore went out, and that other disciple, and they came to the sepulchre.

4 And they both ran together, and that other disciple did out-run Peter, and came first to the sepulchre.

6 And when he stooped down, he saw the linen cloths, lying; but yet he went not in.

6 Then cometh Simon Peter, following him, and went into the sepulchre, and saw the linen cloths lying,

7 And the napkin that had been about his head, not lying with the linen cloths, but apart, wrapped up into one place.

8 Then that other disciple also went in, who came first to the sepulchre: and he saw, and believed.

9 For as yet they knew not the scripture, that he must rise again from the dead.

10 The disciples therefore departed again to their home.

11 But Mary stood at the sepulchre without, weeping. Now as she was weeping, she stooped down, and looked into the sepulchre,

12 And she saw two angels in white, sitting, one at the head, and one at the feet, where the body of Jesus had been laid.

13 They say to her: Woman, why weepest thou? She saith to them: Because they have taken away my Lord; and I know not where they have laid him.

14 When she had said this, she turned herself back, and saw Jesus standing; and she knew not that it was Jesus.

15 Jesus saith to her: Woman, why weepest thou? Whom seekest thou? She, thinking that it was the gardener, saith to him: Sir, if thou hast taken him hence, tell me where thou hast laid him, and I will take him away.

16 Jesus saith to her: Mary. She turning, saith to him: Rabboni (which is to say, Master).

17 Jesus saith to her: Do not touch me, for I am not yet ascended to my Father. But go to my brethren, and say to them: I ascend to my Father and to your Father, to my God and your God.

18 Mary Magdalen cometh, and telleth the disciples: I have seen the Lord, and these things he said to me.

19 Now when it was late that same day, the first of the week, and the doors were shut, where the disciples were gathered together, for fear of the Jews, Jesus came and stood in the midst, and said to them: Peace be to you.

20 And when he had said this, he showed them his hands and his side. The disciples therefore were glad, when they saw the Lord.

21 He said therefore to them again: Peace be to you. As the Father hath sent me, I also send you.

22 When he had said this, he breathed on them; and he said to them: Receive ye the Holy Ghost.

23 Whose sins you shall forgive, they are forgiven them; and whose sins you shall retain, they are retained.

24 Now Thomas, one of the twelve, who is called Didymus, was not with them when Jesus came.

25 The other disciples therefore said to him: We have seen the Lord. But he said to them: Except I shall see in his hands the print of the nails, and put my finger into the place of the nails, and put my hand into his side, I will not believe.

26 And after eight days again his disciples were within, and Thomas with them. Jesus cometh, the doors being shut, and stood in the midst, and said: Peace be to you.

27 Then he saith to Thomas: Put in thy finger hither, and see my hands; and bring hither thy hand, and put it into my side; and be not faithless, but believing.

28 Thomas answered, and said to him: My Lord, and my God.

29 Jesus saith to him: Because thou hast seen me, Thomas, thou hast believed: blessed are they that have not seen, and have believed.

30 Many other signs also did Jesus in the sight of his disciples, which are not written in this book.

31 But these are written, that you may believe that Jesus is the Christ, the Son of God: and that believing, you may have life in his name.

Taken from the Gospel according to St. John, Chapter 21

1 After this, Jesus showed himself again to the disciples at the sea of Tiberias. And he showed himself after this manner.

2 There were together Simon Peter, and Thomas, who is called Didymus, and Nathanael, who was of Cana of Galilee, and the sons of Zebedee, and two others of his disciples.

3 Simon Peter saith to them: I go a fishing. They say to him: We also come with thee. And they went forth, and entered into the ship: and that night they caught nothing.

4 But when the morning was come, Jesus stood on the shore: yet the disciples knew not that it was Jesus.

5 Jesus therefore said to them: Children, have you any meat? They answered him: No.

6 He saith to them: Cast the net on the right side of the ship, and you shall find. They cast therefore; and now they were not able to draw it, for the multitude of fishes.

7 That disciple therefore whom Jesus loved, said to Peter: It is the Lord. Simon Peter, when he heard that it was the Lord, girt his coat about him, (for he was naked) and cast himself into the sea.

8 But the other disciples came in the ship, (for they were not far from the land, but as it were two hundred cubits,) dragging the net with fishes.

9 As soon then as they came to land, they saw hot coals lying, and a fish laid thereon, and bread.

10 Jesus saith to them: Bring hither of the fishes which you have now caught.

11 Simon Peter went up, and drew the net to land, full of great fishes, one hundred and fifty-three. And although there were so many, the net was not broken.

12 Jesus saith to them: Come, and dine. And none of them who were at meat, dared ask him: Who art thou? Knowing that it was the Lord.

13 And Jesus cometh and taketh bread, and giveth them, and fish in like manner.

14 This is now the third time that Jesus was manifested to his disciples, after he was risen from the dead.

15 When therefore they had dined, Jesus saith to Simon Peter: Simon, son of John, lovest thou me more than these? He saith to him: Yea, Lord, thou knowest that I love thee. He saith to him: Feed my lambs.

16 He saith to him again: Simon, son of John, lovest thou me? He saith to him: Yea, Lord, thou knowest that I love thee. He saith to him: Feed my lambs.

17 He said to him the third time: Simon, son of John, lovest thou me? Peter was grieved, because he had said to him the third time: Lovest thou me? And he said to him: Lord, thou knowest all things: thou knowest that I love thee. He said to him: Feed my sheep.

18 Amen, amen I say to thee, when thou wast younger, thou didst gird thyself, and didst walk where thou wouldst But when thou shalt be old, thou shalt stretch forth thy hands, and another shall gird thee, and lead thee whither thou wouldst not.

19 And this he said, signifying by what death he should glorify God. And when he had said this he saith to him: Follow me.

20 Peter turning about, saw that disciple whom Jesus loved following, who also leaned on his breast at supper, and said: Lord, who is he that shall betray thee?

21 Him therefore when Peter had seen, he saith to Jesus: Lord, and what shall this man do?

22 Jesus saith to him: So I will have him to remain till I come, what is it to thee? Follow thou me.

23 This saying therefore went abroad among the brethren, that this disciple should not die. And Jesus did not say to him: He

should not die; but, So I will have him to remain till I come, what is it to thee?

24 This is that disciple who giveth testimony of these things, and hath written these things; and we know that his testimony is true.

25 But there are also many other things which Jesus did, which, if they were written every one, the world itself, I think, would not be able to contain the books that should be written. Amen.

WEEK FIVE

INTRODUCTION TO WEEK FIVE:
FINAL PREPARATIONS

We now enter the final stage of our preparation for our *True Devotion Consecration to Mary*—or more strictly speaking, our *Consecration to Jesus through Mary*. We may feel unworthy in proceeding with this Consecration, perhaps due to some negligence during the last four weeks of preparation. It is rare and unlikely that anyone will have made an entirely perfect and truly acceptable preparation, but that is not a sufficient reason for not making the Consecration. I remind you that St. Louis only recommends a 33-day preparation, but adds that this may be shortened or lengthened at will. I also remind you of the fact that "just man sins seven times a day" and so it would be surprising if you did not fail in some way or another in your preparations. Nothing would please the devil more, than to make you miss the Consecration through feelings of inadequacy or guilt. And nothing would please Our Lord and Our Lady more than a humble admission of your inadequacy as you proceed on your way. Just as children are largely inadequate when they start a coaching session, only to improve with each successive session, so too should each annual renewal show an improvement in our preparation.

In the first week we uncovered the *Spirit of the World* and then in the second week we examined ourselves to how that spirit had affected us or contaminated us—with the intention of leaving that worldly, fleshly, devilish spirit behind us, in our ascent towards God. However, nature abhors a vacuum, and so we had to replace the spirit of the world by another spirit. This was the spirit of Jesus and Mary. Thus, in order to acquire that spirit, the third week saw us grow in a knowledge, appreciation and imitation of the Our Blessed Lady; whereas last week we studied Our Blessed Lord in order to imitate Him and acquire His spirit.

To finish our 5-week long preparation we will now examine the Ceremony itself; meditate a little on some of the words of Consecration and then have a brief look at the consequences of our Consecration by examining the devotional practices that St. Louis recommends for "Life after Consecration."

We would like to remind those making the Consecration for the first time, that *they are simply planting the seeds of True Devotion for the first time.* They should not expect to see a fully grown *"Tree of Life"*— which Mary is—the next day! Just as in nature, this *"Tree of Life"* will gently grow day by day, year by year, until one day you will be able to say: *"It is no longer I that live, but Mary that lives in me!"*

RECOMMENDED PRAYERS FOR WEEK FIVE

Litany of the Holy Ghost

Litany of the Sacred Heart

St. Louis de Montfort's "Prayer to Jesus"

O Jesus Living in Mary

Litany of the Blessed Virgin Mary

Ave Maris Stella

St. Louis de Montfort's "Prayer to Mary"

(Each prayer need not be said daily.)

Litany of the Holy Ghost

Lord, have mercy on us,
Christ, have mercy on us
Lord, have mercy on us
Father, all powerful,
Have mercy on us.
Jesus, Eternal Son of the Father,
Redeemer of the world, *Save us.*
Spirit of the Father and the Son, boundless life of both,
Sanctify us.
Holy Trinity, *Hear us.*
Holy Ghost, Who proceedest
from the Father and the Son, *Enter our hearts.*
Holy Ghost, Who art equal to the Father and the Son,
Enter our hearts.
Promise of God the Father, *Have mercy on us.*
Ray of heavenly light,
Author of all good,
Source of heavenly water,
Consuming fire,
Ardent charity,
Spiritual unction,
Spirit of love and truth,
Spirit of wisdom and understanding,
Spirit of counsel and fortitude,
Spirit of knowledge and piety,
Spirit of the fear of the Lord,
Spirit of grace and prayer,
Spirit of peace and meekness,
Spirit of modesty and innocence,
Holy Ghost, the Comforter,
Holy Ghost, the Sanctifier,
Holy Ghost, Who governest the Church,
Gift of God, the Most High,
Spirit Who fillest the universe,
Spirit of the adoption of the children of God,

Holy Ghost, *inspire us with horror of sin.*
Holy Ghost, *come and renew the face of the earth.*
Holy Ghost, *shed Thy light in our souls.*
Holy Ghost, *engrave Thy law in our hearts.*
Holy Ghost, *inflame us with the flame of Thy love.*
Holy Ghost, *open to us the treasures of Thy graces.*
Holy Ghost, *teach us to pray well.*
Holy Ghost, *enlighten us with Thy heavenly inspirations.*
Holy Ghost, *lead us in the way of salvation.*
Holy Ghost, *grant us the only necessary knowledge.*
Holy Ghost, *inspire in us the practice of good.*
Holy Ghost, *grant us the merits of all virtues.*
Holy Ghost, *make us persevere in justice.*
Holy Ghost, *be Thou our everlasting reward.*

Lamb of God, Who takest away the sins of the world,
    Send us Thy Holy Ghost.
Lamb of God, Who takest away the sins of the world,
    Pour down into our souls the gifts of the Holy Ghost.
Lamb of God, Who takest away the sins of the world,
    Grant us the Spirit of wisdom and piety.

V. Come, Holy Ghost! Fill the hearts of Thy faithful.
R. And enkindle in them the fire of Thy Love.

Let us pray

Grant, O merciful Father, that Thy Divine Spirit enlighten, inflame and purify us, that He may penetrate us with His heavenly dew and make us fruitful in good works; through our Lord Jesus Christ, Thy Son, Who with Thee, in the unity of the same Spirit, liveth and reigneth forever and ever. *R. Amen.*

Litany of the Sacred Heart

Lord, have mercy on us.
Christ, have mercy on us.
Lord, have mercy on us.
Christ, hear us.
Christ, graciously hear us
God the Father of heaven, *Have mercy on us.*
God the Son, Redeemer of the world,
God, the Holy Ghost,
Holy Trinity, one God,
Heart of Jesus, Son of the eternal Father,
Heart of Jesus, formed by the Holy Ghost in the Virgin
Mother's womb,
Heart of Jesus, substantially united to the Word of God,
Heart of Jesus, of infinite Majesty,
Heart of Jesus, holy Temple of God,
Heart of Jesus, tabernacle of the Most High,
Heart of Jesus, house of God and gate of Heaven,
Heart of Jesus, glowing furnace of charity,
Heart of Jesus, vessel of justice and love,
Heart of Jesus, full of goodness and love,
Heart of Jesus, abyss of all virtues,
Heart of Jesus, most worthy of all praise,
Heart of Jesus, King and center of all hearts,
Heart of Jesus, wherein are all the treasures of wisdom and
knowledge,
Heart of Jesus, wherein dwelleth all the fullness of the Godhead,
Heart of Jesus, in Whom the Father is well pleased,
Heart of Jesus, of Whose fullness we have all received,
Heart of Jesus, desire of the everlasting hills,
Heart of Jesus, patient and rich in mercy,
Heart of Jesus, rich unto all who call upon Thee,
Heart of Jesus, fount of life and holiness,
Heart of Jesus, propitiation for our offenses,
Heart of Jesus, overwhelmed with reproaches,
Heart of Jesus, bruised for our iniquities,

Heart of Jesus, obedient even unto death,
Heart of Jesus, pierced with a lance,
Heart of Jesus, source of all consolation,
Heart of Jesus, our life and resurrection,
Heart of Jesus, our peace and reconciliation,
Heart of Jesus, victim for our sins,
Heart of Jesus, salvation of those who hope in Thee,
Heart of Jesus, hope of those who die in Thee,
Heart of Jesus, delight of all the Saints,
Lamb of God, Who takest away the sins of the world,
    Spare us, O Lord.
Lamb of God, Who takest away the sins of the world,
    Graciously hear us, O Lord.
Lamb of God, Who takest away the sins of the world,
    Have mercy on us.

V. Jesus, meek and humble of Heart,
R. Make our hearts like unto Thine.

Let us pray
    Almighty and everlasting God, look upon the Heart of Thy well beloved Son and upon the praise and satisfaction which He offers unto Thee in the name of sinners; and do Thou, of Thy great goodness, grant them pardon when they seek Thy mercy, in the name of the same Jesus Christ, Thy Son, who liveth and reigneth with Thee for ever and ever. *R. Amen.*

St. Louis De Montfort's Prayer to Jesus

    O most loving Jesus, deign to let me pour forth my gratitude before Thee, for the grace Thou hast bestowed upon me in giving me to Thy holy Mother through the devotion of Holy Bondage, that she may be my advocate in the presence of Thy majesty and my support in my extreme misery. Alas, O Lord! I am so wretched that without this dear Mother I should be certainly lost.

    Yes, Mary is necessary for me at Thy side and everywhere: that she may appease Thy just wrath, because I have so often offended Thee; that she may save me from the eternal punishment of Thy justice, which I deserve; that she may contemplate Thee, speak to Thee, pray to Thee, approach Thee and please Thee; that she may help me to save my soul and the souls of others; in short, Mary is necessary for me that I may always do Thy holy will and seek Thy greater glory in all things.

Ah, would that I could proclaim throughout the whole world the mercy that Thou hast shown to me! Would that everyone might know I should be already damned, were it not for Mary! Would that I might offer worthy thanksgiving for so great a blessing! Mary is in me. Oh, what a treasure! Oh, what a consolation! And shall I not be entirely hers? Oh, what ingratitude! My dear Savior, send me death rather than such a calamity, for I would rather die than live without belonging entirely to Mary.

With St. John the Evangelist at the foot of the Cross, I have taken her a thousand times for my own and as many times have given myself to her but if I have not yet done it as Thou, dear Jesus, dost wish, I now renew this offering as Thou desire me to renew it. And if Thou seest in my soul or my body anything that does not belong to this august princess, I pray Thee to take it and cast it far from me, for whatever in me does not belong to Mary is unworthy of Thee.

O Holy Spirit, grant me all these graces. Plant in my soul the Tree of true Life, which is Mary; cultivate it and tend it so that it may grow and blossom and bring forth the fruit of life in abundance. O Holy Spirit, give me great devotion to Mary, Thy faithful spouse; give me great confidence in her maternal heart and an abiding refuge in her mercy, so that by her Thou mayest truly form in me Jesus Christ, great and mighty, unto the fullness of His perfect age. Amen.

Litany of the Blessed Virgin Mary

Lord, have mercy on us.
Christ, have mercy on us.
Lord, have mercy on us.
Christ, hear us.
Christ, graciously hear us.
God the Father of heaven, *Have mercy on us.*
God the Son, Redeemer of the world,
God the Holy Ghost,
Holy Trinity, one God,
Holy Mary, *Pray for us.*
Holy Mother of God,
Holy Virgin of virgins,
Mother of Christ,
Mother of divine grace,
Mother most pure,
Mother most chaste,
Mother inviolate,
Mother undefiled,
Mother most amiable,
Mother most admirable,
Mother of good counsel,
Mother of our Creator,
Mother of our Savior,
Virgin most prudent,
Virgin most venerable,
Virgin most renowned,
Virgin most powerful,
Virgin most merciful,
Virgin most faithful,
Mirror of justice,
Seat of wisdom,
Cause of our joy,
Spiritual vessel,
Vessel of honor,
Singular vessel of devotion,
Mystical rose,

Tower of David,
Tower of ivory,
House of gold,
Ark of the covenant,
Gate of heaven,
Morning Star,
Health of the sick,
Refuge of sinners,
Comforter of the afflicted,
Help of Christians,
Queen of angels,
Queen of patriarchs,
Queen of prophets,
Queen of Apostles,
Queen of martyrs,
Queen of confessors,
Queen of virgins,
Queen of all saints,
Queen conceived without original sin,
Queen assumed into heaven,
Queen of the most holy Rosary,
Queen of peace,

Lamb of God, Who takes away the sins of the world,
Spare us, O Lord.
Lamb of God, Who takes away the sins of the world,
Graciously hear us, O Lord.
Lamb of God, Who takes away the sins of the world,
Have mercy on us.

V. Pray for us, O holy Mother of God.
R. *That we may be made worthy of the promises of Christ.*

Let us pray

Grant unto us, Thy servants, we beseech Thee, O Lord God, at all times to enjoy health of soul and body; and by the glorious intercession of Blessed Mary, ever virgin, when freed from the sorrows of this present life, to enter into that joy which hath no end. Through Christ our Lord. R. *Amen.*

Ave Maris Stella

Hail, bright star of ocean,
God's own Mother blest,
Ever sinless Virgin,
Gate of heavenly rest.

Taking that sweet Ave
Which from Gabriel came,
Peace confirm within us,
Changing Eva's name.

Break the captives' fetters,
Light on blindness pour,
All our ills expelling,
Every bliss implore.

Show thyself a Mother;
May the Word Divine,
Born for us thy Infant,
Hear our prayers through thine.

Virgin all excelling,
Mildest of the mild,
Freed from guilt, preserve us,
Pure and undefiled.

Keep our life all spotless,
Make our way secure,
Till we find in Jesus
Joy forevermore.

Through the highest heaven
To the Almighty Three,
Father, Son and Spirit,
One same glory be. Amen.

St. Louis De Montfort's Prayer to Mary

Hail Mary, beloved Daughter of the Eternal Father! Hail Mary, admirable Mother of the Son! Hail Mary, faithful Spouse of the Holy Ghost! Hail Mary, my dear Mother, my loving mistress, my powerful sovereign! Hail my joy, my glory, my heart and my soul! Thou art all mine by mercy, and I am all thine by justice. But I am not yet sufficiently thine. I now give myself wholly to thee without keeping anything back for myself or others. If thou still seest in me anything which does not belong to thee, I beseech thee to take it and to make thyself the absolute mistress of all that is mine. Destroy in me all that may be displeasing to God, root it up and bring it to nought; place and cultivate in me everything that is pleasing to thee.

May the light of thy faith dispel the darkness of my mind; may thy profound humility take the place of my pride; may thy sublime contemplation check the distractions of my wandering imagination; may thy continuous sight of God fill my memory with His presence; may the burning love of thy heart inflame the lukewarmness of mine; may thy virtues take the place of my sins; may thy merits be my only adornment in the sight of God and make up for all that is wanting in me. Finally, dearly beloved Mother, grant, if it be possible, that I may have no other spirit but thine to know Jesus and His divine will; that I may have no other soul but thine to praise and glorify the Lord; that I may have no other heart but thine to love God with a love as pure and ardent as thine. I do not ask thee for visions, revelations, sensible devotion or spiritual pleasures. It is thy privilege to see God clearly; it is thy privilege to enjoy heavenly bliss; it is thy privilege to triumph gloriously in heaven at the right hand of thy Son and to hold absolute sway over angels, men and demons; it is thy privilege to dispose of all the gifts of God, just as thou willest.

Such is, O heavenly Mary, "the best part" which the Lord has given thee and which shall never be taken away from thee—and this thought fills my heart with joy. As for my part here below, I wish for no other than that which was thine: to believe sincerely without spiritual pleasures; to suffer joyfully without human consolation; to die continually to myself without respite; and to work zealously and unselfishly for thee until death as the humblest of thy servants. The only grace I beg thee to obtain for me is that every day and every moment of my life I may say: Amen—so be it, to all that thou didst do while on earth; Amen—so be it, to all that thou art now doing in heaven; Amen—so be it, to all that thou art doing in my soul, so that thou alone mayest fully glorify Jesus in me for time and eternity. Amen.

O Jesus Living In Mary

O Jesus living in Mary
Come and live in Thy servants;
In the spirit of Thy holiness,
In the fullness of Thy might,
In the truth of Thy virtues,
In the perfection of Thy ways,
In the communion of Thy mysteries,
Subdue every hostile power,
In Thy spirit, for the glory of the Father. Amen.

SUGGESTED ORDER FOR THE CEREMONY

Before Mass

On some day before the consecration, write out your Act of Consecration on a sheet of paper which you will sign after Mass (typing is permissible, pre-prepared certificates are also permissible, but St. Louis recommends writing it out by hand).

If the church has no side altar to Our Lady, then a statue of Our Lady could be placed in the sanctuary.

Before the Offertory of the Mass

The tabernacle doors are opened
Everyone kneels and reads aloud the Act of Consecration.
The tabernacle doors are closed and Mass continues as usual.

After Holy Communion

Everyone renews the Act of Consecration privately and silently, as part of their thanksgiving.

After Mass

Everyone comes forward to sign their Certificate (if they have one) or Act of Consecration, which they should have written beforehand...

(a) at Our Lady's side altar, or,

(b) at a table set in front of Our Lady's statue in the sanctuary, or,

(c) at the Communion Rail in front of Our Lady's statue/ altar.

Penance

St. Louis de Montfort recommends that everyone perform some small act of penance on the day of Consecration.

Obligations Before and After the Consecration

Listed in this book (see page 401 ff.).

Act of Consecration to Jesus Christ, the Incarnate Wisdom, by the Hands of Mary

O Eternal and Incarnate Wisdom! O sweetest and most adorable Jesus! True God and True Man, only Son of the Eternal Father and of Mary, always Virgin! I adore Thee profoundly in the bosom and splendors of Thy Father during eternity, and I adore Thee also in the virginal bosom of Mary Thy most worthy Mother, in the time of Thy Incarnation.

I give Thee thanks that Thou hast annihilated Thyself, taking the form of a slave in order to rescue me from the cruel slavery of the devil. I praise and glorify Thee that Thou hast been pleased to submit Thyself to Mary, Thy Holy Mother, in all things, in order to make me Thy faithful slave through her.

But, alas! Ungrateful and unfaithful as I have been, I have not kept the promises which I made so solemnly to Thee in my Baptism. I have not fulfilled my obligations; I do not deserve to be called Thy child nor yet Thy slave; and as there is nothing in me which does not merit Thine anger and Thy repulse, I dare not any more come by myself before Thy most holy and august Majesty. It is on this account that I have recourse to the intercession of Thy Most Holy Mother, whom Thou has given me for a mediatrix with Thee. It is through her that I hope to obtain of Thee contrition, the pardon of my sins, and the acquisition and preservation of Wisdom.

Hail then, Immaculate Mary, living Tabernacle of the Divinity, where the Eternal Wisdom willed to be hidden and to be adored by angels and by men! Hail, Queen of Heaven and earth, to whose empire everything is subject which is under God! Hail, O sure Refuge of sinners; whose mercy fails no one! Hear the desires which I have of the Divine Wisdom, and for that end, receive the vows and offerings which in my lowliness I present to Thee.

I (*here say your own name*), a faithless sinner, renew and ratify today in thy hands the vows of my Baptism: I renounce forever Satan, his pomps and works; and I give myself entirely to Jesus Christ, the Incarnate Wisdom, to carry my cross after Him all the days of my life and to be more faithful to Him than I have ever been before.

In the presence of all the heavenly court, I choose thee this day for my Mother and Mistress. I deliver and consecrate to thee, as thy slave, my body and soul, my goods, both interior and exterior, and even the value of all my good actions, past, present and future; leaving to thee the entire and full right of disposing of me and all that belongs to me, without exception, according to thy good pleasure, for the greater glory of God, in time and in eternity.

Receive, O benignant Virgin, this little offering of my slavery, in honor of, and in union with, that subjection which the Eternal Wisdom deigned to have to thy maternity, in homage to the power which both of you have over this poor sinner, and in thanksgiving for the privileges with which the Holy Trinity has favored thee. I declare that I wish henceforth, as thy true slave, to seek thy honor and to obey thee in all things.

O admirable Mother, present me to thy dear Son as His eternal slave, so that as He has redeemed me by thee, by thee He may receive me! O Mother of Mercy, grant that I may obtain the true Wisdom of God, and for that end receive me among those whom thou lovest and teachest, whom thou leadest, nourishest and protectest as thy children and thy slaves.

O faithful Virgin, make me in all things so perfect a disciple, imitator and slave of the Incarnate Wisdom, Jesus Christ thy Son, that I may attain, by thine intercession and by thine example, to the fullness of His age on earth and of His glory in heaven. Amen

MEDITATIONS ON THE ACT OF CONSECRATION

WEEK 5: DAY 1–FIRST MEDITATION

EXTRACT FROM THE ACT OF CONSECRATION: *"Eternal and Incarnate Wisdom! O sweetest and most adorable Jesus! True God and True Man, only Son of the Eternal Father and of Mary always Virgin! I adore Thee profoundly in the bosom and splendors of Thy Father during eternity, and I adore Thee also in the virginal bosom of Mary Thy most worthy Mother, in the time of Thy Incarnation."*

MEDITATION: In his little book, *Love of Eternal Wisdom,* St. Louis-Marie de Montfort gives us a valuable abridgment of his spirituality which can be summed up in the words of St. Paul: "Christ living in us." Christ lives in all Christians who are in the state of grace. In the great majority, however, the Christian life is only, as it were, in its embryo and never really gets beyond that embryonic stage. St. Louis' aim is to develop that embryo until Christ has come to the fullness of His age in us. That is, until we have become perfect Christians.

According to Montfort this perfect Christian life is acquired by an ardent desire, continual prayer, universal mortification and a tender and true devotion to the Blessed Virgin Mary. Among these four means, Montfort stresses devotion to Mary as the surest, the easiest and the quickest way to the perfect development of the Christ-life in us. We see this doctrine embodied in the renowned prayer: *Jesus vivens in Maria,* which, translated, reads as *Jesus Living in Mary.*

O Jesus living in Mary,
Come and live in Thy servants,
In the spirit of Thy holiness,
In the fullness of Thy might,
In the truth of Thy virtues,
In the perfection of Thy ways,
In the communion of Thy mysteries,
Subdue every hostile power
In Thy spirit, for the glory of the Father. Amen.

WEEK 5: DAY 1–SECOND MEDITATION

EXTRACT FROM THE ACT OF CONSECRATION: *"I give Thee thanks that Thou hast annihilated Thyself, taking the form of a slave in order to rescue me from the cruel slavery of the devil. I praise and glorify Thee that Thou hast been pleased to submit Thyself to Mary, Thy Holy Mother, in all things, in order to make me Thy faithful slave through her."*

MEDITATION: A slave obeys his master's will. What did our Master say to us? "Learn of me, for I am meek and humble of heart!" It is this humility, this meekness, this gentleness that we should set as our goal. Meek does not mean weak! It is said that grace operates *suaviter et fortiter* —that is to say *gently and firmly.* It was this gentleness, yet firmness, that made souls flock to Christ. St. Francis De Sales so rightly says: "A spoonful of honey attracts more flies than a hundred barrels of vinegar." It is this gentleness, yet firmness, that we should seek to acquire in the months and years following our Consecration.

As Divine Wisdom became Man for the purpose of drawing the hearts of men to love and imitate Him, He was pleased to clothe Himself with all human gentleness and kindness, in such an attractive and visible manner, as to present no defect nor unsightliness. This same disposition, towards gentleness, should also be our goal—it is something that will not be acquired overnight, but only when that seed of the True Devotion starts to take root in us and begins to grow into that gentle, yet strong, *Tree of Life* that is Mary.

If we consider Him in His origin, He is but goodness and meekness. He was born of the sweetest, the most tender and the most beautiful of all mothers, the Immaculate Mary. If you would appreciate the gentleness of Jesus, then consider first the gentleness of Mary, His Mother, whom He resembles by His pleasing character. Jesus is Mary's child; in Him there is no haughtiness, no harshness, no unpleasantness; and still less, infinitely less, in Him than in His Mother, because He is Eternal Wisdom; He is gentleness and beauty itself. There should be no place for haughtiness, pride, harshness, sarcasm, *etc.*, in our lives. These are the weeds that will choke the Tree of Life before it even has a chance to grow!

The Prophets foretold that because of His gentleness, "He would not break the bruised reed, nor quench the smoking flax," which means that because of His abundant mercy He will not allow the loss of a poor sinner, even though the sinner may be broken-down, blinded, depraved by sin, and having already as it were, one foot in hell—unless the sinner should compel Him to do so. What does the name of Jesus, which is the proper name of Incarnate Wisdom, signify, if not an ardent charity, an infinite love and attractive meekness? Jesus, Savior, He Who *saves* man, and Whose characteristic is *to love and to save* man.

Jesus is gentle in His looks, in His words, in His actions. The face of this loving Savior is so serene and gentle that it charmed the eyes and the hearts of those who beheld Him. The shepherds who came to the stable to see Him were so spellbound by the serenity and beauty of His face, that for several days they remained to gaze upon Him in rapture. The Kings, exalted as they were, had no sooner than seen the loving features of this beautiful Child, laying aside their dignity, they fell on their knees by His crib. Tradition tells us that when Jesus was still very young, afflicted people and children in the vicinity went to see Him to find comfort and joy.

Jesus is also gentle in His words. When on earth, He conquered all by the meekness of His words. Never was He heard to cry out loudly or to argue heatedly. This was foretold by the Prophets. Those who listened to Him with good will, were charmed by the words of life which fell from His lips. They said: "Never did man speak like this man." Those who hated Him, were surprised upon hearing His eloquence and wisdom. Never did a man speak with such meekness and unction. Whence did He have so much wisdom in His speech?

Multitudes of poor people left their homes and families to go and hear Him, even in the desert. They spent many days without eating and drinking, but they were filled by the meekness of His words. This meekness of His words was the bait which drew the Apostles after Him; it was the balm which healed the most incurable, and which comforted the most afflicted. To the disconsolate Mary Magdalen He spoke but one word, "Mary," and she was overwhelmed with joy and happiness.

Finally, Jesus is gentle in His actions. This gentleness may be observed throughout the whole course of His life. It was said of Him that "He *hath done all things well.*" Which means all that Jesus Christ did, was done with such exactitude, wisdom, holiness and meekness, that nothing faulty or wanting can be found in what He did. Let us consider how gently this loving Incarnate Wisdom acted in all His ways.

The poor and the little children followed Him everywhere as one of their own. When they came near Him He embraced and blessed them. O, what sweetness and kindness! The poor, seeing Him dressed like the poor, simple in His manners, without ostentation or haughtiness, enjoyed His company. They stood by Him against the rich and the proud, when these calumniated and persecuted Him. He, in His turn, praised and blessed them upon every occasion.

But who will explain to us the gentleness of Jesus in His dealings with poor sinners? His gentleness with Mary Magdalen, the public sinner? His gracious condescension in converting the Samaritan woman? His mercy in pardoning the adulterous woman? His charity when He sat down to eat with public sinners in order to win them?

Did not His enemies take His great kindness as a pretext to persecute Him, saying that He countenanced the transgression of the law of Moses, and tauntingly called Him the friend of sinners and of publicans? How kindly and humbly did He not try to win over the heart of Judas who intended to betray Him, when He washed his feet and called him friend! And how charitably did He ask the pardon of God, His Father, for His executioners, pleading their ignorance as an excuse!

Oh, how beautiful, how meek, how charitable is Jesus, Incarnate Wisdom! How loving and gentle He is with all of us, poor sinners whom He came to seek visibly in this world, and whom He now seeks invisibly every day! Do you think that Jesus, now that He is triumphant and glorious, is any the less loving and condescending? On the contrary, His glory perfects, as it were, His mercy. He wishes to forgive rather than to be exalted, and to display the riches of His mercy rather than those of His glory.

WEEK 5: DAY 1–THIRD MEDITATION

EXTRACT FROM THE ACT OF CONSECRATION: *"But, alas! ungrateful and unfaithful as I have been, I have not kept the promises which I made so solemnly to Thee in my Baptism. I have not fulfilled my obligations; I do not deserve to be called Thy child nor yet Thy slave; and as there is nothing in me which does not merit Thine anger and Thy repulse..."*

MEDITATION: Most probably, the devil has at some point or another tried to make us feel totally inadequate and unworthy in the making of this Consecration. For some of us may well have been "ungrateful and unfaithful" to this tremendous grace that God has given us in being able to make this Consecration.

We are, or at least have been, sinners. Perhaps some of us have even been great sinners. How true, then, will be the words which we will pronounce on the day of Consecration: "I have not fulfilled my obligations; I do not deserve to be called Thy child nor even Thy slave; and as there is nothing in me which does not merit Thine anger and repulse, I dare no longer come by myself before Thy most holy and august Majesty."

Yet, there was no sinner that Our Lord was not prepared to receive—He forgave and accepted Mary Magdalen amongst his followers, the woman caught in adultery and possessed by seven devils! He accepted the confession of guilt by the Good Thief on the cross, at the very last moment of his sin-infested life! He was even prepared to forgive Judas, who had betrayed Him to his enemies, trying to hint at this readiness by calling him "friend"! How then, can He refuse to accept us miserable sinners, when Scripture also says: "Is it my will that a sinner should die, saith the Lord God, and not that he should be converted from his ways and live?"

WEEK 5: DAY 1–FOURTH MEDITATION

EXTRACT FROM THE ACT OF CONSECRATION: *"I dare not any more come by myself before Thy most holy and august Majesty. It is on this account that I have recourse to the intercession of Thy Most Holy Mother, whom Thou has given me for a mediatrix with Thee. It is through her that I hope to obtain of Thee contrition, the pardon of my sins, and the acquisition and the preservation of Wisdom.*

"Hail then, Immaculate Mary, living Tabernacle of the Divinity, where the Eternal Wisdom willed to be hidden and to be adored by angels and by men! Hail, Queen of Heaven and earth, to whose empire everything is subject which is under God! Hail, O sure Refuge of sinners; whose mercy fails no one! Hear the desires which I have of the Divine Wisdom, and for that end, receive the vows and offerings which in my lowliness I present to Thee."

MEDITATION: The greatest means of all, and the most wonderful of all secrets for obtaining Mercy and keeping God's grace in our souls, is a tender and true devotion to the Blessed Mary. No one but Mary has ever found grace with God for herself and for the whole human race. No one but Mary has had the power to conceive and give birth to Him, and no one else has the power to bring Him to life in the soul of a sinner, as it were, through the operation of the Holy Spirit in the souls of those chosen by Him.

It is to the Mother of Mercy that we turn, asking her to turn those Eyes of Mercy towards us. For if she pleads to God on our behalf, then we can be sure that He will turn His Justice to Mercy, just as her pleading made her Son turn water into wine at Cana. How many sinners owe their salvation to this Merciful Mother! Listen to what the saints say of this Compassionate Queen:

St. Bernard says that: "She is impetuous in mercy, she is resistless in mercy. The duration of her mercy is unto the limits of the earth. The height of her mercy is unto the lowest abyss of sin and sorrow. She is always merciful. She is only merciful. She is our Mother of Mercy."

St. Albert the Great says: "They who are not thy servants, O Mary, shall perish." While St. Bonaventure repeats the same thought, saying: "They who neglect the service of Mary shall die in their sins....For them, from whom Mary turns away her face, there is not even a hope of salvation."

The renowned St. Ignatius of Antioch, a martyr of the 2nd century, says: "A sinner can be saved through the Holy Virgin, who, by her merciful prayers, obtains salvation for so many, who, according to strict justice, would be lost."

O, happy the souls who have won the favor of Mary! The Fathers of the Church tell us that Mary is the immense ocean of the perfections of God, the great storehouse of all His possessions, the inexhaustible treasury of the Lord, the treasurer and the dispenser of all His gifts. It is the will of God that since He gave His Son to Mary, we should receive all through her hands, and that no heavenly gift should flow down upon the earth without passing through Mary as through a channel.

Of her plenitude we have all received. If there is any grace, any hope of salvation in us, it is a gift which comes to us through Mary. She is so truly the Mistress of God's possessions, that she gives to whom she wills and as she wills, all the graces of God, all the virtues of Jesus Christ, all the gifts of the Holy Spirit, all good things in the order of nature, of grace and of glory.

Mary is the secret magnet which, wherever it is, draws Christ so powerfully that He cannot resist. This magnet drew Him down upon earth for the benefit of all men in general, and it still draws Him in particular every day to every man who possesses it. Once we possess Mary we shall easily and in a short time possess the Divine Wisdom through her intercession. Of all the means to possess Jesus Christ, Mary is the surest, the easiest, the shortest way and the holiest.

Were we to practice the most frightful penances; were we to undertake the most painful journeys and the most laborious works; were we to shed all our blood for the acquisition of the Divine Wisdom, all these efforts would be useless and insufficient to obtain Him without Mary's intercession and solicitude. But if Mary speaks a word in our favor; if we love her; if we bear the mark of her faithful servants who do her will; then we shall quickly and easily possess Divine Wisdom.

WEEK 5: DAY 2–FIRST MEDITATION

EXTRACT FROM THE ACT OF CONSECRATION: *"It is through her that I hope to obtain…the acquisition of and preservation of Wisdom."*

MEDITATION: Here we are asking for heavenly wisdom, not human wisdom. When Eternal Wisdom communicates Himself to a soul, He confers upon it the gifts of the Holy Spirit and all the great virtues in an eminent degree. That is, He bestows the theological virtues: faith, hope, charity; the cardinal virtues: temperance, prudence, justice, fortitude; moral virtues, such as: religion, humility, meekness, obedience, detachment, mortification, prayer. These, and other admirable virtues are the heavenly gifts which the Holy Spirit describes divinely in but a few words: "If a man love justice; her labors have great virtues, for she teaches temperance and prudence, and justice and fortitude, which are such things as man can have nothing more profitable in life."

Lastly, as Eternal Wisdom is "more active than all active things," He does not allow those who enjoy His friendship to languish in sloth and negligence. He sets them on fire and makes them do great things for the glory of God and the salvation of souls.

To prove them and make them worthy of Him, He gives them occasion for great combats and keeps in store for them contradictions and crosses in almost everything they undertake. He allows the devil to tempt them, the world to calumniate and abuse them, their enemies to have the upper hand and to crush them, their friends and relatives to forsake and betray them.

Sometimes, He will cause them to suffer the loss of their goods or of their health; at other times He will load them with reproach, sadness and despondency. In a word, He will try them variously in the crucible of tribulation "but," the Holy Spirit reminds us, "afflicted in few things, in many they shall be rewarded, because God has tried them and found them worthy of Himself. As gold in the furnace He has proved them; and as a victim of a holocaust He has received them; and in time there shall be respect had to them."

WEEK 5: DAY 2–SECOND MEDITATION

EXTRACT FROM THE ACT OF CONSECRATION: *"I (here say your own name), a faithless sinner, renew and ratify today in thy hands the vows of my Baptism: I renounce for ever Satan, his pomps and works..."*

MEDITATION: The devil is the Prince of the World and never was the world so corrupt as it is now, because it was never so astute, so wise in its own conceit, so cunning. It is so skillful in deceiving the soul seeking perfection that it makes use of truth to foster untruth, of virtue to authorize vice and it even distorts the meaning of Christ's own truths to give authority to its own maxims. "The number of those who are fools according to God, is infinite."

The earthly wisdom spoken of by St. James is an excessive striving for worldly goods. The worldly wise make a secret profession of this type of wisdom when they allow themselves to become attached to their earthly possessions, when they strive to become rich, when they go to law and bring useless actions against others in order to acquire or to keep temporal goods; when their every thought, word and deed is mainly directed toward obtaining or retaining something temporal. As to working out their eternal salvation and making use of the means to do so, such as reception of the Sacraments and prayer, they accomplish these duties only carelessly, in a very offhand manner, once in a while, and for the sake of appearances.

Sensual wisdom is a lustful desire for pleasure. The worldly-wise make a profession of it when they seek only the satisfaction of the senses; when they are inordinately fond of entertainment; when they shun whatever mortifies and inconveniences the body, such as fasting and other austerities; when they continually think of eating, drinking, playing, laughing, amusing themselves and having an agreeable time; when they eagerly seek after soft beds, merry games, sumptuous feasts and fashionable society. Then, after having unscrupulously indulged in all these pleasures—perhaps without displeasing the world or injuring their health—they look for "the least scrupulous" confessor (such is the name they give to those easy going confessors who shirk their duty) that they may receive from him, at little cost, the peaceful sanction of their soft and effeminate life, and a plenary indulgence for all their sins. I say, at little cost, for these sensually wise want as penance the recitation of only a few prayers, or the giving of an alms, because they dislike what afflicts the body.

Devilish wisdom consists in an unlawful striving for human esteem and honors. This is the wisdom which the worldly-wise profess when they aim, although not openly, at greatness, honors, dignities and high positions; when they wish to be seen, esteemed, praised and applauded by men; when in their studies, their works, their endeavors their words and actions, they seek only the good opinion and praise of men so that they may be looked upon as pious people, as men of learning, as great leaders, as clever lawyers, as people of boundless and distinguished merit, or deserving of high consideration; while they cannot bear an insult or a rebuke; or they cover up their faults and make a show of their fine qualities.

With Our Lord Jesus Christ, the Incarnate Wisdom, we must detest and condemn these three kinds of false wisdom if we wish to acquire the true one which does not seek its own interest, which is not found on this earth nor in the heart of those who lead a comfortable life, but which abhors all that which is great and high in the estimation of men.

The worldling, or the man ruled by these three wisdoms, bases his conduct upon his *honor*, upon *what people say*, upon *convention*, upon *good cheer*, upon *personal interest*, upon *refined manners*, upon *witty jokes*. These are the seven innocent incentives, so he thinks, upon which he can rely that he may lead an easy life.

He has virtues of his own for which he is canonized by the world. These are *manliness, finesse, diplomacy, tact, gallantry, politeness, sprightliness*. He considers as serious sins such traits as lack of feeling, silliness, dullness, sanctimoniousness. He adheres as strictly as possible to the commandments which the world has given him:

1. Thou shalt be well acquainted with the world.

2. Thou shalt be an "honest" man.

3. Thou shalt be successful in business.

4. Thou shalt keep what is thine.

5. Thou shalt get on in the world.

6. Thou shalt make friends.

7. Thou shalt be a society man.

8. Thou shalt make merry.

9. Thou shalt not be a killjoy.

10. Thou shalt avoid singularity, dullness and an air of piety.

The wisdom of the world is that of which it is written: "I will destroy the wisdom of the wise" according to the world. "The wisdom of the flesh is an enemy to God." "This is not the wisdom descending from above but earthly, sensual, devilish."

WEEK 5: DAY 2–THIRD MEDITATION

EXTRACT FROM THE ACT OF CONSECRATION: *"...and I give myself entirely to Jesus Christ, the Incarnate Wisdom, to carry my cross after Him all the days of my life and to be more faithful to Him than I have ever been before."*

MEDITATION: The Cross is the greatest secret of Eternal Wisdom. O how different are the thoughts and the ways of Eternal Wisdom from those of man! This great God wishes to redeem the world, to cast out and shackle the demons, to close hell and to open heaven to man. What means will be chosen by the Divine Wisdom?" His arm is almighty. In an instant He can destroy all that is opposed to Him. He can create whatever He wills. By one word of His mouth He can annihilate and create.

But, O wonder! He perceives a thing which is a scandal and a stumbling block to the Jews, an object of foolishness to the Gentiles. He sees a piece of vile and contemptible wood which is being used to humiliate and torture the most wicked and most unfortunate of men; it is called a gibbet, a gallows, a Cross. He looks upon this Cross. He takes delight in it. He loves it and chooses it before all that is great and resplendent in heaven and on earth. He chooses it to be the instrument of His conquests, the adornment of His majesty, the riches and delight of His empire, the friend and spouse of His heart.

"O the depth of the wisdom and of the knowledge of God!" How amazing His choice! How deep and incomprehensible His way of acting and judging! But how ineffable His love of the Cross!

The Incarnate Wisdom loved the Cross from His infancy. He placed it "in the midst of His heart," there to reign. During His life He eagerly sought after the Cross. All His journeying, all His eagerness, all His pursuits, all His desires were directed toward the Cross, because to die in its embrace was for Him the very height of glory and success.

At last His wishes were fully satisfied. Loaded with infamy He was attached to the Cross, fixed to it, and joyfully died in the embrace of His dear friend as upon a couch of honor and triumph. Do not think that, to be more triumphant, He relinquished or rejected the Cross after His death. Far from it. He united Himself so closely to it and became, as it were, so incorporated with it, that no angel or man, no creature in heaven or on earth can separate Him from it. Their bond is indissoluble; their union is eternal. NEVER THE CROSS WITHOUT JESUS; NOR JESUS WITHOUT THE CROSS.

WEEK 5: DAY 2–FOURTH MEDITATION

EXTRACT FROM THE ACT OF CONSECRATION: *"...leaving to thee the entire and full right of disposing of me and all that belongs to me, without exception, according to thy good pleasure, for the greater glory of God, in time and in eternity."*

MEDITATION: When Our Lady appeared to St. Bernadette at Lourdes, she said to the young girl: "I do not promise to make you happy in this life, but in the next." Our Lady chose to dispose of Bernadette in a seemingly harsh manner, but in giving Bernadette crosses, she was actually doing her a great good. The Cross is good and precious for many reasons:

1. Because it makes us resemble Jesus Christ.

2. Because it makes us worthy children of the Eternal Father; worthy members of Jesus Christ; worthy temples of the Holy Spirit: "God the Father...scourgeth every son He receives." Jesus Christ receives as His follower only him who carries his cross. The Holy Spirit cuts and polishes all the souls seeking perfection.

3. The Cross is good because it enlightens the mind and affords more knowledge than all the books in the whole world. "He that has not been tried, what does he know?"

4. Because when well borne, the Cross is the cause and the proof of love. The Cross inflames the heart with the fire of Divine Love by detaching it from creatures; it keeps this love alive and increases it. As wood is the fuel of fire, so is the Cross the fuel of love. The Cross is the surest proof that we love God. The Cross was the proof God gave of His love for us, and it is also the proof He requires of us to show our love for Him.

5. The Cross is good because it is an abundant source of all kinds of delight and consolation. It brings joy, peace and grace to the soul.

You, who are wise and honest by worldly standards, do not understand this mysterious language. You are too fond of sensual pleasures; you seek too much your own comfort; you love too much the things of this life, you fear too much to be held up to scorn and to be humiliated; in a word, you are too hostile to the Cross of Jesus. In general, indeed, you esteem and praise the Cross in theory, but not your personal crosses. These you shun as much as you can, or else you drag them along unwillingly, with murmurings, impatience and complaints.

Eternal Wisdom tells us that the number of fools and unfortunate people is infinite. This is because the number of those who do not know the value of the Cross is infinite and they carry it despite themselves. But, if you have trials and afflictions, if you suffer many persecutions for justice sake, if you are treated as the refuse of the world, be comforted, be glad, thrill with joy, because the cross you carry is a gift so precious, for your reward is great in heaven. Even on earth your reward is great, because of the spiritual graces which the Cross obtains for you.

Friends of Jesus Christ, drink of His bitter cup, and your friendship with Him will increase. Suffer with Him and you will be glorified with Him. Suffer patiently and even cheerfully. Yet a little while and the moment of suffering will be changed into an eternity of happiness. Since it was necessary for Eternal Wisdom to enter heaven by the way of suffering, it is necessary for you to enter by the same way.

Whithersoever you turn, you will always find the Cross. Jesus and Mary have fixed their abode in the Cross, so that you will not find them in this world save in the Cross. They have so truly incorporated and united themselves with the Cross, that in all truth we can say: WISDOM IS THE CROSS, AND THE CROSS IS WISDOM.

WEEK 5: DAY 3–FIRST MEDITATION

EXTRACT FROM THE ACT OF CONSECRATION: *"I choose thee this day for my Mother and Mistress. I deliver and consecrate to thee, as thy slave, my body and soul, my goods, both interior and exterior, and even the value of all my good actions, past, present and future"*

MEDITATION: Mary is *charitable*. She loves us as her children and servants. Let us give her all, and we shall lose nothing. She will turn everything to our gain.

Mary *is generous*. She gives back more than is given to her. Let us give her unreservedly all that we possess. She will render us a hundredfold.

Mary *is powerful*. No one can take away from her what we place in her hands. Let us, then, commit ourselves to her care and she will defend us against all our enemies and help us to conquer them.

Mary is *faithful*. She does not allow anything that we give her to be lost or wasted. She is, *par excellence*, the Virgin faithful to God and faithful to man. She faithfully guarded and kept all that God entrusted to her, never allowing a particle of it to be lost. She still keeps every day, with special care, all those who place themselves entirely under her protection and guidance.

Let us, then, confide everything to this faithful Virgin. Let us attach ourselves to her as to an immovable pillar, as to an anchor that cannot be lifted, or rather as to Mount Sion which cannot be shaken.

Thus, whatever may be our natural blindness, our weakness and inconstancy; whatever may be the number and the wickedness of our enemies, we shall never be deceived nor misled, and we shall never have the misfortune of losing the grace of God and the infinite Treasure of Eternal Wisdom.

WEEK 5: DAY 3–SECOND MEDITATION

EXTRACT FROM THE ACT OF CONSECRATION: *"Receive, O benignant Virgin, this little offering of my slavery, in honor of, and in union with, that subjection which the Eternal Wisdom deigned to have to thy maternity, in homage to the power which both of you have over this poor sinner, and in thanksgiving for the privileges with which the Holy Trinity has favored thee. I declare that I wish henceforth, as thy true slave, to seek thy honor and to obey thee in all things."*

MEDITATION: How can we seek her honor and obey her in all things? St. Louis De Montfort gives the answer in his book *True Devotion to Mary*. The first thing that he lists is being truly devoted to Mary. This is nothing else than Our Lady's message at Fatima, wherein she stated that God wanted the whole world to be devoted to her Immaculate Heart. Thus, by making this Consecration to Jesus through Mary, we are fulfilling the most important and essential part in that obligation of *honoring and obeying* the Blessed Mother.

There are many other ways in which to honor the Blessed Virgin. A little later, we will present St. Louis De Montfort's list of recommendations for showing an external honor and devotion to Our Lady.

WEEK 5: DAY 3–THIRD MEDITATION

EXTRACT FROM THE ACT OF CONSECRATION: *"O admirable Mother, present me to thy dear Son as His eternal slave, so that as He has redeemed me by thee, by thee He may receive me! O Mother of Mercy, grant that I may obtain the true Wisdom of God, and for that end receive me among those whom thou lovest and teachest, whom thou leadest, nourishest and protectest as thy children and thy slaves."*

MEDITATION: Loving and teaching refer to the will and the intellect—two powers of the soul. Thus we see here the necessity of not only an exterior devotion to Mary, but also an interior devotion that embraces both powers of the soul—the will (which loves) and the intellect (which learns and understands).

"Whom thou lovest and teachest..." Let us never doubt Our Lady's love for us! When Our Lord said to her, as He died on the cross: "Behold thy son!" Our Lady took us under her maternal care. Regardless of our ungratefulness towards her, she has always loved us miserable sinners more than we have ever loved ourselves. Yet love is meant to be reciprocal, it is meant to be returned. By this devotion and consecration, we are taking the first steps, like a little baby, towards our Blessed Mother. By this Consecration, we will, in a certain manner, be born again. We will be treasured all the more by our heavenly Mother, since by our Consecration to her, we become, as it were, her first born, those closest to her heart. Let us not be as ungrateful as we have been in the past. Let us live as the first born, let us take up our responsibility in looking after the other children of this great family of the Mystical Body of Christ, by bringing them to a greater knowledge, love and service of our spiritual Mother.

To be able to achieve this, we must first of all make sure that we, ourselves, are ever growing in knowledge and love of our Heavenly Queen, and becoming ever more diligent in her service. There is a philosophical axiom that says: "Nobody can give what they have not got." This is so very true with regard to Our Lady. We have to know her thoroughly, we have to love her ardently, we have to work for her tirelessly. It is only then that we will succeed in bringing others to her.

This Consecration has been a start along these lines. Let us never take this Consecration for granted, whereby we let all our knowledge, love and service go to waste. There are many who have made the Consecration, and then have fallen back into a Marian lukewarmness! Let us not become such ungrateful wretches, who expect so much, in having given so little!

Let us remember the words of St. Alphonsus Liguori, who says: "It is impossible that a servant of Mary be damned, provided he serves her faithfully and commends himself to her maternal protection." Or the words of St. Bonaventure, who says: "They who neglect the service of Mary shall die in their sins!"

WEEK 5: DAY 3–FOURTH MEDITATION

EXTRACT FROM THE ACT OF CONSECRATION: *"O faithful Virgin, make me in all things so perfect a disciple, imitator and slave of the Incarnate Wisdom, Jesus Christ thy Son, that I may attain, by thine intercession and by thine example, to the fullness of His age on earth and of His glory in heaven. Amen"*

MEDITATION: This making of us into disciples, "in all things so perfect" and "imitators and slaves of the Incarnate Wisdom," leads us to the practice of virtue and the practical aspects of the True Devotion Consecration. In his book *Love of the Eternal Wisdom*, St. Louis De Montfort sets forth the *Spiritual Maxims of the Eternal Wisdom,* to whom we shall consecrate ourselves through a perfect devotion to Mary. I give these twelve Maxims below. These give a wonderful foundation to the spiritual life and can be profitably returned to, time and time again, over the course of many years. By following these maxims you shall truly become "in all things so perfect a disciple, imitator and slave of the Incarnate Wisdom" that you will certainly attain "to the fullness of his age on earth and of his glory in heaven."

SPIRITUAL MAXIMS OF THE DIVINE WISDOM

by St. Louis De Montfort

The following maxims or spiritual counsels were originally composed by St. Louis De Montfort and intended for his newly-founded community, the Daughters of Wisdom. For the benefit of the general public we have decided to insert them in this edition, adapting them to the conditions of those living in the world and seeking to acquire a closer union with Christ, the Eternal and Incarnate Wisdom.

WEEK 5: DAY 4–FIRST MEDITATION

FIRST MAXIM
Voice of the Eternal Wisdom
True happiness on earth lies in voluntary poverty and in following Me.

1. My son, have no attachment to any created good, however holy it may be, whether interior or exterior, spiritual or corporal.
2. Always be on your guard against anything which draws your affection.
3. Beware of the purely natural affections of your relatives and friends when they are an obstacle to your salvation or to your perfection.
4. Do not be afraid to disoblige or to displease others, if you must do so to carry your cross after Me.
5. After My example, carry your cross of contradiction, persecution, renunciation and contempt, every day.
6. Do not be ashamed to practice any act of virtue before others, and do not omit any good deed for fear of scorn or praise, when you know that God demands it of you.

SECOND MAXIM

Voice of the Eternal Wisdom

You are truly blessed if the world persecutes you, opposing your plans though they are good, thinking evil of your intentions, calumniating your conduct, and taking away unjustly your reputation or your possessions.

1. My son, beware of complaining to others, rather than to Me, of the bad treatment you receive, and do not seek ways of justifying yourself, particularly when you are the only one to suffer from it.

2. On the contrary, pray for those who procure for you the blessings of persecution.

3. Thank Me for treating you as I Myself was treated on earth, a sign of contradiction.

4. Never be discouraged in your plans because you meet with opposition; it is a pledge of future victory. A good work which is not opposed, which is not marked by the sign of the cross, has no great value before Me and will soon be destroyed.

5. Regard as your best friends those who persecute you, because they procure for you great merit on earth, and great glory in heaven.

6. Regard as unfortunate those who live in luxury, who feast sumptuously, who frequent the world of fashion, who make their way in the world, who succeed in business, and who spend their lives in pleasures and amusements.

7. Never do anything, either good or evil, out of human respect to avoid any blame, insult, mockery, or praise.

8. When through your own fault some loss or disgrace befalls you, do not be disturbed by it, but rather humble yourself before God and accept it from His hands as punishment for your fault.

WEEK 5: DAY 4–SECOND MEDITATION

THIRD MAXIM

Voice of the Eternal Wisdom

If anyone comes to Me and does not hate his father and mother, and wife and children, and brothers and sisters, yes, and even his own life, he cannot be My disciple. (Lk. 14:26).

1. My son, hate your own mind with its thoughts, rejecting them if they are bad, dangerous, or useless.

2. Do not rely exclusively on your own ideas, thoughts, knowledge, visions, or contemplations, and never constitute yourself the final judge of their goodness or their malice.

3. Believe that the judgment of others, in any indifferent matter, is always more accurate and more solid than your own, however much you would like to believe the contrary.

4. Beware of your imagination and your memory, rejecting evil thoughts, extravagant and useless plans, and vain, dangerous, or at least idle representations of the past or the future.

5. Strive to empty your memory of every object other than the presence of God.

6. Do not voluntarily dwell on the evil that has been done to you or on the good that you have done.

7. Despise your own will, submitting it to that of your superiors and always renouncing it, even in matters that seem excellent to you.

8. Do nothing of any importance without taking counsel, so that you may not have to repent of it after it is done.

9. Do not anxiously crave for things you do not possess, even though they might seem useful to your neighbor and glorious to My majesty.

10. Ask Me earnestly for particular favors, but request them only because it is My will that you should ask for them, and let conformity to My will be the basis of your prayer.

FOURTH MAXIM

Voice of the Eternal Wisdom

Take up your cross daily and follow Me.

1. My son, renounce the pleasures of your senses, innocent though they be.

2. Mortify your eyes, by avoiding the sight of dangerous or curious things.

3. Mortify your ears, closing them to evil, vain, and useless discourse.

4. Mortify your tongue, by avoiding idle conversations, speaking frequently of Me or of things that concern Me, and maintaining a continual silence, if you can, on the good that you have done, on the faults of your neighbors, and on your own good qualities.

5. Mortify your taste, by not eating unnecessarily between meals, by fasting in a spirit of obedience, by eating something unpleasant, by eating with restraint and modesty when appetite and hunger make you eager for food.

6. Mortify your sense of smell, by abstaining from superfluous use of perfumes.

7. Mortify your hands, by avoiding superfluous and unseemly gestures.

8. Mortify your feet, avoiding hurried and unbecoming steps. Do not walk with affectation or haste, but with simplicity and modesty.

9. Mortify your sense of touch, by preferring less expensive clothing and furniture and by performing acts of penance daily.

10. Mortify your whole body, by doing your work in a spirit of penance, and by accepting joyfully the discomforts of the seasons, and the various illnesses that attack the body.

WEEK 5: DAY 4–THIRD MEDITATION

FIFTH MAXIM

Voice of the Eternal Wisdom

The way and the gate that lead to heaven are narrow, and few there are who find the way and enter by the gate.

1. My son, do continual violence to your natural inclinations and dispositions, that you may be one of the small number who find the way of life, and who enter by the narrow gate to heaven.

2. Take care not to follow the majority and the common herd, so many of whom are lost.

3. Do not be deceived—there are only two ways: one that leads to life, and is narrow; the other that leads to death, and is wide; there is no middle way.

4. If your eye or your hand or your foot scandalize you, cut it off without delay lest you perish. In other words: avoid the occasions of sin.

SIXTH MAXIM

Voice of the Eternal Wisdom

Watch and pray without ceasing.

1. My son, you must apply yourself continually to vocal or mental prayer.

2. Do everything in the spirit of prayer, that is to say, for the love of God and in the presence of God.

3. Never give up prayer, no matter what difficulty or what dryness you may experience.

4. Never give yourself up entirely to external things, for the kingdom of God is within you.

5. Esteem more highly than all exterior things, those that are within the heart.

6. Believe that the greatest things that are done on this earth, are wrought interiorly, and in the hearts of faithful souls.

7. Do everything in a spirit of faith, and let this virtue be the food of your meditations, and the quality that gives value to your actions.

SEVENTH MAXIM

Voice of the Eternal Wisdom

Love your enemies, do good to them that do evil to you.

1. My son, pray for them that persecute you, heap insults upon you, and rob you of your honor and property.

2. Never do to others what you would not have them do to you.

3. Bear with the faults of others for the love of God Who is patient with you.

4. Rebuke those who offend Me, without fearing

EIGHTH MAXIM

Voice of the Eternal Wisdom

I converse familiarly with the simple, and I reveal My secrets only to the little ones.

1. My son, be simple as a dove, without malice, without duplicity, without dissimulation.

2. The greater you are, the more you should humble yourself, that is to say, be the servant of others. Choose the lowest place, the lowliest employment, the poorest clothing.

3. As God gives His grace to the humble, do all your actions with deep humility of heart, in order to obtain My grace, and My friendship.

4. Beware of what is great, illustrious and dazzling in the eyes of men, for that is valueless in My sight.

5. Love the life that is hidden, poor, and worthless in the eyes of the world for such is the object of My delight.

6. You must become like a little child, if you would enter heaven, that is to say, simple, obedient, innocent, and gentle as a little child.

7. Those who for the kingdom of God, have made themselves the last; and the servants of others are the first and the most exalted in My sight.

8. If you exalt yourself higher than I desire, you will be brought lower than you desire, in this world and in the next; if, on the contrary, you set yourself below others, I will exalt you above others, even in this world.

WEEK 5: DAY 4–FOURTH MEDITATION

NINTH MAXIM

Voice of the Eternal Wisdom

He who is faithful in little things will be faithful also in those that are great, and he who is unfaithful in little things will be unfaithful also in those that are great.

1. My son, be very faithful to the little rules, the little inspirations, the little practices of virtue.

2. Do not neglect anything that can help you to acquire perfection.

3. If you are faithful in a few things, I assure you that I will set you over many things; that is to say, that if I see you corresponding faithfully to the few graces you receive, to the little amount of devotion you feel, *etc.*, I will give you a share in a greater abundance of graces.

4. Take care not to neglect the little things, for otherwise you will gradually fall into lukewarmness and a lack of devotion; you will lose, little by little, your inspirations, your devotion, your merits, and your graces.

TENTH MAXIM

Voice of the Eternal Wisdom

I choose the least things of this world to confound and destroy what is greatest.

1. My son, humble yourself and remain humble, and I will make something of you.

2. Give your garment to him, who takes from you your cloak.

3. Turn the other cheek to him who strikes you.

4. Suffer everything without complaining.

5. Be the first to accuse yourself, and to take the blame upon yourself.

6. Believe all that is good of others and all that is evil of yourself.

7. Choose, if you have the grace to do so, the least agreeable in everything.

8. Rejoice amid all sorts of difficulties and contradictions especially when you are found worthy to suffer something for My sake.

9. Never despair, and never be disturbed, when you fall into sin, but humble yourself, begging My forgiveness.

ELEVENTH MAXIM
Voice of the Eternal Wisdom
Beware of false prophets. My son, you must deeply distrust:

1. The lights of your own mind, however spiritually-minded you may be;

2. The feelings of your heart, however just and sincere they may seem to you;

3. The spiritual maxims of the lukewarm;

4. The beautiful and lofty thoughts and the holy undertakings which the evil spirit, disguised as an angel of light, often inspires in the most zealous and spiritual souls to bring about their downfall by his wiles and deceits.

TWELFTH MAXIM
Counsels of St. Louis De Montfort
To distinguish and avoid the subtle snares of self-love, of the flesh, and of the devil, these are the important counsels I give you.

1. Never willingly take pleasure in, or still less rely on, what you have thought, imagined, or decided; but put your pleasure, your confidence, and your reliance only in the merits and intercession of Mary, whose slave you are, with Jesus; in the blood and the merits of Jesus before the Father; and in the infinite mercy of God your Father.

2. Do not set yourself up as your own judge, for no one is a legitimate judge of his own case; but reveal all your thoughts, ideas, *etc.*, to your spiritual director or to your confessor; do not hide from him anything you have in your heart or anything that has affected you.

3. Obey your confessor in all spiritual matters and profit by his advice.

THE EXTERNAL PRACTICES OF THE INTERNAL DEVOTION AS RECOMMENDED BY ST. LOUIS DE MONTFORT

Before the Consecration...

WEEK 5: DAY 5–FIRST MEDITATION

1. The Day of the Consecration:

> At the end of the three weeks they should go to Confession and Communion, with the intention of giving themselves to Jesus Christ in the quality of slaves of love, by the hands of Mary. After Communion, which they should try to make according to the method given further on, they should recite the formula of their consecration, which they will also find further on. They ought to write it, or have it written, unless they have a printed copy of it; and they should sign it the same day on which they have made it (*True Devotion* §231).

WRITING OUT THE CONSECRATION: Though by no means obligatory, this practice is however strongly recommended—at least for those making the Consecration for the first time. For by doing so, it becomes even more personal and deliberate. However, one may also type out the text of the Consecration.

CONFESSION: St. Louis says that those making the Consecration "should go to Confession and Communion." This is desirable, but not obligatory. There might even be circumstances (*e.g.,* large numbers making the Consecration) that will prevent everyone from going to Confession on the actual day of Consecration. One should not become anxious over this and a Confession can be made within days of the Consecration, either before or after it takes place.

THE MOMENT OF CONSECRATION: The actual offering of ourselves to Jesus through Mary would be most appropriately done immediately before the Offertory at Mass (after the Creed). A solemn consecration would be ideal, whereby the priest would open the doors of the tabernacle, so that all those making the

Consecration can read aloud their Consecration in the presence of the Blessed Sacrament.

If only a few are making the Consecration, they could come to the Communion rail to do so. If it is a case of large numbers, they should do so from the pews. If the priest does not wish to participate, then the person(s) can silently make the Consecration during the Offertory of the Mass.

Once they have made their Consecration, they can renew it in the presence of Our Lord, once they receive Holy Communion.

SIGNING THE CONSECRATION: Once Mass is over, those having made (or renewed) their Consecration could come forward to the Communion rail, or to an Altar of Our Lady, and there sign the text of the Consecration. The more solemnly this can be done, the better it would be. If large numbers are making the Consecration, we recommend that several hymns in honor of Our Lady be sung and, perhaps, interspersed by some decades of the Holy Rosary. If possible, the hymns should include the *Ave Maris Stella* and the *Magnificat*. Thus by reciting the Rosary and singing these hymns, those having made the Consecration actually start practicing a devotion to those very prayers that St. Louis recommends for our external devotion.

2. Acts of Penance on the Day of Consecration

> It would also be well that, on that day, they should pay some tribute to Jesus Christ and our Blessed Lady, either as a penance for their past unfaithfulness to the vows of their Baptism, or as a testimony of their dependence on the dominion of Jesus and Mary. This tribute ought to be according to the devotion and ability of each one, such as a fast, a mortification, an alms or a candle. If they had but a pin to give in homage, and gave it with a good heart, it would be enough for Jesus, who looks only at the good will (*True Devotion* §232).

Once again, this adds seriousness and deliberation to our Act of Consecration. The penance or alms need not be great. As to the alms, we suggest that an offering might be made to help the work of the Legion of Mary, which is responsible, among other things, for the spreading of St. Louis de Montfort's True Devotion Consecration to Mary.

3. Renewal of the Consecration

Once a year at least, and on the same day, they should renew the same consecration, observing the same practices during the three weeks. They might also, once a month or even once a day, renew all they have done, in these few words: "I am all Thine and all that I have is Thine, O most loving Jesus, through Mary, Thy most holy Mother" (*True Devotion* §233).

However, this renewal, and time of renewal, is not of strict obligation. St. Louis says that they *should* make it once a year and on the same date. One can, nevertheless, renew it more frequently or less frequently; on one feast or another. The time of preparation for the renewal is also left to each individuals personal choice. It is to be remembered that, in his *True Devotion to Mary*, St. Louis says that the recommended time of preparation (33 days) can be lengthened or shortened at will.

LIFE AFTER CONSECRATION...

WEEK 5: DAY 5–SECOND MEDITATION

"Although what is essential in this devotion consists in the interior, we must not fail to unite to the inward practice certain external observances. "We must do the one, yet not leave the other undone" (Mt. 23:23); because the outward practices, well performed, aid the inward ones; and because they remind man, who is always guided by his senses, of what he has done or ought to do; and also because they are suitable for edifying our neighbor, who sees them; these are things which inward practices cannot do. Let no worldling, then, or critic, intrude here to say that because true devotion is in the heart, we must avoid external devotion; or that devotion ought to be hidden, and that there may be vanity in showing it. I answer, with my Master, that men should see our good works, that they may glorify our Father who is in heaven (Mt. 5:16); not, as St. Gregory says, that we ought to perform our actions and exterior devotions to please men and get praise—that would be vanity; but that we should sometimes do them before men with the view of pleasing God, and glorifying Him thereby, without caring either for the contempt or the praise of men.

I will allude only briefly to some exterior practices, which I call "exterior" not because we do not perform them interiorly, but because they have something outward about them to distinguish them from those which are purely inward (*True Devotion* §226).

1. Reciting the Little Crown of the Blessed Virgin Mary

They may recite every day of their life, without however making a burden of it, the Little Crown of the Blessed Virgin, composed of three *Our Father's* and twelve *Hail Mary's*, in honor of Our Lady's twelve privileges and grandeurs. This is a very ancient practice and it has its foundation in Holy Scripture. St. John saw a woman crowned with twelve stars, clothed with the sun, and with the moon under her feet (Apoc. 12:1); and this woman, according to the interpreters, was the most holy Virgin. (*True Devotion* §234).

There are many ways of saying this Crown well, but it would take too long to enter upon them. The Holy Ghost will teach them to those who are the most faithful to this devotion. Nevertheless, to say it quite simply, we should begin by saying: "Grant that I may praise thee, holy Virgin; give me strength against thy enemies." After that, we should say the Apostles' Creed, then an *Our Father* with four *Hail Mary's* and then one Glory be to the Father; then another *Our Father*, four *Hail Mary's,* and *Glory be to the Father* and so on with the rest; and at the end we should say the *Sub Tuum Praesidium i.e.,* "We fly to thy patronage" (*True Devotion* §235).

You will find a little prayer card containing the *Little Crown*, as part of your *True Devotion Package*. It is recommended that you say it daily—but as St. Louis says, without it becoming a burden to you. It may be well to set it aside for a little while if it starts to become too burdensome. Similarly, it would not constitute a sin to have omitted it on some days due to a crowded daily schedule. St. Louis does not tie us down with a multiplicity of devotions of an obligatory nature. He suggests certain things and then leaves the rest up to each individual soul and the Holy Ghost—"The Holy Ghost will teach them to those who are the most faithful to this devotion."

WEEK 5: DAY 5–THIRD MEDITATION

2. Wearing Chains to Signify our Slavery to Jesus and Mary

It is a most glorious and praiseworthy thing, and very useful to those who have thus made themselves slaves of Jesus in Mary, that they should wear, as a sign of their loving slavery, little iron chains, blessed with the proper blessing. It is perfectly true that these external insignia are not essential, and a person who has embraced this devotion may very well go without them; nevertheless, I cannot refrain from warmly praising those who, after having shaken off the shameful chains of the slavery of the devil, in which Original Sin, and perhaps actual sin, had bound them, have voluntarily surrendered themselves to the glorious slavery of Jesus Christ, and glory with St. Paul in being in chains for Christ (Eph. 3:1; Philem. 9), chains that are a thousand times more glorious and precious, though of iron, than all the golden ornaments of emperors (*True Devotion* §236).

Once there was nothing more infamous on earth than the cross, and now that wood is the most glorious boast of Christianity. Let us say the same of the irons of slavery. There was nothing more ignominious among the ancients; there is nothing more shameful even now among the heathens. But among Christians, there is nothing more illustrious than the chains of Jesus; for they unchain us and preserve us from the infamous fetters of sin and the devil. They set us at liberty and chain us to Jesus and Mary; not by compulsion and constraint, like galley-slaves, but by charity and love, like children (*True Devotion* §237).

The following are the reasons for wearing these little chains:

Firstly, to remind the Christian of the vows and promises of his Baptism, of the perfect renewal he has made of them by this devotion, and of the strict obligation under which he is to be faithful to them. As man, who shapes his course more often by the senses than by pure faith, easily forgets his obligations toward God unless he has some outward thing to remind him of them. These little chains serve marvelously to remind the Christian of the chains of sin and the slavery of the devil from which Baptism has delivered him, and of the dependence on Jesus which he has vowed to Him in Baptism, and of the ratification of it which he has made by the renewal of his vows. One of the reasons why so few Christians think of their baptismal vows, and live with as much license as if they had promised no more to God than the heathen, is that they do not wear any external sign to remind them of their vows (*True Devotion* §238).

Secondly, to show that we are not ashamed of the servitude and slavery of Jesus Christ, and that we renounce the slavery of the world, of sin and of the devil. Thirdly, to protect ourselves against the chains of sin and of the devil; for we must wear either "the chains of sinners or the chains of charity and salvation" (*True Devotion* §239).

These loving slaves of Jesus Christ, "the chained of Christ" (Eph. 3:1; Philem. 9), can wear their chains on their feet or on their arms, around their body or around their neck. Fr. Vincent Caraffa, seventh Superior General of the Jesuits, who died in the odor of sanctity in the year 1643, used to wear an iron band around his feet as a mark of his servitude; and he said that his only regret was that he could not publicly drag a chain. Mother Agnes of Jesus, of whom we have spoken before, used to wear an iron chain around her body. Others have worn it around their neck in penance for the pearl necklaces which they had worn in the world; while others have worn it around their arms to remind themselves, in their manual labors, that they were slaves of Jesus Christ (*True Devotion* §242).

The chain we recommend above all chains, is a chain that has the *Miraculous Medal* hanging from it. On November 27, 1830, Our Lady appeared to St. Catherine Labouré, at the Rue de Bac, in Paris and charged her with the mission of seeing that a medal be made according to the design shown to St. Catherine by Our Lady herself. Mary said that this medal, if worn with confidence around the neck, would draw upon the wearer an abundance of great graces. Obviously, the Medal is also worn on a chain. So what better sign of slavery, than to wear the Miraculous Medal on a chain!

There have been many saints who have worn chains as a penance—one of the most recent ones was the converted alcoholic of this century—St. Matthew Talbot, who, after they found him dead on the street, was found to have been wearing penitential chains under his clothing. However such acts of penance should never be undertaken without the permission of your spiritual director. Furthermore, I think that the Miraculous Medal would attract more notable graces than the imprudent wearing of other kinds of penitential chains!

WEEK 5: DAY 5–FOURTH MEDITATION

3. Enrollment in the Brown Scapular

St. Louis De Montfort was a tireless advocate of the Brown Scapular of Our Lady of Mount Carmel. The Scapular was first given to an Englishman, St. Simon Stock, on July 16, 1251. It was Heaven's response to a plea from St. Simon Stock to save the then dwindling Carmelite Order, from the increasing waves of opposition that it was undergoing. Attached to this Brown Scapular of Our Lady of Mount Carmel, is the promise that nobody who dies clothed in this Scapular will suffer the fires of hell: "This shall be a sign to you and to all Carmelites: whosoever dies wearing this, shall not suffer eternal fire."

For a long time the Habit or Scapular was the exclusive property of the Carmelite Order, a sign of profession in it, and a sign of a life totally consecrated to Mary—but in the 14th century, we find a bridge appearing between Carmel and the world. Pious people living in the world became anxious to live its Marian-form life and to share in its spiritual treasury of prayers and good works. They affiliated themselves to the Order and were given the Scapular as a sign of that affiliation.

In a comparatively short time, the wearing of the Scapular spread to the whole Church and became the unmistakable mark of devotion to Mary. Popes, kings, princes, nobles and humble folk alike, all lived and died in the hope of participating in the Scapular Promise. Throughout time, it has kept generation after generation aware of its filial duty towards the Queen of Heaven and the Mother of Mercy.

Pope Pius XII, on the occasion of the 7th centenary of the Brown Scapular, said:

> The Holy Scapular, which may be called the Habit or Garment of Mary, is a sign and a pledge of the protection of the Mother of God. But not for this reason, however, may they who wear the Scapular think that they can gain eternal salvation while remaining slothful and negligent of spirit, for the Apostle warns us: "In fear and trembling shall you work out your salvation." May it be to them a sign of their Consecration to the most sacred Heart of the Immaculate Virgin, which consecration we have so strongly recommended in recent times.

WEEK 5: DAY 6–FIRST MEDITATION

4. Devotion to the Mystery of the Incarnation

Those who undertake this holy slavery should have a special devotion to the great mystery of the Incarnation of the Word (March 25th). Indeed, the Incarnation is the mystery proper of this practice, inasmuch as it is a devotion inspired by the Holy Ghost: first, to honor and imitate the ineffable dependence which God the Son was pleased to have on Mary, for His Father's glory and our salvation—which dependence particularly appears in this mystery wherein Jesus is a captive and a slave in the bosom of the divine Mary, and depends on her for all things—secondly, to thank God for the incomparable graces He has given Mary, and particularly for having chosen her to be His most holy Mother, which choice was made in this mystery. These are the two principal ends of the slavery of Jesus in Mary (*True Devotion* §243).

A very practical way of cultivating this devotion to the Mystery of the Incarnation is fidelity in praying the *Angelus* three times a day—morning, noon and evening. One can also find a host of meditative thoughts to ponder upon, while reciting the vocal prayers of the *Angelus*. St. Louis De Montfort's book, *The Love of Eternal Wisdom,* provides so many appropriate themes and ideas for us to dwell upon.

5. Devotion to the *Hail Mary*

Those who adopt this slavery ought also to have a great devotion to saying the *Hail Mary* (the Angelical Salutation). Few Christians, however enlightened, know the real value, merit, excellence, and necessity of the *Hail Mary*. It was necessary for the Blessed Virgin to appear several times to great and enlightened saints to show them the merit of it. She did so to St. Dominic, St. John Capistran and Blessed Alan de la Roche (*True Devotion* §249).

They have composed entire works on the wonders and efficacy of that prayer for converting souls. They have loudly proclaimed and openly preached that, salvation having begun with the *Hail Mary*, the salvation of each one of us in particular is attached to that prayer. They tell us that it is that prayer which made the dry and barren earth bring forth the fruit of life; and that it is that prayer well said which makes the word of God germinate in our souls, and bring forth Jesus Christ, the Fruit of Life (*True Devotion* §249).

They tell us that the *Hail Mary* is a heavenly dew for watering the earth, which is the soul, to make it bring forth its fruit in season; and that a soul which is not watered by that prayer bears no fruit, and brings forth only thorns and brambles, and is ready to be cursed (Heb. 6:8) (*True Devotion* §249).

Let us remember the divine origins of this beautiful prayer. God the Father sent the Angel Gabriel with those opening words: "Hail, full of grace! The Lord is with thee! Blessed art thou among women!" While God the Holy Ghost spoke through the mouth of St. Elizabeth, saying: "Blessed art thou among women and blessed is the fruit of thy womb!" These words, carefully chosen by God Himself, should be engraved with love and reverence upon our hearts. I recommend that you read parts of St. Louis De Montfort's book, *The Secret of the Rosary*, in order to have a greater understanding and love of this beautiful Angelic Salutation.

WEEK 5: DAY 6–SECOND MEDITATION

6. Devotion to the Holy Rosary

St. Louis writes the following in his book, *True Devotion to Mary:*

> Listen to what Our Lady revealed to Blessed Alan de la Roche, as he has recorded in his book on the dignity of the Rosary: "Know, my son, and make all others know, that it is a probable and proximate sign of eternal damnation to have an aversion, a lukewarmness, or a negligence in saying the Angelical Salutation, which has repaired the whole world (*True Devotion* §250).

These words are at once terrible and consoling, and we should find it hard to believe them, if we had not that holy man for a guarantee, and St. Dominic before him, and many great men since. But we have also the experience of several ages; for it has always been remarked that those who wear the outward sign of reprobation, like all impious heretics and proud worldlings, hate or despise the *Hail Mary* and the Rosary. Heretics still learn and say the *Our Father*, but not the *Hail Mary* nor the Rosary. They abhor it; they would rather wear a serpent than a Rosary. The proud also, although Catholics, have the same inclinations as their father Lucifer; and so have only contempt or indifference for the *Hail Mary*, and look at the Rosary as at a devotion which is good only for the ignorant and for those who cannot read (*True Devotion* §250).

On the contrary, it is an equally universal experience that those who have otherwise great marks of predestination about them love and relish the *Hail Mary*, and delight in saying it. We always see that the more a man is for God, the more he likes that prayer. This is what Our Lady also said to Blessed Alan, after the words which I have just quoted (*True Devotion* §250).

I do not know how it is, nor why, but nevertheless I know well that it is true; nor have I any better secret of knowing whether a person is for God than to examine if he likes to say the *Hail Mary* and the Rosary. I say, if he likes; for it may happen that a person may be under some natural inability to say it, or even a supernatural one; yet, nevertheless, he likes it always, and always inspires the same liking in others (*True Devotion* §251).

The *Hail Mary* well said—that is, with attention, devotion, and modesty—is, according to the saints, the enemy of the devil which puts him to flight, and the hammer which crushes him. It is the sanctification of the soul, the joy of the angels, the melody of the predestinate, the canticle of the New Testament, the pleasure of Mary, and the glory of the most Holy Trinity. The *Hail Mary* is a heavenly dew which fertilizes the soul. It is the chaste and loving kiss which we give to Mary. It is a vermilion rose which we present to her; a precious pearl we offer her; a chalice of divine ambrosial nectar which we proffer to her. All these are comparisons of the saints (*True Devotion* §253).

"I pray you urgently, by the love I bear you in Jesus and Mary, not to content yourselves with saying the Little Crown of the Blessed Virgin, but to say five decades, or even, if you have time, fifteen decades of the Rosary every day. At the moment of your death you will bless the day and the hour in which you followed my advice. Having thus sown in the blessings of Jesus and Mary, you will reap eternal blessings in heaven. "He who soweth in blessings, shall also reap blessings" (II Cor. 9:6) (*True Devotion* §254).

All this is reinforced upon all sides. Our Lady appeared at Lourdes and Fatima asking for the Rosary to be prayed. The Rosary has been endorsed by a long succession of popes and saints. The often miraculous consequences of reciting the Rosary have been much and well chronicled. Our Lady has requested that, in today's age, it be recited everywhere.

Even though St. Louis says that it is better to say one *Hail Mary* well than thousands badly, we must nevertheless remember that she said of little Francisco at Fatima that *he would have to recite many Rosaries before he would get to heaven!* What evil and harm could such a small child have accomplished in his sheltered, short life back in 1917—when the world was much less corrupt than it is today? How much more applicable should that phrase be today—*you will have to recite many Rosaries before you can get to heaven?* Let us recite those Rosaries—not out of routine, not mechanically, not distractedly, not in haste, but with dignity, attention and devotion!

WEEK 5: DAY 6–THIRD MEDITATION

7. Devotion to Our Lady's Own Prayer—*The Magnificat*

To thank God for the graces He has given to Our Lady, those who adopt this devotion will often say the *Magnificat*, as Blessed Mary d'Oignies did, and many other saints. It is the only prayer, the only work, which the holy Virgin composed, or rather, which Jesus composed in her; for He spoke by her mouth. It is the greatest sacrifice of praise which God ever received from a pure creature in the law of grace. It is, on the one hand, the most humble and grateful, and on the other hand, the most sublime and exalted, of all canticles (*True Devotion* §255).

There are in that canticle mysteries so great and hidden that the angels do not know them. The pious and erudite Gerson employed a great part of his life in composing works upon the most difficult subjects; and yet it was only at the close of his career, and even with trembling, that he undertook to comment on the *Magnificat*, so as to crown all his other works. He wrote a folio volume on it, bringing forward many admirable things about that beautiful and divine canticle (*True Devotion* §255).

Among other things, he says that Our Lady often repeated it herself, and especially for thanksgiving after Communion. The learned Benzonius [Rutilio], in explaining the *Magnificat*, relates many miracles wrought by virtue of it, and says that the devils tremble and fly when they hear these words: "He hath showed might in His arm; He hath scattered the proud in the conceit of their heart." (Lk. 1:51) (*True Devotion* §255).

This wonderful hymn of thanksgiving is an ideal prayer to recite after receiving Holy Communion. And if done so, it almost reproduces the circumstances in which it was first recited by the Blessed Virgin herself. For at the moment of the Visitation, when Our Lady prayed the *Magnificat*, she was carrying Our Lord within the temple of her womb. Similarly, at Holy Communion, we are carrying Our Lord in the temple of our soul. If, according to the learned Gerson, Our Lady was wont to say it after her own Communions, how much more should we not rush to imitate her in our own Communions. Perhaps we too shall bring about some of the above-mentioned miracles, wrought in virtue of the *Magnificat*.

WEEK 5: DAY 6–FOURTH MEDITATION

8. Performing All Our Actions *with* Mary

We must do all our actions with Mary; that is to say, we must in all our actions regard Mary as an accomplished model of every virtue and perfection which the Holy Ghost has formed in a pure creature for us to imitate according to our little measure. We must therefore in every action consider how Mary has done it, or how she would have done it, had she been in our place. For that end we must examine and meditate on the great virtues which she practiced during her life, and particularly, first of all, her lively faith, by which she believed without hesitation the angel's word, and believed faithfully and constantly up to the foot of the cross; secondly, her profound humility, which made her hide herself, hold her peace, submit to everything, and put herself the last of all; and, thirdly, her altogether divine purity, which never has had, and never can have, its equal under heaven; and so on with all of her other virtues. Let us remember, I repeat, that Mary is the great and exclusive mold of God, proper to making living images of God at small cost and in a little time; and that a soul which has found that mold, and has lost itself in it, is presently changed into Jesus Christ, Whom that mold represents to the life (*True Devotion* §260).

9. Performing All Our Actions *in* Mary

We must do our actions in Mary. To thoroughly understand this practice, we must first know that our Blessed Lady is the true terrestrial paradise of the New Adam, and that the ancient paradise was but a figure of her. There are, then, in this earthly paradise, riches, beauties, rarities and inexplicable sweetness which Jesus Christ, the New Adam, has left there; it was in this paradise that He took His complacence for nine months, worked His wonders and displayed His riches with the magnificence of a God (*True Devotion* §261).

This most holy place is composed only of a virginal and immaculate earth, of which the New Adam was formed, and on which He was nourished, without any spot or stain, by the operation of the Holy Ghost, who dwelt there. It is in this earthly paradise that there is the true tree of life, which has borne Jesus Christ, the Fruit of Life, and the tree of the knowledge of good and evil, which has given light unto the world (*True Devotion* §261).

There are in this divine place trees planted by the hand of God, and watered by His divine unction, which have borne and daily bear fruits of a divine taste. There are flower beds adorned with beautiful and varied blossoms of virtues diffusing odors which delight the very angels (*True Devotion* §261).

There are meadows green with hope, impregnable towers of strength, and the most charming houses of confidence. It is only the Holy Ghost who can make us know the hidden truth of these figures of material things (*True Devotion* §261).

There is in this place an air of perfect purity; a fair sun, without shadow, of the Divinity; a fair day, without night, of the Sacred Humanity; a continual burning furnace of love, where all the iron that is cast into it is changed, by excessive heat, to gold (*True Devotion* §261).

There is a river of humility which springs from the earth, and which, dividing itself into four branches, waters all that enchanted place; and these are the four cardinal virtues (*True Devotion* §261).

10. Performing All Our Actions *for* Mary

Finally we must do all our actions for Mary. As we have given ourselves up entirely to her service, it is but just to do everything for her as servants and slaves. It is not that we take her for the last end of our services, for that is Jesus Christ alone; but we take her for our proximate end, our mysterious means and our easy way to go to Him. Like good servants and slaves, we must not remain idle, but, supported by her protection, we must undertake and achieve great things for this august sovereign (*True Devotion* §265).

We must defend her privileges when they are disputed; we must stand up for her glory when it is attacked; we must draw all the world, if we can, to her service, and to this true and solid devotion; we must speak and cry out against those who abuse her devotion to outrage her Son, and we must at the same time establish this veritable devotion; we must pretend to no recompense for our little services, except the honor of belonging to so sweet a Queen, and the happiness of being united through her to Jesus her Son by an indissoluble tie, in time and in eternity. Glory to Jesus in Mary! Glory to Mary in Jesus! Glory to God alone! (*True Devotion* §265).

WEEK 5: DAY 7–FIRST MEDITATION

11. Going to Holy Communion with Mary

Manner of practicing this devotion when we go to Holy Communion

1. You must humble yourself most profoundly before God.

2. You must renounce your corrupt interior and your dispositions, however good your self-love may make them look.

3. You must renew your consecration by saying: "I am all thine, my dear Mistress, with all that I have."

4. You must implore that good Mother to lend you her heart, that you may receive her Son there with the same dispositions as her own (*True Devotion* §266).

You will explain to her that it touches her Son's glory to be put into a heart so sullied and so inconstant as yours, which would not fail either to lessen His glory or to destroy it. But if she will come and dwell with you, in order to receive her Son, she can do so by the dominion which she has over all hearts; and her Son will be well received by her, without stain, without danger of being outraged or unnoticed: "God is in the midst thereof, it shall not be moved" (Ps. 45:6) (*True Devotion* §266).

You will tell her confidently that all you have given her of your goods is little enough to honor her; but that by Holy Communion you wish to make her the same present as the Eternal Father gave her, and that you will honor her more by that than if you gave her all the goods in the world and finally, that Jesus, who loves her in a most special manner, still desires to take His pleasure and repose in her, even in your soul, though it be far filthier and poorer than the stable where He did not hesitate to come, simply because she was there. You will ask her for her heart, by these tender words: "I take thee for my all. Give me thy heart, O Mary" (*True Devotion* §266).

After the *Our Father*, just before receiving Jesus Christ, you say three times: "Lord, I am not worthy." Say the first one to the Eternal Father, telling Him you are not worthy, because of your evil thoughts and ingratitude toward so good a Father, to receive His only Son; but that He is to behold Mary His handmaid—

"Behold the handmaid of the Lord" (Lk. 1:38)—who acts for you and who gives you a singular confidence and hope with His Majesty: "For thou singularly hast settled me in hope" (Ps. 4:10) (*True Devotion* §267).

You will say to the Son: "Lord, I am not worthy"; telling Him that you are not worthy to receive Him because of your idle and evil words and your infidelity to His service; but that nevertheless you pray Him to have pity on you, because you are about to bring Him into the house of His own Mother and yours, and that you will not let Him go without His coming to lodge with her: "I held Him; and I will not let Him go, till I bring Him into my Mother's house and into the chamber of her that bore me" (Cant. 3:4) (*True Devotion* §268).

You will pray to Him to rise, and come to the place of His repose and into the ark of His sanctification: "Arise, Lord, into Thy resting place: Thou and the ark which Thou hast sanctified." (Ps. 131:8). Tell Him you put no confidence at all in your own merits, your own strength and your own preparations, as Esau did; but that you trust only in Mary, your dear Mother, as the little Jacob did in Rebecca. Tell Him that, sinner and Esau that you are, you dare to approach His sanctity, supported and adorned as you are with the virtues of His holy Mother (*True Devotion* §268).

You will say to the Holy Ghost: 'Lord, I am not worthy'; telling Him that you are not worthy to receive this masterpiece of His charity, because of the lukewarmness and iniquity of your actions, and because of your resistance to His inspirations; but that all your confidence is in Mary, His faithful spouse. You will say, with St. Bernard: "She is my greatest security; she is the source of all my hope." You can even pray Him to come Himself in Mary, His inseparable spouse, telling Him that her bosom is as pure and her heart as burning as ever; and that, without His descent into your soul, neither Jesus nor Mary will be formed nor worthily lodged (*True Devotion* §269).

After Holy Communion, inwardly recollected and holding your eyes shut, you will introduce Jesus into the heart of Mary. You will give Him to His Mother, who will receive Him lovingly, will place Him honorably, will adore Him profoundly, will love Him perfectly, will embrace Him closely, and will render to Him, in spirit and in truth, many homages which are unknown to us in our thick darkness (*True Devotion* §270).

Or else you will keep yourself profoundly humbled in your heart, in the presence of Jesus residing in Mary. Or else you will sit like a slave at the gate of the King's palace, where He is speaking with the Queen; and while they talk to each other without need of you, you will go in spirit to heaven and over all the earth, praying all creatures to thank, adore and love Jesus and Mary in your place: "Come, let us adore" (Ps. 94:6) (*True Devotion* §271).

Or else you will yourself ask of Jesus, in union with Mary, the coming of His kingdom on earth, through His holy Mother; or you will sue for divine wisdom, or for divine love, or for the pardon of your sins, or for some other grace; but always by Mary and in Mary; saying, while you look aside at yourself: "Lord, look not at my sins"; "but let Your eyes look at nothing in me but the virtues and merits of Mary." And then, remembering your sins, you will add: "It is I who have committed these sins" (Cf. Mt. 13:28); or you will say: "Deliver me from the unjust and deceitful man" (Ps. 42:1); or else: "My Jesus, You must increase in my soul, and I must decrease" (Jn. 3:30); Mary, you must increase within me, and I must be still less than I have been. "O Jesus and Mary, increase in me, and multiply yourselves outside in others also" (Cf. Gen. 1:22 ff.) (*True Devotion* §272).

There are an infinity of other thoughts which the Holy Ghost furnishes, and will furnish you, if you are thoroughly interior, mortified and faithful to this grand and sublime devotion which I have been teaching you. But always remember that the more you allow Mary to act in your Communion, the more Jesus will be glorified; and you will allow Mary to act for Jesus and Jesus to act in Mary in the measure that you humble yourself and listen to them in peace and in silence, without troubling yourself about seeing, tasting or feeling; for the just man lives throughout on faith, and particularly in Holy Communion, which is an action of faith: "My just man liveth by faith" (Heb. 10:38) (*True Devotion* §273).

WEEK 5: DAY 7–SECOND MEDITATION

12. Join the *Legion of Mary* as an *Active Member* or an *Auxiliary Member*

The Legion of Mary is a lay organization which is, in effect, an extension of the priest. It is entirely based upon the spirituality of St. Louis De Montfort's *True Devotion to Mary* and is, therefore, a natural progression or practical consequence of the True Devotion Consecration. The consecration plants the seed of True Devotion, whereas the Legion of Mary is that same seed grown into a mature "Tree of Life."

The Active Members of the Legion of Mary form a body of lay men and women, who meet weekly to discuss and report upon their allocated apostolic work, given to them by their parish priest. Work can include working with fallen-away Catholics; potential converts; teaching the Catechism at varying levels; visiting the sick and elderly at home, in hospitals and nursing homes; working with the youth; distributing Catholic literature; spreading the True Devotion of St. Louis De Montfort; organizing and running a Fatima Pilgrim Virgin Statue campaign; organizing Rosary Rallies; working in various ways to raise the spiritual fervor of their local parish, *etc.*

The parish priest, when faced by the multitude of possible apostolates, can do very little with the time he has at his disposal. Hence the need for dedicated co-workers, under his guidance and encouragement, in order to be able to reach more places and more souls.

The Auxiliary Members of the Legion of Mary do not do any active work. On the contrary, they supply the active workers with the graces that they so badly need in order to successfully accomplish their work. Their sole obligation is to recite the Rosary daily, together with a few other short Marian prayers that are contained on a Legion Prayer Sheet called the *Tessera*.

Conclusion

These are the many different ways, not obligatory but recommended, by which we can nurture and express our devotion to Our Blessed Lady. At times we may focus more earnestly upon one, then upon another. It is not hard to perform all of them, but let us avoid "performing" them in the thespian sense of the word. Routine can soon creep in and before we know it, we have perhaps slipped into a mere perfunctory devotion, that in no way